IDIOT'S GUIDES®
AS EASY AS IT GETS!

Real Estate Licensing Exams

WITHDRAWN
Anne Arundel Co. Public Library

by Raymond D. Modglin, the Real Estate Monkey

ALPHA

A member of Penguin Random House LLC

Publisher: Mike Sanders
Associate Publisher: Billy Fields
Acquisitions Editor: Jan Lynn
Development Editor: Christy Wagner
Cover Designer: Lindsay Dobbs
Book Designer: William Thomas
Compositor: Ayanna Lacey
Proofreader: Lisa Starnes
Indexer: Tonya Heard

First American Edition, 2017
Published in the United States by DK Publishing
6081 E. 82nd Street, Indianapolis, Indiana 46250

Copyright © 2017 Dorling Kindersley Limited
A Penguin Random House Company
17 18 19 10 9 8 7 6 5 4 3 2 1
001-305394-July2017

ISBN: 9781465462749
Library of Congress Catalog Card Number: 2016962253

Note: This publication contains the opinions and ideas of its author(s). It is intended to
provide helpful and informative material on the subject matter covered. It is sold with
the understanding that the author(s) and publisher are not engaged in rendering professional services in the book. If the reader requires personal assistance or advice, a
competent professional should be consulted. The author(s) and publisher specifically
disclaim any responsibility for any liability, loss, or risk, personal or otherwise, which
is incurred as a consequence, directly or indirectly, of the use and application of any
of the contents of this book.

Trademarks: All terms mentioned in this book that are known to be or are suspected
of being trademarks or service marks have been appropriately capitalized. Alpha
Books, DK, and Penguin Random House LLC cannot attest to the accuracy of this
information. Use of a term in this book should not be regarded as affecting the validity of any trademark or service mark.

DK books are available at special discounts when purchased in bulk for sales promo-
tions, premiums, fund-raising, or educational use. For details, contact: DK Publishing
Special Markets, 345 Hudson Street, New York, New York 10014 or SpecialSales@
dk.com.

Printed and bound in USA

Contents

Part 5: Evaluation and Financing   171

Part 6: Practice Exams and Solutions   234

Appendixes

Introduction

As a REALTOR, I enjoy my work immensely. I love the interaction with people, helping them make life-defining decisions on their housing needs, solving problems, and the freedom to manage my own schedule. After several years in a corporate job, I became a licensed agent, and to this day I have no regrets. After 13 years and almost $100 million in sales, I have decided to pass along some knowledge that I have acquired over the years as a broker and an instructor to new prelicensing according to the style sheet students in my school.

The test is by far the hardest part of this process, and studying for the test is a long, arduous task, but it will pay off in the end when you pass. The test, in Indiana, is comprised of two sections: 80 questions of general information, which is covered in this book, and 50 state-specific law questions. Check with your state on the exact layout of your exam.

This book is designed to give you insight into the information and knowledge required to take and pass the real estate salesperson/broker exam. Topics covered include the latest information on brokerages, federal laws, financing and the new Consumer Financial Protection Bureau (CFPB), appraisals and valuation of real estate, title work, real estate taxes, and more. With nearly 500 practice questions and a 100- question practice exam complete with answers that explain key concepts, this book is the go-to guide to preparing for your state licensing exam.

How This Book Is Organized

This book is divided into six parts:

In **Part 1, Introduction to the Real Estate Business,** I discuss how real estate is sold and why a professional such as you is needed in the process. I also cover the differences between a salesperson, broker, and REALTOR.

In **Part 2, The Job Basics,** I introduce you to the day-to-day job expectations as well as the skills you'll need to excel as a real estate professional. I also review the ethics, skills, and activities a successful real estate agent must practice.

In **Part 3, Ownership and Transference,** we take an in-depth look at the different types of ownership and deeds that transfer ownership. I go over the covenants that are promised and transferred during a sale and some of the involuntary ways property can get transferred, such as foreclosure, tax sales, and more.

In **Part 4, Legal Ramifications,** I discuss the federal, state, and local laws a new agent needs to know to ensure they're practicing legally. I cover fair housing, federal finance laws, and numerous others laws that could potentially give a practicing REALTOR issues.

In **Part 5, Evaluation and Financing,** I share information about appraisals and the valuation models appraisers use. I talk about key factors at play in the valuation process and how to recognize them as a real estate agent. I also discuss the financing options available to a buyer and how a licensed agent can play a role in helping a client find the right financing.

In **Part 6, Practice Exams and Solutions,** I give you 500 practice questions, with answers, that cover many common real estate problems a licensed agent faces in the real world, including real estate tax calculations, loan and interest valuations, commission splits, and much more.

At the back of the book, I've included a number of appendixes, including a handy glossary of real estate-specific terms, a national sample test with 100 unique questions and answers, a list of state real estate commissions, and some useful sample real estate forms.

Extras

Throughout the book, we include three kinds of sidebars to enhance the text. Here's what to look for:

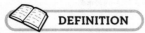 **DEFINITION**

Read these sidebars for easy explanations of common real estate-related terms and concepts.

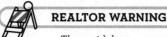 **REALTOR WARNING**

These sidebars present warnings on issues I have seen in practice that can cause severe problems if left out or forgotten during the buying and selling process.

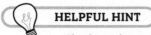 **HELPFUL HINT**

Check out these sidebars for insights I would suggest you follow as best practice procedures and other interesting information.

Acknowledgments

I wish to thank my wife, Kelly, for understanding and accepting all the hours I spent completing this book. I also want to thank my children, Brandon, Justin, Ian, Connor, Olivia, and Sean, for encouraging me to undertake this glorious adventure. And lastly, I want to thank you, my students, for trusting me as I guide you on the way to a successful career in real estate.

Introduction to the Real Estate Business

Real estate transactions happen every day across the country: from the owner-occupied single-family residential home to the high-rise development. At some point in almost everyone's life they will be involved in some type of real estate transaction: buying, selling, investing, or development of real property. When that time comes, they will turn to the licensed REALTOR for guidance, advice and support. Real estate is big business involving many different professionals, realtors, appraisers, mortgage brokers, attorneys, etc., and millions of dollars exchanging hands.

Despite the complexity of a real estate transaction, many people believe that a REALTOR is the key component and often seek them out first when getting started. Having a successful career as a real estate professional requires many skills and specific knowledge. The first step is obtaining your education and passing the state's licensing exam.

Why Real Estate as a Career?

The career of a licensed real estate professional has greatly expanded over the last few years and offers one of the widest career selections in the business world today. Helping clients buy and sell residential homes, along with investment properties, commercial buildings, property management, home inspection, and appraisals are just a few of the aspects of a career in real estate. Let's get started!

In This Chapter

- The career benefits of real estate
- What to expect from your real estate career
- The future of real estate

Career Benefits

As a *real estate professional,* your actions help make the difference between someone relocating to a new city or staying in the area, or a child growing up in a small bungalow versus playing on a farm. The effect of a real estate professional on his or her client's life can be immeasurable.

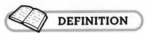

DEFINITION

A **real estate professional** is any person who practices real estate brokerage and is licensed under the laws of his or her state. A *REALTOR* is a member of the National Association of REALTORS (NAR). A real estate professional might not be a REALTOR, but he or she might still practice real estate brokerage.

As a real estate professional, you are in control of your own business as an independent contractor. You can make a six-figure income with minimal required education, and your income is unlimited and based solely on your activities. You set your own work hours, and your day-to-day activities are varied and constantly growing. Perhaps most importantly, you help people achieve their dreams and can feel pride about your career choice.

Although it sometimes can be expensive to establish, owning your own business can provide a lifetime of benefits. By becoming a real estate agent, you can start your own business with a relatively low initial investment. The cost of getting an education, taking a license exam course and your state's test, and marketing your business is really all it takes to get started in this potentially lucrative career.

HELPFUL HINT

New data from NAR shows that more than 1.7 million homes were listed in 2016 with an average U.S. median price of $250,000. That's a market value of more than $425 *billion* in potential real estate transactions to be had!

As an independent contractor, you choose the hours you want to work and create your own flexible work schedule. Real estate professionals often put in more than a standard 40-hour week, regularly work evenings and weekends, and are usually on call to respond to the needs of clients. That's not always a bad thing, though. I've enjoyed the option of taking personal time during the week knowing I had scheduled showings with a client on Saturdays or during evening hours. The flexibility of a real estate career is the single biggest benefit afforded me, even over the income.

Advances in technology and the capability to retrieve data about properties over the internet allow many real estate professionals to work out of their homes instead of real estate offices. Even with this convenience, they still may spend much of their time away from their desks, showing properties to clients, analyzing properties for sale, meeting with prospective clients, or researching the real estate market.

Another great plus to this career is that you decide your own pay. Determining the number of hours you want to work also determines the amount of pay you receive. You can increase your income in other ways, too. For example, you can increase the value of the transactions you close for your clients. You can generate more income with fewer deals by increasing the average selling price of the properties you represent and sell.

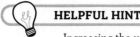

HELPFUL HINT

Increasing the value of the properties you sell, which sometimes is easier than increasing the number of clients you help, can make you more money.

No other career affords you the opportunity to be walking a plot of farmland, talking to the farmer about listing his house on one day and speaking with a company president about selling their manufacturing site the next. Even residential transactions vary, enabling you to expand your abilities and experience for future clients down the road.

Perhaps the biggest benefit to this career is knowing you play a large role in helping your clients' home-ownership dreams come true. Seeing the faces of your clients after closing, knowing you helped them with a major life decision, is a wonderful gift for a REALTOR. The fact that you get paid to do it is nice, too!

Career Responsibilities

Real estate professionals spend a significant amount of time helping their clients buy or sell real estate.

They obtain *listings,* which are agreements signed by property owners placing their properties for sale with real estate firms. When listing a property for sale, real estate professionals compare the listed property with similar properties in the area that recently sold to determine a competitive market price for the property. Following the sale of that property, both the agent who sold it and the agent who obtained the listing receive a portion of the commission from the sale. The same agent can represent the buyer and the seller by creating a *dual* or *limited agency.* An agent who sells a property they themselves have listed can increase their commission.

Before showing residential properties to potential buyers, agents meet with them to get an idea of the type of home they want to purchase. During this process, the agent determines how much the buyers can afford to spend. He or she might guide the buyer to a *mortgage broker* from the onset to determine the buyer's true financial strength before showing any properties.

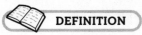

DEFINITION

A **listing** is a legal agreement between a seller and a real estate professional to list a property for sale. With a **dual** or **limited agency,** a real estate professional represents both the selling and buying parties on the same deal. A **mortgage broker** works with a buyer to qualify them financially for a loan.

The agent and the buyer usually sign an agency contract, which states that the agent will be the only one to show houses to the buyer. A real estate professional then generates lists of properties for sale, with their location and description, and available sources of financing. In some cases, real estate professionals can give buyers a virtual tour of properties that interest them on their computer.

A real estate professional may meet several times with prospective buyers to discuss and visit available properties. They also will identify and emphasize a property's most pertinent selling points. To a first-time home buyer, for example, they might emphasize the convenient floor plan, the area's low crime rate, and the proximity to schools and shopping. To a potential investor, they might point out the tax advantages of owning a rental property and the ease of finding a renter.

If bargaining over price becomes necessary, a real estate professional must follow his or her client's instructions carefully and might have to present offers and counteroffers to get the best possible deal for their client.

After the buyer and seller have signed a contract, the real estate professional must ensure all special terms of the contract are met before the closing date. The real estate professional must also be sure any legally mandated or agreed-upon inspections, such as termite and radon inspections, take place. In addition, if the seller agrees to any repairs, the real estate professional ensures they are made. Increasingly, the real estate professional may be handling environmental problems as well, ensuring the properties they list or sell meet local environmental regulations.

Most real estate professionals sell residential property through the local real estate board and *MLS*, or *multiple listing service*. A small number, usually employed in large or specialized firms, sell commercial, industrial, agricultural, or other types of real estate. Every specialty requires knowledge of that particular type of property, clientele, business practices, trends, and locations.

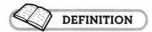 **DEFINITION**

> **MLS (multiple listing service)** is a database listing agents use to place a seller's home for sale. When a real estate professional works with a buyer, they search the MLS for properties that meet the buyer's wants and needs.

Who Becomes Real Estate Professionals?

The choice to become a real estate professional often comes after other careers. According to information from the NAR Member Profile Study, only 7 percent of REALTORS report that real estate was their first career. REALTORS tend to be former managers, salespersons, law enforcement officers, teachers, nurses, homemakers, or administrators. The average REALTOR has 13 years of experience in the industry, which supposes that many got into the profession at about the age of 39. Furthermore, the study goes on to say the following:

- The average REALTOR is a 52-year-old female grossing approximately $47,700 annually.

- 74 percent of REALTORS are married, with median gross household incomes of $92,800.

- 80 percent of REALTORS have some college education, compared to 51 percent of U.S. adults, according to the U.S. Census Bureau.

- 9 out of 10 REALTORS own a home, and nearly half own rental properties.

- REALTORS with a bachelor's degree earns 30 percent more than REALTORS without a degree.

Look at what the average REALTORS have in common: they have more education than the public, experience that comes with age, usually another wage earner in the household, and enough wherewithal to own and buy more property. Does that indicate an economic barrier for the entry level? Yes, it does, which could explain why people don't typically enter the profession right out of school.

In fact, the average age of REALTORS has increased over the last few decades, from age 42 in 1978 to age 50 and even older today. This is creating a crisis of youth in the profession. Almost a third of brokers are 60 years old, and 16 percent of brokers are older than 60. Only 12 percent of sales agents are under 35, as compared to 29 percent in 1978. Becoming a real estate professional could simply boil down to whether or not you have the money to get started. Facts show that the older you are, the more likely you are to be able to afford to finance your new profession. You must have seed money and good money-management skills because in most cases, you'll be paid irregular amounts on an irregular basis. You must have enough to cover yourself and your expenses until you start making enough commission to survive financially.

Other Real Estate Positions

In most states, *real estate brokers* hire salespersons to be their agents. Salespersons are also licensed by the state and can perform real estate duties acting as representatives of the broker, working either in the managing broker's name or in his or her company's name. Any commission earned with that client belongs to the managing broker, who splits a portion with the salesperson.

Salespersons' licenses are much easier to obtain than brokers' licenses because brokers' licenses generally require both time and experience in addition to testing. Salespersons can start working as soon as they're licensed and *hang* their licenses with a broker.

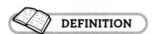 **DEFINITION**

A **real estate broker** is a real estate professional who holds the highest degree of licensure and whose responsibilities may include management of office personnel and other real estate professionals and holding fiduciary responsibilities to clients. In real estate, **hang** means to contractually and legally have one's real estate license assigned to a managing broker. The managing broker then accepts responsibility for the actions of the salesperson under each state's license law.

In most cases, salespersons are hired to bring in business to the brokerage and are paid a portion of the listing's commission. Very seldom will you find an opportunity to sell real estate for a salary, and if you do, expect to be paid on a draw against commission, or a salary against a goal—meaning if you don't meet the production goal, you don't get paid and are likely out of a job.

Financial Expectations

Typical commissions may vary from listing to listing but average between 4 to 7 percent.

In most cases, the listing broker shares a portion of the listing commission to entice another broker to bring the buyer to the deal. The listing broker keeps a portion of the listing commission, or the "house split." The listing broker then splits that portion with the salesperson, based on a pre-determined split amount.

If you represent both sides of the deal as a dual or limited agency, you can make as much as 3 percent with the broker keeping the balance. If you are a managing broker and do your own selling or buying for clients, you can make the full commission.

Getting started as a real estate professional can include meeting educational requirements of as many as 45 to 120 hours of education and paying significant expenses, depending on state requirements, testing fees, state licensing fees, and local real estate board fees so you can access the MLS to have inventory to sell. Local real estate boards are the unions of real estate—they protect the industry and make it easier to do business. In most states, you have to become a member of a local board to gain access to the MLS system. Most local memberships' dues include membership to the state and national associations as well.

A large portion of homes sold in the United States are listed by real estate professionals and found in the MLS. Some states allow all licensees to access their local MLS without requiring a membership. However, most states maintain a closed MLS and require a licensee to be a member of the local, state, and national REALTOR association to gain access. These costs, although worthwhile to most members, can run into the hundreds or thousands of dollars. In addition, you have to purchase access to the company running the MLS system for the board, which can also run hundreds of dollars.

Most real estate professionals use smartphones, but they also employ laptops, tablets, lockbox technologies, mobile apps, and more to do business, which also cost money at the onset. Advertising costs to promote homes and get name recognition can run in the hundreds or thousands of dollars as well.

According to the NAR, the average REALTOR spent more than $1,000 on self-promotion in 2014. Seven out of ten REALTORS also maintain a home office, in addition to using office space supplied by their brokers. All these require money spent before you even begin to earn commission. All totaled, the average real estate professionals spend approximately 14 percent of their personal gross income on business-related expenses. Real estate professionals grossing more than $100,000 annually spend $26,300 on business-related expenses.

All these costs can be overwhelming, so I often tell new students in my prelicensing class to take it a little at a time. Take the prelicensing course while you're still employed elsewhere. Build up approximately 6 months of income so you can survive a job change. Start telling everyone you know of your intentions to enter the real estate business. Begin building a database of names and contact information so you'll have prospects to call when you start selling real estate. Interview brokers and find out what training programs they offer to new real estate professionals. You may be better off taking a job with a brokerage that offers lower commission splits if the broker brings in business and shares it with agents or has a great training program for new agents. Offer to become a team member for a top agent until you can break away on your own so you can be paid while you learn and watch how a pro brings in business. Some agents pay well enough that you may never need to leave the team.

There's no way to tell you exactly how much money you need to become a real estate professional because every market is different. To learn more, interview local brokers and ask them their opinions. Tell them you would like to become a real estate professional and ask what you should expect. A good broker will suggest you write a business plan so you can measure your progress. When you present the plan to the broker, he or she will tell you if your expenses and sales goals are reasonable.

 HELPFUL HINT

If you don't fit the average real estate professional demographic, don't despair. The industry offers a lot of growth opportunities and is actively seeking new people, especially young people, to bring fresh perspectives to an aging profession. In fact, membership in the NAR and local associations is at record-high levels.

Outlook for the Future

According to a recent report by realtor.com, employment of real estate brokers and sales agents is projected to grow 3 percent from 2014 to 2024. Although this growth is slower than, say, the growth of careers in technology, the growth of real estate careers is projected to increase as the real estate market improves.

Both the financial and nonfinancial sectors spur demand for home sales. Real estate is often perceived as a good long-term investment, and many people want to own their homes.

 REALTOR WARNING

The U.S. housing bubble of 2007 and 2008 affected more than half of U.S. states after housing prices peaked in early 2006. In 2008 alone, the U.S. government allocated more than $900 billion to special loans and rescues related to the U.S. housing bubble, with more than half going to Fannie Mae and Freddie Mac (both government-sponsored enterprises) as well as the Federal Housing Administration (FHA). On December 30, 2008, the Case-Shiller Home Price Index all capitalized reported its largest price drop in U.S. history. The real estate market fluctuates, which is something you should prepare for if you enter this field.

Population growth also stimulates the need for new real estate professionals in the real estate field. The large millennial generation is entering the job market and will start to purchase homes over the next decade. Although this generation has delayed home ownership because of financial and debt considerations, it's projected that many will enter the housing market and need the help of a real estate professional.

In addition to the millennial first-time home buyers' market, purchasers need help from real estate professionals when they're looking to upgrade to larger homes, downsize to smaller ones, or relocate due to a job or any other myriad reasons.

Geography is another factor in determining your job outlook. In certain areas of the country where the population is booming, the job market is thriving and the high cost of living provides numerous real estate sales opportunities. Coastal areas have been and will continue to be strong real estate markets providing strong job prospects. However, some areas of the country may have low job opportunities for a real estate professional simply due to the lack of population.

An improving job market and rising consumer spending also drives demand for real estate professionals to handle commercial, retail, and industrial real estate transactions.

The real estate market is sensitive to fluctuations in the economy, and employment of real estate professionals varies accordingly. In periods of economic growth or stability, employment should grow to accommodate people looking to buy or sell homes and businesses and/or to expand commercial rental space. Alternatively, during periods of declining economic activity or rising interest rates, the amount of work for real estate professionals slows and employment may decline. In recent years, the real estate bubble made it difficult for a real estate professional to thrive; however, an adaptation in business strategy and a historical proven track record of past success will allow you to be a successful real estate professional even in the lean years.

The Least You Need to Know

- Real estate is big business.
- A real estate professional plays an integral part in helping people make their home-ownership dreams come true.
- Getting your education and passing the state exam to get your real estate license is the first step toward your new career.
- Based on the job outlook predictions, real estate professionals can have very successful and lucrative careers.

Taking the Real Estate Exam

Congratulations on passing the first hurdle of your licensing process—the education! Now you must take and pass the state licensing exam to be able to apply for your license. The exam tests your knowledge so you can be an effective, successful, and knowledgeable licensee for your client. As I tell my students all the time, "Think about all the REALTORS you know … they all passed this exam." Soon, hopefully, you will be among their ranks.

In this chapter, we will cover the real estate exam: the requirements to register for the exam, strategies for passing the exam, what to do when you pass the exam, and many more concepts. We will discuss the requirements needed to join a local REALTOR board, plus the differences in each state's real estate commission. Finally, we will cover what happens should you not pass the exam on the first attempt and how to study for the reexamination test.

In This Chapter

- How to register, take, and pass the state licensing exam
- Getting your license after you pass the exam
- Local, state, and national board membership requirements
- The forms needed to apply for your license
- Finding a broker to work for
- What if you don't pass the exam?

Registration Requirements

Before registering for the state licensing exam, you must determine who is your state's testing authority. It might be a third-party company the state has contracted to proctor the exams, or it might be the state itself. Your prelicensing course instructor can give you the details specific to your particular state.

Typically, to gain entrance into the exam, the state (or its assigned proctor) requires proof of course completion, such as a certificate of completion, and two pieces of identification, one of which must contain a current picture.

 HELPFUL HINT

Be sure your certificate of completion has the correct spelling of your legal name as it appears on your state-issued identification. Also, it must have the date of completion of the course as well as the authorizing signature of the school's director or instructor.

A common mistake I see students make is registering for the class in a name other than their legal name. For example, I had a student whose name was Clarence, but his nickname was Buddy. He registered for the exam under the name Buddy and was denied admission because the testing facility claimed Clarence and Buddy were two different people. If you're newly married or divorced and use a different name than the one on your state-issued identification, that could be a problem, too. Most testing centers won't let you in to take the exam if there's a name discrepancy. You'll still be charged for the exam you missed, and after you get the issue corrected with your school, you'll have to reschedule and pay a second testing fee for another chance to take the exam.

All states require some degree of prior education before you can sit for the state licensing exam. Furthermore, all states have a mechanism in place to bypass the education requirement, providing that certain college-level real estate courses were taken. In Indiana, the required course can be waived by the commission, providing that the student has taken 8 credit hours in real estate at an accredited college or university. You can ask your state's real estate commission for any instances in which the course and/or the state exam maybe waived. This small effort may pay huge dividends if they agree to waive the requirements based on any previous coursework you may have completed.

The schedule of most testing centers is 4 to 6 days a week, so you can schedule an exam at your convenience, providing an open seat is available on that date. Remember, you are not the only potential licensee using the testing center. When you sit down to take your exam, others in different occupations might be taking their own licensing tests—plumbers, private detectives, etc. The testing center likely provides testing for the all the careers for which the state requires a licensing examination.

With the advent of the internet, most testing centers now offer an online exam that's proctored by a testing center employee. This enables you to take the exam in any approved location throughout your state. When you schedule your exam, the testing center installs the approved real estate exam on a computer for you to take. You can schedule to take the exam at any location of your choice.

Security at the exam is of utmost importance, and most testing centers won't allow you to take anything into the testing room. In Indiana, the testing center provides lockers in which you can place your purse, briefcase, backpack, and any other belongings for safekeeping during the exam. The testing center also doesn't allow smartphones, tablets, smartwatches, or calculators with the capability to store notes, items, or formulas.

REALTOR WARNING

As technology advances, such as with the advent of the Apple Watch, state testing centers now ask test-takers to remove their watches. The Apple Watch can access a paired iPhone even if it's not in the test-taker's possession, giving him or her potential access to help during the exam.

Registering for the Exam

Registering for the exam is simple and straightforward. However, there are a few decisions to be made before you call to schedule it:

- How soon after the end of the course should I take the exam?

- What locations for the exam are available, and which one is right for me?

- What time of the day should I take the exam?

After you've answered these questions, determine who your state's testing proctor is and contact them via telephone or internet to schedule your exam.

Because you know the course's end date when you start the course, you can schedule your state licensing exam any time during your coursework. Completing the course isn't a requirement for scheduling the exam; you only need to complete the course to qualify to *take* the exam. I've had many students schedule the exam within the first week of school to ensure the date, time, and location they wanted would be available. Don't worry about unforeseen issues that might change the course's completion date. All testing centers allow students to move or cancel their exam, with a full refund of the examination fee with 24 to 48 hours' notice.

When calling the testing center to schedule your exam, be prepared to answer several questions to validate your coursework. In general, you'll need to provide the following:

- Your full, legal name

- Your school's name or *approval code*

- Your proposed graduation date from the course

- Your choice of exam location, date, and time

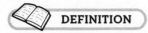

DEFINITION

When a school is approved by the state to teach real estate prelicensing, it is issued an **approval code.** In some states, this code might be called a *license number* or *registration number*. The testing center uses this code to track the number of students from each school and to verify the student did attend a state-approved school.

Sometimes your choice of exam dates or times may be full and you'll need to select a second or even third choice. Remember, you also can seek alternate locations within your state if you need a certain date or time.

Nowadays, most schools offer an online version of the course, which you can complete at your own pace, making a course's end date often hard to determine. Most testing centers want the date on your printed completion certificate to match the end date you declared when you registered for your exam. Contrast that with a live course that has scheduled class meeting times and, therefore, a known completion date.

Several of my students use the state licensing exam as a motivational tool to force them to complete the course within a given time period. By calling the testing center and scheduling a testing date, it encourages online students to finish the course within their self-imposed allotted times. Of course, should something happen to cause a delay in your finishing the course, you can call the testing center and reschedule within the required timeframe.

The Pass/Fail Method of Licensing

You've completed the course, registered for the exam, and the fateful day of testing has arrived. You will take your exam at the proctor's approved place of testing. You will need to complete two separate exams: a general body exam that covers the general theories, concepts, and ideas of real state, and a state-specific exam that deals with license law requirements for your particular state.

REALTOR WARNING

The information provided in this book is intended to give you a general insight into the testing process. Please check with your state for specific testing and registration requirements. Your prelicensing course instructor should be able to give you a good idea of the composition of your state's testing parameters.

During the course, you'll be required to take and pass several exams and/or quizzes over the course's subject material, plus any other requirements your state might impose. These items are used to determine if you are able to pass the course based on each state's guidelines. For example, in Indiana, you must achieve a three-exam average score of 75 percent or better, plus attend 80 percent of your scheduled classes to pass the course.

The second requirement of class attendance is a huge benefit to students taking the course online. Because the online course can be taken around your schedule, there's no such thing as being absent from class. You can merely move the class to the next day you're free. However, be sure to note that all online courses have an expiration date from their date of purchase to their date of completion. Some schools provide a 6-month window to complete the course, while others have given as much as a year to complete the class.

The exams and/or quizzes during the course are graded, and you'll receive scores like any other educational institution. However, when it comes to taking the state licensing exam, a different manner of scoring is used by most states. When you earn the required minimum exam score declared by the state as passing, which is usually 70 to 75 percent, you'll only be given a grade of *pass* and not an actual quantifiable number such as 94 percent. The general reasoning for this among most educators is so there's no way to determine if one person is a better or worse agent because he or she scored higher or lower on the exam. This also plays into the hiring process as well, so no agent can say, "I scored higher than him; therefore, I should get more money."

Should you fail the exam, you are given a quantifiable grade so you can see exactly how close you came to passing. In addition, you receive a note explaining what areas you were strongest and weakest in, which enables you to tailor your studying for future exams.

State Agencies and Getting Licensed

All states have a governing body for the real estate profession typically called the *real estate commission*. This group oversees all the license laws for the state and can issue, deny, suspend, or revoke real estate licenses.

DEFINITION

A **real estate commission** is a governing body of individuals appointed or elected in some states to administer, enforce, and uphold license laws within the state. This governing body is comprised of any number of individuals who collectively work as one group. For example, the Indiana real estate commission contains twelve members, including nine brokers—one from each geographic district, two citizen members who are unaffiliated with real estate in any way to represent the consumer's point of view and one "at-large" broker from any of the nine state districts.

Local Board Membership

Once you are licensed by the state to practice real estate activities, you must decide if you want to join a local board of REALTORS. Remember, a member of the local board and, therefore, a member of the state and national boards (i.e., the National Association of REALTORS, or NAR) can use the term *REALTOR*, whereas a nonmember may not.

All states have local real estate boards specific to different areas of the state. To join such boards, you are required to become an MLS member so you can list your own residential properties for sale and search those other agents have listed. Gaining access to the MLS is *the* main reason licensed residential real estate professionals choose to join the local, state, and national boards. Commercial brokers who choose to not list or sell residential property likely won't join a local board because the MLS isn't as much of a benefit to their businesses.

Some states allow nonboard members access to the MLS, but this is very rare. Membership dues to the local board typically include dues to cover the state board of REALTORS as well as the NAR. Dues for membership can range from a few hundred to thousands of dollars, as it also covers the dues for the state and national boards. You also must declare a *primary board* of REALTORS on your application to the local board.

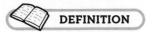

DEFINITION

A **primary board** is the board you choose where you will do the majority, if not all, of your work.

In some certain circumstance, REALTORS may need to become a member of a secondary board of REALTORS as well. If so, the cost is reduced because there's no need to pay the portion of the secondary board's fee to the state or national boards because it was paid in full upon joining the primary board. The reason for joining a secondary board is usually because the city in which you work straddles the geographic boundaries of two boards and you want to market your houses to both boards.

Finally, because you're an agent of your managing broker, you are required join the primary board he or she belongs to and, conversely, cannot join a board in which he or she is not a member.

What Happens After You Pass?

Although you've passed the exam, you're not immediately licensed. Passing the exam simply means you can apply to the real estate commission for a license.

Along with the exam questions, expect to be asked several other questions to validate the licensing process, such as these:

- Did you attend an approved school?

- Were you solicited for employment by the course instructor?

- Have you ever been arrested?

- Did you use any device to aid you in passing this exam?

The answers to these questions will be turned into the state. Note that the question about your criminal past varies greatly from state to state, so please check with your state for its definition. One state might mention a felony, while other states might decree it as any arrest within the past 5 years. In Indiana, the wording is as follows:

An applicant for licensure cannot have a conviction for any of the following:

- An act that would constitute a ground for disciplinary sanction

- A crime that has a direct bearing on the individual's ability to practice competently

- Fraud or material deception in the course of professional services or activities

- A crime that indicates the individual has the propensity to endanger the public

There's a major problem with this issue. If a student, or potential student, knows of an issue that might cause their application to be rejected under their state's license law, they won't know for sure until their application is sent to the real estate commission. Therefore, the student will have gone through the entire process of paying for, taking, and passing the course; taking and passing the exam; and applying for licensure before the commission can rule on their ability to be licensed. In my many years of experience, the commission never has preemptively told a prospective student before they actually apply.

After you pass the exam but before you submit application to the state for licensing, you must get a managing broker to agree to hang your license and accept responsibility for your actions. Your managing broker must first sign your application as the managing broker responsible for you before you can submit it to the state for consideration (more on managing brokers in a bit).

Forms Required to Get Licensed

The form you receive when you pass the state exam enables you to apply to the state licensing board. This form is given to you only after you pass the exam. In some states, the application is multiple pages, while in others, it's simply one.

Some states also require more information for the application process than others. For example, Florida requires the applicant to submit a set of fingerprints with their application. This process can vary from state to state.

Managing Broker Requirements

As mentioned earlier, in most states, if not all, the application must be signed by a managing broker who accepts responsibility for that licensee once he or she is licensed.

As a new licensee, selecting the managing broker you work for may be one of the biggest decisions in your new career. There are numerous variations when it comes to managing brokers and their brokerages. They can be part of a franchise or independent, be sole proprietors or any form of a company, with a single location or many throughout the city, and/or a full-service brokerage or limited-service brokerage.

The key question you as a new agent need to ask yourself is, "What am I looking for in a managing broker?" Are you looking for a broker who provides ongoing training? A broker who offers agents high-split compensations? One who specializes in certain types of real estate you are interested in? Or something else?

Ongoing training is usually the number one thing newer agents want from their managing broker. If this is what you want, know there's a cost associated with that training, usually in the form of a lower split to you on commission.

I suggest that as a new agent, you interview with several different managing brokers around the areas where you plan to work. Keep in mind, however, that even nationally recognized franchise real estate firms might vary within the same area because they're all independently owned and operated. One might have different training programs, pay compensation, and rules from another similar franchised company down the street. You also might decide to interview with a smaller firm rather than a large franchised firm.

Typically, smaller firms have less amenities than larger firms; however, they tend to pay higher commissions to the salespersons. At first glance, one would ask why an agent would want fewer amenities, such as a desk in the office, access to a copy machine, etc. Simply put, most agents work as independent contractors and are rarely in the office to use these amenities, so why pay for them? An agent can get copies at Kinkos, use the free Wi-Fi at Starbucks or sit in a library. So the less an agent's use of the amenities can translate into a higher commission that can be paid to the agent when they close a deal. Furthermore, smaller firms operate more like a family and close community of friends, whereas larger firms often treat agents more like a number.

Another strong factor that might influence your decision is the relationship you have, or will have, with a managing broker on a personal level. I have seen many agents go to work for, and subsequently leave, a managing broker's firm due to personal issues with the broker rather than the job itself.

What Happens If You Fail Your Exam?

When you schedule your exam and arrive to take the test, it probably will be unlike any experience you have encountered to date. The stress of passing the exam and entering a new career combined with the tension of the testing environment itself may cause you to not perform your best. Should you fail the exam, your first question likely will be, "What now?"

Don't worry! Some states claim a first-time passing rate of as low as 30 percent. The best thing to remember is that you can retake the test again and again as needed. Of course, there's an exam fee for *each* exam retake. As discussed previously, you'll likely take two separate exams: one for the general body and one for the state laws. The good news is that you can pass or fail each independently. If you pass the general body but fail the state, or vice versa, you only have to retake the section of the exam you failed.

In addition, when you fail the exam, you're given a printed report detailing the areas of the exam where you did poorly. This report directly details the parts of the course in which you need to strengthen your knowledge.

Retesting Timeframe

If you need to reschedule your test, you can do it almost immediately. I say *almost* because most states have a requirement that you cannot schedule an exam on the same day you failed it.

In a perfect world, the testing facility would have an opening the next day, making the shortest timeframe between the two tests. Sometimes, however, the testing facility may have a packed schedule, and you can't reschedule until a later date.

Also, most students like to restudy the material and choose to not reschedule that quickly anyway.

HELPFUL HINT

As mentioned earlier, you are allowed to take your state licensing exam at any approved location. So if your preferred location is full and not accepting anymore appointments on the date you need, you can take the test at another approved location. Of course, there may be other associated costs with this, such travel, lodging, etc., so keep that in mind.

There's a time limit to taking and passing your state licensing exam, whether it's your first or forty-first try. Most states have a license law section describing the timeframe by which the exam must be passed. If it isn't, the student must start the entire process all over again—including retaking the prelicensing course. In Indiana, this timeframe is 1 year from the day of course completion. Every state's license law addresses this issue in some form or manner, so be sure to check with your state.

Retesting Strategies

If you failed your first attempt at the exam, don't give up. There are strategies you might consider before retaking the exam.

As stated earlier, if you fail the exam, you are given insight into the testing areas where you were weaker as well as stronger. Using this information, you can customize your studying plans to concentrate on those areas where you had difficulty. Your prelicensing instructor might be a great source of other helpful material you can use for those areas. In addition, you can purchase real estate licensing practice exams, quizzes, and even refresher courses online as study aids.

Creating flashcards can help you practice for the exam as well. I suggest you create a system of handwritten flashcards using blank 3×5 index cards with the definitions of important terms written on the back. The key here is that the definition should not be a long, drawn-out definition, but rather a short, 8- to 10-word definition you've written in your own words to help you remember it. I recommend handwritten cards as opposed to printed cards because hand-writing the words and definitions gives you a head start on learning the material. Practice with these flashcards until you know the definitions of the words on sight.

You also might want to hire a private tutor to help you in your weakest areas of the exam. A great choice here would be the managing broker who intends to hang your license. He has a vested interest in you passing the exam so he can get you started in your new career. Similarly, an active REALTOR/mentor or a family member who already has his or her license can be a great source of help.

The Least You Need to Know

- The state licensing exam's registration process is simple and straightforward.
- Be sure your name on your course certificate matches your state identification card exactly.
- The exam consists of two tests: one on the general body and another on state laws.
- The state exam is pass/fail. If you do fail, you can retake the exam.
- You must pass the course before you can take the exam and apply for your license.
- You must have a managing broker accept responsibility for you before you can apply for your license.

Successful Exam Strategies

Passing the state licensing exam on the first attempt is the dream of all students as they enter the testing facility. The fact is, the outcome has been determined long before any student ever stepped foot in the testing facility. Understanding how to study in the most efficient way, realizing the manner in which the questions are written, and creating successful study habits can determine the outcome before you even take the exam.

In This Chapter

* Strategies for taking and passing the state licensing exam

* Using practice tests, quizzes, and other test-prep tools

* How the internet can help you study

* Understanding the exam questions

* Basic math and mathematical formulas used in real estate

Successful Studying Strategies

I'm not going to sugarcoat it; the state licensing exam is hard. You shouldn't expect to be able to pass it by simply listening to the instructor and not doing your homework. Failing to put in the hours of study after the lectures will result in a very disappointing exam result on your first attempt. I dare say that if this is the strategy you employ, the result may be so horrendous, you might never make a second attempt at the exam.

HELPFUL HINT

If you follow the standard rule of thumb for studying in college, where for every single hour spent in class you spend another hour studying, you'll spend a significant amount of time dedicated to the completion of the course. It also should result in a more desirable outcome on exam day.

Instead, let's discuss some other ideas that will certainly help you become more successful at comprehending the course and passing the exam.

Read After Class

Immediately after class, find a quiet place free from distractions to read the chapter material covered in the lecture.

I tell my students to "read behind me rather than in front of me." Don't read the material your instructor is going to discuss; instead, wait until he's explained it and then read the specific chapter in the book after the class. You'll have a greater level of comprehension because when you're reading it, you'll have already heard it explained by your instructor.

Like I do, your instructor might change the order of the sections in each chapter of the book to follow a more logical progression based on his knowledge of the material. He also could skip an entire section of the book. If you read beforehand, you might get confused on material that may not flow directly from the book.

Don't Take Notes During Class

I am a huge proponent of not taking notes during the class lecture. Yes, you read that correctly, *don't take notes*.

All the information you need is explained in the book. Note taking can be distracting because you're too busy focusing on taking notes instead of really listening to the instructor's lecture.

Furthermore, once you get behind in taking notes, you'll hardly ever be able to catch up to the rest of the class.

Concentrate as You Read

After class, as you read the chapter material covered during the lecture, pay careful attention to remembering the lecture as you read each page, section, and chapter. Now is when you can take extra notes on important items you find within the text or highlight terms and concepts you feel are important.

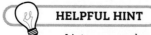 **HELPFUL HINT**

It's important that you study 1 hour on your own for every 1 hour of lecture time in order to gain the maximum understanding of the material.

Complete Your Homework

Always do the end-of-chapter questions, exercises, and homework immediately after you finish reading the material. This produces the best results because the information is fresh in your mind and readily available. Of course, you also should check your answers against the answer key to see what you've retained and what you need to study more, and to get a good, quantifiable answer for each practice exam or quiz.

Remember, most state exams require a passing score of 70 to 75 percent. Using these practice questions as a benchmark for those scores is a good method of measuring your comprehension of the material.

If you find that your practice exams or quizzes are not at or above the state's required passing rate, you should study more. It also would benefit you to notify your instructor immediately so he or she can help you create a study plan. Don't wait until the last day or two to schedule office hours and claim you're having trouble comprehending the material. Remember, your instructor wants to see you pass the exam and become successful just as much as you do. Furthermore, he or she has all the information at their fingertips you need to pass the course and state exam. Waiting until near the end of your coursework is the wrong time to start seeking help.

Ask for Clarification

Prepare a list of questions about any material that isn't clear to you. At the beginning of the class, or perhaps even before class, you can offer up these questions for explanations, debate, or instruction. Chances are that if you have a question, others students may benefit from a discussion on that particular topic as well.

Study with a Group or Partner

You should create a study group, or find a study partner, with which to exchange ideas, concepts, and questions. Using a fellow student as a study partner works great from an accountability aspect and often forces one student to do the homework knowing he has to be responsible to another.

Having a study partner (or group) to turn to for help, especially someone who might excel in a different area from you, can be beneficial in helping you learn topics that are hard for you and vice versa.

More Study Tips

Here are some other study strategies that might help:

- Create flashcards for sight word recognition.

- Seek outside material or textbooks to use as study guides.

- Interview practicing REALTORS to help you understand more difficult concepts.

- Schedule an office hour with the instructor for private custom instruction on a specific topic.

Using any or all of these strategies helps you prepare for the state exam. It's virtually impossible to *over*study for this exam.

HELPFUL HINT

Using all available avenues to prepare for the exam and understanding that it isn't an easy exam both go a long way in helping you pass on the first attempt.

Practice Test and Quizzes

Using any combination of the previously mentioned study strategies to help you pass the state exam is a worthwhile endeavor. Practice tests and quizzes are also valuable study aids. One of the greatest benefits of practice tests and quizzes is that they serve one purpose before they are taken and serve a completely different purpose after they are taken. This dual-purpose result is what makes this strategy an important concept to use when trying to pass the state exam.

The Benefits of Practice Tests and Quizzes

The first purpose of a practice exam is to test your knowledge in the field of real estate, either as a whole or by section. This is accomplished by asking general questions and grading your answers in the fashion you should expect from an exam.

The second purpose of this strategy is one in which most students fail to take advantage: using the practice exam as a guide for studying the material. Most students completely overlook the value of these practice tests, thinking that after they've taken the test, it can be tossed aside and serves no further purpose. That's not the case. The practice text gives you a set of real-word questions—and answers—you can use to better understand how concepts are used, how words are defined, and much more in your state exam. To the same extent, smaller quizzes produce the same results. After you've completed them, you can use them as study guides for smaller, more topic-specific concepts.

As mentioned, the completed practice exam represents more practical, real-world applications of the concepts your instructor covered. Many people learn better, faster, and in a more complete manner using concrete examples with answers rather than trying to understand a conceptual lecture. Plus, it can further help you by giving you insight to answers you got wrong.

I've told my students that another good way to gain insight on a completed test is to determine *why* the correct answer was correct. For a good practice in comprehension, write a short sentence or two that explains why each answer is correct. For most students, this usually can be the bridge between the concept and the question's concrete answer.

It may help to do a similar exercise by writing a sentence or two outlining why the wrong answer was wrong. This exercise helps two-fold: it explains why an answer is wrong for that particular question, and it helps you understand what sort of question it might be the correct answer for.

Technology-Assisted Study

The incorporation of technology in learning has become a viable and inexpensive option. As a result, it's becoming increasingly clear that traditional textbooks will be cast aside, resulting in the adoption of the ebook. Even with the rise in the internet, responsive websites, smartphones, tablets, apps, etc., technology-aided studying strategies don't differ much from traditional ones. The old strategies haven't changed, but access to them has gotten easier.

Many technologies offer every method of study options. These are the same strategies discussed earlier, just more easily accessible. Thanks to technology, students can now see an unlimited number of practice questions, concept explanations, and example questions from many different sources. This information can provide different views from myriad instructors, using varying teaching styles and techniques for that concept. Furthermore, the access to this information can now be held in the palm of your hand, which enables a student to maximize his or her studying over small intervals of free time. No longer does a student need to carry books and notes to study. Rather, they can access the information via smartphone while on the go and in remote places not normally conducive to studying.

 HELPFUL HINT

Smartphones provide students access to information, practice exams, concept explanations, flashcards, etc. in almost any location. This enables students to review materials on the go in their free time.

Book and Paper Study

The one downside to technology-aided study is the lack of concrete material for a student to touch, hold, and feel in their hands like traditional books and paper. Many students learn and comprehend better through the process of tactile learning—being able to hold the material. A study completed by Jan Noyes and Katie Garland, "Computer- vs. Paper-Based Tasks: Are They Equivalent?" found "… that information presented on video display terminals (VDTs) resulted in a poorer understanding by participants than information presented on paper." My own students have said they feel more comfortable learning from hardcopy materials than from computers or tablets. These students have even mentioned they used technology to find the information, but then they printed it so they would have the "touch" factor when studying.

Another factor of book and paper studying is the inherent belief that studying should be done in the traditional manner the students were exposed to in their formative years. This fact plays a role, specifically with older students who have not embraced technology as of yet.

In addition, traditional book and paper study methods enable a student to curate information in one place for easy access. They can group their completed exams, notes, and papers, which enables them to flip through the information faster rather than switching back and forth between websites or apps.

How to Read the Questions

Many strategies are available for maximizing your success on the state exam. The best way to improve your chances is to study carefully before the exam. There's no good substitute for knowing the correct answer.

Even a well-prepared student can make silly mistakes on a multiple choice exam, however, falling prey to distracters that look very similar to the correct answer.

For many reasons, students commonly consider multiple choice exams easier than essay exams. After all, the correct answer is guaranteed to be among the possible responses, and it's possible to score points with a lucky guess. Also, many multiple choice exams tend to emphasize basic definitions or simple comparisons rather than asking you to analyze new information or apply theories to new situations. And because multiple choice exams usually contain many more questions than essay exams, each question has a lower point value and, therefore, comes with less risk.

Despite these factors, however, multiple choice exams actually can be very difficult. Because multiple choice exams contain many questions, they force you to be familiar with a much broader range of material. Multiple choice exams also usually expect you to have a greater familiarity with general concepts. And because it's much more difficult for an exam writer to write good multiple choice questions, students often face higher risks due to unintended ambiguity.

 HELPFUL HINT

The best way to answer a question correctly is to eliminate any and all possible wrong answers. Even eliminating one or two wrong answers can increase your odds of guessing correctly to 50 or 75 percent.

When taking the state exam, reading the questions correctly is perhaps the single most important factor to getting the correct answer. I tell my students to answer the question that's asked. Many times the exam will ask a question and students will mentally alter the question by unintentionally injecting some other information into the question. Some questions might trip you up by changing units within the question or answers. For example, the question might ask about years and give the answers in months. Or perhaps a question is asked in square feet and the answers are given in acres. This is very common and can be easily missed if you don't read the *exact* question asked.

The state exam is designed to test your understanding of overall concepts of real estate, rather than your memorization of facts. As an instructor, I tell my students to be sure they understand the underlying theories of brokerage, agency, etc., rather than memorizing specific data and facts.

Sometimes the easiest way to determine the right answer is to eliminate the wrong answers. Do this by looking for answers that obviously cannot be correct. Responses that use absolute words, such as *always* or *never* are less likely to be correct than ones that use conditional words such as *usually* or *probably*.

Look for grammatical clues as well. If the question ends with the indefinite article *an*, for example, the correct response probably begins with a vowel.

A response that repeats the keywords found in the question is likely to be correct as well.

Also, the longest response is often the correct one because exam creators tend to load longer answers with qualifying adjectives or phrases.

Remember, these are just guidelines and should never be taken as the absolute truth when answering questions. If you are truly at a loss for the answer, go with your gut feeling. You've probably covered the topic in class and subconsciously know the answer.

Finally, never change an answer after you've completed the question. With that said, if you can determine without a doubt your answer is wrong, such in the case of a math question, you should change it. Perhaps another question in the exam shed light on a previous question, confirming you answered it incorrectly.

Solving Math Problems

It's a given that your real estate exam will contain math. Many students enter my classroom and immediately say, "I hate math, and I'm not good at it." I am a firm believer in self-affirmation, so with that attitude, such students probably won't be good at math. Always tell yourself that the math is easy and will be a common activity in your career. Convince yourself you are good at it.

 HELPFUL HINT

As stated before, the greatest advantage to multiple choice exams is that the correct answer is given among the answer options. So the worst-case scenario is that you can guess and have a 25 percent chance of getting the answer correct (if four answer options are offered).

Even with math questions, you can eliminate wrong answers, increasing your chances of getting the right answer with each wrong answer thrown out. After you have eliminated the obviously wrong options, take the remaining answers and work backward by using the answers as your starting point. Work the question backward and see if you find the question asked. If not, try another answer. Repeat this process until you find the question you were asked. It must be the correct answer.

Here's an example of what I mean:

> What percent commission did Jon charge his client if he earned $18,000 on a house that sold for $300,000?
>
> A. 5 percent
>
> B. 6 percent
>
> C. 20 percent
>
> D. 50 percent

You obviously can eliminate answers C and D because they aren't within the realm of possibility. Through the process of eliminating two answers, you've raised your guessing percent from 25 to 50 percent without even doing any calculation at all.

Using the backward concept, let's try answer A first:

> 5% × $300,000 = $15,000

Is this commission amount equal to the commission amount stated in the question? No. Therefore, it is not the correct answer. Move on to the next answer, B. Working backward, we can see that:

> 6% × $300,000 = $18,000

Is this commission amount equal to the commission amount stated in the question? Yes. Therefore, answer B is the correct answer.

Often students are concerned about the time required to answer math questions, worrying they might take too long and put themselves in jeopardy of not finishing. The time given to take the state exam is sufficient and takes into consideration the time needed to answer math questions. You shouldn't be concerned about not finishing because of the math questions.

The Least You Need to Know

- Using good study strategies increases your chances of passing the state exam.
- Many different study strategies can help you comprehend the information. Choose the one that best works for you.
- Practice exams and quizzes are great tools to test your knowledge and can be great study guides as well.
- New technology increases your access to more study material.
- Learning to read the questions correctly is a key element of passing the state exam.
- Using the backward-solution method can be a great help in solving math problems.

The Job Basics

The real estate agent is the crucial cog of the real estate industry. Oftentimes he is a salesman for the customer looking to buy a home, a seller's advocate the next; A great real estate professional is a real estate consultant, a financial analyst, an expert negotiator, a networking specialist, as well as a social and industrial media marketer. The job requires strong dedication to its clients, often after normal workhours—with some weeks requiring well beyond forty hours a week.

Getting your license is the first step to becoming a super-agent. First you must attend a state-approved course and pass the state's licensing exam. Once you pass, you will work with another real estate broker for a period before starting your own business. During this period of apprenticeship, you will learn the basic knowledge of the business as well as the skills needed to successfully help your clients achieve their life dream of home ownership.

The REALTOR Job

Becoming a REALTOR can be a very lucrative and successful career. But more than that, it can be a very self-rewarding career. As a REALTOR, your ultimate goal is to help your clients fulfill their goals of home ownership. Helping people is the definitive self-reward a person can achieve. It's a bonus you get paid to do it.

If helping people is your dream, you have chosen the right career. Let's look at the job of a REALTOR.

In This Chapter

- Understanding the REALTOR role and its requirements
- The different levels of real estate licenses
- Determining which brokerage is right for you
- How a REALTOR gets paid
- Key business laws that affect real estate

REALTOR 101

REALTORS help people buy, sell, trade, exchange, manage, or lease *real property,* be it single family homes, doubles, vacant land, condos, or in some cases, commercial property. REALTORS work with property buyers or sellers, landlords, and tenants, assisting them as they navigate the complex world of the property market. REALTORS talk with clients to find out what kind of property they want to buy or lease, including price points, square footage, locations, and many more specific amenities they're seeking. They also meet with clients about property they might want to sell.

DEFINITION

Real property includes real estate, and it adds a bundle of rights. This bundle of rights consists of the rights for property owners to use their property as they see fit.

REALTORS may use their local multiple listing service (MLS), personal websites, social media, and flyers to market their sellers' properties and to find properties for sale for their buying clients. REALTORS often work nights and weekends, showing properties to buyers, conducting open houses for properties they have listed, and other pertinent activities.

During the process, the REALTOR might write an offer and subsequent counteroffers for their client. As part of their responsibilities, the REALTOR guides their client to get the best possible deal using their insight, expertise, and knowledge of the local real estate market.

When the offer is accepted and the property is pending, the two REALTORS (the buyer's REALTOR and the seller's REALTOR) work together, along with many other professionals, to facilitate a smooth closing and transfer of the property from the current owner to the new owner.

REALTORS help their clients in four main phases:

1. **Marketing for new clients**   The time prior to finding a client.

2. **Working for active clients**   The time between creating agency with a client and writing the offer.

3. **Pending the client's deal**   The time from the initial offer to the acceptance of a property.

4. **Closing the client's deal**   The time between pending a property and closing the property.

Let's take a look at each in more detail.

Marketing for New Clients

Marketing for new clients is the first phase of the REALTOR's activities. Searching for clients is the life-blood of a REALTOR, taking up the largest portion of their time and day-to-day activities—typically 40 to 50 percent.

What marketing activities does a REALTOR do? How often does he market? In what manner does he market and where? These are just a few of the questions a REALTOR must answer to find a client. Here's the tricky part—there are no magic answers to these questions. And worse, it's not the same for any other REALTOR, client, location, etc. One marketing technique, type, social platform, etc., might work in Florida, but it might not be effective in New York.

The marketing phase is perhaps the hardest to master and the easiest to botch. Spending time, effort, and money on this phase that yields no clients can cause many REALTORS to get frustrated and quit the business.

HELPFUL HINT

Successful marketing is a process of figuring out what works best for you in your area.

Once you have found a client who wants to sell their home or buy another, you then proceed into the next phase of working with your client.

Working for Active Clients

Now that your client is ready to buy or sell, you'll start working with the client toward an eventual closing. This phase is the second longest phase and will occupy approximately 20 percent of your time.

If the client is a seller, you'll list the property on the local MLS for other REALTORS and their buyer clients to view. You might list the property on your own personal website as well as any other real estate-related websites. You'll use pictures, plus a description of the property, to entice other REALTORS, and their buyers, to come view the property.

If your client is a buyer, you'll need to meet with them to determine their wants and needs for their new property. Then, you'll scour the local MLS and other sites to find the best properties that fit your client's goals. When you've found suitable properties in the MLS, you'll escort your buyer to view the properties until you find the perfect one. Calling on your REALTOR expertise, the buyer will determine his or her offer amount and direct you to write the purchase offer for the property.

Pending the Client's Deal

The third phase spans from when the initial offer is written until the offer, or counteroffers, is accepted. This phase is typically the shortest of all the phases, but it's perhaps the most important. This is when all the finer points of the purchase agreement get offered, countered, and finalized.

In some situations, however, purchase offers and any subsequent counteroffers may never end in an accepted offer. I have experienced some deals in which the buyer and seller could never agree on key terms, even after numerous counteroffers were presented by both parties. Some deals just never are mutually agreed upon.

Closing the Client's Deal

After the purchase agreement has been accepted and the deal is considered *formed*, the real work begins for both the buyer and the seller.

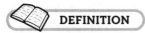

DEFINITION

As is the case with other contracts, real estate contracts are **formed** when one party makes an offer and another party accepts the offer.

During this phase, other professionals usually step in and assist with the process, including home inspectors, lenders, appraisers, etc. The extent of a REALTOR's interaction is limited to reactionary measures, such as if something happens and a client needs help to rectify the issue. The culmination of this phase results in the closing and transfer of the real estate from the seller to the buyer.

It's important to note that at any time during one of the four phases, a client might fall out of the process, either by his own accord or someone else's. For example, if a buyer does not qualify for a mortgage due to bad credit, he or she might withdraw from the process. A seller might also withdraw if they've reconsidered and decided to not sell their property. It's possible that a client can move between phases during the process as well. For example, if a buyer makes an offer on a property that ultimately gets accepted, but upon inspection it's revealed the property has major damages, the seller can withdraw and terminate the deal. They may then choose to restart the process and begin looking at other properties.

To be a successful REALTOR, you'll need to have different clients in different phases at the same time. Time management is a crucial skill all successful REALTORS need to master. Keeping track of each client and their respective phase is an art, and many REALTORS may decide to create a team of assistants, or other licensed REALTORS, to help control the flow of the client's deal. Many REALTORS are adopting *real estate teams* to increase their output, deal flow, and overall efficiency with their clients.

DEFINITION

A **real estate team** is a group of licensed REALTORS working together to increase their efficiency or deal flow as a whole. There are two team concepts. The first is comprised of many different REALTORS working under one main REALTOR yet doing their own deals with their own clients, usually because the main REALTOR has a strong and favorable reputation within the local market. In the other, one REALTOR performs one phase or part of a phase for a client and then hands them off to another REALTOR for the next phase, creating a division of labor. Typically, this method is used because each REALTOR excels at one phase more than another.

Several types of software are available that enable a REALTOR to achieve a similar level of effectiveness as a team concept on their own. This software varies in style, brand, ease of use, and cost and should be vetted thoroughly before use.

Licensing Levels

All states require a REALTOR to have a license in order to broker real estate deals for clients. However, different states utilize different licensing models.

Almost half of the states utilize a model whereby all licensees acquire a broker's license after they pass the state licensing exam. A second licensing model requires that a newly licensed person, upon passing the state exam, acquire a salesperson's license first. This model then requires time in the industry, more education, and testing to gain a broker's license.

The Single Broker License Model

Some states have adopted a licensing model in which a person passing the state licensing exam earns a broker's license. These states usually require that a student complete higher initial educational hours in order to be eligible to sit for the state exam.

This model is slightly misleading, however, because these states still require you to spend some time in service before starting your own brokerage company. This time frame can range from 1 to 3 years. Furthermore, most of these states also require some postlicensing education within the initial year or two as part of the licensing process.

States that use this model also have a designation, not a license level per se, that's required to start a brokerage. This designation typically requires more education and testing before the designation of managing broker can be achieved. It's important to note that the designation of managing broker doesn't need to be attained unless you want to start a brokerage company.

The Salesperson/Broker Model

The other licensing model used by the remainder of the states grants a new licensee an entry-level license, which is called a *salesperson's license*. While a licensee maintains his salesperson's license, he cannot start a real estate brokerage firm. Salespersons don't need to take the test for a broker's license if they have no desire of ever owning a real estate brokerage. They can simply maintain a salesperson's license forever and continue to practice under a principal broker.

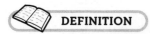 **DEFINITION**

> In the states that use the salesperson/broker licensing model, the **salesperson's license** is the entry-level license granted to all new agents that pass the exam. To obtain a **broker's license** an agent must have time in service plus pass a second exam, the **broker's exam.**

To obtain a broker's license within this model, a salesperson must gain some time in service, complete more education, and pass a second exam, which is referred to as a *broker's exam*. Upon passing this second exam, he or she is conferred a higher level of license, called a *broker's license*. However, if the goal of the newly licensed broker is to still practice under another broker's license, they are granted an associate broker's license. If, after passing the exam, they want to start their own brokerage company, they are granted a principal broker's license. A person holding a principal broker's license is allowed to start their own company, hold the license of other salespersons and associate brokers, and be responsible for their actions. Once a person passes the broker exam, they can apply to the state for either an associate broker's or principal broker's license. They declare which type of broker's license they seek on the licensure application.

Once the broker's license has been attained, it can easily be switched between the two different designations of associate and principal broker. Most states only require an application requesting the change from one to the other and an application fee.

A principal broker's license cannot be held under another principal broker's license. Therefore, if an owner wishes to close his company and go to work for another broker, he must apply to the state for an official license change to switch to an associate broker's license. Similarly, an associate broker may not start a company without notifying the state of his intention and officially applying for his license change to principal broker.

HELPFUL HINT

In the states that use the single broker model, the main responsible REALTOR is called a managing broker. In the states that use the salesperson/broker model, he is known as the principal broker.

Which Brokerage Is Right for You?

No matter what licensing model a state chooses to use, all new licensees, either licensed as a broker or salesperson, must have a managing or principal broker hold their license for an initial period. Consider this period an apprenticeship for new agents to learn the business.

So how do you determine which real estate brokerage firm you should work for? Before you can answer this question, you must think about, understand, and be comfortable with many factors.

To begin, let's talk about the three types of real estate brokerage offices: *big-box brokerages, boutique brokerages,* and *independent brokerages.*

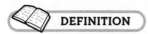

DEFINITION

Big-box brokerages are national franchise companies that broker real estate throughout the United States and abroad. **Boutique brokerages** are nonfranchised real estate brokerage companies that typically consists of a few REALTORS up to a couple dozen. In **independent brokerages,** a REALTOR works for him- or herself with no other REALTORS working under them.

As a new licensee, you need to know what type of brokerage best suits your needs. Each one of these brokerage types can offer advantages and disadvantages to a new licensee.

The Big-Box Brokerage

These are the companies that have spent millions of advertising dollars to make their names household entities, such as RE/MAX, Keller Williams, Century 21, Coldwell Banker, ERA Realty, etc.

These brokerages are most often franchised by an owner, typically the principal or managing broker. The franchisor provides the broker-owner with ongoing help, support, and branding to gain market share in the broker-owner's local area. In exchange, the broker-owner pays a small portion of their commission (typically 2 to 6 percent) from every seller or buyer transaction completed to the franchisor.

A big-box brokerage offers many other perks and benefits to the broker-owner and the other REALTORS under him, including preprinted marketing material, access to free legal advice, and robust company websites to name a few. Furthermore, due to the top-heavy managerial structure, most big-box brokerages have a staff of trainers, IT specialists, and receptionists assisting the broker-owner and his REALTORS.

The downside to this model for the new licensee is the cost to maintain these personnel and benefits. This cost comes in the form of a lower commission split to the agent and higher split to the company to cover the overhead. However, traditionally this price is only paid when a deal is closed, so most new licensees don't see this as an immediate downside.

The Boutique Brokerage

A boutique brokerage, sometimes called a nonfranchised brokerage, is very similar to big-box brokerages in their day-to-day operation; however, they lack any national franchise backing. A 2015 National Association of REALTORS (NAR) report states that 59 percent of all licensed REALTORS in the United States work for a boutique brokerage.

These companies try to mirror the big-box model for the most part, but the fact that they owe no commissions percentage to a franchisor enables the boutique to keep more commissions as a whole, often passing down that increase to their REALTORS.

This model is the most varied of the three, depending on the size of the boutique. I have seen a few agents working diligently on their own deals for the broker where there's no administrative help other than the broker himself. I also have seen a boutique that boasted more than 100 agents and the largest brokerage in the city based on volume closed. That company had more than 10 administrative support staff members for all the REALTORS in the office. In this particular case, the brokerage collected a similar portion of the commissions from each deal, but rather than pay the collected monies to a franchisor, they kept it as a general fund to pay the administrative staff.

The Independent Brokerage

The third model is the easiest to understand: one REALTOR working by himself and keeping all the commissions earned. This model seems great at first glance—no one to worry about, no commissions paid out to others, etc. Yet upon further inspection, you can see several large issues that arise from this model.

First, the fact that there's only one person means the REALTOR is his or her own administrative support, trainer, boss, etc., possibly creating logistical problems throughout the day. No staff is available to call for support if the REALTOR forgot a form for a client meeting or needs to show a property. Also, if no commissions are generated in a given month, the REALTOR is still responsible for any bills the brokerage needs to pay.

There are upsides and downsides to each brokerage model. Determining your needs as a new licensee helps you determine which brokerage you might want to work for. Generally speaking, most new licensees go to large, big-box brokerages to begin their careers so they can take advantage of the training and mentorship available. They view the lower commission split of the big-box model as a cost of gaining experience and doing business during their initial years. However, after they feel they've learned as much as they can, they tend to move their license to a smaller boutique firm to take advantage of a potential higher commission split.

Some new licensees that come from a sales background have opted to go directly for the higher split and forego the training. They feel their previous sales training and experience is sufficient enough for them to excel at real estate. This mind-set may or may not be true. I have seen it both work and fail miserable. You have to ask yourself what you want from your broker.

Understanding the Commission Structure

When a new licensee finally decides which brokerage firm and broker he or she wants to hold their license, they sign an *independent contractor agreement*. This agreement lists the many terms and conditions created between the agent and the broker.

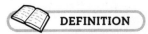 **DEFINITION**

> An **independent contractor agreement** is a legal contract entered into by the new licensee and her broker. This contract spells out many terms and conditions they both agree on. One major term is the split of the commissions earned and paid to the new agent. They also agree that the broker will withhold no income taxes and pay the entire amount earned by the new agent. The new agent is responsible to pay her own taxes at year's end.

In the independent contractor agreement, the commission split is determined through negotiations during the initial hiring period between the two parties. This agreement is usually for a year and automatically renews on the anniversary of the initial agreement date. I have seen many different types of splits created; they're limited only by the imagination of each party.

The commission split between the new agent and broker can be thought of in terms of a plan, much like an insurance policy that has different plans. Most brokers have one or two different plans they like to offer to new agents. Typically, a specific commission plan is offered based on the broker's guess as to how much business the new agent will bring to the brokerage. Sometimes the split offered may be based on the amount of time, training, and help a broker thinks he'll have to give the new agent.

Many possible plans can be agreed upon by the new licensee and the broker. Here are few types of common splits:

- A straight split on all commission earned

- A graduated split on all commission earned

- A split with a cap fee paid to the brokerage

- A flat-fee paid to the broker for each deal closed by the agent

Let's review each type of split.

A Straight Split on All Commission Earned

A straight split on all commission earned is by far the simplest and most common commission split used by a broker with his agents. A 60/40 split, for example, means an agent gets 60 percent of the commission earned, while the broker earns 40 percent. I've never seen a broker receive a larger portion than an agent.

A Graduated Split on All Commission Earned

A graduated split works the same as a straight split. However, when the company has earned a predetermined dollar amount, the commission adjusts upward to benefit the agent. This concept was created as an incentive to encourage agents to do more business so they'll earn more money on the later deals.

For example, a 60/40 split is in place until a company receives $5,000 and then the split is adjusted to 70/30 until another predetermined number is hit, enabling the split to be readjusted again to an even higher split like 90/10.

The downside to this plan is that the split returns to the original 60/40 rate after the agents hit the anniversary of the initial signing date of the independent contractor agreement.

A Split with a Capped Fee Paid to the Brokerage

This plan has been increasing in popularity with brokerages in recent years because they can use it to draw other agents to their brokerage firm. It's very similar to the graduated plan but with one major difference: after the new agent reaches the predetermined dollar amount, usually a higher number, it adjusts one time only to a very high split, such as 95/5 or even 100 percent of the commission earned. Upon the agent's signing anniversary, it resets and they start again at their beginning split.

For example, an agent may be at a 60/40 split until he or she earns the brokerage $17,000. Then, they receive 100 percent of their commission earned for the rest of that year.

This plan is growing in popularity because a broker can create their annual budget and determine how many agents they'll need to cover their costs due to the capped payout of the new agent.

A Flat-Fee Paid to the Broker

Another new concept gaining popularity is the flat-fee plan. In this setup, which is more agent-centric, the broker keeps a flat fee from every closing, and the agent keeps the remaining portion of the commission.

For example, if the commission earned on a deal is $5,000, the broker only retains the flat-fee of $600 and the remaining $4,400 goes to the agent. This plan is almost exclusively offered only to experienced agents who need little in the way of support from their brokers; the agents deserve the lion's share of the money earned.

Desk Fee

Another factor that's common in some areas is a *desk fee*. This is a fee the agent pays to the broker every month to cover any overhead used by the agent, such as electricity, rent, phone, etc. Most brokers use this fee as a way to cover their fixed monthly costs. Agents view it as the cost of doing business they would incur anywhere they opened an office. Think of it as being a base monthly rent paid by the agent to the broker, even if the agent hasn't earned commissions in that given month.

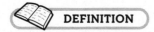 **DEFINITION**

> A **desk fee** is a fixed fee the agent pays to the broker to cover a broker's fixed costs. This fee is paid every month in addition to, or in the absence of, any commission paid by the agent.

Sometimes, the desk fee can be used in conjunction with one of the other plans or to boost the split of the agent. For example, one version of the plan a broker may have is a 50/50 split with no desk fee, or the agent could choose a 75/25 with a $300/month desk fee. If the agent is new and unsure of his abilities to earn commission, he might opt for the no desk fee plan. However, if the agent is sure he can close three, four, five, or more deals per month, he may opt for the higher split and pay the desk fee, making his overall monthly agent's portion higher.

All desk fees the agent pays to the broker are tax deductible as an expense on the agent's taxes.

The Sherman Antitrust Issues in Real Estate

The real estate brokerage business is like any other business in that it must file business documents and reports such as annual reports, company taxes, etc. Like other businesspeople, real estate brokers need to be aware of the do's and don'ts of Sherman Antitrust laws.

Sherman Antitrust laws prohibit price fixing, group boycotting, the allocation of customers or markets, and tie-in agreements. It's an area where both federal and state enforcement authorities are active, and where a violation can result in criminal as well as civil penalties. The process is anything but comfortable and could bring about irreparable damage, even when the person subjected to an investigation is ultimately vindicated.

Price Fixing

Price fixing is prohibited. It means that competing brokers, real estate governing bodies, or multiple listing organizations can't agree to set sales conditions, fees, or management rates.

Listing brokers typically price their commissions on a percentage of the sales price. At the same time, they usually offer a share of that commission to the selling broker to entice him to find a buyer. From my own experience in various real estate markets, it appears that these commissions and cooperating splits are surprisingly similar, almost fixed within certain markets.

There are many reasons the commissions could end up similar in value due to similar cost structures, company expenses, overall market sensitivity to price, etc. But real estate brokers should understand that any agreement, express or implied, with a competing brokerage to charge a certain commission is a violation of the Sherman Antitrust laws with both criminal and civil consequences. Brokers should always independently set their prices or risk antitrust liability. Of course, brokers negotiating a particular transaction must discuss pricing, but for that transaction only.

Group Boycotting

Group boycotting is illegal under the Sherman Antitrust laws as well. A group boycott can be an organized refusal by competing businesses to deal with a particular business or person. The purpose of such a boycott is to force the company to change its ways or even force it out of business.

It should be emphasized that it's never illegal for one party to refuse to deal with another. However, as soon as two or more competitors acting in concert participate in a refusal to deal, their conduct crosses the line and becomes an Antitrust violation.

The Allocation of Customers

The allocation of markets or customers could occur when brokers agree to divide their markets or customers and not compete for the other's business. The biggest concern and detriment to the customer is when a customer is moving outside the boundaries determined by the brokers.

For example, two brokers might determine that one will service all the north-side clients and the other will service all the south-side clients in their real estate transactions. If a customer on the north side of the city wants to move to the south side, they would like the knowledge and expertise of that south-side REALTOR. However, the illegal allocation of the customers between those two brokers would prevent that from happening, making it an antitrust violation.

Tie-In Agreements

A tie-in agreement, sometimes called a *tying agreement,* is where a broker ties one service or product to another service or product. For example, a real estate broker owns 10 acres of vacant land. A builder wants to buy the land, but the broker refuses to sell to the builder unless the builder agrees to list the property with their brokerage firm. This tie-in arrangement is illegal.

If it's determined that a violation of the Sherman Antitrust laws has occurred, an individual may be fined a maximum of $100,000 and sentenced up to 3 years in prison, and a corporation may be fined up to $1 million per violation. In a civil suit, an aggrieved person may recover up to triple the value of the actual damages plus attorneys' fees and costs.

It's best to know and understand the Sherman Antitrust laws and avoid any violations of those laws.

The Least You Need to Know

- A REALTOR's main job is to help their client complete a successful real estate transaction.
- Some states use a two license business model of a salesperson and broker, while other states only have one license level of broker.
- A time-in-service period is required by all states prior to opening your own brokerage firm.
- Boutique real estate brokerages account for more than half of all licensed REALTORS.
- Commission splits between the new licensee and his or her broker vary and can be negotiated.
- Work carefully to avoid violating the Sherman Antitrust laws.

Agency Law

This chapter covers two types of laws: statutory and common. In statutory law, a law is passed by the legislature at the state or federal level. Statutes set forth general concepts of law that courts apply to specific situations. Common law, sometimes called case law, is borne out of the decisions of prior court cases and can change with new cases being determined every day.

Agency is common law and can change throughout the years.

In This Chapter

- What is agency?
- Creating agency with a client
- Terminating agency with a client
- The relationship between an agent and his or her broker
- Paying agents and calculating splits
- Avoiding issues within agency agreements

Understanding Agency

Agency is an area of law dealing with contractual, fiduciary relationships that involve a person, called the agent, who is authorized to act on behalf of another, called the principal. It may be referred to as an equal relationship between a principal and an agent whereby the principal authorizes the agent to work under his direction and on his behalf. Under their fiduciary responsibilities, the agent is required to negotiate on behalf of the principal and bring him the best deal.

Before we begin, it's important that you understand some basic terms used in the real estate profession. These definitions are very specific and must be understood to protect both the agent and client when performing agency duties.

Customer   A person with whom there is no agency agreement.

Client   A person with whom agency has been created. This person sometimes is called the principal or seller/buyer.

Agent   A person contractually bound to a client.

Fiduciary responsibilities   The duties and obligations that define each particular agency.

Listing agent   An agent who represents the seller, or landlord, of property in a transaction.

Selling agent   An agent who represents the buyer, or tenant, of property in a transaction.

Dual agent   Also called a limited agent, an agent who represents both the buyer and the seller on the same real estate transaction.

Nonagent   An agent who represents neither party in a transaction but does aid in the preparation of the documents. Often referred to as a transactional agent.

 HELPFUL HINT

Generically speaking, agency can cover many different professions, including talent agency, sports agency, or real estate agency. All basically work the same: an agent represents his or her client to a third party in a specific transaction.

The law of agency is created under common law, often called the common law of agency. Agency, therefore, can and has changed throughout the life of real estate. This is why REALTORS are required to take continuing education. Should a change occur, the required continuing education keeps practicing agents abreast of any changes.

In the real estate world, agency is created in two ways: express and implied.

Express Agency

The most preferred agency is created by either an oral or a written agreement between the principal and the agent that indicates their express intent for this representational status. Although a written agreement is the preferable method to create express agency, some states allow oral contracts in real estate and consider them legally binding. The *statute of frauds,* which requires a contract to be written to be legally enforceable, is used in most all real estate contracts.

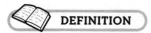 **DEFINITION**

> The **statute of frauds** is a law that requires that certain contracts be in writing and that those contracts be signed by the parties who are to be bound by the contract.

The most common method of creating express agency with the seller is through a listing agreement. Similarly, express agency can be created with a buyer through a buyer's agency agreement.

Implied Agency

It's also possible to create an agency relationship by the actions of the parties. Oftentimes, most customers fail to understand the complexities of agency law and assume that when they contact an agent for help, the agent is their agent.

If a real estate agent takes on responsibilities that are normally those of an agent but hasn't signed an agency agreement, he still may be considered an agent via implied agency. By the same token, if the customer asks the agent for advice or actions that are normally reserved for express agency, an implied agency could be created.

Sometimes, in the course of casual conversation, it may be possible to accidentally create an implied agency relationship. This may occur when the real estate agent casually provides insight, advice, or expertise that would be reserved for clients, but that consumer relies on that advice.

For example, a customer, not a client, phoned to discuss home buying in general. During the course of the conversation, the caller asked the agent his opinion regarding the listing price and wondered if the seller was willing to negotiate that price. That's the kind of question that requires insight, expertise, and knowledge to answer, and an agent cannot risk answering with a customer without fear of creating implied agency.

 HELPFUL HINT

> This job is entirely based on finding customers and converting them to clients through an agency relationship. The capability of a REALTOR to do this is the key to becoming successful.

Some states have specific legislation that states no agency can exist without a written agency agreement. This helps avoid accidental implied agency.

Single Agency

Single agency is the most common type of agency. In it, the agent represents only one side of the deal—the seller or the buyer. The listing agent represents the seller, and the selling agent represents the buyer.

The terminology is critical to understand and confusing at best. The easiest way to understand these two terms is to look at their primary function within the listing process. The listing agent markets, or lists, the seller's property on the multiple listing service (MLS). The buyer works with the agent who ultimately sells them on the attributes of the property and, therefore, sells the house.

Dual or Limited Agency

In some cases, the listing agent also represents the buyer of the property. This is known as dual or limited agency. To become a dual agent, the agent must have permission in writing from both parties prior to showing the house to the buyer.

Some states have enacted laws that prohibit dual agency to avoid potential problems for the agent or either party involved. Many agents use the term "me-me" when representing both parties to signify they are collecting both sides of the real estate commission.

Gratuitous Agency

Compensation does not create agency, and it's possible for an agent to work for free. This is known as gratuitous agency or *gratis,* or free, agency. This is analogous to an attorney working a case pro bono.

An agent does not have to be paid by the principal in order to be his agent. The fact that the agent entered into the agency agreement of his own free will is what creates the agency between the parties.

The Fiduciary Responsibilities of Agency

The main reason agency becomes an important factor is due to the service given to clients versus the service given to customers. A client is a person with whom agency has been created, either express or implied. Once this agency is created, the customer is entitled to a range of fiduciary responsibilities, including care, obedience, loyalty, disclosure, accounting, and confidentiality.

 HELPFUL HINT

Remember the six fiduciary responsibilities by thinking of the anagram *COLD AC:* **c**are, **o**bedience, **l**oyalty, **d**isclosure, **a**ccounting, and **c**onfidentiality.

Care

An agent must exercise a degree of reasonable skill and care to ensure the client does not suffer any harm during the business dealings when buying or selling real property. This is why it's important that an agent know and understand the client's wants and needs, whether that client be a seller or buyer.

When an agent works with a seller, the fundamental way to exercise reasonable skill and care is to give the client the benefit of their expertise and knowledge to obtain the best deal. When working with a seller, the same care and skill include helping the client determine the correct listing price, making the property available for showings to other buyer's agents, and holding open houses.

An agent who represents a buyer must exercise reasonable skill and care to locate a property suitable for the buyer to purchase. Other duties include helping the buyer find suitable financing, evaluating properties and neighborhoods, as well as writing offers and counteroffers, to name a few.

If an agent fails to exercise reasonable skill and care, he or she might be found negligent by a court or state association. If found in violation of his or her fiduciary responsibilities, an agent could be liable for any loss to their client.

Obedience

An agent must act in good faith to represent his or her client at all times by obeying the client's directions based on the written purchase agreement. The directions the client presents to the agent also must be in good faith to give a true and honest picture of the property and all facets of the deal.

An agent is not bound by obedience if any instructions from the client violate local, state, or federal law, like failing to disclose lead-based paint. However, an agent should not act without the direction of the client, nor exceed the authority granted to him or her by the contract, or risk potential liability for such actions.

Loyalty

An agent should always place the interest of the client above his or her own during the course of all real estate dealings. The agent is hired to gain the best deal for the client, not the agent.

For example, you should never ask your client to make a higher offer solely because the commission payout would be greater for you.

Disclosure

An agent must disclose all pertinent facts about the property, buyer, and seller, if known. Furthermore, you must disclose these facts even if your client hasn't asked you to.

Disclosure also can hurt your client or his interest in the property. For example, a buyer makes an offer on a property. However, the buyer's agent knows the buyer recently filed for bankruptcy, which could affect his ability to obtain a mortgage.

In some states, disclosure also could be defined as the timeframe with which you make known to your client any offers you receive. An agent must give all offers to his or her client promptly.

The agent also must disclose material defects regarding the property to give all potential buyers a true and accurate picture of the property. A *latent defect,* once known, must be disclosed in future dealings with buyers unless the issue has been rectified.

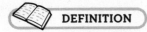 DEFINITION

A **latent defect** is an unforeseen or hidden defect in the property. Typically, latent defects cannot be determined by someone other than a professional specifically seeking that defect. For example, a pest inspection service would be able to determine if wood-destroying insects were present at a property.

Accounting

The accounting of all monies for each deal must be carefully tracked and identified during the process of closing a deal. The misplacement, loss, or misuse of funds can be both a criminal and civil violation for the agent and his broker.

Confidentiality

All agents will eventually know intimate details about their clients' financial and personal reasons as to why they are selling or buying property. This information was given under the context of confidentiality between the agent and the client. Therefore, the agent cannot reveal this information to any person connected to the deal for any reason, even if he or she thinks the disclosure will not harm the client.

These fiduciary responsibilities are present during the entire course of the agency, from beginning to end. After agency has terminated (discussed later in this chapter), the agent is not required to be responsible for care, obedience, loyalty, and disclosure to his client. However, the agent will maintain accounting and confidentiality forever.

Customers, as opposed to clients, are entitled to a lesser degree of responsibilities: fair and honest dealings. An agent is not allowed to misguide the customer and deal with him in a manner inconsistent with the profession. An agent is allowed to give factual information regarding the property and must disclose any material defects of the property. Factual information that can be given under customer-level service might include sales price, location, school system, bed/bath configuration, etc.

How Is an Agency Created?

In real estate, agency is created by either a written listing agreement with a seller or a buyer agency agreement with a buyer. Some states allow verbal agreements, but most do not.

Several different types of listing agreements are available, and all create varying degrees of agency.

Listing Agreements

An *exclusive-right-to-sell listing* agreement is the most common listing contract that grants one broker the sole right to list a property for sale. Under this agreement, a broker lists a property, markets the property for sale, and represents the seller on any purchase offers and counteroffers. Under this listing, the agent is seen as the *procuring cause* and, therefore, receives the commission regardless of who brings the buyer. This listing agreement is considered the most protective of all the listing agreements.

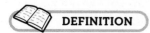 **DEFINITION**

A **procuring cause** is a broker who, by their actions, brought about the sale of a property. For the listing agent, this might be simply getting the seller to sign the listing agreement. For the buyer's agent, it might be the agent who showed the property to a buyer who ultimately entered into a purchase agreement with the seller.

An *exclusive-agency listing* agreement is one in which the agent is granted the right to list a property for sale. However, the seller retains the right to bring the ultimate buyer. In this case, the seller owes no commission to the agent. The seller is only obligated to pay the commission should the agent bring a buyer, which includes a buyer's agent bringing a buyer as well.

An *open listing* is one in which the seller retains the right to enter into as many agreements, with as many different brokers, as he or she wants to employ. The agent who brings the buyer is granted the listing, creating a dual, or limited, agency with the seller and buyer. The seller also retains the right to bring the buyer in an open listing and owes no commission to any broker. Sometimes a seller sells the property "by owner" and says he is "protecting brokers" or some other method of indicating payment to the buyer's agent. This signifies he will pay a buyer's agent's portion of the commission but does not create an open listing. Of course, every participating broker in an open listing must agree to the open listing in advance. Most brokers see this as the least-protective listing and often won't agree to participate.

A *net listing* can be dangerous and is illegal in some states. Under this agreement, the seller tells their agent the net price they want for their home. The listing agent can then add the desired commission onto this net price when presenting it to buyers. If the agent obtains a purchase offer far above the seller's net listing price, the seller may feel cheated and accuse the listing agent of not disclosing the home's true market value. Or if the agent receives a low purchase offer close to the net price, yielding the listing agent little or no commission, the agent might be tempted to not present the offer to the seller. Most states that allow net listings require they to be disclosed to all parties at a minimum.

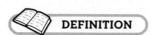 **DEFINITION**

An **exclusive-right-to-sell listing** allows the listing agent to be paid no matter who brings the buyer. An **exclusive-agency listing** allows the property seller to bring the buyer without paying a commission to the listing agent. An **open listing** is one in which the agent who brings the buyer also gets the listing, creating dual agency. The seller can enter into as many open listings as he or she chooses. A **net listing** is one in which the seller needs to "net" a certain amount of money and the agent adds his commission on top of that value.

Buyer Agreements

For many years, real estate was practiced in such a manner that agency relationships were only extended to sellers. Any real estate agent who brought a buyer to the table was actually working as a subagent to the seller. Many states have abolished subagents for a more protective agency to the buyer.

Agency laws continue to vary by state, but even in states that recognize buyer agency, the client might not receive fiduciary responsibilities from the agent automatically during the home-buying process.

With an *exclusive buyer agency* agreement, a completely exclusive agency agreement, the buyer is legally bound to compensate the agent at the time when the buyer purchases any property of the same type as described in the contract. Regardless of whether the agent locates the property or not, the agent is entitled to payment. Even if the buyer finds the property on his or her own, the agent is still owed payment.

Similar to an exclusive buyer agency agreement, an *exclusive-agency buyer agency* agreement is an exclusive contract between the agent and the buyer. But with this type of agreement, a limit is placed on the broker's right to payment. The broker is entitled to payment only if he or she actually finds the property the buyer purchases. The buyer is free to locate a suitable property with no obligation to pay the agent.

An *open buyer agency* agreement is a nonexclusive agency contract between a buyer and an agent permitting the buyer to enter into similar agreements with an unlimited number of other agents. Only the agent who actually locates the property the buyer eventually purchases is entitled to compensation. This is a common buyer agency for real estate investors. They may engage several different agents who specialize in certain types of investment property, such as residential rentals, multifamily apartments, land, commercial buildings, etc. If they entered into an exclusive buyer agency agreement, the investor could be liable for paying two commissions, one to the agent who found the property and one to the other agent as well.

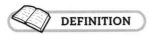 **DEFINITION**

> An **exclusive buyer agency** allows the buyer's agent to be paid no matter who brings the buyer. An **exclusive-agency buyer agency** allows the buyer to pay no commission if the buyer finds the property on his or her own without the agent. An **open buyer agency** is one in which the agent who brings the buyer a property gets compensated for his or her work. A buyer can enter into as many open buyer agencies as he or she chooses.

A buyer's agent compensation must be discussed in detail prior to starting the search for properties. The most common method of payment for a buyer's agent comes from the listing agent. Most MLS systems and local boards allow for the listing agent to pay a portion of the listing commission to the buyer's agent to entice them to bring the buyer.

Another less-common method of payment a buyer's agent could receive is a flat fee for services or an hourly rate paid by the buyer. In some cases, an agent may request a retainer fee upon signing the agreement. This retainer fee may be applied as a credit toward any fees received at the time of closing.

Buyer agency agreements provide agents a comforting level of reassurance that their efforts will not go unrewarded and motivate them to work even harder for the buyer. Buyers must balance the financial guarantees to agents against the risk of limited or poor performance by that agent.

How to Terminate an Agency

An agency relationship lasts for a specific term until the goal of the agency is accomplished, expires by date, or is terminated by the parties, either by breach or mutual agreement. The specific term of the agency is defined as the term of the listing or buyer's agreement. Depending on the reason for the termination, the particular circumstances, and what's negotiated, the broker may or may not be entitled to compensation.

The ability to terminate an agency relationship unilaterally does not mean there may not be legal consequences for either party. In real estate, such consequences often become an issue when the seller wants to terminate the listing before it expires. The seller's right to terminate the listing agreement as a contract is not the same as his or her right to terminate the agency relationship.

Terminating the agency can be achieved by several methods, including completion of the agency, expiration of the agency contract, death by either party to the contract, mutual agreement by the parties, an operation of law, a breach of the contract by either party, or destruction of the property.

 HELPFUL HINT

Remember that the fiduciary duty of accounting and confidentiality survives the termination of an agency relationship. A broker is not relieved of accounting responsibilities after the agency has ended for any reason. A broker also may not reveal information received from a client even after that client stops being the broker's client.

Completion of the contract is the most common method to end agency. Selling the property for the seller or buying a suitable property for the buyer would be considered completion of the goal of the agency.

Expiration of the agency happens when an agent fails to complete the agency agreement within a predefined period of time. Most states don't require a set time frame for agency to be completed, but rather allow it to be negotiated by the agent and the client. Perpetual, or self-renewing, agency agreements are not permitted in most states. If an agent wants to extend his agency period, he must get the permission of the client to do so. This method of expiration allows for the client to "soft" fire his agent by not renewing the agreement, allowing the client to look elsewhere for another agent.

The death or incapacitation of a client or the managing, or principal, broker also is grounds for agency termination. Remember, the client belongs to the managing broker; therefore, should one of the agents designated to work for him die, agency is not terminated. The managing broker would simply reassign the listing to another agent under him.

Mutual agreement between the agent and client also can terminate the agency agreement. The key term is *mutual*. A unilateral termination, without grounds, is not allowed by either party and could create legal liability for either party. Real estate agents often confuse termination of the agency relationship with performance or breach of the listing contract.

Usually there are provisions in the listing agreement about damages if the seller breaches the agreement by unilaterally withdrawing consent to act. Breach of contract issues, however, have nothing to do with whether or not the broker can continue to act on the seller's behalf to market the property. An agent cannot continue to represent a seller without the seller's consent even if withdrawing that consent breaches the listing agreement and entitles the broker to damages.

Bankruptcy, foreclosure, or insanity are examples under the "operation of law" clause set forth in most agency agreements that also would terminate the agency.

Should either party breach the agency contract during the life of the contract, termination may be invoked by either party. Failure to abide by the fair housing clause within the listing agreement by the seller would be an example of breach. The agent must immediately send notification to the client stating the violation, date of the breach, and notice of release from the agency agreement. In this example, failure to terminate the agency contract immediately could result in civil and criminal charges being brought against the client and the agent.

Destruction or condemnation would result in the agency contract being terminated. This method of agency termination only applies to the listing agency because the buyer's agency is not bound to only one property.

The Relationship Between Salesperson and Broker

The relationship between the broker and his agent is one of an independent contractor. The Internal Revenue Service (IRS) states that "People who are in an independent trade, business, or profession in which they offer their services to the general public are generally independent contractors. The general rule is that an individual is an independent contractor if the payer has the right to control or direct only the result of the work and not what will be done and how it will be done." You are not an independent contractor if you perform services that can be controlled by an employer—i.e., what will be done and how it will be done. This applies even if you are given freedom of action.

As an independent contractor, you are self-employed and are subject to self-employment tax as well as income tax. An advantage of being self-employed is that most every expense you incur to successfully perform your job is deductible against the income you earn. Education, marketing costs, licensing fees, etc., are examples of costs you will incur that can be deducted. Good record-keeping is crucial to ensuring you get the deductions you deserve.

As stated earlier, your broker won't have the right to control your activities in the manner they are performed or the method in which they are completed. If you choose to work in a specific geographic location, with a specific type of buyer, or during specific days and hours, he will have no control over those, for example.

Calculating Your Commission

The goal of any real estate transaction for the clients is the exchange of money for property. It also means agents get paid for doing the duties they were contracted to perform, whether it be for the buyer or the seller.

Agents are paid a portion of the commission the broker earns. A listing broker earns a commission for listing the property and then gives a portion of that commission to the buyer's agent. The listing agent determines the amount given to the buyer's broker at the time he lists the property. The portion kept by the listing agent is split with the agent who represented him during the deal. As discussed, that split is determined when the agent signs the independent contractor agreement with the broker.

Let's look at an example: A listing broker charges 7 percent listing commission to list a seller's house. Of that commission, he gives 50 percent to the buyer's agent, or 3.5 percent of the total commission. Therefore, only 3.5 percent of the commission is retained by the listing broker. Suppose his agent was on a 60/40 split. If the house's final selling price is $150,000, the agent's portion of the commission is determined as follows:

$$\$150,000 \times 0.07 = \$10,500 \text{ for the total commission}$$

However, the listing broker only retains 50 percent of the commission, or $10,500 \times 0.50 = \$5,250$.

The agent receives 60 percent of the listing broker's portion based on the independent contractor agreement he signed with the broker. So for this example, the agent receives $5,250 \times 0.60 = \$3,150$ for his part in closing the deal.

Here's another example: A listing broker charges 7 percent listing commission to list a seller's house. However, the agent also finds the buyer for this property, making him a dual or limited agent for the buyer and seller. Assuming all the proper paperwork is in order and both parties agree to the dual agency, the listing broker receives the entire 7 percent. Therefore, the agent, who was on a 60/40 split with the broker, gets 60 percent of the entire listing commission earned. If the house's final selling price is $150,000, the agent's portion of the commission is determined as follows:

$$\$150,000 \times 0.07 = \$10,500 \text{ for the total commission earned with the total amount going to the listing broker}$$

The agent receives 60 percent of the listing broker's portion based on the independent contractor agreement he signed with the broker. So for this example, the agent receives $10,500 \times 0.60 = \$6,300$ for his part in closing the deal.

Avoiding Common Issues

REALTORS face many issues daily during the process of completing their job. Let's look at some issues you must keep in mind to become successful.

Mishandling Escrow Accounts

All brokers must maintain a clearly identified escrow account, sometimes called an impound account. The escrow account is created, maintained, and administered by the broker of the company for the benefit of holding a buyer's earnest money. A broker may be found liable for *commingling* if he places the earnest money into a nonearnest money account. He also might be guilty of *conversion* if he uses the earnest money for his own benefit.

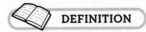

DEFINITION

Commingling is the act of a broker placing a client's earnest money into a personal or business account, other than the earnest money account. **Conversion** is the act of a broker spending the client's earnest money for a bill, expense, or payment.

Earnest money accounts can bear interest; however, the broker may not profit from that interest earned. He must return the interest earned to the buyer when he presents the earnest money to the closing or to the buyer if it gets returned. Some states might require interest to be paid, so check with your specific state statute regarding earnest money. Placing personal money into an identified earnest money account also would be considered commingling unless the money is used to either start the account or maintain the account.

A broker can elect to have as many earnest money accounts as he wants. In my practice, I have seen many brokers utilize different account for different deals—i.e., one for residential deals and one for commercial deals. This method is a personal preference and should be considered if you plan on starting your own brokerage firm.

Puffing, Fraud, and Negligent Misrepresentation

Puffing is exaggerating the good points of real estate. Although it's not illegal, it is very borderline, and many states have strict views against the use of puffing in real estate.

Fraud is a misrepresentation of a material fact or facts used to induce someone to do something, such as buy real property. *Actual fraud* occurs when you intentionally deceive a person by misrepresenting facts that influence a person's decision. *Negative fraud* can be intentionally failing to disclose facts that make a statement misleading.

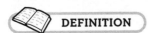

DEFINITION

Actual fraud is lying about true facts to present a better picture of the property, while **negative fraud** is the omission of some detrimental information to present a better picture of the property.

There's a lesser form of fraud called negligent misrepresentation. If an agent makes a mistake and unintentionally misrepresents a material fact about a property, they may not mean to cause anyone harm. However, if their mistake does end up being relied upon by a buyer and that buyer is harmed because of it, the agent and his broker may be liable for the resulting harm. The agent can be held financially responsible for the damages and harm caused by the failure in their duty of care, even if it was a mistake on their part and they meant no harm. In these situations, their professional insurance may provide coverage for the harm and damage the buyer or seller incurred.

Not Disclosing Stigmatized Properties

Typically, stigmatized properties include those in which death (either from natural causes, homicide, or suicide), gang-related activity, the commission of a felony, the manufacture of illegal substances, or the discharge of a weapon by a police officer in the line of duty has occurred. Some states have adopted the potential of a house being haunted as a stigma. This might seem silly, but the reputation of being haunted may cause a property not to sell in a reasonable time or for a reasonable price.

> **HELPFUL HINT**
>
> According to the National Association of REALTORS (NAR), Alaska and South Dakota are the only two states that mandate the seller's agent disclose whether a homicide or suicide occurred in the listed home over the last 12 months.

Stigmatized properties have been found to take longer to sell compared to similar properties. They also tend to sell for about 3 percent less, according to a study conducted by Wright State University professors of 102 stigmatized homes in Ohio. Researchers found that the stigmatized homes took 45 percent longer to sell than comparable homes.

Check your local and state laws regarding stigmatized properties, but as a general rule, the rule of *caveat emptor* applies, which is Latin for "let the buyer beware." Simply said, the seller is not liable.

The main exception to this rule, however, is where the seller makes a fraudulent misrepresentation, or lies, about an aspect of the property. A seller has a duty to reply truthfully about important facts and in a manner not aimed toward misleading buyers.

In some states, not disclosing an answer isn't a violation of the law. For example, you could say "Our brokerage firm chooses to not discuss this topic." This isn't the same as committing fraud, either actual or negative. Other states require you disclose those certain activities that may be deemed stigmatized.

The Least You Need to Know

- Agency is based upon common law, known as the common law of agency.
- Single agency, either express or implied, works with only one party in a deal; dual agency works with the buyer and the seller on the same deal.
- Agency is created through an agency agreement—a listing agreement for the seller and a buyer's agency agreement for the buyer; however, agency can be terminated in several manners.
- The relationship between an agent and his broker is created by an independent contractor agreement.
- Fraud is knowingly giving false or misleading information to induce a buyer to buy property.
- Stigmatized properties are not required to be disclosed voluntarily in most states.

Contract Law

Before we begin this chapter, I want to make a key issue clear: "drafting legal documents for third parties is conduct that requires a license to practice law. However, there is an exception that permits a real estate licensee to fill in the blanks on common preprinted forms that have been prepared by an attorney. This is because such conduct is perceived as falling within the ordinary course of a licensee's business duties." Most states have legal precedence with verbiage of something very similar to this. So during the course of this chapter, the phrase *writing a contract* will mean "filling in blanks in a preprinted form that was written by your state REALTOR Association."

The real estate world abounds with contracts between agents and sellers, agents and buyers, buyers and sellers, and more. Being able to understand, read, and help your client write a contract, at least fill in the blanks in a preprinted form, is a paramount factor in your success. Therefore, understanding what a makes a contract, the different types of contracts used in real estate, and when to use specific contracts is an important concept for all REALTORS to understand.

In This Chapter

- Key elements of contracts
- How contracts are created
- The requirements to make a contract valid
- Types of contracts used in real estate
- Risk management and mitigation of contract law

What Makes a Contract?

A contract is a binding promise or agreement between legally competent parties to perform, or not perform, a legal activity for compensation. A contract must contain five specific elements to be valid: a voluntary offer and acceptance, an agreement or promise, legally competent parties, a legal purpose, and valuable compensation.

Voluntary Offer and Acceptance

Two essential components of a valid contract are a meeting of the minds and communication back to the offeror. An offer is an intention to enter into a legally binding agreement. In a real estate contract, the offer must be communicated to the seller and be definite and certain, with all terms in writing. Acceptance means that both parties must know the intentions of the other and be informed immediately. A contract is not accepted until the original party has been made aware of the acceptance in writing. Upon acceptance of all terms of the offer, a valid contract is considered *formed*.

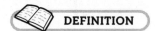 DEFINITION

A contract is considered **formed** when the buyer and seller have agreed upon all terms, assuming all the parts of the contract are valid.

An Agreement or Promise

The agreement or promise for a contract is a legally binding agreement to perform, or not perform, some activity as described by the contract. In a real estate purchase agreement contract, the agreement is to transfer the property from one party to another under the specifications of the contract.

Legally Competent Parties

In order for an agreement to be legally binding, the parties must have contractual capacity. This means both parties are able to understand that a contract is being formed, are of legal age, and understand the basic nature of the contract. It is not necessary to understand every detail of a contract, as long as they know they're entering into a contract and grasp its general nature.

Legal Purpose

A contract must be for a legal purpose to be considered valid. A contract that, at its intention, has some illegal activity cannot be enforced or defended in a court of law.

Valuable Compensation

There must be compensation from one party to the other that's sufficient to balance the contract for the actions stated. In real estate, the compensation is typically money.

Other Items in Contracts

Contracts can be either bilateral or unilateral in nature. Real estate contracts are almost exclusively bilateral in nature. The only unilateral contract used in real estate is the option (discussed later in the chapter).

A bilateral contract has at least two parties involved, and each makes promises to the other party. For example, a real estate purchase agreement is a bilateral contract. A buyer promises to pay the seller some money, the purchase price, in exchange for the promise to transfer title of seller's property.

A unilateral contract has only one party involved, and he or she makes a promise. For example, a real estate option is a unilateral contract. The seller can give the buyer an option to buy the property. The buyer is under no obligation to buy. If he exercises his right to buy, however, the seller is obligated to sell.

Status of Contracts

When a contract is executory, it means the contract has not yet been completed. Obligations still must be fulfilled. For example, a real estate transaction in process of closing is considered executory until closing.

An executed contract is complete. No more obligations are to be fulfilled. For example, after a real estate closing has occurred, the transaction is considered executed. All parties have fulfilled their obligations, and there are no outstanding obligations by either party.

A valid contract is one in which all five elements are in place and enforceable.

A void contract is one in which at least one element is missing from the offer, such as no mention of compensation. This term is often a misnomer due to the fact that with one missing element, the form was never really a contract. A void contract is unenforceable by either party.

A voidable contract is one in which all elements are present and appear to be valid, but upon further inspection, one of the elements is defective, such as one party is not of minimum age or not mentally capable due to an illness. Voidable contracts may be reaffirmed by the offending party prior to being cancelled or dismissed by the other party.

A contract can be deemed unenforceable when it appears valid on the surface, but a statute or law renders one party unable to sue for performance. For example, if an oral contract to sell real estate is in place between two parties, it might appear to be valid. But due to the *statute of frauds* requirement, it's rendered unenforceable in a court of law.

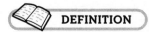 **DEFINITION**

The **statute of frauds** comes from English law that states, "particular contracts cannot be enforced unless a written note or memorandum of agreement exists that is signed by the persons bound by the contract's terms or their authorized representatives."

An unenforceable contract may still be valid between the parties. This means that once the contract is executed and the title is transferred between the parties without any issues, there's no reason to initiate a lawsuit by either party.

After a contract is formed by two parties, it can be express or implied. An express contract is one in which both parties know and understand their rights and responsibilities. A listing agreement between a seller and a broker is an express contract describing the seller's duties as well as the broker's duties. An implied contract is one in which one party or the other may not be aware that a contract exists or is unaware of his or her rights or responsibilities. For example, if a REALTOR fails to get a buyer to sign a written buyer's agency agreement but continues to work on the buyer's behalf, he may be working under an implied contract.

Types of Contracts in Real Estate

The real estate world is full of different types of contracts and uses for them.

 **REALTOR WARNING**

Remember, unless you are a licensed, practicing attorney, you are not allowed to write contracts for your clients.

The agency agreement is probably the single most used contract in real estate. This contract is an express contract, due to both parties understanding their rights and responsibilities. It's also written based on the requirements of the statute of frauds and would be valid when used correctly by the REALTOR.

Similarly, the buyer's representation agreement is another common contract used by REALTORS.

Both of these contracts are, in fact, not real estate contracts but rather employment contracts between the client and the agent, yet they still must fulfill all the requirements of a valid contract. These contracts establish the agency between the parties as well as discuss the commission charged by the listing broker. Most state or local agencies utilize preprinted forms for the REALTOR to engage their client that can be accessed as part of your membership fees.

Another common form used in real estate is the purchase agreement. This contract is between the buyer and seller for the sale of real property. Again, this form has been standardized and is usually provided by your state board of REALTORS.

HELPFUL HINT

New agents should acquire copies of these forms at their first company and read the entire contracts so they can understand and explain them to clients when questions arise.

Sometimes the need arises for other contracts not provided by any board, such as the lease, land contract, or option to buy. In these cases, remember that you cannot write a contract and must seek help from a licensed attorney.

Leases

Leases, although common in real estate, are still contracts and must fulfill all the necessary requirements. Leases are often very specific to a landlord, tenant, and property of location, and quite custom. The customization requirement makes it virtually impossible to have a preprinted form, so leases aren't provided by any board of REALTORS.

A *leasehold estate* is for a defined period during which the *lessor* transfers a portion of the rights to a *lessee* for the term of the lease. At the end of the designated time frame, the rights passed to the lessee return to the lessor. These rights are known as revisionary rights, or revisionary interests, and are willable to the lessee's heirs and/or successors.

Just as a *freehold estate* has many different types, so does the leasehold estate (more on this in Chapter 15).

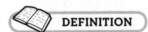

DEFINITION

A **lease** is a legal binding contract between the two parties. A **lessor** is the person doing the leasing (i.e., the landlord). A **lessee** is is the person the lease is done to (i.e., the tenant). A **leasehold estate** is for a limited, or defined, period of time, while a **freehold estate** is forever, or indefinite. An easy way to remember these is to notice the *L* in *leasehold* and *limited* time and the *F* in *freehold* and *forever.*

An estate for years, sometimes called a lease for term, is the most common leasehold estate. This type of leasehold estate has a defined beginning and ending date, and the term can be days, weeks, months, or years. The lessee knows the date of termination the day they enter into the leasehold estate. Because of this requirement, the lessee has to do nothing for the lease to terminate. Upon the termination date, the lessee's rights are extinguished and returned to the lessor under his or her reversionary interest in the property. The lease may be terminated without cause prior to the defined expiration date by agreement of both parties. If the parties fail to agree on an early termination, the contractual lease is still in place. Of course, the lease may be terminated with cause if declared by a court of law.

An estate from period to period, sometimes called a periodic tenancy, can be created when a lessor and lessee enter into an agreement that does not specify an end date. This type of lease has a defined beginning and runs for a defined period of time, such as a day, week, or month. However, at the end of the defined period, the lease automatically renews for that same period of time again … and again … and again—virtually forever. To terminate this type of lease, proper written notice must be given by either party at least one period prior to the proposed end date.

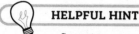

HELPFUL HINT

Sometimes an estate for years will convert to an estate from period to period after the initial lease terminates.

A tenancy at will is a lease containing all the terms and conditions under which a landlord will rent a specific property, for an undetermined time, at a stated rent, to a tenant. However, this type of lease has no defined beginning nor ending dates and can be terminated by either the landlord or the tenant by written notice to the other or by death of either party. The length of the notice may be governed by state law, but it may be longer if the parties agreed. A tenancy at will also can be legally created by the parties after the end of any lease, which allows a tenant to remain.

The tenancy at will gives more flexibility to both parties, in that you can end the tenancy with the written proper notice (i.e., at will or by death of either party). Under this tenancy, a landlord can adjust the rent with no recourse by the tenant. Some states require a proper notice to alter the rent even within a tenancy at will.

A tenancy at sufferance exists when a tenant wrongfully holds over after the expiration of a lease without the landlord's consent, typically where the tenant fails to surrender possession after termination of the lease. A tenancy at sufferance is the lowest estate in real estate, and no notice of termination may be required from the landlord to evict the tenant. This kind of tenancy is designed to both protect the tenant from being classified as a trespasser and prevent his acquisition of title by adverse possession.

A *holdover tenant,* created by tenancy at sufferance, is a tenant who continues to occupy the premises without the landlord's consent after the original lease has expired. The tenant is responsible for payment of the monthly rental at the existing rate and terms, which the landlord may accept without admitting the legality of the occupancy. If a holdover tenant does not leave after a written notice to quit, he is subject to a lawsuit for unlawful detainer. A holdover tenant differs from a tenant at will in that the latter has the landlord's permission to stay beyond the agreement's expiration date, while the holdover tenant does not.

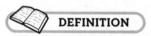

DEFINITION

A **holdover tenant** is a tenant who once occupied a property legally under a lease but is now there illegally without permission from the landlord. This is not a trespasser due to the fact he occupied the property legally at some point under a valid lease.

Options, Lease Options, and Lease Purchase Agreements

An option to purchase, a lease option, and a lease purchase agreement are three variations of financing documents that can be used between a buyer and seller. These may be used for many reasons, such as to secure the rights to an investment by an investor without having to buy the property today, when a buyer may not be able to get a loan immediately but doesn't want to lose out on getting the property, or when other situations prevent the purchase immediately by the buyer.

An option to purchase gives the buyer the right to purchase the property from a seller at a later date. The buyer and seller may agree to a purchase price now, or the buyer may agree to pay market value at the time the option is exercised; it's negotiable. However, most buyers want to lock in the future purchase price upon inception of the option. The term of the option agreement is negotiable as well, but the common length is generally from 1 to 3 years. The buyer deposits with the seller some form of option consideration, or a nominal amount paid now to acquire the option. The option consideration is rarely refundable if the buyer fails to exercise the option but is usually, but need not be, applied to the overall sales price when the buyer exercises his option. During the period of option time agreed upon by the buyer and the seller, no one else can buy the property. The buyer is not obligated to buy the property but merely has the option to buy. If the buyer does not purchase the property at or before the end of the option period, the option expires and the seller is free to sell to another buyer.

The option is the only unilateral contract used in real estate. The buyer does not have to exercise their right to buy, but should they decide to do so, the seller must sell the property under the terms agreed upon in the option agreement.

The lease option is two separate documents—a lease combined with an option—and can be used when a buyer wants to buy the property but may not be financially able to get a loan at the moment. The buyer and seller could enter into a lease with an option to buy at some future date. In this situation, the buyer becomes a tenant for a specific period of time and pays monthly lease payments. At the end of the lease, or anytime during, the tenant has the option to buy the property at the predetermined price established by the buyer and seller. However, they could agree that the purchase price will be determined by market value at the time the option is exercised. The fact the price is not determined prior to the exercise date does not invalidate the option.

The seller may require a deposit for the lease portion and a separate option consideration for the purchase portion of the deal. Typically, the security deposit for the lease may be applied to the purchase price, if exercised by the tenant, or refunded to the tenant at the end of the lease if not exercised. The option consideration would not be refunded if the tenant/buyer fails to exercise the purchase option. During the lease portion of the agreement, the tenant may or may not be responsible for the maintenance, insurance, and taxes on the property.

A lease purchase is very similar to the lease option; however, at the time the lease ends, the tenant/buyer is contractually responsible to buy the property. Should he fail to exercise the purchase, he could be subject to liability to the seller for damages under the *specific performance* clause. The lease purchase is seen as a stronger purchase agreement than a lease option due to the contractual obligation of the tenant/ buyer.

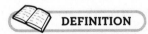 **DEFINITION**

Specific performance is where one party or the other fails to complete a contract without cause. The harmed party may seek specific performance from the other party to compensate that harm, typically in the form of money.

For example, I had a client agree to sell a small investment property to a qualified buyer for $10,000. The buyer later decided to not buy the property for no legal cause. My client sued the buyer in court, where the judge said, "I cannot make you buy the property, but I can make you pay for it." The judge found for the entire balance of the purchase price against the buyer. He ultimately did buy the property after the judge's ruling.

Land Contracts

Another possible contract used to finance real estate is the land contract, sometimes called a contract for deed or installment sale. A *vendee* can enter into an agreement with the *vendor* to buy a piece of property in regularly scheduled payments, typically monthly. At the signing of the land contract, the vendee receives "equitable title" and possession of the property, and the vendor keeps a legal title interest in the property. The land contract sets the purchase price and monthly payments based on the agreement between the parties. The vendee makes payments to the vendor as described in the land contract, and after the vendee has made all the payments, the legal title transfers and the vendor must deliver good legal title of the property to the vendee by way of a deed.

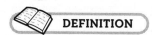 **DEFINITION**

> The **vendor** (not called a seller here) is the party who is passing equitable title and retains actual, or legal, title. The **vendee** (not called the buyer here) is the party receiving equitable title as well as possession of the property.

This differs from lease option in many ways. In a lease, if the tenant defaults, he may be subject to a small claims court case, called an actual eviction. However, if a vendee defaults on a land contract, whereby equitable title was given, the vendor has to file a foreclosure lawsuit to regain the title passed to the vendee. This lawsuit can cost more money and take longer than evicting the tenant.

The vendee often takes on the responsibilities of maintenance, property insurance, and real estate taxes in a land contract. In most states, they also are allowed to file for the homestead exemption to help defer some of the real estate taxes.

The difference between buying a home with a mortgage and through a land contract is that the deed transfers to the buyer right away when buying with a mortgage. With a land contract, the deed does not transfer until after all the payments have been made. So although the vendee lives on the land, the property actually belongs to the vendor until all the payments have been made.

Many times a vendee wants to record a land contract to help with issues regarding the tax record or if he will be claiming the homestead exemption. Furthermore, a vendee may want it recorded as protection against the vendor trying to falsely sell the property to another party. Oftentimes, a vendor may not want the contract recorded due to the fact he may have an underlying mortgage on the property. In this case, the lender for that property may exercise their right to call the loan due when they find out he has transferred the property via a land contract.

A land contract is a viable method to transfer property, but it can be a very difficult task to do correctly. I advise all my clients to seek the aid of a real estate attorney when using this method of financing.

Real Estate Risk Management

When owning real estate, many inherent risks can be present, both personally and financially. There are four ways to handle risk: avoid it, control it, retain it, or transfer it.

The easiest way to handle risk is to completely avoid the potential for any danger. This includes not performing an activity that could carry risk and vigorously eliminating the possibility of the threat. For example, the easiest way to avoid drowning in a residential pool is for the owner to completely remove the pool.

Controlling risk includes employing approaches that reduce the severity of the loss or the likelihood of the loss from occurring due to the risk thereby reducing the exposure to unwanted outcomes. For example, use access cards to get into certain areas of an office building, or add automatic fire extinguishers to a building.

You could retain the risk, providing you're willing to accept small risks or large catastrophic risks, because the cost of guarding against them is greater than the total loss of the property. For example, the cost of hurricane insurance may be more expensive than the outright cost of replacing the property.

You also could pay someone to accept the risk for you and transfer the risk to them. This is a very common concept and is the basis of insurance companies. After all, that's all you're doing when you buy insurance—transferring the risk to someone else.

Insurance companies are merely companies that will accept the transfer of a risk from you for a cost, called a *premium*. The more you transfer, the less you retain, the more it costs you. Likewise, the more you retain, the less you transfer, the less it costs you.

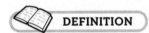 **DEFINITION**

An insurance **premium** is a monthly cost a client pays to an insurance company to accept the risk of a given outcome for a given activity.

Types of Insurance

Many different types of insurance cover many different types of losses that can occur in a person's lifetime.

Hazard insurance protects a homeowner against the costs of damage from fire, smoke, vandalism, and more. When you take out a mortgage, the lender requires you to take out hazard insurance to protect their investment; many lenders incorporate the insurance payment into your monthly mortgage payment. Hazard insurance may protect only against specifically named damages, or it can cover all forms of damage except those specifically excluded.

 HELPFUL HINT

Hazard insurance is not synonymous with homeowners' insurance because it only covers physical damage. Homeowners' insurance typically includes liability protection and hazard insurance.

Contents and personal property insurance covers personal contents not covered within the structural insurance of the property. This type of insurance, sometimes referred to as renters' insurance, is often used by people who don't own the real property themselves. Clients living in a condo also may utilize this insurance due to the fact the condo association may have insurance on the structure itself and the owners would want protection of their personal items.

Consequential loss insurance, or business interruption insurance, protects clients against the loss of income while the building is being replaced or rebuilt. Typically, consequential losses are not covered by ordinary insurance policies, unless specifically included on payment of additional premium.

Liability insurance is about financial protection for you and your family. The personal liability coverage within your homeowners' policy provides coverage for bodily injury and property damage sustained by others for which you or your family members are legally responsible. For example, should someone fall down your stairs, or your child accidentally throws a ball through a neighbor's window, you may be held responsible for the damages.

Flood insurance provides protection to a home or other property against damage from flooding. A variety of events can cause flood damage, including high water from creeks and rivers entering a home, leaking basement walls, and rainwater runoff. Many homeowners are unaware that standard homeowners' insurance policies do not cover flood damage. Insurance companies sell flood insurance as a separate product from homeowners' insurance. If a home is designated to be in a flood plain, most lenders won't allow the borrower to buy a property without proof of flood insurance coverage.

A multi-peril insurance policy is one in which a client has two or more types of insurance policies in place at the same time. One of the main benefits of multi-peril insurance is that the scope of coverage is more in depth and applies in a wider range of scenarios. For example, a single peril plan that protects a home in the event of fire does not provide any real benefits in the event that a flood destroyed the home. By contrast, a multi-peril insurance plan that includes protection in the event of fire or flooding provides benefits in either scenario.

Insurance Reimbursements

Your insurance company can calculate the amount it will pay you for a loss in several different ways. Payment based on the replacement cost of damaged or stolen property is usually the most favorable figure from your point of view because it compensates you for the actual cost of replacing property.

Actual cash value is the standard method insurance companies prefer when reimbursing policyholders for their losses. Actual cash value is equal to the replacement cost minus any depreciation of the item over time. It represents the dollar amount you could expect to receive for the item if you sold it in the marketplace. The insurance company determines the depreciation based on a combination of objective criteria as well as subjective assessment.

For example, if you bought a television 5 years ago for $500 and it gets damaged today, the replacement cost policy would pay to replace it at today's cost. However, the actual cash value policy would take into consideration the depreciation over the last 5 years and determine today's value at $100. Therefore, you would receive $100, not $500.

The premiums of these obviously differ in price, with the premiums for the replacement cost policy being higher than the actual cash value policy premiums.

Mitigating Risk in Real Estate

Litigation and arbitration cannot be avoided forever. They are a fact of life in today's litigious society and a cost of doing business. This is especially true in those professions in which fiduciary relationships are created between the consumer and the service provider. REALTORS are but one of the targets for litigation because of the nature of the service they provide. Trust is an essential by-product of these relationships therefore, liability is high. But this doesn't mean the risk inherent in these professions cannot be effectively managed.

Risk mitigation is the process by which an organization introduces specific measures to minimize or eliminate unacceptable risks associated with their operation. In real estate, risk mitigation is the technique used to reduce activities that could bring about potential harm to an agent, the broker, or the brokerage company.

Perhaps the best risk mitigation tool available to a real estate company is training. Ensuring all agents are correctly trained in the state laws governing real estate, proper code of ethics, and actions of professional REALTORS can make the difference between being liable and being protected if a court case is leveled against an agent, the broker, or the brokerage firm. Ensuring that all agents are trained uniformly and continuously is a key issue as well.

Some agents may be more at risk than others simply due to the type of real estate they practice. High-risk activities in real estate include foreclosures and short sales, investor properties, real estate owned (REO) properties, and commercial properties. Agents that hold themselves out as specialists may need more in the way of training and closer supervision due to these high-risk real estate activities.

Another factor that can be paramount in reducing risk is the ratio of agents to broker. If too many agents are working for a broker, the chances of personal interaction are small. A brokerage might want to adopt a policy concerning the number of agents allowed or perhaps the target number of agents who would require a new manager, or team leader, to be hired.

A final thought about risk management: companies should acquire errors and omissions (E&O) insurance. E&O insurance is a type of professional liability insurance that protects companies and their workers or individuals against claims made by clients for inadequate work or negligent actions. E&O insurance often covers both court costs and any settlements up to the amount specified by the insurance contract. E&O insurance is based on the financial exposure of a company and the activities it undertakes. For example, a brokerage that closed $1 million in transactions would pay lower premiums than a company that closed $10 million. In my experience, brokerage companies that deal with commercial real estate property management also have higher premiums than companies that do not.

 REALTOR WARNING

An agent, broker, or brokerage company that has had numerous litigation problems has a higher underwriting risk and is likely to find E&O insurance more expensive or its terms less favorable.

In the real estate industry, lawsuits happen, regardless of how baseless the claims may be. Clients sometimes sue an agent or broker after a deal goes sour, even if the risks were well known and within the guidelines established by the client. In these cases, even if a court or arbitration panel finds in favor of a broker, the legal fees can be very high, making E&O insurance vital.

The Least You Need to Know

- A contract is a legally binding agreement between parties that can be executed or in executory status, express or implied.
- The listing agency agreement is a contract between the client and the broker.
- A lease is for a defined period of time.
- An option is the only unilateral agreement in real estate.
- A land contract gives equitable title to the vendee.
- Risk can be controlled and mitigated.

Fair Housing

Fair housing is the right for a buyer or tenant to choose housing free from unlawful discrimination by a seller or landlord. Federal, state, and local fair housing laws protect people from discrimination in housing transactions. Fair housing is the key to all people owning real estate. It guarantees that regardless of your race, color, religion, national origin, sex, disability, or familial status, you have the right to choose the property that's best for your needs with no outside bias or discrimination.

Discrimination in the housing sector is a terrible activity that is still present in today's world. We will look at the evolution of the Fair Housing Act, including the laws that brought us to today's current legislation. The Fair Housing Act is a federal law that enforces the restraint of certain actions and activities that limit the free choice of a person's housing desires. We will cover the illegal activities and the repercussion of those activities, as well as discuss the importance of each protected class within the law.

In This Chapter

- The history and evolution of fair housing laws
- A look at the federally protected classes
- Violations of fair housing laws
- Enforcement of fair housing laws
- Fair housing laws and real estate professionals

What Is Fair Housing?

The need for federal fair housing legislation evolved out of a long history of discriminatory housing practices in the United States. For much of the past centuries, the nation existed as a racially segregated society in which black and white citizens occupied separate and vastly unequal neighborhoods. Personal prejudice, business practices, and government policies at all levels promoted and maintained residential divisions. African American members of Congress have long understood the serious consequences of neighborhood segregation and fought to pass legislation ensuring the nation's residents have the right to the housing of their choice.

The Civil Rights Act of 1866

The Civil Rights Act of 1866, enacted on April 9, 1866, was the first U.S. federal law to define citizenship and affirm that all citizens are equally protected by the law. It was mainly intended to protect the civil rights of persons of African descent born in or brought to America in the wake of the American Civil War. The act declared that people born in the United States, and not subject to any foreign power, are entitled to be citizens without regard to race.

 HELPFUL HINT

In 1892, Homer Adolph Plessy was arrested on an East Louisiana Railway train for refusing to move to the car designated for "colored passengers." The case eventually reached the U.S. Supreme Court in 1896 as *Plessy* v. *Ferguson*, named for the New Orleans Criminal District Court judge who first ruled against Mr. Plessy.

Plessy v. *Ferguson* created a landmark decision regarding segregation and discrimination. Here is an excerpt, written by Justice Henry Billings Brown: "… as long as racially separate facilities were equal they did not violate the Fourteenth Amendment's guarantees of equal protection of the law." All justices but one, John Marshall Harlan, agreed with Brown's arguments. The *Plessy* ruling provided legal justification for segregation in transportation, public accommodations, and education.

In 1954, the U.S. Supreme Court decided another landmark case, *Brown* v. *Board of Education of Topeka*. The Supreme Court concluded that racially segregated schools are inherently unequal. The Court found support for its decision in studies that indicated that minority students learn better in racially mixed classrooms. The *Brown* v. *Board of Education* decision effectively overruled the 1896 *Plessy* v. *Ferguson* decision. It is inherently impossible to have "separate but equal" standards for all citizens.

The Civil Rights Act of 1968

On April 11, 1968, President Lyndon Johnson signed the Civil Rights Act of 1968, which was meant as a follow-up to the Civil Rights Act of 1964. Within the Civil Rights Act of 1968, the Fair Housing Act of 1968, also known as Title VIII of the Civil Rights Act of 1968, was created. Congress passed the act in an effort to impose a comprehensive solution to the problem of unlawful discrimination in housing based on race, color, sex, national origin, or religion. The Fair Housing Act has become a central feature of modern civil rights enforcement, enabling persons in the protected classes to rent or own residential property in areas that were previously segregated.

Even while Congress debated, the U.S. Supreme Court was hearing arguments in *Jones* v. *Alfred H. Mayer Co.* and ruled in June 1968 that the Civil Rights Act of 1866 prohibited race discrimination in housing even among private parties. Before then, the case had been successfully applied only in cases of governmental housing discrimination or restrictive covenants based on race.

Jones v. *Alfred H. Mayer Co.* held that Congress could regulate the sale of private property to prevent racial discrimination: "… bars all racial discrimination, private as well as public, in the sale or rental of property …." The buyer, Joseph Jones, filed a complaint arguing that the seller, Alfred H. Mayer Co., had refused to sell him a home for the sole reason that he was black. The Civil Rights Act of 1866 passed by Congress provided the basis for this case's decision.

The Housing and Community Development Acts of 1974

The Housing and Community Development Acts of 1974 brought about many social reform changes in public housing and discrimination. However, one of the main aspects was the amendment to the Civil Rights Act of 1968 to include sex as a protected class.

The Fair Housing Amendments Act of 1988

The Fair Housing Amendments Act of 1988 establishes an administrative enforcement mechanism, provides stiffer penalties than the previous act, and expands its coverage to include disabled persons and families with children. The act, among its more important provisions, bans discrimination in the sale or rental of housing on the basis of a disability and requires the design and construction of new, covered, multifamily dwellings to meet certain adaptability and accessibility requirements. It also bans discrimination in the sale or rental of housing because there are children in a family, but exempts housing for older persons, and modifies the definition of a discriminatory housing practice to include acts of interfering, coercing, threatening, or intimidating a person in the exercise or enjoyment of their rights.

Currently, the federal Fair Housing Act does not specifically address discrimination on the basis of sexual orientation, gender identity, or gender expression. However, such complaints may raise jurisdictional claims under the act's current provisions. Upon receipt of an inquiry that involves sexual orientation, gender identity, or gender expression, the U.S. Department of Housing and Urban Development (HUD) must thoroughly review all allegations to determine if the claims are jurisdictional under the act's prohibitions on discrimination based on one or more of the protected classes.

The 1988 act also established that people diagnosed with AIDS are a protected class. According to HUD, it's illegal for real estate agents to make unsolicited disclosures that a current or former occupant of a property has AIDS.

 HELPFUL HINT

If a prospective purchaser asks an agent if the current or former occupant has AIDS, and the agent knows this is in fact true, HUD advises the agent not to respond.

The Housing for Older Persons Act of 1995

The Housing for Older Persons Act of 1995, sometimes called HOPA, was exempted from the Fair Housing Act's prohibition of discrimination against families with children in two categories: 100 percent of the occupants must be 62 years of age or older or 80 percent of the occupied units must be occupied by at least one person who is 55 or older. The new requirements under HOPA are equivalent to the original provisions of the Fair Housing Act regarding the age categories.

HOPA also requires that a facility or community seeking to claim the 55 and older exemption show the following factors:

- The HUD Secretary has determined that it is specifically designed for and occupied by elderly persons under a federal, state, or local government program.

- The housing is intended and operated for persons 55 years of age or older.

- The housing facility publishes and adheres to policies and procedures that demonstrate its intent to qualify for the exemption.

- The housing facility also complies with rules issued by HUD for the verification of occupancy.

State Versus Federal Fair Housing Requirements

All states must follow the federal guidelines for fair housing and the administration of the policies and procedures. However, it's possible for state, local, or regional guidelines to be more (but not less) restrictive than federal guidelines. For example, a state may add a protected class to the list of federally protected classes; however, they cannot remove a class.

The seven protected classes named by statute within the Fair Housing Act are race, color, religion, national origin, sex, disability, and familial status. These are the only federally protected classes.

Most states have adopted the federal guidelines of the Fair Housing Act, but some states, cities, counties, and other municipalities may have additional housing discrimination laws to protect additional groups. Consult with your specific state to get a list of additional protected classes, if any.

 HELPFUL HINT

All states have a state or local department of housing to oversee any questions, concerns, or possible violations within their own state.

Understanding the Federal Protected Classes

When it comes to protected classes and the Fair Housing Act, the key to compliance is whether a seller or his agent treats buyers differently because of an underlying characteristic the buyer may have.

Remember, the Fair Housing Act includes these seven protected classes: race, color, religion, national origin, sex, disability, and familial status.

Race

One of the central objectives of the Fair Housing Act was to prohibit race discrimination in sales and rentals of housing by either the seller or the buyer. The majority of the Justice Department's discrimination cases involve claims of race discrimination by the seller or his agent.

Color

Even though race and color overlap, they are not synonymous. Color discrimination can occur between sellers and buyers of different races or between persons of the same race. Although Title VII of the Civil Rights Act of 1964 does not define color, the courts have commonly understood the meaning to be a pigmentation, complexion, or skin shade or tone. Color discrimination occurs when a client is discriminated against based on the person's lightness, darkness, or other color characteristic.

Title VII of the Civil Rights Act of 1964 further prohibits color discrimination against all persons, including Caucasians.

Religion

The First Amendment to the U.S. Constitution prohibits the U.S. government from establishing a national religion and interfering with its citizens' free exercise of religion. The Fair Housing Act raises delicate issues relating to the establishment and free exercise of religion in private and in public. Discriminating against one party by the other or their agent solely based on their religious beliefs, practices, or observances is a violation of the Fair Housing Act when it comes to the sale of real property.

On the other hand, the Fair Housing Act exempts dwellings owned or operated by religious organizations from some of the prohibitions in the act.

National Origin

National origin discrimination is closely related to race, color, and religious discrimination. However, national origin refers to a person's place of birth, ancestry, or ethnicity. National origin discrimination includes treating buyers or sellers differently because of customs, culture, dress, and food associated with their country of origin. It also refers to a buyer's or seller's language, including whether or not they speak English or have an accent. Actions based on stereotypes associated with particular national origins are also discriminatory.

Discrimination based on immigration status is considered a type of national origin discrimination because it's often linked with stereotypes about certain groups of immigrants. It's also a practice that unfairly impacts only those born outside the United States or those whose national origin is not American. It also may be considered discriminatory if a seller or his agent threatens to call U.S. Citizenship and Immigration Services on a buyer.

Sex

One of the most confusing and misunderstood protected class is sex, as defined by the Fair Housing Act. The original interpretation is intended to mean gender, either male or female. However, in today's society, many broad interpretations have been applied to this term, including sexual orientation, sexual identification, and sexual preference.

Under federal law, the Fair Housing Act does not protect buyers against housing discrimination based on any of these. However, some states have included sexual orientation as a protected class in their housing discrimination laws.

 HELPFUL HINT

Many states have added sexual orientation as a protected class, including California, Colorado, Connecticut, Hawaii, Illinois, Maine, Maryland, Massachusetts, Minnesota, New Hampshire, New Jersey, New Mexico, New York, Rhode Island, Vermont, Washington, and Wisconsin.

Disability

The Fair Housing Act bars sellers and landlords from discriminating against buyers or tenants based on the fact they have a disability. This federal law also may require landlords to make reasonable accommodations or modifications to physical structures when a tenant requests them in connection with a disability during the rental term.

According to the Fair Housing Act, a disability is a physical or mental impairment that substantially limits the quality of a major life activity, including functions such as caring for one's self, performing manual tasks, walking, seeing, hearing, speaking, breathing, learning, and working. Although this definition appears to be broad in nature, there are some important points to be aware of when it comes to what's considered a disability under the act.

A buyer's or tenant's disability doesn't have to be obvious to be considered a disability. A seller or landlord does not have to be able to visibly discern the disability in order for the buyer to gain the law's protection. Similarly, there's no requirement that a buyer use a device for assistance to aid the disability, such as a wheelchair, cane, or hearing aid. Furthermore, a buyer's disability doesn't have to be physical. The Fair Housing Act protects buyers who have mental impairments as well.

An addiction may count as a disability. However, buyers or tenants who currently use illegal drugs or who have been convicted of the illegal manufacture or distribution of drugs aren't protected under the disability discrimination act. Likewise, a buyer or tenant isn't entitled to the act's protection if they pose a direct threat to others' health or safety.

It's also important to note that the act's definition of *disability* also encompasses less common situations, such as if a buyer has a "record of" having a disability or is "regarded as" having a disability. The first situation applies when a seller takes action based on knowledge of a disability that a buyer used to have or was just misclassified as having and never actually had. In the second situation, the seller's actions are based on a mistaken belief that a buyer has a disability.

Housing discrimination because of HIV or AIDS is illegal. This includes the unlawful denial of housing or access to housing and housing-related services.

Finally, keep in mind that the Fair Housing Act also protects people who live with a buyer who has a disability because adverse, discriminatory housing decisions affect everyone in that person's household.

Familial Status

Familial status refers to the presence of at least one child under 18 years old and also protects women who are pregnant or in the process of adopting a child.

 HELPFUL HINT

You may legally turn away families with children if your property qualifies as senior housing under the HOPA exemption rules.

Exceptions to the Fair Housing Act

Any seller engaging in discriminatory conduct may be held liable unless they fall within an exception to the act's coverage. Courts have applied the act to individuals, including property owners, lenders, real estate agents, and brokerage services. Under specific exceptions to the Fair Housing Act, some activities of the act do not apply to a private owner who sells his own home. Some exemptions include the following:

* A religious or private organization may give preference to other members unless membership is restricted based on one of the seven protected classes.

* An owner who owns four units or fewer and lives in one unit.

* A private individual owner who does not own more than three single-family houses, if the owner does not use the services of a broker, if the owner does not use discriminatory advertising, and if the owner has not participated in three or more rental or sales transactions in a 1-year period.

* Housing for elders may exclude families with children under the HOPA exemptions.

There are no exemptions to the advertising provision of the Fair Housing Act, which stipulates that you cannot make, print, or publish a discriminatory statement. And no one is exempt from the Civil Rights Act of 1866, which prohibits all racial discrimination in the sale or rental of property.

Violations of Fair Housing

When illegal discrimination occurs, it's rare that the wrongdoer announces the intent to discriminate overtly, where the intent to discriminate is clear. However, under the law, even people who do not mean to discriminate are responsible for discrimination. Even if the person intended for something good to happen, they can still be found to have acted illegally.

For housing-related violations, the act provides both a civil remedy in the form of monetary compensation for injury, including emotional distress and injunctive relief, and a criminal remedy, including fines and jail time for the perpetrator or their agent.

 REALTOR WARNING

Although the making, printing, or publishing (and/or to cause the making, printing, or publishing) of housing advertisements that discriminate against a protected class are illegal according to the Fair Housing Act, internet providers have not been subject to the law. This is due to an interpretation of the Communications Decency Act that determines internet providers are not publishers and, consequently, are not liable for Fair Housing Act violations on the websites they host.

Steering

Steering refers to the practice in which real estate brokers guide prospective home buyers toward or away from certain neighborhoods based on any one of the protested classes. Steering can be divided into two broad classes of conduct: advising customers to buy or not buy a home in a particular neighborhood based on a protected class and failing to show, not show, or inform buyers of homes that meet their specifications based on a protected class.

At times, steering can be confusing to real estate agents because they may think they're trying to help; however, they still could be in violation.

The courts have distinguished illegal racial steering from cases in which a REALTOR or broker merely responded to a customer's preferences. The line may not always be clear. For example, a client asked you to find him properties in an area that was Hispanic because he doesn't speak English very well. If you only show him properties in an area you think is heavily Hispanic influenced, even though you think you are helping him, your actions could be construed as steering.

Blockbusting

Blockbusting, or panic selling, is an unlawful act under the fair housing laws. It was a particularly prevalent practice in the 1950s and 1960s, but it continues today, although perhaps somewhat more subtly.

Blockbusting exists when REALTORS or investors persuade people to sell their homes or leave a neighborhood because of the prospective entry of home buyers of another race in the neighborhood. This results in panic selling, whereby white homeowners feel compelled to leave a neighborhood and are induced to sell at reduced prices—also known as "white flight." The homes are then resold to minority buyers at a profit.

Redlining

With redlining, real estate brokers, mortgage lenders, or insurance companies in effect write off an entire neighborhood and refuse to do business there because of certain minorities. There has been a long history of redlining in African American neighborhoods. The name comes from the fact that the perpetrators literally would draw a red line around a geographic area on the map.

Redlining may be difficult to prove. Insurance and mortgage companies traditionally argue that certain neighborhoods present too much risk or loss potential to justify doing business there. Unfortunately, it's not illegal for a company to charge higher premiums due to higher risks, and higher risks may well be present in some minority communities.

The key might depend on how the company defines neighborhood area boundaries and whether those boundaries are intentionally drawn in a manner to include only minorities in the high-risk neighborhoods. Redlining can occur if these companies offer different products to "neighborhoods of color" or if certain neighborhoods are targeted for predatory lending or inferior loans or if loan modifications or refinancing is not equally available. Redlining also may be evidenced by the type and extent of advertising in or to particular neighborhoods.

Appraising

Any person who appraises or gives value to a property, whether written or oral, may not use any of the protected classes in determining that value. This also includes a real estate professional who gives comparative market values to their clients.

Advertising

Advertising under the Fair Housing Act doesn't just mean ads in newspapers. The law says you can't "make, print, or publish … any notice, statement, or advertisement … that indicates any preference, limitation, or discrimination based on a person's race, color, religion, sex, handicap, familial status, or national origin." That includes such things as applications, flyers, brochures, deeds, signs, banners, posters, billboards, and even pictures in your office. This prohibition applies even if the particular housing is itself exempt under the Fair Housing Act.

This provision covers all advertising and not just the traditional newspaper advertisement. It also applies to spoken statements and visual representations made to sellers or buyers. For example, if an advertisement contains only white models, or if the advertisement appears to discourage persons with disabilities from living in the particular environment, the advertisement may be in violation of the law.

Anyone who publishes an advertisement is responsible for its content. Newspapers, for example, are strictly liable for the content of advertisements printed in their papers, as are providers of community bulletin boards. Sellers, or their agents, who post discriminatory advertisements on the internet are liable for what they post; however, courts have held that website providers that do not solicit specific information from the persons posting internet advertisements have immunity under the federal Communications Decency Act. Furthermore, the law states that "… words, phrases, photographs, illustrations, symbols or forms of any kind" that give the impression that your property is available or not available to certain types of people is illegal.

Advertisements cannot state a preference or limitation based on race or color, but statements such as *master bedroom* and *desirable neighborhood* are not illegal. And although religious discrimination is illegal, using phrases like *kosher meals served on the premises, Merry Christmas,* or *Happy Easter* in an ad is not discriminatory either.

Obviously, statements such as *no handicapped* are illegal. However, using phrases such as *great view, walk-in closets,* or *walk to bus stop* are acceptable. You still should avoid certain illegal words or phrases that have been associated with discriminatory practices in the past, including *restricted, exclusive, limited,* and so on.

HUD considers the use of certain advertising words evidence of your compliance with the Fair Housing Act. For example, using *Equal Housing Opportunity* or the fair housing logo in your ads is good. Displaying a fair housing poster in your office is another way to advertise in a positive manner. Another way to produce positive advertisements is to vary the use of human models in your ads so both majority and minority groups in your community, both sexes, persons with disabilities, and, when appropriate, children of all ages are represented.

Fair Housing Enforcement Procedures

HUD is charged with enforcement of the Fair Housing Act. It issues regulations and institutes investigations into discriminatory housing practices.

Any person who claims to have been injured by a discriminatory housing practice or who believes he or she will be injured by such a practice about to occur may file a complaint with HUD. HUD will offer assistance to persons preparing a complaint. Alternatively, an aggrieved person can file a private civil suit or work directly with a state or local agency that HUD identifies through its substantial equivalence certification. A certified agency enforces a law with rights, procedures, remedies, and judicial review provisions that are substantially equivalent to the Fair Housing Act. The state's Commission on Human Rights and Opportunities (CHRO) is a certified agency. HUD must refer complaints to certified agencies whenever possible.

The complaint must contain a brief summary of the facts regarding the alleged discrimination. The complaint may be directed against a person engaged in the sale, rental, advertising, financing, or brokerage of real property who is alleged to have engaged in a discriminatory housing practice. A complaint also can be filed against a person who directs or controls the property owner. The complaint can be amended, but it must be filed with HUD within 1 year after the alleged discrimination occurred or terminated. After the complaint is filed, HUD may process it or refer the matter to an appropriate state or local agency for further action.

Within 10 days of the filing of the complaint, HUD or the state or local agency will serve the complaint to each person named in the complaint. Within 10 days of service, each person named may respond to the allegations.

Upon the filing of the complaint, HUD will initiate its investigation. HUD's general counsel will make a determination as to whether or not reasonable cause exists that a discriminatory housing practice has occurred. Although the investigation is to be completed within 100 days of the filing of the complaint, this time period is routinely extended.

During the investigation phase, HUD will attempt to conciliate the complaint. In so doing, HUD will bring the parties together to obtain an amicable resolution of the dispute. Through *conciliation,* HUD will seek assurances that respondents will remedy any violations of the rights of the complainant and take action to eliminate discriminatory housing practices in the future. HUD may terminate conciliation if the complainant or respondent fails to participate in good faith.

 **DEFINITION**

Conciliation is the process of adjusting or settling disputes in a friendly manner through extrajudicial means. It means bringing together two opposing sides to reach a compromise in an attempt to avoid taking a case to court.

Unless the parties have executed a conciliation agreement approved by HUD, HUD will prepare a final investigative report. The report is made available to the complainant and respondents and forwarded to HUD's general counsel for a "reasonable cause" determination.

HUD's counsel reviews the Final Investigative Report to determine "whether there is sufficient evidence to believe that housing discrimination may have occurred or is about to occur." If HUD determines that there is reasonable cause to believe discrimination has or is about to occur, it will issue a "charge" against the respondents. Otherwise, HUD will dismiss the complaint.

If HUD issues a charge, either party may elect to have the charge litigated in the U.S. District Court, where the charge will be prosecuted by the Department of Justice. If no one makes an election to litigate within the prescribed time, the charge will be handled before a HUD Administrative Law Judge. Regardless of whether the charge is handled through litigation or administrative proceedings, the respondents may be ordered to pay damages, complainant's legal fees, and provide services and amenities if the alleged discrimination is proven.

If found to be in violation, compensatory and punitive damages can be awarded. Compensatory damages include actual out-of-pocket expenses or losses, called special damages, which range from actual expenses incurred by the discriminatory act to losses that directly result from the discrimination. Compensatory damages also include general damages for humiliation, embarrassment, or emotional distress. These damages are available "… for distress which exceeds the normal transient and trivial aggravation attendant to securing suitable housing." Courts are less inclined to award damages if the harm is considered more of an "inconvenience" than detrimental.

Punitive damages also may be awarded by federal courts. These aren't damages to reimburse the complainant, but rather damages to punish the wrongdoer when there's clear evidence of willful or malicious intent. Attorney's fees and court costs may be awarded to the prevailing party as well.

On March 28, 2014, the U.S. Department of Justice published a notice increasing the civil monetary penalties for violations of the Fair Housing Act. Under the new rule, which applies to violations that occur on or after April 28, 2014, the maximum civil penalty for a first violation increases from $55,000 to $75,000, and for subsequent violations the new maximum is $150,000.

HUD keeps a record of all charges that are filed through them and makes that information publicly available. You can read all HUD charges going back to 2004.

What Fair Housing Means to Real Estate Licensees

As a member of the National Association of REALTORS (NAR), you've made a commitment to equal treatment, not just because it's the law, but as part of the REALTORS Code of Ethics. NAR requires that members stay up to date on the code, completing training at least every 4 years. In addition, states and localities often have their own fair housing laws, so state and local associations administer specific fair housing training for their members. Typically, licensees are required to take a 2- or 3-hour course every 2 to 4 years.

If you are not a member of the NAR, you still should provide equal service to all clients regardless of their race, color, religion, national origin, sex, disability, or familial status.

As a licensed professional, you are responsible for practicing ethically, legally, and honestly. You have a social and legal responsibility to help maintain an open real estate market through knowledge, expertise, and understanding of the fair housing laws. You should strive to educate your clients in the same.

In almost all cases of discrimination, whether overt or unintentional, the REALTOR was named as a co-party to the suit. This can cause great concern for you as a real state professional. Not only can you lose money in the form of fines, fees, and penalties if you're found in violation, but you also can lose your ability to practice real estate if your license is suspended or revoked.

That the offense was unintentional is no defense in fair housing. Whether the discrimination was innocent of any intent or not, the effect of feeling discriminated against is the key test as to whether a violation occurred. The fair housing law is an effects law, not an intent law.

The Least You Need to Know

- Fair housing laws protect people from discrimination in housing transactions against race, color, religion, national origin, sex, disability, or familial status bias.
- Some properties are exempt from fair housing in certain situations.
- Violations to fair housing laws can warrant civil and criminal penalties against all violators, including the REALTOR.
- Enforcement of the fair housing laws falls to the Department of Housing and Urban Development, and fines for first-time violations can be a maximum of $75,000.
- Fair housing is an effects law, not an intent law.
- Real estate professionals can lose their licenses if they're found violating fair housing laws.

Ethics

Ethics can be defined as a "set of principles of right conduct." That's all well and good—simple, clear, and concise. But is it?

Ethics is a vast combination of decisions in each situation for a given set of criteria that has to be assessed. What may be ethical in one situation, given a set of certain conditions, may not be ethical with a different set of conditions.

Ethics changes over time, and it does indeed evolve to reflect the changing needs of society. For example, slavery was once held has widely acceptable and ethical; however, as society has evolved and recognized the errors brought about by slavery, people have a completely different view on the topic today. Birth control was once seen as hush-hush among polite society. Today, however, it's a widely discussed and prevalent topic.

Even within the real estate industry, the past view with buyers when selling a house was *caveat emptor*. It has only been within the past 30 years that buyers are now being represented by their own agents due to a change in what's considered ethical treatment of both parties.

In this chapter, we will cover the need for ethics in a professional society such as the NAR, along with the basic ethical practices mandated by them. We will cover the ethical activities practiced by working REALTORS and how they benefit their clients and the overall profession as a whole. There will be a discussion on *ethical*

In This Chapter

- Understanding ethics
- Applying ethics in your everyday life
- How to be an ethical real estate professional
- Ethical versus legal
- The REALTOR Code of Ethics

versus *legal* and how, in some cases, a person may act legally but not ethically and vice versa. Finally we will cover the basic canons of the NAR's code of ethics and see how they are the minimum actions that should be used by a REALTOR.

What Is Ethics?

In a recent study by sociologist Raymond Baumhart, people were asked, "What does ethics mean to you?" Here are some of their responses:

- Ethics has to do with what is right or wrong.

- Ethics has to do with my religious beliefs.

- Ethics is doing what the law requires.

- Ethics consists of the standards of behavior our society accepts.

As you can see by these answers, ethics can mean different things to different people. Therein lies the problem: your standards of ethics might not necessarily match someone else's view of ethics, and problems can arise with the interaction of people with different perceptions of what is ethical.

Many people tend to equate ethics with their feelings, religious beliefs, or the law.

Basing ethics on your feelings is clearly not a valid answer. People tend to have feelings that often might fly in the face of ethics, in fact. If a person were to follow his feelings, he may resist doing what is right.

Nor should one identify ethics with religion. Most religions strive to achieve a high level of ethical standards. However, if that were true, only religious people would be ethical. Furthermore, if religion was the basis for ethics, the question would arise, "What religion?" Could that cause you to have a different view of ethics if you were Buddhist versus Christian? Religion can, and often does, set high ethical standards and can provide intense motivations for ethical behavior. Ethics, however, cannot be confined to religion, nor is it the same as religion.

Nor should following the law be considered ethical. The law often incorporates ethical standards to which most citizens subscribe. But laws, like feelings, can deviate from what is ethical. Slavery is one example where past laws and ethics collided.

Finally, being ethical is not the same as doing whatever society accepts. If this were true, then ethics could simply be determined by polling the populous to find answers. Abortion, for example, cannot be decided by asking your friends what they think and then simply adopting the majority point of view. Further, the lack of social consensus on many issues makes it impossible to equate ethics with whatever society accepts. Some people accept abortion, but many others do not. If being ethical were doing whatever society accepts, one would have to find an agreement on issues which does not exist.

So what is ethics? Ethics is two things. First, ethics refers to well-founded standards of right and wrong that prescribe what humans ought to do, usually in terms of rights, obligations, benefits to society, fairness, or specific virtues, and standards that relate to unalienable rights, such as the right to life, the right to freedom from injury, and the right to privacy. These standards are a great basis of ethics because they're supported by consistent, conscious, and well-founded reasoning.

Secondly, ethics refers to the study and development of one's own ethical standards. Ethics also means, then, the continuous effort of studying your own moral beliefs and moral conduct and striving to ensure that you, and others, live up to those standards.

The Role of Ethics in Real Estate

In a 2015 study conducted by Gallup, REALTORS ranked thirteenth in the "most ethical and honest" professionals, with doctors and nurses being number one and two, respectively. Furthermore, 78 percent of people polled thought REALTORS were only average, or below, with respect to being ethical.

When it comes to buying or selling a home, people place a huge amount of trust in their agent. The process of buying and selling a home is fraught with complex activities, concepts, and processes that most buyers or sellers don't know or understand. Therefore, they rely on the advice, insight, and expertise of their agent. This trust given to the agent is predicated on the fact the agent will serve the client with ethical practices.

Therefore, ethics should be the cornerstone for all real estate professionals. If you are a member of the National Association of REALTORS (NAR), you must legally abide by the Code of Ethics. If you are not a NAR member, as a good practice, you still should abide by a set of standards and principles to treat your clients with honesty, fairness, and respect.

 REALTOR WARNING

Failing to practice according to the REALTOR Code of Ethics can cause your license to be suspended or even revoked. Please make sure that you know, are aware of and practice by the Code of Ethics daily.

As a real estate professional, ethics must play a large role in your practice. Many people might think all real estate professionals are obligated to follow a code of ethics. However, if you're not a REALTOR, or a member of the NAR, you might not necessarily have a code of ethics you practice. As a REALTOR, you are held to a higher standard of ethics.

In general, a code of ethics is a set of principles of conduct within an organization that guides decision-making and behavior. The purpose of the code is to provide members with a set of guidelines for making ethical decisions in the conduct of their practice. Members of an organization adopt a code of ethics to share a dedication to ethical behavior and adopt this code to declare the organization's principles and standards of practice.

The REALTORS Code of Ethics sets forth the standards by which all REALTORS treat customers, clients, and other agents. This is arguably the most important part of being a REALTOR. The Code of Ethics includes a preamble that introduces the basic concepts of the code, followed by the 17 principles REALTORS must use during their real estate practices.

Many of these principles deal with how clients are treated. For example, the key principle is that REALTORS have to put their clients' needs ahead of their own self-interest. This means they always have to do what's in the best interest of their client, no matter what. Another principle says the REALTORS have to work in conjunction with other REALTORS if it can benefit their client. The Code of Ethics also states REALTORS are not allowed to discriminate against any parties associated with a real estate transaction. REALTORS have to treat everyone equally and provide everyone with equal service.

In addition to ethics, truth is another prevalent concept that runs throughout the REALTORS Code of Ethics. REALTORS must engage in truthful practices always. For example, a REALTOR cannot misrepresent any details about a house they are selling. They cannot exaggerate any details or leave out any important information when advertising a house. They have to engage in full disclosure.

REALTORS also must be truthful when advertising. They cannot make any misleading statements that could be used to induce a sale of a house, acquire a listing, or create an agency relationship with a client. Furthermore, they are not allowed to "lie by omission" or withhold important facts, details, or information specifically to give a misleading picture of the house.

Other ethical practices include how you treat the other REALTORS and how you treat the other REALTORS' clients. You are not allowed to speak negatively about any other REALTORS, nor are you allowed to try to take clients from any other REALTORS in the area.

The Difference Between Ethical and Legal

Ethical and legal are often used and considered equal in concept and meaning. Although there's a relationship between the two, the concepts can be mutually exclusive of each other.

Being ethical is not the same as following the law. The law often may incorporate ethical standards to which most citizens subscribe. But laws, like feelings, can greatly deviate from what is ethical.

And sometimes what is ethical may not be legal. For example, the medical use of marijuana may be ethical when used to relieve pain and symptoms in patients with certain maladies, but in many states, it is illegal to do so.

 HELPFUL HINT

Both legal and ethical concepts can be applied in almost any situation, private or public, even in the realm of professions like real estate.

License Law and Code of Ethics

Both license law and the REALTORS Code of Ethics are comprised of a set of rules designed to provide guidelines for agents and brokers on how to honestly and ethically represent buyers and sellers. These two sets of rules may be very similar in most respects, but they differ in others, as shown in the following table.

All real estate professionals must abide by license laws that govern their state. In addition to these license laws, REALTORS are subject to the NAR's Code of Ethics rules and regulations.

License Law Versus Code of Ethics

Similarities	Differences
Both must disclose their status as principals in real estate transactions.	Under license law, a written listing agreement and consent of the owner is required before a property can be advertised for sale.
Both must disclose the receipt of any monies or fees from vendors.	Under license law, agents can receive payment only from their brokers. The Code of Ethics allows for payments from other REALTORS to an agent with the consent of the principal broker.
Both must have a separate account in which to place client monies.	Under the Code of Ethics, REALTORS must disclose to the seller the amount of commission they intend to share with cooperating brokers.
Both must provide copies of all relevant documents to clients.	Under the Code of Ethics, REALTORS must disclose the existence of accepted offers to other REALTORS.
Both must have authority to advertise a seller's property for sale.	Under the Code of Ethics, REALTORS must disclose variable rate commissions.
Both must be truthful and not misleading in their advertising.	Under the Code of Ethics, REALTORS must disclose their status as an owner when buying or selling property.
Both must refrain from discrimination or fair housing violations.	
Both prohibit licensees from contacting sellers who have outstanding exclusive agency agreements with other licensees for the purpose of negotiating about properties or seeking listings.	

In certain areas, the license law and Code of Ethics are different. Should there be a discrepancy between the two, license law always trumps the Code of Ethics.

Reporting Ethics Violations

Many of the difficulties that arise between real estate professionals result from misunderstandings or poor or inadequate communication. If you have a problem with another real estate professional, you might want to speak with them or their principal broker. Open, constructive discussion often resolves questions or differences, eliminating the need for further action.

If, after discussing matters with the other real estate professional or his principal broker, you still aren't satisfied, you might want to contact your local board or association of REALTORS. In addition to processing formal ethics complaints against member REALTORS, many boards and associations offer informal dispute resolution services. Often, parties are more satisfied with informal dispute resolution processes because they're quicker, less costly, and often help repair damaged relationships.

REALTORS are different from non-NAR-member real estate professionals in that they voluntarily subscribe to a strict Code of Ethics. If you believe a REALTOR has violated one or more Articles of the Code of Ethics, you can file an ethics complaint alleging a violation through the local association of REALTORS where the REALTOR holds membership or participates in a REALTOR association-owned/operated multiple listing service (MLS). As a condition of membership, REALTORS agree to arbitrate contractual disputes and specific noncontractual disputes as provided for in Article 17 of the NAR Code of Ethics. However, if the real estate professional you are dealing with is not a REALTOR, your only recourse may be the court system.

Boards of REALTORS determine whether the Code of Ethics has been violated. Local boards do not regulate whether the license law has been broken; that's decided by the state real estate commission. If the board determines there has been a Code of Ethics violation, disciplinary actions can be taken, including the following:

- Require increased continuous education specifically designed for the ethics.

- Issue a letter of reprimand and appropriate fines.

- Suspend or terminate a REALTOR's membership from the local board for serious or repeated violations.

Boards of REALTORS cannot do the following:

- Require REALTORS to pay money to parties filing ethics complaints.

- Issue jail time to a REALTOR.

- Award punitive damages for violations of the Code of Ethics.

- Suspend or revoke a REALTOR's license. Only the state real estate commission has the power to do this.

 HELPFUL HINT

Only local boards of REALTORS can hear complaints on the Code of Ethics. Only the state real estate commission can deal with license law violations.

The local board of REALTORS can provide you with information on the state specific procedures for filing an ethics complaint. However, there are some general guidelines you should keep in mind.

Ethics complaints must be filed within 180 days from the time a complainant knew, or reasonably should have known, that potentially unethical conduct took place. The NAR's Code of Ethics consists of 17 Articles with the duties imposed by many of the Articles. Further explanations and illustrations of the Articles are present through the accompanying Standards of Practice as well. Your complaint should include a very detailed description of the circumstances that lead you to believe there has been, or will be, a Code of Ethics violation. Your complaint must specifically cite one or more of the Articles of the Code of Ethics that may have been violated.

The board of REALTORS's hearing panels decide whether the Articles expressly cited in the complaint were violated, not whether Standards of Practice were violated. Most local boards of REALTORS provide technical assistance in preparing a complaint in proper form and with proper content.

Your complaint will be reviewed, typically by a grievance committee. The committee's job is to review complaints to determine if the complaint made, if true, might be a violation of the Code of Ethics. The grievance committee either dismisses your complaint or forwards it for a hearing. If it dismisses your complaint, it's most likely due to the fact that it does not feel your complaint would support a hearing panel's conclusion that the Articles had been violated. You might want to review your complaint to see if you cited the appropriate Articles. If your complaint is dismissed as not requiring a hearing, you can appeal the dismissal to the board of directors of the local board or association of REALTORS.

If the grievance committee forwards the complaint for hearing, it feels your complaint, if found to have actually occurred, might give the hearing panel reason to believe a violation of the Code of Ethics has occurred. It doesn't mean it has decided the Code of Ethics has been violated.

Hearing panels base their decisions on the evidence and testimony presented during the hearing. It's up to the hearing panel, during the hearing process, to determine what actually happened. The hearing panel pays careful attention to what you say and how you say it.

When the hearing panel's *findings of fact* are made and handed down to all the parties, review them carefully. Findings of fact are the conclusions of an impartial hearing panel based on its reasoned assessment of all the evidence and testimony presented during the hearing. The hearing panel's findings of fact are not appealable.

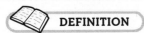 **DEFINITION**

> **Findings of fact** is the term applied to the conclusion reached by the panel, arbitrators, or court. It's the determination of truth after consideration.

If you believe the hearing process was seriously flawed to the extent you were denied a full and fair hearing, appellate procedures can be involved to request a new hearing. The fact that a hearing panel found a violation or no violation is not appealable. Refer to the procedures used by your local board of REALTORS for detailed information on the bases and time limits for appealing decisions. Appeals must be based solely on a perceived misapplication or misinterpretation of one or more Articles of the Code of Ethics, a procedural deficiency or failure of due process, or the nature or gravity of the discipline proposed by the hearing panel.

Basically, many ethics complaints result from misunderstandings or failures in communication. Before filing an ethics complaint, make reasonable efforts to communicate with the real estate professional or a principal broker in his or her firm. If these efforts are not fruitful, state boards of REALTORS can share options for dispute resolution, including the procedures and forms necessary to file an ethics complaint.

The Least You Need to Know

- Ethics is not a set of laws, religious beliefs, nor societal points of view but rather a "set of principles of right conduct."
- Ethics is the cornerstone for real estate professionals.
- Ethical and legal are not the same.
- Local boards deal with Code of Ethic violations, while license law is the purview of the state real estate commission.
- Ethics violations must be filed within 180 days.
- A hearing panel determines the findings of fact, which cannot be appealed.

Ownership and Transference

If you have real estate that you would like to sell, or give away, to a friend, relative, or some other third-party, for money, there are a few issues that need to be covered with your REALTOR and other legal advisers. Before you buy or sell any real estate, make sure you are doing it correctly to save yourself from any court actions trying to interfere with the process. Furthermore, make sure you are selling the property at the right time for the tax purposes.

Using a knowledgeable REALTOR to guide you through the process is the safest and surest way to avoid any pitfalls that may occur during the process. To help you during the selling or buying process, your real estate agent will guide you to other knowledgeable professionals such as: a title company, a home inspector, a mortgage broker.

Estates and Interests

Most real estate transactions cover real property or personal property. Many of the legal concepts and rules associated with these types of property are derived from English common law. Modern law has incorporated many of these concepts and rules into statutes, which define the types and rights of ownership in real and personal property.

A third type of property that can be owned by a person or entity is intellectual property. Ownership of intellectual property, which traditionally includes patents, copyrights, trademarks, and trade secrets, cannot be defined as clearly as the other types of property because intellectual property is intangible—it cannot be held, touched, or defined by physical boundaries. Instead, intellectual property is the ownership interest a person or entity has in creations of the human mind. Ownership of intellectual property means ownership of a concept or idea rather than ownership of a parcel of property or object. Like real property and personal property, intellectual property can be bought, sold, or otherwise conveyed.

We won't discuss intellectual property rights in this book. Instead, in this chapter, we'll concentrate on real and personal property rights.

In This Chapter

- Real estate versus real property
- An estate in real property
- Types of estates in real estate
- Passing an estate to a buyer
- Surface, subsurface, air, and water rights

What Is Real Property?

Real property can be defined by three areas: land; man-made items, called *real estate;* and the rights associated with the property, called *real property.*

Land

Land is comprised of the physical dirt and earth within a given area and any naturally growing plants on it. When a person buys land, it is thought to mean from the center of the earth to the heavens above. However, many previous court cases have defined the "heavens above" to have a specific meaning based on the buildings built on it.

Land can be further divided into three subcategories: surface, subsurface, and air rights (more on these later in this chapter).

An appurtenance is a right or benefit that is associated with a property but not necessarily attached to the property itself, such as a dock sitting in the lake that would be included in the purchase of the house on the water. Another example would be a parking spot in a basement garage that is included with the condo on the third floor.

Real Estate

Real estate is land plus any man-made items on the land, often called *improvements.*

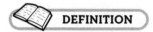 **DEFINITION**

> An **improvement** is any permanent structure on real property, or any work on the property (such as planting trees) that can increases its value.

Real Property

Real property is land plus real estate plus the legal bundle of rights. The bundle of rights consists of five rights, sometimes called "twigs," including possession, control, exclusion, disposition, and enjoyment (sometimes called quiet enjoyment).

Bundle of rights is a term used to describe property rights belonging to the property owner. The right of possession is the right to occupy the property. The right of control is the right to determine how the owner will use the property. The right of exclusion is the right to refuse others legal entrance, use, or interference of the property. The right of disposition is the right to determine how the property is sold or given away to another party. The right of enjoyment, also called quiet enjoyment, is the right to use, or enjoy, the property without any third-party interference.

As a real property owner, you have the fullest rights to the property, providing you are not breaking any local, state, or federal laws doing so.

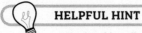

HELPFUL HINT

The legal bundle of rights consists of five rights, or *twigs*, as they're often called. This comes from the old English tradition of passing a twig from a tree on the land to symbolically show the passing of ownership from the seller to the buyer.

Personal Property

Personal property, or chattel, is anything other than land that can be the subject of ownership. Common items in a real estate transaction that would be considered personal property are couches, dining room tables, dressers, etc.

An easy way to identify personal property is by looking as if the item is movable. If it's movable, it's personal property. If it's not, it's real property. This is often called the movability test.

However, some items appear to be personal property but in fact may be real property. These are called fixtures.

Fixtures

Fixtures are items that appear to be personal property but are affixed in such a way they become real property. Ceiling fans, miniblinds, and curtain rods are examples of such items.

You can determine if an item is real or personal in three ways.

First, apply the movability test and consider if the item is affixed to the property. For example: A microwave may be personal property if it's sitting on the countertop; however, if it's bolted above the stove and is a permanently affixed part of the cabinet, it's real property. This is called the movability test. If an object can be easily moved, then it is often considered personal property.

You also could determine if the item a part of system. For example: A refrigerator may be personal if it's movable and easily can be taken with the seller. If the refrigerator is a component of a cabinetry system and would be obviously missed if it was removed, it may be real property.

Finally, the parties can decide whether an item is real or personal in the purchase agreement. For example: A ceiling fan may be considered real property by its method of annexation, but if both parties agree the fan will be removed and taken with the seller, it's deemed personal property.

Furthermore, trade fixtures are used in commercial real estate as well. A trade fixture is a tenant's personal property that's affixed to the landlord's real property. Trade fixtures not removed by the tenant at or before the end of the lease can become a landlord's real property though *construction annexation*, or accession.

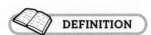

DEFINITION

Constructive annexation is an action whereby a landlord's property value is increased by labor, material, or items added to the property by a tenant. This can come in the form of a tenant improving the landlord's property, in any manner, and not returning it to the original condition at the end of the lease.

Severance and Annexation

The characteristics of real and personal property can be altered at times by severance or annexation.

The process of creating personal property from real property is called severance. For example: An apple tree may be considered real property, but if you remove an apple from it by severance, the apple would become personal property.

The process of turning personal property into real property is known as annexation. When a load of wood is dropped at your property, it would be personal property. But if you use that wood to build a deck on the house, that wood has been annexed into real property.

Plants

When dealing with plants, there are two distinct different types: *fructus industriales* and *fructus naturales*.

Fructus industriales are the industrial fruits, called emblements, planted on an annual basis and harvested. Examples include corn, oats, hay, barley, tobacco, etc. These are considered the personal property of the seller, and he has the right to remove them at, or before, the time of sale of the property. He also could return later, after the sale, to collect the crop, but that should be negotiated at the time of the sale.

Fructus naturales are naturally occurring fruits, such as trees, bushes, and flowers. *Fructus naturales* are considered real property and remain with the real property at the time of sale.

What Is an Estate in Land?

An estate in land can be defined as the degree or nature of interest enjoyed by the property owner. An interest in the property must allow for possession and enjoyment to be considered an estate. Often an interest is defined by the time or length of possession.

Freehold estate, leasehold estate (discussed further in Chapter 15), life estate, and legal life estate are types of estates. They vary in nature and are classified based upon the duration of ownership, with freehold being the longest and life estate being the shortest duration of ownership.

Freehold Estates

A freehold estate is an estate held for an indeterminable amount of time, as in forever or a lifetime. One type of freehold estate is a fee simple estate, whereby a property can be passed to an owner's heirs. A life estate, although still a freehold estate, terminates when the life estate holder passes away.

Many different types of freehold estates can be passed from person to person.

A fee simple estate occurs when all five rights (possession, control, exclusion, disposition, and enjoyment) are transferred from the seller to the buyer in some form. The highest form, or degree, would be fee simple absolute. When a fee simple absolute estate is passed to a new owner, he would have the enjoyment "to the fullest extent" of the property. Under fee simple absolute, when the property owner dies, the property may pass it to any co-owners, to any heirs, or by a legal will. A fee simple absolute is only subject to restrictive covenants and local, state, or federal laws, including zoning laws.

A fee simple defeasible is similar in that all rights are transferred; however, there is some limiting, or qualifying, condition that must be met. Two fee simple types are fee simple determinable and fee simple condition subsequent. Fee simple determinable means "as long as" or "during." Fee simple condition subsequent means "as a condition of." Both degrees of ownership, although not absolute, give the property owner all the rights of the property but limit the control through a defeasance, or restriction.

Fee simple determinable is used to ensure there's some activity or event, or lack thereof, that's continued during the ownership of the new owner. The former owner retains the right, called the possibility of reverter, which allows for the property to revert automatically to the holder of the right, without any court intervention, should the current owner fail to maintain the defeasance. For example, if a property owner transfers property to a church as long as it's used for religious functions, he may use a fee simple determinable. "As long as it's used for religious functions" is key. If, or when, the church fails to meet the required activity, the property reverts to the original owner without any court proceedings.

The fee simple condition subsequent is based on the condition that's placed on the new owner by the seller. However, if the condition is not met, the previous owner has to seek court remedies for the property to revert to him. For example, if an owner transfers property as fee simple condition subsequent that states that no alcohol will be sold, bought, or consumed on the property and the condition is violated, the previous owner has to seek court remedies to get the property back.

These rights are transferrable to subsequent heirs and successors, known as inheritable rights.

Life Estate

While it is considered a freehold estate due to the indeterminable amount of time owned, a life estate is not forever, but rather determined by the life of a tenant, or someone else, identified during the creation of the life estate. The right of disposition is not granted to the new owner but retained by the current owner to be decided later, making a life estate not inheritable. The receiver of a life estate is known as a life tenant.

An ordinary life estate is when the life tenant's death will trigger a transfer of the property to someone else. A *pur autre vie* life estate is when the death of someone other than the life tenant triggers the transfer of ownership of the property.

 **DEFINITION**

> **Pur autre vie** is an old French saying that means "by the life of another" or "for another's life."

For example, if a wealthy father gives his son a house as a life estate under an ordinary life estate, the son would become the life tenant with all the legal bundle of rights except for disposition. The death of the life tenant triggers the transfer of the property back to the father, or his heirs or successors. However, if the son cannot care for himself, the father, under a *pur autre vie* life estate, can transfer the property to an agency to care for him. In this case, the agency would be the life tenant. However, the death of the son, not the life tenant, would trigger the transfer of the property back to the father, or his heirs or successors, or someone else he has named in the creation of the life estate.

When the life tenant dies, the property transfers to another person identified during the creation of the life estate. If that person is the original creator of the life estate, he is granted a revisionary interest. However, if the person named is someone other than the original creator of the life estate, this person or entity is granted a remainderman's interest.

Legal Life Estate

A legal life estate is created by law rather than by property owners. Dower, curtesy, and homestead are examples of legal life estates used by most states.

Dower is the life estate of a wife in her deceased husband's real estate. Curtesy is the husband's life estate in his deceased wife's real estate. Upon the death of the wife or the husband, the surviving spouse is granted an interest in the property to protect them from the property being transferred without their consent or knowledge. The surviving spouse can release their dower or curtesy right upon the sale or voluntary transfer of the property. Therefore, it's necessary to gain both spouses' signatures when listing a property so there's no question of ownership when it comes time to transfer the property.

The homestead is a legal life estate that protects the family and their primary residence against unsecured creditors. In most states that use the homestead estate, only a portion of the value of the real property is protected against debts, judgments, or charges; other states protect the entire amount of the property. It's important to note that the homestead estate only protects against unsecured creditors and not secured debts such as mortgage or real estate tax liens. Furthermore, some states require the homeowner, or head of household, to apply for the homestead estate while other states require it by statute.

Surface, Subsurface, Air, and Water Rights

Land can be further divided into three areas: surface, subsurface, and air rights.

Water rights are the statutory rights granted to property owners in or around bodies of water that can include rivers, streams, and lakes.

Surface Rights

The ownership rights in a parcel of land are limited to the surface of the property and do not include the air rights above it or the subsurface or minerals below it. Surface rights implies that the owner may do whatever he wishes to the land as far as law permits.

Subsurface Rights

Under common law, an owner of land also owns down to the center of the earth. As for how much of the land below your property you own, there's no real limit enforced by courts, and there have been cases of people being prosecuted for trespassing on other people's property for digging even in the thousands of feet below the ground in the search of oil.

Of course, in reality, there's a practical limit in that if there is a country on the other side of the world from your land, it's probably not one where your country has jurisdiction. Further, there's the matter of the giant layer of magma in between. But beyond that, you can generally dig as deep as you like as long as you're not breaking any environmental laws and have the appropriate permits.

Also associated with subsurface rights are mineral, gas, oil, and water rights (more on water rights in a bit).

In most countries, all mineral resources belong to the country's government. This includes all valuable rocks, minerals, oil, and gas found on or within the earth. However, in the United States and a few other countries, ownership of mineral resources is granted to the individuals who own the surface rights.

Mineral rights can be described as the unseen value associated with a tract of land. Historically, land was transferred among owners with the royalty rights commingled with the surface rights. As oil and gas production began in the United States, these rights started to be viewed independently. This separation allows for an owner to split out the mineral rights as a separate entity and sell or lease the rights to someone else.

HELPFUL HINT

In most states, gas and oil rights are typically considered within the mineral rights; however, they can be segregated from the mineral rights if negotiated in such a manner. Coal, natural gas, and other subsurface entities also are considered within the realm of mineral rights.

Air Rights

Historically, property owners owned to the center of the earth and to the top of the heavens, which included the right to all the air above the property. That gave property owners the right to exclude trespassers from their air.

Until the invention of aircraft, the matter typically arose only in disputes over the right to remove tree limbs extending over one's property. In 1926, Congress created what we now call the Federal Aviation Administration and declared that the air above 500 feet is the public domain.

As an accommodation to modern technology, courts allow reasonable trespasses to air rights. The question at the core of these court cases is, "Who owns the air?"

Thomas Causby was a chicken farmer in North Carolina who lived near a tiny airport. During World War II, the Army took over the airport, and suddenly big military planes were flying over Causby's chicken coops all the time, scaring his chickens and causing them to fly into the walls of the coop and die. Causby sued the government, and the case went all the way to the Supreme Court. In the end, the Court sided with Causby, ruling that landowners own the sky above their homes up to at least 83 feet. But the *United States* v. *Causby* decision still left a gap. If the air above 500 feet is public property, and the air below 83 feet is private property, what about the space in between?

Many examples exist of air rights being bought, sold, or traded separate from the surface or subsurface rights. The owners of the MetLife Building in New York, formerly built as the Pan Am Building, purchased the air rights from the Grand Central Station and built a 59-story skyscraper.

Water Rights

Water rights generally emerge from a person's ownership of land that borders the banks of a body of water or from a person's actual use of the water. Water rights are conferred and regulated by common law, state and federal legislative bodies, and other government departments. Water rights also can be created and transferred by contract.

Riparian rights are common law rights granted to property owners along rivers, streams, or creeks. Most states have specific laws that govern the exact ownership interest, but they typically allow for unrestricted use of the body of water.

If a stream is navigable, as determined by the U.S. Coast Guard, the owner would only enjoy the ownership to the edge of the water. Navigable waters are considered public right of ways and use and travel by the public is allowed. Furthermore, the ground beneath all navigable water is owned by the state.

If the stream is non-navigable, the property owner owns to the center of the water.

The only restrictions for either property ownership situation would be to not contaminate the water nor impede the flow of water to other people's land because all running water eventually flows into the public ocean.

Littoral rights are a landowner's claim to use water in large navigable lakes and oceans adjacent to his or her property. The ownership rights to land bordering these bodies of water goes up to the high-water mark. The government owns the land below that point. These rights concern the ability of the littoral property owner to use the shore and the adjoining water.

Littoral rights are appurtenant to the land, which means they go with the land when you sell it.

The Least You Need to Know

- Real property is comprised of the land, improvements, and the rights to the property.
- You can convert real property to personal property via severance. Conversely, you can convert personal property to real property via annexation.
- Plants can be considered real or personal depending on the type of plant: fructus industriales (personal) or fructus naturales (real).
- Fee simple is the transfer of all five rights (possession, control, exclusion, disposition, and enjoyment) to the property in some form.
- The land can be further divided into three areas—surface, subsurface, and air rights—which can be sold or leased independently of each other.
- Riparian rights, dealing with rivers, and littoral rights, dealing with lakes or oceans, are two types of water rights.

Forms of Ownership

Buyers acquire ownership via several different methods. Although real estate professionals must be knowledgeable in all the different types, ultimately, it's the buyer who will choose the correct type for their circumstance. Each state may have specific laws that govern the type of ownership, but in general, they are taken by the owner in one of three ways: as a single owner, as a form of co-ownership, or in a trust.

Every real estate transaction involves a buyer and a seller; however, the government often plays an unseen role in the transaction, too. In this chapter, we will talk about the ways a new owner can take title and how the government has some control in the selling, financing, and ownership rights of the property. Government intervention, control, and withholding of certain activities on a property has spawned many lawsuits over the years. We will take a look at the rights of property owners that are not conferred to the new owner for the sake of public safety and welfare.

In This Chapter

* The role of government in real estate
* A look at how fee simple absolute is not absolute
* Different methods of taking ownership

Governmental Powers in Real Estate

I previously discussed acquiring real estate in fee simple absolute, whereby the owner has the absolute ownership and fullest extent of bundle of rights. Unfortunately, that's not completely correct.

Some powers are reserved for the government and are not transferred to any owner, including police power, eminent domain, taxation, and escheat. The purpose of these governmental powers is "to enact measures to preserve and protect the safety, health, welfare, and morals of the community."

Police Power

Police power is the right of states to make laws governing safety, health, welfare, and morals derived from the Tenth Amendment to the U.S. Constitution, which states, "The powers not delegated to the United States by the Constitution, nor prohibited by it to the states, are reserved to the States respectively, or to the people." State legislatures exercise this power by enacting statutes, and they delegate much of their police power to counties, cities, towns, villages, and large boroughs within the state through enabling acts.

Police power does not specifically refer to the right of state or local municipalities to create police forces, although that is one right encompassed within the police power. Police power is used as the basis for enacting a variety of laws designed to safeguard the public. Areas such as zoning and building codes fall within the police power, as do gambling rules and regulations, antidiscrimination laws, crime statutes, licensing of professionals, schooling, sanitation, etc.

If a law is enacted under police power and does not promote the health, safety, or welfare of the public or community, it may be deemed to be an unconstitutional deprivation under the takings clause of the Fifth Amendment, which states "No person shall be deprived of life, liberty, or property, without due process of law; nor shall private property be taken for public use, without just compensation." The most common challenge to a statute enacted pursuant to police power is that it constitutes a taking.

Under the takings clause within the Fifth Amendment, a landowner whose property is taken for the betterment of the public must receive just compensation. Typically, the compensation can be negotiated between the landowner and the public agency to arrive at a fair market value acceptable to both parties. In some cases, however, the landowner is not willing to negotiate in good faith with the public agency and essentially forces the state to take the property through *condemnation*.

Another possible method would be for the landowner to freely dedicate the property in the best interest of the public.

Eminent Domain

Eminent domain is the power to take private property for public use by a state, municipality, or private person or corporation authorized to exercise functions of public character, following the payment of just compensation to the owner of that property. Federal, state, and local governments may take private property through their power of eminent domain or may regulate it by exercising their police power. Either way, the government must provide fair compensation to the landowner.

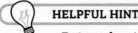

HELPFUL HINT

Eminent domain is the right of the government to take private property. **Condemnation** is the process used to exercise eminent domain.

All property rights are subject to eminent domain proceedings, including land, air, and water rights. Throughout these proceedings, the property owner has the right of due process.

In 2005, the U.S. Supreme Court heard the case of *Kelo* v. *City of New London,* in which private property was taken via condemnation and subsequently given to a private land developer. The City of New London decided to use the right of eminent domain as a means for economic development and incorporated a new meaning of "public use" by declaring that taxes paid by a private developer on property would be greater than taxes paid by private users and, therefore, would be "for the betterment of the public." Suzette Kelo and her colleagues resisted the city and tried to defend their actions under the broad terms of "public use" to be the more commonly understood definition of roads, bridges, school, parks, etc., and not for commercial ventures. The Supreme Court ruling, a 5 to 4 decision, decided that the states can establish the rules that must be followed when exercising eminent domain proceedings. This ruling significantly changed the meaning of "public use."

Inverse condemnation is a situation in which a landowner, who owns property adjacent to land that's been taken by a public agency, suffers a devaluation of his property yet receives no immediate compensation. For example, when an airport builds a new runway, it may use eminent domain to take certain properties for the construction of that runway. The affected landowners will receive some compensation for the lost land; however, the adjacent property owners, whose property value has been diminished due to its location now immediately next to a runway, receive no compensation. These property owners may bring a lawsuit of inverse condemnation action to be compensated for their loss. The hard part is determining the value of loss that's occurred and is often negotiated between the landowner and the public agency.

Taxation

Taxation is a charge on real property owners to cover the funds needed to operate the government facilities, services, and special projects.

The taxes on real property include reoccurring annual taxes based on the assessed value of the property, special taxes and fees levied for special projects to improve the real property of the owners, and profits realized from the sale of real property.

Escheat

Escheat is a legal process by which the state or local government takes property from a deceased person who dies with no legal heirs or a will directing the property to be transferred to a third party. The purpose of this law is so that no property remains ownerless or left in disrepair.

Escheat can benefit the county where the property is located or the state.

 **HELPFUL HINT**

Easily remember the governmental powers using the anagram *PETE:* **p**olice power, **e**minent domain, **t**axation, and **e**scheat.

Taking Ownership in Real Estate

Ownership of real property may appear to be transparent to onlookers, but the method of acquisition is important to the ultimate disposition of the property in most cases.

There are three common methods to take ownership: severalty (one owner), co-ownership, and trusts.

Severalty

Severalty is a common form of ownership and occurs when only one person acquires the rights to a parcel of real property. The name is derived from the concept that a sole owner is severed, or cut off, from all other owners.

In severalty, the owner has all the rights and privileges of the property and can sell, give away, lease, or otherwise transfer the property at his sole discretion.

Co-Ownership

Co-ownership is a form of ownership enjoyed by two or more owners at the same time. Most states commonly recognize several forms of co-ownership, such as tenancy in common (TIC) and joint tenancy.

TIC is a form of co-ownership that may allow for multiple owners to have a disproportional, or fractional, interest in the property, such as when one owner holds 90 percent interest while the other owns the remaining 10 percent interest. This disproportional interest is further considered an undividable interest. An undividable interest does not allow for segregation of the property but rather constitutes owning a portion of the entire property. For example, a 90 percent owner of the TIC does not own 9 of the 10 chairs but rather 90 percent of every chair and, therefore, the property is indivisible. It's the ownership, not the property, that's divided.

Each of these ownership interests can be owned by a single person, a legal entity, or a husband and wife. Due to the nature of the fractional ownership interest in the TIC, each owner may sell, trade, give away, or will his or her portion to whomever they choose without the consent of any other TIC owners. In common practice, most TIC owners have an operating agreement in which they'll offer another owner the first chance to buy the property if they choose to sell.

The deed and subsequent title insurance policy may reveal the fractional interest held by each TIC owner. If the deed does not declare the proportional interest of the TIC, it's assumed to be equal ownership interests for all parties. So if four people own the TIC, they each own 25 percent interest in the property. No one owner can transfer the entire property without the agreement of every owner. If a deed is recorded with no declaration of type of ownership, it automatically defaults to a TIC with equal ownership interests.

The only enjoyment, or unity, shared by the owners of the TIC is the unity of possession—that is, they both can possess the property equally. Furthermore, due to the fact that interest shares in a TIC can be bought, sold, and exchanged, each owner can acquire their interest at a different time.

A TIC is usually a common form of ownership in expensive high-rise buildings where one person may not be able to afford the entire price and invites friends, family, or colleagues to contribute to the purchase price. TICs also are very common in multifamily property ownership investments.

> **REALTOR WARNING**
>
> The formation of TIC is a very difficult process and should not be undertaken without the aid of an attorney to guide you through the process.

Joint tenancy is another form of co-ownership used by most states. Again, the tenant may be a single person or a legal entity. A joint tenancy can be created only by an intentional act of conveying the title through a deed or will. The instrument must state the intention of creating a joint tenancy specifically and clearly identify the recipients of the joint tenancy. Each owner of the joint tenancy shares the unity of possession in the property.

The major difference between the TIC and joint tenancy is that when an owner in a joint tenancy dies, his or her portion transfers equally to the surviving members without any court action needed. This is known as the right of survivorship and is shared by all the owners of the joint tenants. Due to this right, a joint tenancy, even during his own lifetime, cannot sell, give away, will, or trade his interest in the property. Essentially, the ownership is now divided by one fewer owner. This process of survivorship continues until the last-named owner is the only one living. In that case, he now owns the property in severalty and can sell, give away, or lease the property at his discretion. He also can will the property to his heirs or successors upon his death.

Another required right shared by the owners of joint tenancies is the unity of interest, or equal ownership interests. They all must own equal interest amounts. For example, four owners would each own 25 percent interest, five owners would each own 20 percent, etc. These interests are still considered indivisible by nature, much like the TIC.

In the third unity, the unity of time, all owners have received the interest at the same time.

The fourth required unity, called the unity of title, requires that all owners be named on one title instrument stipulating they are owners of joint tenancy. Some states allow for title to be taken by joint owners, which implies the right of survivorship; however, using the express term *joint tenant with right of survivorship* leaves no room for confusion by any party.

> **HELPFUL HINT**
>
> Remember the four unities required by joint tenants by the anagram *PITT*: **p**ossession, **i**nterest, **t**ime, and **t**itle.

In some cases, co-ownership must be dissolved due to irreconcilable differences between the parties. *Partition* is a legal method to separate parties of a co-ownership when the parties do not, or cannot, voluntarily agree.

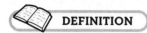 **DEFINITION**

> **Partition** is a court action that can be brought to divide the property into individual shares among the owners, allowing each owner to move forward with his or her share independently.

In extreme cases, a court can order the entire property to be sold if the property cannot be divided without harming its overall value. The proceeds would then be divided among the owners per their pro rata share.

In the case of joint tenants, an action to partition also can be used to separate, or carve out, one owner from the others. In this case, the owner then would be free to sell his share at his discretion. He also could will his share upon his death to his heirs or successors. However, the remaining owners would continue to operate as joint tenants with right of survivorship as originally determined. As a group, they would be a TIC with the owner who brought about the act of partition.

For example, four brothers, Aaron, Bob, Charlie, and David, were willed farmland from their grandfather. In his will, their grandfather intentionally stipulated the brothers were to be joint tenants with right of survivorship. According to the requirements of joint tenancy, they each own 25 percent.

One brother, David, brings an action to partition for his share, and the judge grants the partition. His share is still 25 percent based on the fact there were four brothers. However, David can now sell his interest to a fifth person, Edward. Aaron, Bob, and Charlie, who now own only 75 percent of the property, are joint tenants but together are a tenant in common with Edward.

When Aaron dies, his portion is divided between Bob and Charlie, giving each of them 37½ percent interest, while Edward still has only the original 25 percent interest.

When Bob dies, his portion goes to Charlie, giving him an ownership interest of the full 75 percent, while Edward still has 25 percent interest. Therefore, Bob, at 75 percent ownership, and Edward, at 25 percent ownership, having gotten the property at different times and now having different title work, would be the definition of TIC. So although the original three still maintained joint tenancy, together they were TIC with the new owner, Edward.

Tenancy by the entirety is a special form of joint tenancy reserved for married couples. Most states recognize this form of ownership and use the term *entirety* because married couples are one legal entity under common law. Each spouse owns an equal, undivided interest in the property. Under this special type of joint tenancy, one spouse inherits the other spouse's interest in the property upon their death without any court process required. Furthermore, with the right of survivorship requirement under joint tenancy, neither party may transfer ownership without the consent of the other. During their lives, they both must consent to a sale and signing of a deed to convey the property.

This issue can become interesting when discussing same-sex marriages. If the partners are legally married, they benefit from this special form of joint tenancy when one dies. However, if they weren't married, they could be subject to the decedent's heirs making a claim to the property. If no heirs were involved, they still could be subject to inheritance tax if they were not legally married.

Community property laws are governed by each individual state, and some states have no such laws concerning community property. Currently nine states—Arizona, California, Idaho, Louisiana, Nevada, New Mexico, Texas, Washington, and Wisconsin—plus Puerto Rico have community property laws that determine how debt and property are divided during a divorce. These states typically divide the property equally between the husband and wife. Other states follow equitable distribution, meaning a judge decides what is equitable or fair. Alaska is unique in that it allows divorcing couples to choose.

Typically, all property acquired during marriage by either spouse is presumed to be community property, or marital property, belonging to both spouses. If a spouse who asserts that property should be considered separate property, he or she will bear the burden of proof for claiming sole ownership. Some states recognize the concept of community property, in which all marital property is considered equally owned, but most states allow more flexibility in property division should the couple get a divorce.

On the other hand, separate property is property one spouse owns before the marriage and is not subject to division in a divorce. If a spouse receives property via inheritance or a gift during the marriage, it's normally considered separate property and not subject to being divided if the couple gets divorced.

Trust

A trust is the third form of ownership. A trust is a fiduciary arrangement created by a trustor that allows a third party, or trustee, to hold assets on behalf of a beneficiary. Trusts can be arranged in many ways and can specify exactly how and when the assets pass to those beneficiaries.

For example, a landlord may place a rental property into a trust, thus making him the trustor, and then hire a real estate attorney to oversee the property, who would be the trustee. The rental income generated by that property would be given to the children of the landlord trustor, making them the beneficiaries of the trust. The trustee would have fiduciary responsibilities toward the beneficiaries named within the trust. Although the trustee has limited power over the activities and actions to be taken with the property, he or she ultimately is guided by the trust document itself.

A trust can be created during the life of the trustor, or it can be created by his will after his death. If a person, the trustor, uses his will as a vehicle to create a trust after his death, it's a testamentary trust. If the trust is created during the life of the trustor, it's a living trust, not to be confused with a living will. (A living will, also called a directive to physicians or an advance directive, is a document that lets people state their wishes for end-of-life medical care in case they become unable to communicate their decisions. It has no power after death.) A living trust is often used as an estate planning tool to create and protect the wealth of the owners. A living trust's greatest feature is its ability to decrease the time and costs of *probate*.

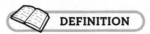 **DEFINITION**

Probate is the legal process whereby a will is proved factual, or validated, in a court and accepted as a valid public document that's the true last testament of the deceased.

In a living trust, a trustor transfers ownership of the property into a trust and often declares himself as the trustee. This way, the control of the asset is never lost or turned over to another person. The trustor also can name himself as the primary beneficiary and maintain the enjoyment of the property. Upon the death of the trustor, who also is the trustee, the property, under the terms of the trust, transfers to a named secondary beneficiary. In this manner, the transfer is seen as a simple transfer of real property from the trust to the beneficiary and not as an inheritance, as it would be from parent to child if the property transferred in that manner.

A land trust, sometimes called an Illinois land trust because Illinois was the first state to recognize this method as a form of ownership and was established by court precedent in *Kerr* v. *Kotz* in 1920, is specifically used to hold real property. One of the greatest benefits of a land trust is that there usually are no public records of the beneficial party holding the interest. The beneficial interest in a trust can be used as collateral for a loan without a mortgage being recorded. And a beneficiary's interest is inheritable and can be transferred upon the death of the beneficiary to another party.

A living trust usually is defined for a given term and must be renewed by the beneficiary or else the trust could expire. Upon expiration of the beneficial interest, the trustee must sell the real property; pay off the underlying note, if any; and give the proceeds to the beneficiary.

All states recognize other legal entities that can hold real property. For instance, a corporation, a limited liability company (LLC), or a partnership may hold title to a property in addition to those already covered. While each one of these entities may be controlled, governed, or operated by multiple people, they would still take the title in severalty as one owner.

A partnership is when two or more people come together to work as co-owners for profit. The general partner controls the day-to-day operation but is fully liable for the partnership's losses, debts, and obligations. A limited partner does not participate in the daily activities of the partnership and is limited in their exposure to losses only up to the amount they are invested. The limited partnership concept is a great method for investors to invest small amounts of money yet remain fairly protected in their losses.

A corporation, run by a board of directors under the direction of a company president and controlled by shareholders, takes property in severalty. In the opinion of U.S. law, the company is an artificial person and owns property as one person—severalty.

An LLC combines the best of both worlds: the corporation and the partnership. An LLC is taxed like a partnership, whereby the income flows directly to the partners, is taxed at their own individual tax rate, and is not subject to double taxation at the corporate level. However, the LLC has the protection of a corporation without the complicated rules and regulations that govern that entity.

The Least You Need to Know

* The governmental powers, police power, eminent domain, taxation, and escheat take precedence over fee simple absolute. These are in place to protect the health, safety, and welfare of the public.

* Eminent domain is the right of the public to take private land for the betterment of the public and is often achieved through condemnation.

* Inverse condemnation occurs when a landowner suffers the harm but gets no compensation.

* Ownership forms include single owners, co-ownerships, and trusts.

* Joint tenants share the right of survivorship as well as four unities: possession, interest, time, and title, whereas tenants in common share only one unity: possession.

* Tenancy by the entirety is a special form of joint tenancy shared by married couples.

Encumbrances

The right of disposition is but one twig within the legal bundle of rights. (Remember those from Chapter 9?) This right allows a property owner to decide the method by which he or she transfers ownership of that property to another person. The owner can sell the property, lease the property, or give it away. Furthermore, upon the owner's death, the property ownership can pass to his or her heirs or successors through a will.

An encumbrance can restrict the owner's right of disposition for the property or lessen its value.

In This Chapter

- The importance of encumbrances
- How encumbrances affect property sales
- The different types of encumbrances
- Zoning ordinances and the laws that govern them

What Is an Encumbrance?

An encumbrance, as a general term, is a charge or legal claim against real estate. This limitation or liability represents the right or claim to a portion of the property or to the use of the property by someone other than the property owner.

In general, an encumbrance is used to allow one person to use the property of another to gain access to their property. Cities and states use encumbrances to allow access to public utilities for repair and maintenance; while private encumbrances may be used to share property by two adjoining property owners—such as a fence or driveway. Commercial easements may be placed to allow consumers to cross parking lots to gain access to other retail establishments within the same area.

Types of Encumbrances

In general, an encumbrance can take the form of a money or nonmoney encumbrance. A money encumbrance, called a lien, can be placed on a property in the form of a claim, which is collateral held for a debt, such as a tax lien, mechanic's lien, or mortgage. A nonmoney encumbrance relates to how a property can be utilized, controlled, or accessed by someone other than the property owner.

Other types of nonmoney encumbrances are considered private restrictions, such as deed, or builder, restrictions; covenants, conditions, and restrictions (CCRs); and homeowner associations (HOAs).

Liens

A lien is a future ownership interest in a property secured by a debt against a piece of real property used as collateral. A mortgage is the most common lien placed on real property.

A lien is typically a public record. It's generally filed in the county where the property is located with the county records office, sometimes called the recorder's office.

If this debt is unpaid, the holder of the lien can pursue a motion in court to have the property sold so the debt is paid off, called foreclosure.

Another common money encumbrance, or lien, would be a mechanic's lien. A mechanic's lien is a claim held against a property by a person who has completed work on it yet has not been paid. When this occurs, they file the mechanic's claim. If the property is sold to a new owner before the debt is paid, the lien transfers to the new owner.

Encumbrances

An encumbrance can limit the enjoyment of the property owner through a diminished use of the property, such as an easement, license, or an encroachment.

An easement is the right to use another person's land for a specific purpose, such as access to your property, including airspace easements as well as right-of-way easements. Easements are very common and can be bought, sold, leased, or given away.

There are many different types of easements based on the need, the creation of the easement, or the usage of the easement. There are voluntary easements, such as the easement appurtenan, the party wall easement, and the easement in gross. However, some easements may be created involuntarily, such as the easements by necessity and prescriptive easements.

The easement appurtenant is an easement that benefits one parcel of land, known as the *dominant tenement*, to the detriment of another parcel of land, known as the *servient tenement*. Easements appurtenant are attached to the land (sometimes they are said to "run with the land") and are transferred automatically when the servient or dominant tenement is sold to a new owner. An easement appurtenant would be considered for public use by all parties accessing either property.

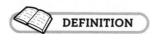 **DEFINITION**

> A **dominant tenement** is the party, or tenement, taking the use of the property. A **servient tenement** is the party, or tenement, giving up the use of the property.

For example, Aaron, the owner of a 10-acre tract of land, decides to section off 5 acres and build a house, which he sells to Bob. However, from the house, Bob has no access to any major road due to the surrounding woods. Aaron grants an appurtenant easement across his property for Bob to gain access to the road. In this scenario, Aaron is the servient tenement because he's giving up the use of his land to Bob, the dominant tenement. Furthermore, Aaron kept an easement to the lake on Bob's 5-acre parcel when he divided it. In this case, Bob is the servient tenement because he's giving up the use, or access, to the lake to Aaron, the dominant tenement.

As you can see, dominant tenement and servient tenement are determined based on which easement appurtenant is being considered. In the road easement, Aaron is the servient tenement, yet with respect to the lake easement, he's the dominant tenement, and vice versa.

A party wall easement is an exterior wall that straddles the lot line and is used by two buildings. Each party owns half of the wall on their respective property and shares an easement appurtenant with the other owner for the other half of the wall. Generally, all expenses to build and maintain the wall are shared by the owners.

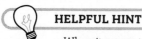 **HELPFUL HINT**

> When it comes to party wall easements, a fence built on the lot line would be considered the same as a party wall.

An easement in gross is the right of only one party to treat something as an easement, not the public. Utility, railroad, and right-of-way easements, such as sewers or pipelines, are examples of easements in gross. Easements in gross are not for public use but are only for the company that owns the easement. For the rest of the public, they are considered the private property of the owner. Commercial easements in gross are sellable, assignable, and inheritable whereas private easements in gross are not.

Most easements are voluntary and their creation is agreed upon by the owners of the property, but some are created without the voluntary agreement of the parties. An easement by necessity is created when a landowner sells a parcel of property that has no legal access for entry—it is landlocked, so to speak. This easement is granted by court order due to necessity rather than convenience. The right of possession is one of the property rights granted in a sale and, therefore, must be granted to the new owner. The right of ingress (to enter) and egress (to exit) are implied within the right of possession.

An easement by prescription, or a prescriptive easement, is where one party claims use of another's property per state statute. Most states require 10 to 21 years of usage before a claim can be made for an easement by prescription. Furthermore, the usage must be continuous, hostile (without the owner's permission), and nonexclusive (the owner isn't excluded from the use of the property). The use must be visible, open, and notorious, and the owner must have been able to learn about it.

The concept of tacking allows for a successive party owner to tack, or add to, the previous owner's time-frame of usage to meet the required state law timeframe. They must be *successors in interest,* such as heirs from an owner's will or a buyer and seller, creating a continuous and uninterrupted usage.

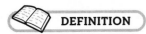 **DEFINITION**

Successors in interest is the right of a party to acquire a usage or control of real property directly from a successive property owner through a voluntary sale or inheritance.

For example, a property is located in a state that requires 10 years for a prescriptive easement. For the last 11 years, a neighbor has driven across a property owner's land to gain entrance to his own garage in the back of his lot. He has a prescriptive easement.

Or consider a property located in a state that requires 10 years for a prescriptive easement. For the last 7 years, a neighbor has driven across a property owner's land to gain entrance to his own garage in the back of his lot. During the sale of his property to a new owner, he states, "I've been doing it for years." The new owner continues for another 3 years. He can claim a prescriptive easement through tacking.

A license is a personal privilege granted to a property owner by an adjacent landowner to use his property. The difference between a license and an easement is that the license is not usually formally recorded but rather created orally between property owners. A license can be terminated at will by either party, upon the death of either party, or upon the sale of either property.

An encroachment refers to a physical piece of permanent property from a neighbor's house that illegally lies on an adjoining neighbor's property. For example, a neighbor is unclear about his property line and places a fence 1 foot into his neighbor's property. That's an encroachment. It will be noted in surveys and title insurance policies until it's removed.

The neighbor whose land the fence or other invading element lies on has the right to seek financial damages due to the loss of use or secure removal of the property. If the encroachment exceeds the state's required prescriptive timeframe, it may create a prescriptive easement.

Private restrictions are considered an encumbrance because they limit the right of control of a property. Deed restrictions are used to limit the control of all future property owners who acquire the property through a legal sale. As the name implies, deed restrictions are written into deeds and run with the land. Deed restrictions cannot violate any local, state, or federal law, and any attempt to do so would be considered illegal and unenforceable in a court of law.

Covenants, conditions, and restrictions (CCRs) are often created by the original builder to protect the value of a neighborhood subdivision by demanding compliance with certain requirements, such as the size, shape, or style of all the homes to be built. The CCRs are created and recorded in the public records where the property is located, along with the initial subdivision development plan. They are incorporated by reference into the deeds to the individual purchasers upon the initial sale of the property. Enforcement of the CCRs is assigned to the developer as long as he still maintains an interest in the development; it's then passed to the property owners with future sales.

Homeowner associations (HOAs) are another form of private restrictions that limit the right of control of property. An HOA is created by the actual homeowners and governed by an elected board. The HOA can determine any rules and regulations it thinks will benefit the homeowners that are not already incorporated by any deed restrictions or CCRs. Some HOAs turn over the control of the HOA to professional management companies to govern and enforce the rules and regulations.

Creating Easements

Easements are usually created by conveyance in a deed or some other written document such as a will or contract. Creation of an easement requires the same formalities as the transfer or creation of any other interests in land, such as a written instrument, a signature, and proper delivery of the document. An easement may be express, implied, or by prescription.

An express easement is created by a written agreement between landowners granting or reserving an easement. Express easements must be signed by both parties and are typically recorded with the deeds to each property.

An implied easement may be created only when two parcels of land were at one time treated as a single tract or owned by a common owner. Accordingly, easements appurtenant may arise by implication, but easements in gross may not. An easement is implied by existing use if the easement is necessary for the use and enjoyment of one parcel of land and the parties involved in dividing the tract intended that the use continue after the division. An easement is implied by necessity when one parcel of land is sold, depriving the other parcel access to a public road or utility.

A prescriptive easement, or easement by prescription, arises if an individual has used the property in a certain way for a certain number of years. In most states, a prescriptive easement will be created if the individual's use of the property meets the following requirements:

- The use is open and notorious—i.e., obvious and not secretive.

- The individual actually uses the property.

- The use is continuous for a statutory period, typically between 10 and 20 years.

- The use is adverse to the true owner—i.e., without the owner's permission.

Removing Easements

Most easements run with the land, or pass forward in effect to new owners of the involved properties. But there are reasons that would render an easement of no further use or ways easements can be terminated.

An easement can be removed when the purpose for the easement no longer exists. For example, suppose an easement was created more than 75 years ago, and the original creator of the easement is now deceased.

An easement also can be terminated when a merger of the properties is completed. For example, when two adjacent properties have an easement between the servient tenement and the adjoining dominant tenement and one owner acquires and merges both properties into one legal description, the easement would no longer need to exist.

If both parties agree and execute a release agreement, the easement can be removed. For example, if an easement exists and new owners of both properties find it's no longer of interest or use to the dominant property owner, the easement can be terminated by a release document from the dominant property owner to the servient owner.

The easement also can be abandoned. For example, if the holder of an easement no longer uses the property, this is considered an abandonment, which cancels the easement by showing that the easement holder no longer intends to use the rights granted by the easement. To terminate an easement by abandonment, the easement holder's actions must clearly demonstrate an obvious intent to abandon all future use of the easement

If the reason for the easement is destroyed or terminated, the easement is moot. For example, in the case of an easement created for a party wall that serves two properties, the destruction of the party wall terminates the easement.

Understanding Zoning

Zoning is a restriction on the way land within its jurisdiction can be used. Through community planning and development, zoning laws help local governmental agencies preserve property values and ensure communities are functional and safe places. Where zoning restrictions are in place, violators suffer major consequences for their noncompliance.

HELPFUL HINT

Without zoning, an adult book store could open next to an elementary school; a neighbor could turn his house into a toxic waste dump; or a retail store could open a new store on a residential street. These examples might sound like stretches now, but remember that before zoning was practiced, such situations could happen.

Planning entered the legal realm in the 1920s with two important federal acts prepared by the U.S. Department of Commerce: the Standard State Zoning Enabling Act of 1922 and the Standard City Planning Enabling Act of 1928. Even though the Planning Act was not enacted yet, the Zoning Enabling

Act contained language that a zoning ordinance be prepared "in accordance with a comprehensive plan." Many states have incorporated similar language in their own zoning acts.

The constitutionality of zoning ordinances was upheld in 1926 in the case of *Ohio* v. *Ambler Realty Co.* in which the zoning ordinance of Euclid, Ohio, was challenged in court by a local land owner on the basis that restricting use of property violated the Fourteenth Amendment. Although initially ruled unconstitutional by lower courts, ultimately the zoning ordinance was upheld by the U.S. Supreme Court.

Types of Zoning

Zoning codes have evolved over the years as urban planning theory has changed, legal constraints have fluctuated, and political priorities have shifted. Zoning may be divided into four broad categories: functional, form-based, intensity, and incentive.

Functional zoning, also called block zoning or Euclidian zoning, is the most prevalent form of zoning where land use zones are defined according to their function, such as agricultural, commercial, residential, or industrial. Each kind of zone is subject to specific rules and regulations concerning the type of activities that can be built in that area. Each defined zoning district does not allow for cross-function uses. For example, residential properties can be within residentially zoned areas only and not in any other zoning function type.

Form-based zoning defines zones according to their physical characteristics, mostly from an urban identity perspective such as the downtown area. This form of zoning is usually easier to relate to the general population because it uses well-known zonal definitions.

Intensity zoning, or density zoning, zones land use by the level of permitted intensity, such as the number of residential units per acres or allowed commercial surface. Such regulation enables a level of flexibility in urban development because it permits developers to select which types of development take place in an area as long as these developments abide by density constraints.

In entive zoning, often part of revitalization or development plans, developers are allowed to build residential, commercial, or industrial (manufacturing, warehousing) projects in specific areas through the provision of various incentives such as tax abatements or basic infrastructure like roads, utilities, public transport, services, etc. Further, developers can be granted lower restrictions, namely density limits, if amenities such as park areas, green space, or infrastructure are developed as well.

More types of zoning can be applied, or overlaid, to property to control the use, size, function, etc., including aesthetic zoning, which governs the overall look, style, and design of the property; bulk zoning, which restricts the density of units per given area; buffer zoning, which creates a neutral space between two different types of zoning classifications; and historic zoning, the main goal of which is preserving the historic character of a neighborhood.

Several methods enable the zoning ordinance and its administration to be more flexible, and the *zoning overlay* is one of them. Overlay districts are placed over the original zoning districts and apply additional provisions that are either more restrictive or expansive, or that may provide for different uses or design standards than the original district regulations.

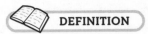 **DEFINITION**

A **zoning overlay** is an additional requirement designed to enhance, or curtail, above and beyond the current zoning classification.

Overlay districts also can be used for infrastructure planning or to manage safety, access, and mobility. They can be used to preserve scenery, wetlands, and conservation areas as well. Clustering, performance zoning, planned unit developments (PUDs), neighborhood design, and historic district preservation are types of zoning overlays that add site flexibility. Here, overlay zoning can benefit both the municipality and individuals seeking to develop the property.

Nonconforming: Conditional Use Permits and Variances

Zoning is purely a county, city, or municipal affair. Although such laws are somewhat universal, the classifications used to describe zoning are not uniform from place to place. It's not uncommon to find that zoning laws that apply to one city in the county are different from another city within the same county, or that one town permits a mix of residential and commercial uses but a neighboring community might not allow for such a mix. Zoning ordinances may permit or prohibit certain uses and may create whole districts devoted only to residence, commerce, or industry.

When a property's use does not conform to a zoning ordinance but the property existed before the adoption or amendment of the zoning ordinance, the structure is granted a nonconforming use status, sometimes called legal nonconforming use. Basically, the property is grandfathered and the property owner is allowed to maintain his current use, even though it's in direct conflict with the new zoning classification, unless it's abandoned or terminated. It's a property right that cannot be taken away without just compensation. However, the nonconforming use structure may not be expanded; its use may not be changed; and under many state laws, if it's destroyed by fire or other cause and not rebuilt within a specific timeframe, it will lose the nonconforming status.

Property owners can request deviations, alterations, or changes to zoning ordinances by filing for a zoning change with the board of appeals or zoning board. Conditional use permits and variances both require a public hearing.

The most important distinction between a conditional use permit and a variance is the type of deviation from the zoning ordinance.

A conditional use permit involves uses that generally are not consistent within a zoning district but are allowed in specific circumstances set forth in a zoning ordinance. A conditional use permit is designed to allow flexibility within the zoning laws. A zoning ordinance cannot account for every situation, and exceptions such as the conditional use permit gives the zoning authority discretion to allow uses otherwise prohibited in the specific district for the benefit of the neighborhood. A conditional use permit is commonly granted to add commercial, educational, or religious services to residential zones. Churches, schools, and small or home-based businesses in residential neighborhoods are all products of the conditional use permit that allows exceptions to the zoning law.

A variance is a request to deviate from current zoning requirements. If granted, it permits the owner to use his or her land in a way that's ordinarily not permitted by the zoning ordinance. It's not a change in the zoning law but a waiver from the requirements of the zoning ordinance.

A variance would likely be granted for unusual circumstances, such as an especially narrow lot or a stream on the property making it especially difficult to comply with the local zoning ordinance.

The Least You Need to Know

- An encumbrance is a limitation to the use, control, or disposition of real property and is considered monetary or nonmonetary in nature.
- A lien is a future interest in ownership, not actual ownership.
- Easements are the rights of one person to use another person's property.
- Private restrictions are comprised of deed restrictions; covenants, conditions, and restrictions; and homeowner associations.
- An easement can be created by law, by convenience, or by agreement and can be terminated, cancelled, or abandoned.
- Zoning is controlled by zoning ordinances granted by the state through the enabling acts.

Deeds and Titles

A title is an ethereal object. You can't touch it, see it, feel it, or hold it. You can see the title insurance policy or the deed, but not the title itself. It doesn't physically exist. However, the title is a very important concept in the real estate transaction.

In this chapter, we will cover the aspects of title: what it is, how it's created, its purpose, and how to transfer title to a new owner. The deed, a physical representation of the title, is a legal contract and as such must meet all the requirements of a valid contract. We will discuss the parts of a deed and how they are created. We will discuss the different types of deeds used and what guarantees, or warranties, the seller makes to the buyer. We will also discuss the mechanics of a closing and how the deed and title play an important role in the transfer of the real property between the parties.

In This Chapter

- Titles and how they work
- The requirements for a valid deed
- The different types of deeds used in real estate
- An exploration of closings

What Is a Title?

A title serves two purposes: it provides evidence of ownership of the property, and it provides evidence that you have the right to sell or transfer the property to another person.

A title also can be defined as the possession of the legal bundle of rights, in whole or in parts. The possession of the legal bundle of rights is not the same as possession of the property itself. A person may hold possession through a lease but not hold the full bundle of legal rights.

A title also can be held as actual ownership in the property, called legal title, or by holding an interest in the property, called equitable title, through such vehicles as a *land contract*.

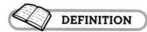

DEFINITION

A **land contract** is a form of ownership conveyance between a vendor seller and vendee buyer. With a land contract, land ownership is transferred based on the portion of equity earned through each payment from the vendee to the vendor, giving the vendee an interest in the property based on the equity earned, hence equitable title.

What Is a Deed?

A deed is a document used to transfer ownership from one party to another, such as in a sale, gift, or transference by will. All 50 states, under the statute of frauds, require the deed to be a written instrument used in the transfer of real property.

Using the deed as the vehicle, the person transferring the property, called the grantor, transfers ownership to the person receiving the property, called the grantee. The grantor executes, or signs, the deed; the grantee does not.

HELPFUL HINT

Two distinct legal suffixes are used throughout the real estate industry, -or and -ee. -or is used to determine, explain, or identify the person doing the action in question: *grantor, lessor, mortgagor, vendor,* etc. -ee is used to identify the person receiving the action: *grantee, lessee, mortgagee, vendee,* etc.

Contractual Requirements for Valid Deeds

A deed is a legal contract, and as such, it must fulfill all the requirements of a legal contract. State laws may vary, but for a deed to be valid, it must contain the following necessary elements:

- Legal competency for both the grantor and grantee

- A statement of consideration—typically a nominal value placed within the deed itself

- A granting clause to identify the conveyance of the property

- The habendum clause to identify the degree of ownership the grantee receives

- An accurate legal description of the property being transferred

- Any deed restrictions or other exceptions placed on the property

- An acknowledgement of the grantor's signature

The grantor must be of legal age to hold or transfer property; in most states, the age of consent is 18 years old. A deed executed by a minor would generally be considered voidable in a court of law. However, after the minor reaches age 18, he or she can choose to accept the deed as *valid* conveyance or have the conveyance recognized as nonlegal and, therefore, nonbinding.

Furthermore, the grantor must be legally competent, or of sufficient mental capacity to understand the ramification of the sale, often called sound mind. If a person is mentally impaired, the deed is not automatically *void*, but rather *voidable* on its face. However, if a person is determined by a court of law to be incompetent, the deed would be automatically void. A person who has been judged legally incompetent cannot transfer property without the permission of the court.

 **DEFINITION**

> A **valid** contract is one in which all elements are intact and enforceable in a court of law. A **void** contract is of no legal force because one or more elements are missing from the contract. A **voidable** contract appears to be valid on the surface, but after inspection, one element is defective. An **affidavit of one and the same** is a legal contract that declares that a person is the same person using a different name, such as after a marriage, divorce, or legal name change.

The grantor's legal name must be mentioned and maintained throughout the deed in its entirety. In the case of a name change, either through marriage, divorce, or a legal action, the deed may state both the former and current names, such as "Susan Smith, formerly Susan Jones." Some states allow for supporting documents, such as marriage certificates or legal divorce decrees, to help identify the person. An acceptable but less-preferred method is for a person to sign an *affidavit of one and the same.*

The grantee's name must be specified for a deed to be valid. It must identify the grantee in such a way as to not be questionable, but rather specifically stated. For example, a deed that names "my best friend Kenneth" would be unacceptable; however, one that identifies "Kenneth John Turner" would be acceptable.

If a deed contains more than one grantee, the granting clause specifies how they are taking title to the property, be it as joint tenants or tenants in common.

A valid deed also must include a consideration clause stating the grantor is receiving something of value from the grantee for the transfer of the ownership. Most states require a nominal fee stated within the deed itself, such as "for $10 and other good and valuable consideration." If the property is being transferred as a gift between family members, "love and affection" may be sufficient as consideration.

The granting clause states the grantor's specific intention to convey the property to the grantee. Depending on the intention and degree to which he intends to convey the property, the deed uses specific language to identify his intention, such as the following:

"I, [grantor's name], convey and warrant ..."

"I, [grantor's name], remise, release, and alienate ..."

"I, [grantor's name], grant, bargain, and sale ..."

"I, [grantor's name], remise, release, and quitclaim ..."

A conveyance of a deed typically transfers all the rights of the grantor into fee simple unless specified within the deed itself. A deed granting fee simple usually contains the words "to Kenneth John Turner and his heirs or successors"; if the deed conveys less than fee simple, such as a life estate, the wording of the granting clause identifies the intention, like "to Kenneth John Turner for his natural life."

The habendum clause gives rise to the degree of enjoyment conveyed between the grantor and grantee. "To have to hold" is the common understanding of the habendum clause issued by most grantors. However, the provisions of this clause must run parallel with the granting clause. That is, if the granting clause is conveying less than fee simple, the habendum clause must specify the grantee rights conveyed.

A valid deed must include an accurate legal description of the property being conveyed as well. Most real estate transactions require the full legal description rather than the street address to avoid any confusion during the transfer. In the case of a resale, the county surveyor's office can help determine the correct legal address. When selling large parcels of farmland or new construction, a property surveyor might be required to determine the accurate legal address.

Should a deed have any exceptions, reservations, or restrictions placed on the property, they must be noted within the deed. In the case of a new build, a builder may have placed some private restrictions in the form of covenants, conditions, and restrictions (CCRs). A private resale of property may allow for the grantor to place other restrictions on the property, such as a fee simple determinable. Along with any other private restrictions, if any, he received when he bought the property, these also must be included in the new deed to the grantee. Some deed restrictions may have expiration terms that need to be renewed if the intention is to keep them in place at the time of the conveyance.

The signature of the grantor or grantors must be in place to create a bona fide deed. In most states, both spouses must sign the deed to convey clear title and release their interest in the property during a sale or transfer of the property. In a case of a corporate deed transfer, a corporate seal may be required to verify the corporation's agreement of the conveyance.

Some states allow a power of attorney to sign for a grantor. A power of attorney is a person who has been granted legal authority to sign documents, including a deed, for another person. The document granting the power of attorney to the individual may be recorded in the public documents already, or it may be recorded by incorporation into the closing documents collected by the closing company, which then will be subsequently recorded.

An *acknowledgment* of the deed by a notary public is required at the time of conveyance. The acknowledgment by a notary public is a declaration by a state-authorized person, typically a closing agent, that the person signing the document did so voluntarily. The closing agent, acting as a notary public, also verifies that the person signing the deed is, in fact, the person stated on the deed by a verification of identification.

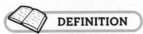

DEFINITION

An **acknowledgment** by a notary public is not a legal validation of the document and does not suppose any legal information at all. Rather, an acknowledgment is merely a verification that the people signing the document are, in fact, who they say they are.

The deed is considered to have passed upon delivery by the grantor and accepted by the grantee. The deed may be delivered by the grantor personally or by a third party acting on their behalf, such as a title company during an insured closing. The effective date of conveyance is considered the date the deed was accepted by the grantee. A deed also may be considered accepted on the date of entering it into the public record with the county recorder.

Types of Deeds

The clear majority of real estate transactions use one of four major types of deeds to convey title, although less common types are also sometimes used. The difference in types of deeds is primarily the covenants and warranties conveyed by the grantor to the grantee. These vary from significant warranties to no warranties at all conveyed with the property. The type of deed used to convey the property can vary, but it must run parallel with the granting clause's intention of conveyance.

Deeds can be very short in length—under a page—or they can be several pages long with many restrictions, covenants, and special granting clauses. In a residential transaction, the deed is normally prepared by an attorney.

Common deeds used in real estate include general warranty deeds, special warranty deeds, bargain and sale deeds, quitclaim deeds, deeds of trust, trustee's deeds, reconveyance deeds, and deeds executed pursuant to a court order.

The general warranty deed, sometimes called just warranty deed, is by far the most common deed used to convey property from the grantor to the grantee. The general warranty deed affords the most protection to the buyer due to the covenants, promises, and warrantees given by the seller. The general warranty deed is the assumed method of conveyance when the granting clause states, "I, [grantor's name], convey and warrant …." Contained within the general warranty deed are specific warranties that may vary by state, but basically state the following:

Covenant of seisin   The grantor warrants that they own the property and have the legal right to convey it.

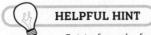

HELPFUL HINT

Seisin, from the feudal system, means "possession."

Covenant against encumbrances   The grantor warrants that the property is free of any liens or encumbrances unless they're specifically stated in the deed.

Covenant of quiet enjoyment   The grantee is guaranteed that the title will be good against third parties attempting to establish title to the property.

Covenant of further assurance   The grantor promises to make the title good and will deliver any document or instrument necessary.

Covenant of warranty forever   The grantor promises these warranties to never expire and compensates the grantee for any losses sustained in the future.

The covenants or warranties in a general warranty deed do not cover just the period of ownership of this grantor; they extend back to the origin of the property. Each grantor of a general warranty deed will defend the title against any defects created by the grantor as well as those previously holding title to the property.

In a special warranty deed, the seller's guarantee does not cover the property's entire history. Generally, the seller only guarantees against problems or claims created during the seller's ownership of the property. A special warranty deed often is used with property seized in a foreclosure situation, where the history prior to the current owner is unsure or questionable. The special warranty deed is the assumed method of conveyance when the granting clause states, "I, [grantor's name], remise, release, and alienate …."

The general warranty deed conveys five covenants, or warranties, but the special warrant deed only conveys two such covenants:

- The grantor has received the title.

- During the ownership of the grantor, they did not allow the property to become encumbered, except as otherwise noted specifically within the deed.

The grantor of the special warranty deed, in effect, only warrants the title against their own actions or omissions. They warrant nothing prior to their taking title. This makes the special warranty deed very useful in cases where a fiduciary, such as a trustee or executor of a will, has no intimate knowledge of the prior owners' actions and lacks the authority to warrant against any such actions.

A bargain and sale deed, used in residential real estate or sales of court-seized properties, conveys ownership of a property from the seller to the buyer. It generally does not guarantee, but rather implies, to the buyer that the seller owns the property free and clear. A bargain and sale deed resembles a quitclaim deed, but the property is sold rather than relinquished. The bargain and sale deed is the assumed method of conveyance when the granting clause states, "I, [grantor's name], grant, bargain, and sale …."

It's permissible to add covenants or warranties to a bargain and sale deed. A covenant against encumbrances could be incorporated within the bargain and sale deed as well, creating a bargain and sale with covenants against encumbrances. This addition would make the deed appear very much like a special warranty deed.

A quitclaim deed is used to transfer an interest, whatever that interest may be, in real property from one individual to another. This type of deed distinguishes itself from all other deeds in that it does not give any covenants, warranties, guarantees, or assurances with the transfer of ownership to the new owner. A quitclaim deed is the assumed method of conveyance when the granting clause states, "I, [grantor's name], remise, release, and quitclaim …."

HELPFUL HINT

Please note the word *quit* rather than *quick* in quitclaim deed. This is a reference to the analogy of "I quit" my rights to the property. The quitclaim deed can be executed and recorded quickly, but *quick* is not the correct choice in the named title of the deed.

A quitclaim deed can convey good title as well as the general warranty deed, apart from any of the covenants that come with the general warranty deed, as long as the grantor holds good title at the time of the issuance of the quitclaim deed.

Often there are instances when a quick transfer of property is needed without the assurances other deeds like the warranty or special warranty deeds give to the new owner. When property is transferred to an ex-spouse as part of a divorce settlement, for instance, a quitclaim deed is used. It also can be useful when adding a new spouse to the title after marriage. Parents often use it to deed a house to their children, and estate planners use it to transfer property into a trust or to an heir.

During regular real estate transactions, quitclaim deeds are quick fixes to cure a *cloud on the title*.

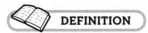

DEFINITION

A **cloud on the title** refers to any mistakes, misspellings, or irregularities in the chain of title that would give a reasonable person pause before accepting title. A cloud on the title reduces the value of a property because any prospective buyer knows they are buying the risk the grantor may not be able to convey good title.

A deed of trust, sometimes called a deed *in* trust, is used to transfer property from the trustor into a trust controlled by a trustee for the benefit of the beneficiary.

A reconveyance deed is used by a trustee to return the property to the original trustor. In states that use the deed of trust theory to take ownership of property, a reconveyance deed is used to transfer the property to the trustor when the last payment is made to satisfy the outstanding loan on the property.

A trustee's deed is a deed executed by the trustee to convey the property to any person other than the trustor. The trustee's deed must include a statement that his actions are authorized under the guidance of the trust.

A deed executed pursuant to a court order is a deed that's conveyed by order of a court and established by state statute. The most common is a family court, in the case of a divorce decree. It also may be used by executors or administrators of a will.

One unique feature of a deed executed pursuant to a court order is that within the consideration clause of the deed, the full consideration price of the property is listed. Instead of "… for $10 and other good and valuable consideration," it states the actual sales price, such as "… for $105,000 and other good and valuable consideration."

Transfer Tax and Calculations

In some states, the sale of nonexempt real property may be subject to a transfer tax, or a grantor's tax. Real estate transfer tax is an excise tax on transactions involving the sale of real property where title to the property is transferred from the seller to the buyer.

A transfer tax is typically paid by the seller; however, it can be paid for by the buyer or even split between the two parties based on local customs or agreed upon contractually. Some states require that the tax be paid in advance and a stamp be placed on the deed to make it eligible to be recorded; other states collect the tax at the time of recording at the recorder's office.

 HELPFUL HINT

Only a few states use the transfer tax on the sale of real property. Check with your state real estate commission to verify if your state uses the tax, and the applicable rate.

States that require transfer tax stamps also mandate a transfer declaration form, or affidavit of real property value, which must be signed by both the seller and buyer and their agents to testify to the actual sales price.

The actual tax rate imposed varies and may be imposed at the state, county, or local level. For example, the transfer tax on a sale of real property is $1 for every $1,000, or any fractional part thereof. If the property sold for $150,500, the transfer tax would be $151:

$$\$150,500 \div \$1,000 = \$150.5$$

However, the "or any fractional part thereof" phrase in the example means there are 151 units within the sale price because there are 0.5 parts it would treat as a single unit. So the transfer tax is $1/unit, or $151 tax.

Some properties may be exempt from transfer tax stamps, such as deeds between certain family members, deeds by government entities, deeds of foreclosure and deeds in lieu of foreclosure, deeds of partition, deeds pursuant to mergers or consolidations of corporations, deeds by a subsidiary corporation or parent corporation, deeds executed by public officials, deeds into or out of trusts, and deeds to charitable conservation organizations or religious institutions.

Closing the Transaction

The culmination of the activities involved in a real estate transaction is the closing, sometimes called the settlement or exchange. The buyer completes the financing arrangements for the mortgage and note, while the seller transfers over title of the property to the buyer. Per the sales contract, both sides of the transaction have promises, or terms, to uphold to the other party for the closing to be a success.

Typically, the closing is held at a title company agreed upon by the buyer and seller within the sales contract. The parties in attendance to the closing are the buyer or buyers, the seller or sellers, agents for both parties, the closing agent, and sometimes also a lender. In some states, an attorney may accompany the buyer or seller to a closing.

Prior to the closing, the buyer and his agent perform a final walk-through of the property to ensure the property he made an offer on, and accepted, is still in the same condition. Typically, he checks that all agreed-upon personal property was left or taken, based on the negotiated sales contract; all the repairs have been made; and the property has been well maintained since the inception of the sales contract.

During the closing, the buyer may seek several documents to ensure the seller can deliver marketable title, the title is free and clear of any liens, and the title can be transferred with no issues. These might include the deed; the title insurance policy; the mortgage and loan documents, if any; a copy of the appraisal; any documents or receipts clearing the liens; any lease agreements, if it's a rental property; or a survey of the property.

The seller's primary role in a closing is to maintain contact with his agent for closing instructions. The title company performs a title search on the property to determine if any outstanding liens and encumbrances exist. It's the job of the seller to remove the liens or provide proof if the lien has been paid in full. The seller may be asked to sign an affidavit of title, or seller's affidavit to certify the seller has not encumbered the property, become involved in a lawsuit, or placed a lien on the property since the original title work was searched upon listing the property. Furthermore, the title company seeks a mortgage payoff statement, also called a mortgage reduction certificate, from the seller's mortgage company stating the exact payoff amount as of a certain date.

The closing agent or officer is a representative for the title company and guides the buyer and seller through the actual closing process. Most closing agents are also notary publics and can notarize documents for recording as the buyer and seller are signing them during the closing process.

The broker's role at closing is to aid his or her client should they need any last-minute help, advice, or insight at the closing table. Some states operate under the minimum level of services act that requires a broker to attend closing with their client, among other responsibilities.

In some cases, a lender may attend the closing as well to ensure their company's interest is well taken care of during the closing. Much like the buyer, the lender seeks the same documents to protect their asset being collateralized for the loan. The lender might request additional requirements, like home hazard insurance policy; home inspection; reserve or impound accounts for real estate taxes, insurance, and flood insurance; and PMI insurance policy, if any. The lender also might seek a *certificate of occupancy* if the property is a new construction.

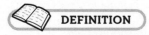 **DEFINITION**

A **certificate of occupancy** is evidence that the building or residence complies substantially with the plans and specifications that have been submitted to, and approved by, the local authority.

Face-to-Face Closings

The face-to-face closing is a scheduled event, with a specific date, time, and location agreed upon by both parties. It's usually held at the title company's office, an attorney's office, or a real estate brokerage office. New *mobile closings* are becoming more in-demand as people's schedules become more hectic.

DEFINITION

A **mobile closing** is one that takes place outside regularly accepted locations or time-frames by allowing a closing agent to travel and meet with the buyer and seller in a remote location. I have heard of closings happening in hospital rooms, backyard picnic tables, and even jail cells.

During a face-to-face closing, the closing agent works for both parties as a disinterested third party to ensure all documents are properly executed, funds are collected, and copies of all paperwork are served to both parties.

When the everyone is confident the paperwork is in order and properly signed, the exchange is made. The seller signs the deed and delivers it to the buyer. The buyer provides the monies required in the form of a loan and possibly earnest money, if any was deposited upon the acceptance of the offer. The title company then has all the documents properly recorded. Due to the *priority of liens,* proper care is taken to ensure the seller's lien is removed first via the payoff. The deed is then recorded, followed by the buyer's mortgage and loan documents. The deed must be recorded first, due to the fact the buyer cannot mortgage a property he doesn't own.

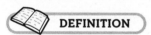

DEFINITION

A **priority of liens** is a theory that states that liens gain priority, or preference, based on the order they are recorded. The first lien recorded gets primary position, hence the name primary lien.

Escrow Closings

An escrow closing, sometimes called a non-face-to-face closing, can be used whenever the buyer and seller cannot physically be together in the same location, either due to geographical or time-related constraints. Should this occur, an agreed-upon escrow agent, or an escrow holder, can be used to close the property in escrow. Most often, the title company serves as the agent for the escrow closing; however, attorneys, certified public accountants, trust companies, or special companies established just to be escrow agents could be used as well.

In an escrow closing, one party attends the closing and executes their portion of the required documentation. If the reason for the escrow is due to a time issue and both parties can be present at one location but not at the same time, the escrow process is a bit easier and quicker to accomplish. If the seller attends first, he signs the deed. Remember, the property only passes hands when the deed is delivered and accepted by the buyer. So if the seller leaves the signed deed in escrow with the agent, the deed has not passed yet. The seller's agent also leaves the earnest money, if any, collected from the buyer with the escrow agent.

The escrow agent collects all the paperwork, seals it in a file, and places all the documents in a safe, usually within the office.

The buyer attends his portion of the escrow closing, and the escrow agent guides him through his portion of the paperwork. Once complete, the escrow agent collects the buyer's paperwork and adds it to the seller's paperwork for recording. Copies are made and handed to the buyer. At this time, the deed is delivered and accepted by the buyer from the escrow agent. The escrow agent then calls the first broker and apprises him of the completed transaction. Sometime later, he returns with his seller client to get their paperwork and closing proceeds from the sale of the property.

If the escrow closing is due to geographical reasons, such as a bank-owned property closing, the escrow agent overnights the seller's portion of the documents to the bank. It then executes the paperwork under the supervision of its notary to verify the authenticity of signatures. It then returns the executed documents to the escrow company for final signatures by the buyer.

In today's ever-more-technological world, expect to see eclosings soon, which will eliminate the need for escrow closings. Both parties will be able to join a website and close the property via electronic signature and wire transfers.

The Least You Need to Know

- A title serves as evidence of ownership and as evidence that you have the right to sell.
- A deed is the physical document used to transfer title from one person to another.
- A deed is a legal contract and must fulfill all contract requirements.
- Most real estate transactions can be completed with one of four types of deeds: warranty, special warranty, bargain and sale, or quitclaim deeds.
- Some states use a transfer tax on the sale of real property.
- The closing is the culmination of an agreed-upon sales contract and can happen face-to-face or as escrow.

Transferring Property

Title to land may be transferred in one of two ways: by conveyance, voluntary or involuntary, or by operation of law. The strictly legal classification is that land is transferred by operation of law only in the case of descent without a will, and every other transfer of title is considered a transfer by purchase. But from the commercial side, all transfers by death, including those by descent and those by devised under a will, are considered transfers by operation of law. All other transfers of title are considered transfers by conveyance.

In this chapter, we will cover the mechanisms used to transfer property, both voluntarily and involuntarily. We will cover the types of voluntary transfers and how the seller and buyer interact to complete the transfer. We will also cover the major ways a property can be taken from an owner, called involuntary alienation, and the processes involved in those scenarios.

In This Chapter

- The ways property can be transferred to other parties
- How property can be taken from an owner
- A look at foreclosures and how to avoid them
- What happens to property upon the owner's death
- Transferring property to heirs

Transfer by Conveyance

One of the important rights of real estate ownership is the right of disposition, or the right to transfer ownership of real property to someone else. In general, the voluntary conveyance of real estate by a person who is still living is accomplished by the execution and delivery of a deed.

A deed, as you learned in Chapter 12, is a legal instrument in writing, duly executed and delivered, in which the owner of the land, called the grantor, conveys to another, called the grantee, some right, title, or interest in or to the real estate.

The involuntary transfer of real estate requires no vehicle of conveyance, or the deed, to be executed by either party involved in the transfer.

Voluntary Alienation

Transfer, or conveyance, of title by voluntary alienation is the normal real estate transaction, whereby either all or some of the owner's rights are voluntarily transferred to another.

Voluntary alienation may occur by gift or sale. Examples of such transfers are a cash sale of real estate or a transfer of title by a deed of trust or mortgage as security for the payment of a note. A gift of real property also is considered a voluntary alienation.

When a person wishes to alienate, or convey, real property from himself to another, he may do so by an agreement consummated with the transfer of a deed.

Involuntary Alienation

Transfer of title by involuntary alienation is a transfer without the owner's consent. Examples of such involuntary transfers are tax sales, foreclosed mortgages, or mechanics' or any other liens enforced. A person also could involuntarily lose his property to the state if he dies without a bona fide will and no legal heirs for the property exist. A local or state government also could involuntarily take an owner's land through the right of eminent domain. (Remember that from Chapter 10?)

Another example is loss of title by adverse possession. In this case, the owner may lose title if he or she isn't making use of the property.

Involuntary alienation also could occur upon the death of a person, or a *testator,* with a will in place, or *testate. Intestate* is when a person dies and has no will. In this case, any real property that person owned is subject to the state's laws of descent.

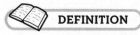 **DEFINITION**

Testate is when a person dies and leaves a last will and testament. The maker of the will would be the **testator. Intestate** is the condition of dying with no will in place.

Adverse possession is a principle of real estate whereby somebody who possesses the land belonging to someone else for an extended period may be able to claim legal title. To prove adverse possession under a typical definition, the person claiming ownership through adverse possession, the claimant, must show that their possession is actual, open, notorious, exclusive, hostile and continuous, and uninterrupted for the statutory period.

HELPFUL HINT

Real estate laws can vary significantly between jurisdictions, and each state may have slightly different requirements to claim ownership by adverse possession. Adverse possession is governed by statute; and the law, definitions of terms, and applicable statute of limitations can vary significantly from jurisdiction to jurisdiction.

The following elements are required to claim adverse possession:

Actual   The person claiming possession actually acted in the manner of an owner of the property.

Open and notorious   The person engaged in acts of possession consistent with the property in a manner that was capable of being seen. This does not mean they must have been actually observed, but rather should have been in a position to be observed. The claimant need not use the property in a manner different from what would be expected of the actual owner. It may be possible to claim adverse possession of a vacant parcel of land by engaging in typical acts of maintenance on the parcel or claim adverse possession of a vacation property based on use only during the vacation season.

Exclusive   The adverse possessor cannot occupy the land concurrently with the true owner or share possession in common with the public.

Hostile   You cannot claim adverse possession if you are engaged in the permissive use of somebody else's land.

Continuous and uninterrupted   All elements of adverse possession must be met continuously throughout the statutory period for a claim to be successful. Tacking (which you learned about in Chapter 11) allows for the possibility of claiming adverse possession even if there's a transfer of ownership. For example, a former owner's 7 years of adverse possession can be added, or tacked, to the new owner's 3 years for a continuous use of 10 years of adverse possession to meet the statutory period.

The statutory period   The statutory period, or statute of limitations, is the amount of time the claimant must hold the land to successfully claim adverse possession. Each state's statutory period requirement may vary.

The Fifth Amendment grants the federal government the right to exercise its power of eminent domain, and the due process clause of the Fourteenth Amendment makes the federal guarantee of just compensation applicable to the states. State governments derive the power to initiate condemnation proceedings from their state constitutions, except North Carolina, which gains its power through statute.

To exercise the power of eminent domain, the government must prove that the four elements set forth in the Fifth Amendment—private property, must be taken, for public use, and just compensation—are present.

The first element requires that the property taken be private. Private property includes land as well as fixtures, leases, options, stocks, and other items.

The second required element of eminent domain refers to the taking of physical property, or a portion thereof, as well as the taking of property by reducing its value. Property value may be reduced because of noise, accessibility problems, or other agents. In general, compensation must be paid when a restriction on the use of property is so extensive it's virtually equal to confiscation of the property. Another property right that's often protected is the right to use the airspace above privately owned land.

HELPFUL HINT

Airports and their flight patterns over private property that significantly interfere with the property owner's use also may be considered a form of taking. The courts have traditionally not recognized the regulation of property by the government as taking.

The third element, public use, requires that the property taken be used to benefit the public rather than specific individuals. Whether a use is considered public is a question decided by the courts. To determine whether property has been taken for public use, the courts first look at whether the property was to be used by a broad segment of the public. The definition of public use has been broadened to include anything that benefits the public, such as trade centers, municipal civic centers, and airport expansions. An even more broad definition of public use was determined to include the benefit to the public by economic means, wherein private property can be taken and given to another private individual if that taking would increase the tax base to the public.

The last element set forth in the Fifth Amendment mandates that the amount of just compensation awarded when property is seized or damaged through condemnation must be fair to the public as well as to the property owner. Because no precise formula for determining it exists, just compensation is the subject of frequent litigation. The courts tend to emphasize the rights of the property owner in eminent domain proceedings over the government's rights. The owner usually has not initiated the action but has been brought into the litigation because his property is needed for public use. The owner must participate in the proceedings, which can create an emotional and financial burden.

The compensation should be paid in cash, and the amount is determined as of the date title is acquired by the public authority. Interest is paid on the award until the date of payment.

The measure of damages is often considered to be the fair market value of the property that's harmed, or taken, for public use. The market value is commonly defined as the most reasonable price that could be achieved from negotiations between a willing owner and a ready, willing, and able buyer. Generally, the amount of compensation should be measured by the owner's loss rather than by the government's, or other public authority's, gain, and the owner should be placed in as good a financial position as he would have been in had the property not been taken.

Escheat is the involuntary transfer of real property to the local or state government based on the fact that the property owner died intestate or in the absence of any legal heirs or claimants. This occurs when the last property owner passed away without naming an adequate owner in succession. As such, escheat property is typically considered abandoned. Escheated property is not treated the same as abandoned property, however, and most states now place a heavy emphasis on finding a legal successor to assume ownership before escheating the property to the government.

Foreclosure is the last method of involuntary alienation of a property. Foreclosure is the sequence of legal proceedings by which a lender exercises his right given to him within the mortgage document to repossesses a home when the homeowner has stopped making payments for any reason. Some states require the lender to take the homeowner to court to foreclose on the home, known as *judicial foreclosure*. Other states utilize *nonjudicial foreclosure*, which requires no court intervention in the foreclosure process, but rather uses the power of sale clause contained within the deed of trust.

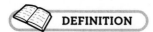 **DEFINITION**

Judicial foreclosure requires a foreclosure to be processed through the state's courts. **Nonjudicial foreclosure** does not require the lender to go to court to force a foreclosure on a home. This means the foreclosure can proceed more quickly.

Transfer by Operation of Law

An operation of law is when an individual acquires real property, certain rights, or liabilities automatically, through no act or cooperation of his own but merely by the application of the established legal rules and not an agreement or court order.

Whether by will or by descent, property that transfers by operation of law must go through a legal process, known as *probate*, to determine the validity of the will, take care of the financial responsibilities of the descendant, and facilitate the transfer of real property to heirs and successors.

In a probate proceeding, the court appoints an *executor*, named in the will if the descendant dies testate, or an *administrator*, if the descendant dies intestate, as a personal representative to collect the assets, pay the debts and expenses, and distribute the remainder of the estate to the beneficiaries, all under the supervision of the court.

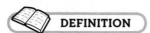 **DEFINITION**

Probate is the legal validation of the will, under the guidance and direction of the named **executor,** if there is will, or by a court-appointed **administrator,** if no will exists.

Transfer by operation of law can include different methods that depend on the estate of the person who dies—namely by will or by descent.

By Will

A will is a legal document by which a person, the testator, expresses his wishes regarding how his property is to be distributed after his death and names one or more persons, the executor(s), to manage the estate until its final distribution.

At times it has been thought that a will was limited to real property while testament applies only to dispositions of personal property, giving rise to the popular title of the document as "last will and testament." Recently, the two terms have become mostly synonymous and are often used interchangeably. *Will* has come to mean both personal and real property. A will also may create a testamentary trust that's effective only after the death of the testator.

HELPFUL HINT

In a will, real property is called a devise while personal property uses the term bequest. Cash is given as a legacy.

Only real property owned by the testator before his death can be passed, or transferred, within a will. The transfer of real property within a will is known as a devise. That means the testator is also the divisor, and the person receiving the gift of the real property is the devisee. Personal property gifted inside a will is known as bequest, and a gift of cash is a legacy.

No will can supersede the state laws of dower, curtesy, and homestead, which were initially created to protect the rights of inheritance by the surviving spouse in certain types of real property owned by the descendant. Furthermore, most states have additional protection for the surviving spouse's interest in the descendant's personal property. Children, of majority age or who have been emancipated, may be disinherited by a parent's will, except in Louisiana, where a minimum share is guaranteed to surviving children. However, minor children are protected by the courts and receive whatever financial support the minor is entitled to receive, assuming the money is available.

Because a will is a legal document, it must obey the requirements of a valid contract to be enforceable. A will must be prepared and executed according to the laws of the state where the testator resides. There's no legal requirement that a will be drawn up by a lawyer, although there are pitfalls into which homemade wills can fall. A will may not include a requirement that an heir commit an illegal, immoral, or other act against public policy as a condition of receipt.

Any person who has the capacity to contract—meaning anyone over the age of majority and having a sound mind—can make a will. In most states, the age of majority is defined as the age in which a person is responsible for his or her own actions, has the capacity to enter into a contract that's enforceable by the other party, is liable for damages for negligence or intentional wrongs without a parent, and can be punished as an adult for a crime. In almost all states, the basic legal age is 18. There are no legal tests, requirements, or measurements to demonstrate a sound mind; that's presumed if the testator has sufficient mental capacity to understand the ramifications of their decision regarding real estate transactions.

Most states require legal wills to be signed by the testator in front of witnesses to be valid. The witnesses sign the will as well. Some states require that real property may only be transferred by formally written and properly witnessed wills. Some states still recognize handwritten, or holographic, wills or oral, or nuncupative, wills.

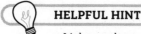

HELPFUL HINT

It's best to be sure a party receiving any benefit from the will is not used as a witness to the signing of the will.

The testator, while still alive, can change the will at any time he or she chooses. Any modification, addition, or deletion of a will that already has been executed and recorded is called a codicil.

By Descent

The term *heirs* usually refers to the person or persons who by operation of law or the application of the established rules of law inherit, or succeed to, the property of a person who dies intestate. Statutes generally confer rights of inheritance only on blood relatives, adopted children, adoptive parents, and the surviving spouse.

The order of persons who have descended, one from the other or all from a common ancestor, is called the line of descent. The direct line of descent refers to persons who are directly descended from the same ancestor, such as father and son or grandfather and grandson. Each generation is called a degree in determining the *consanguinity*, or blood relationship, of one or more persons to an intestate.

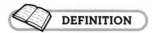

DEFINITION

Consanguinity is the degree of relationship between people of the same kinship, blood, or common ancestry.

When the intestate's next of kin who are entitled to share in the estate are in equal degree to the deceased, such as two or more children, they share equally in the estate. For example, a mother who has two daughters—her only living relations—and dies intestate, leaving an estate of $100,000. The two daughters occupy the same proximity of blood relationship to their mother, so they share her estate equally, each inheriting $50,000.

The succession to the disposition and distribution of personal property, wherever it is located, is governed by the laws of the state where the owner resided at the time of his or her death, unless a statute in the state where the property is located provides otherwise. However, the laws of descent in the state where the real property is located, such as land, houses, and farms, and not the state of primary residency of the deceased owner governs the distribution.

The privilege of receiving property by inheritance is not a natural right but a creation of law, so a state's legislature has complete authority over the descent and distribution of property within the borders of the state. The disposition of the property of an intestate is governed by the statutes in force at the time of death.

Title by descent is the title by which one person, upon the death of another, acquires the real estate as an heir. Title by inheritance is in all cases called descent, although in some states, statute law may require the title to ascend rather than descend.

The rules of descent vary somewhat from state to state and usually are governed by the law of the state in which the deceased party lived. Depending on which relatives survive, the estate may go all or in part to the surviving spouse, then descend to their children. If there are no children or none surviving, it then may go to grandchildren. Depending on the state laws of descent, a property may ascend to surviving parents or go collaterally to brothers and sisters. If there are no survivors among those relatives, then aunts, uncles, cousins, nieces, and nephews may inherit, depending on their degree of consanguinity.

If the deceased person lived in a community property state, where the spouse has a survivorship right to community property, the property goes directly to the spouse first.

Probate

Probate proceedings must take place in the county where the decedent resided as well as in any or every other county the decedent owned real property. The will must be presented for filing with the court by the executor. The court may act on its own volition, through the executor or through a court-appointed administrator, as it determines the validity of the will, takes care of the descendant's financial responsibilities, determines the descendant's assets, and facilitates the transfer of real property to the heirs and successors.

The key goal of probate is to properly allocate and distribute the assets of the decedent. The executor is responsible for ensuring that all the decedent's assets are collected, assessed, and sold to cover his outstanding debts at the time of his death. In addition to paying off all the debts, all outstanding real estate taxes, federal incomes taxes, and applicable inheritance taxes are paid before any distribution is made to his heirs.

The Least You Need to Know

- Real property can transfer by conveyance, either voluntary or involuntary, or by operation of law.
- A sale of real property is an example of a voluntary transfer.
- Anytime property is taken from an owner through a court action, a government agency, or an adverse possession action it's considered involuntary alienation.
- Title also can pass by an operation of law, such as by will or by descent.
- Probate is the legal validation of a will.
- You must probate in the county of the decedent's residency and every county where he owned real property.

Legal Ramifications

Becoming a successful agent often requires more than just specialized knowledge of real estate, it also requires dedication to honing your craft, attention to detail, careful consideration of all facts involved in every deal, and a strong ethical component. Without trying to scare you, this career can be stressful; however, you can prevent almost any issue by understanding the rules and laws of your state.

Real estate agents are particularly prone to getting sued by clients, customers, and sometimes other professionals involved in any deal. A successful REALTOR will have many deals in his career involving numerous contracts, important property details, multiple clients and customers, as well as properties valuing in the millions of dollars, making their exposure too great for some people to ignore. Even the slightest mistake could end up costing you a lot of money, a lot of stress, and worst of all, tarnish your reputation. Luckily, there are proactive steps you can take to protect yourself and your real estate career.

Contracts 101

The law of contracts is at the heart of most business dealings, so it's one of the three or four most significant areas of legal concern and can involve variations of circumstances and complexities. Similarly, contracts are the backbone of the real estate world. Everything real estate brokers, buyers, sellers, mortgage brokers, lenders, etc. do relies on a contractual agreement between parties.

In this chapter, we will cover a contract: how it's formed, the required parts of a contract, the terms used, and how they apply to real estate. A contract is a legally binding agreement between the two parties; in the real estate world, it could be considered the instructions on how a seller will transfer his property to a buyer and for what consideration. We will also cover some of the basic contracts used within the real estate world, such as the listing contract, the purchase contract, and more.

In This Chapter

- What defines a contract
- The clauses required to create valid contracts
- The formation of contracts
- Terminating contracts
- Common contracts in real estate

What Is a Contract?

A contract is a legally binding or valid agreement between two parties. The law considers a contract valid if the agreement contains all the following elements:

- **Agreement**   An intention between the parties to create a binding relationship.

- **Consideration**   Consideration to be paid by the grantee to the grantor.

- **Capacity to contract**   The legal capacity of the parties to enter into a contact.

- **Voluntary assent**   The genuine consent of the parties given freely and without coercion.

- **Legal activity**   The legality of the agreement

An agreement that lacks one or more of these elements is not a valid contract.

Contract law is the governing body by which all contracts are formed, executed, and dismissed, including the real estate contracts used by real estate professionals in the course of their everyday activities.

Express Versus Implied Contracts

A contract can be express or implied. An express contract is one in which all parties have clearly stated their intentions and terms in words. An express contract may be written or oral; however, only written contracts can be enforced in a court of law. Most all the real estate contracts brokers and their agents use should be written to comply with the statute of frauds in effect in most states. In addition, most real estate contracts are express and written as well.

 HELPFUL HINT

A lease less than 1 year in length is the only real estate contract not subject to the statute of frauds.

An implied contract is an unwritten contract. It has the force of law because of the parties' conduct and actions, as well as the circumstances demonstrated by each. There are two types of implied contracts: implied-in-fact and implied-in-law.

An implied-in-fact contract is an unwritten contract that the parties presumably intended to agree on, as can be inferred from their actions, conduct, and the circumstances. The "meeting of the minds" is necessary for a valid contract and is not written in this type of contract, but it can reasonably be inferred to have taken place. For example, when a person goes to lunch at a local restaurant, he will pay the bill after he eats but before he leaves. There's no written agreement stating his action; it's implied.

An implied-in-law contract is one in which there is an obligation imposed by law because of some special relationship between the parties, or because one of the parties would otherwise unjustly benefit from the relationship. For example, if a person at a restaurant begins to choke on a chicken bone, a doctor at the next table might perform the Heimlich maneuver and save the customer's life. The doctor might then send a bill for his services. The courts would probably determine that payment is required. The law looks at fairness and whether you benefitted from the contract.

Bilateral Versus Unilateral Contracts

Contracts can be classified as either bilateral or unilateral in nature. A bilateral contract is one in which both parties make promises to each other in exchange for something of value, or compensation.

A listing agreement is an example of a bilateral contract used in real estate. The seller agrees or promises to allow the broker to list the property for sale; likewise, the broker promises to commit sufficient time and effort to market the property to obtain a buyer. The purchase agreement, or sales contract, is also a bilateral contract between the buyer and seller. With it, the buyer promises to pay a specified amount, and the seller promises to transfer title to the buyer.

 HELPFUL HINT

To remember the difference between bilateral and unilateral contracts, think of bicycles and unicycles. Bicycles have two wheels, and bilateral contracts require that two parties act. Unicycles have one wheel, and unilateral contracts only require one party to act.

With an unilateral contract, only one party is bound to activity, or contractually obligated to act, while the other one is not. For example, if a man loses his dog and places flyers throughout the neighborhood offering a reward for the return of the dog, is anyone bound by contract or obligation to seek the dog? No. However, if they do find and return the dog to the owner, the owner is bound to pay a reward. In the real estate world, the *option* is the only unilateral contract used.

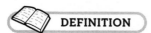 **DEFINITION**

An **option** is the right to buy property at a later date for a price agreed upon in the present time that's sealed by some option consideration.

Executed Contracts

Contracts can be considered executed if they have been completed to the satisfaction of both parties. Do not confuse this term with the legal term *to execute,* which attorneys define as signing a contract. However, if the contract has not been completed due to one party or the other still working on completing their required portion, the contract is said to be *executory.*

The listing agreement real estate brokers use is formed on the agreement and acceptance of the seller and the broker to list a house for sale. During the marketing activities to sell the property, the contract is in executory status. However, once the real estate broker has brought a ready, willing, and able buyer to the seller, completing his obligation under the listing agreement, the listing agreement has been executed, or complete.

Terms Within Contract Law

For a contract to be considered valid and binding on the parties involved, it must contain essential elements, including an offer and acceptance, terms and conditions, consideration, agreement and consent, the capacity to contract, and legal activity. I touched on some of these earlier in the chapter. Let's take a closer look now.

A contract, at its essence, is an offer from one party to another to do some legal activity, or not do some activity, with compensation by legally competent parties. The offer is the set of rules, obligations, and requirements made by the offeror. (In real estate, this is the buyer.) The other party, called the offeree (or the seller in real estate), can accept the offer. If there's acceptance, the contract has been formed, or agreed upon. This acceptance is often referred to as mutual assent, or a meeting of the minds, and binds the two parties and requires them to complete the contract under the weight of law.

Sometimes, a buyer's offer is not sufficient to induce the seller to accept the offer. The seller may counter-offer to the original buyer a modified set of terms based on the original offer. The counteroffer is a legal rejection of the original offer and, therefore, releases the buyer from obligation to fulfill the contract under the original terms offered.

The offer can be terminated, by the seller, through an outright rejection of the offer. The seller also can terminate a contract by withholding acceptance of the offer past the expiration date.

An offeror may *rescind,* or revoke, an offer prior to being accepted by the offeree, even if it's still within the timeframe given to respond. For example, the buyer makes an offer on a property and gives the seller 5 days to reply. Before the seller has formally accepted the offer, the buyer may rescind the offer at any time at his discretion. However, a written letter of revocation must be communicated to the seller to give notice of the revocation.

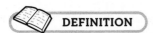 **DEFINITION**

To **rescind** an offer means to withdraw, or take back, an offer presented by the offeror to the offeree.

The terms and conditions of the contract must be expressly stated and in writing, in the case of real estate. The offer must expressly state the intention of the offeror to enter into a lawful and binding contract with the offeree. Most courts look at the objective intent of the offer to determine if they are willing to enter in a binding contract.

The terms and conditions would include other items contained within the contract, such as price, closing date, financing arrangements, etc. Terms and conditions typically are the heart of most contractual agreements.

The consideration is an essential element within a contract and a required item to ensure its validity. The courts have determined that consideration must be given as an element of a contract or it may be considered a gift rather than a contract.

Consideration can take the form of money, a promise, or something of value by both parties. Consideration also could consist of "love and affection," such as in a marriage contract. However, in most all real estate contracts, consideration's most acceptable definition is money.

For a contract to be binding, all parties must signal their agreement to its terms. In most cases, this means signing it. However, a written signature need not be present for a contract to be considered valid. If both parties behave in ways required in the contract, a court may assume consent has been reached.

However, a contract forced on someone via intimidation, such as duress or a threat to bodily harm of any kind, is considered legally invalid. Claims of duress are filed by parties to a contract seeking to prove that their assent to a contract was not genuine and did not fulfill the essential requirements needed to form a contract.

When it comes to contracts, misrepresentation is referring to, engaging in, or utilizing a false statement by one party to another party which induces that party into agreeing to the contract. A finding of misrepresentation allows for a remedy of rescission and sometimes damages, depending on the type of misrepresentation

 HELPFUL HINT

> All state level REALTOR organizations will provide a set of pre-written contracts for their members to use throughout the buying and selling process. This allows for REALTORS to merely fill in blanks in pre-printed forms that were crafted by attorneys using each state's set of laws. Remember, unlicensed attorneys cannot write true contracts; however, we can fill in the blanks for our clients.

To have a binding contract, all parties to it must have the capacity to contract. This means they must all be at least 18 years old, or legally emancipated, and have sufficient mental capacity to make sound decisions.

A contract involving a legal minor, or someone who is under 18 and not emancipated, would be considered voidable. The same goes for a contract with someone suffering from any form of mental incapacitation.

The contract itself must be legal on its face for the court system to enforce it. For example, a contract between a contractor and a subcontractor that requires the subcontractor to pay a bribe to win the job bid, is neither a contract nor legal. It would be considered void.

A contract can be determined to be valid, void, voidable, or unenforceable depending on the surrounding circumstances. A contract is said to be valid if all the essential elements are in place and enforceable if it's binding in a court of law. A voidable contract is one in which all the essential elements appear to be in place, but one element may be defective upon inspection, such as mental capacity or age of one of the parties to the contract. Contracts made under duress or misrepresentation by either party also may be voidable.

The act of making a contract voidable requires the ability, by either party, to rescind or revoke the contract based on some legal principle. A contract is said to be void when one of the essential elements is missing, left out, or completely disregarded in the contract. In essence, a void contract is a misnomer, as it never was a contract to begin with due to the missing element.

An unenforceable contract is one that has all the elements of a valid contract, yet neither party can sue the other to force performance of it. For example, an unsigned contract is generally unenforceable. This could also happen because the terms of the contract are ambiguous or the statute of limitations expired. The statute of limitations requires that lawsuits be filed within a certain period of time following a breach.

Another reason a contract might be unenforceable could be because of the *doctrine of laches*. This principle states that a court has determined a contract is unenforceable due to needless delay or neglect in filing a claim even though the statute of limitations may not have expired.

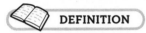 **DEFINITION**

The **doctrine of laches** is a failure to bring a legal claim in the proper, or a reasonable, time.

An unenforceable contract is still said to be valid between the parties. Upon the execution of a contract and if both parties are satisfied, there's no need to litigate or force performance of a party.

Formation and Discharge of Contracts

A contract is said to be formed when all parties agree on the terms included and are satisfied with their individual rights, responsibilities, and obligations under those terms. Contracts must be discharged at some point after their formation. An executed, or satisfied, contract is one method to discharge a contract.

A contract is comprised of many terms and concepts that are required to make it a living and viable document. And each party has their obligations and duties they must fulfill to execute the contract. One such term required in real estate contracts dealing with the performance of a contract is *time is of the essence*. This has nothing to do with the formation of the contract but everything to do with the completion of the contract. *Time is of the essence* means that once the parties are past the date incorporated in the contract and one has not completed their portion of the contract, they may be held liable, often called breach of contract.

If a contract fails to have a date specifically mentioned within one of its terms, the courts may rule the agreement void and unenforceable by either party. Similarly, a judge may determine a reasonable time frame for completion based on the intent, wording, or understanding of the parties involved.

A contract is an agreement between parties, simply stated. That contract easily can be changed providing both parties agree and are willing to do so. Duties and obligations can be added or deleted, and dates can be changed, as can specific issues within the contract.

A novation is a change or alteration of an element, or elements, of an already executed contract between willing parties. The new contract is formed between the same parties; however, it is possible to change one of the parties involved in the contract. This is called a novation of parties. Common changes seen in real estate contracts include the closing date, the purchase price, the personal property left or taken from the property, or the financing type being used at closing.

A novation usually is exercised in one of two methods: with an addendum or amendment. An addendum is a separate form used to add language not already incorporated in any agreement, such as a purchase agreement between sellers and buyers. However, an amendment is an alteration, addition, or removal of words or terms already in the original contract.

HELPFUL HINT

The amendment amends, or changes, words already discussed in the contract. An addendum adds new words or terms that were never covered in the formation of the contract.

Another means of changing a contract is called an assignment. This is where one party transfers his or her rights and obligations to another party. Most states require that a contract specifically allow for an assignment before it can be exercised by either party. Some states are silent to assignments, meaning that without specific permission to do so, the right is not guaranteed and can be denied by the other party at their discretion. Some contracts may specifically deny the right of assignment as one of the incorporated terms of the original contract. Many residential leases contain a clause prohibiting a tenant from assigning their lease to another tenant without the landlord's knowledge.

Termination and Breach of Contract

There are many ways to terminate a contract other than complete satisfaction, including partial performance, substantial performance, impossibility of performance, mutual agreement, and operation of law.

Partial performance is when (where) either party does only part of what is agreed upon in the contract. This partial performance must be accompanied by agreement of the party accepting the partial performance.

Moreover, a contract may be a group of smaller individual contracts that can be distinguished from one another. For example, if a lease of real property or an apartment is breached before the entire term has expired, the tenant is liable for the remaining rent as each month occurs but not prior to that time. In effect, the court treats the lease as a contract for each month, with rent due on the first of each month.

Substantial performance is similar to a partial performance requirement, but in this case, the contract can be divisible and is seen as one complete entity. If both parties agree that a substantial part of the contract is complete, they may, at their discretion, agree that the contract is satisfied. For example, if a home builder has completed the build of a new home but has not yet washed the windows, as per the agreement, the builder and buyer may agree that the contract is substantially close enough to satisfied to move forward with the closing.

An impossibility of performance is where the contract has become impossible to perform due to some outside or unforeseen force that neither party can rectify. Examples might include a natural disaster that prevents the delivery of goods, weather conditions that cancel a performance or competition, a new law or decree that makes the contract performance illegal, or a play's key performer getting injured with no one to replace them.

Mutual agreement is perhaps the easiest to understand because both parties simply agree to terminate a contract for whatever reason. However, the fact that a party agrees to terminate the contract does not automatically relieve one party or the other from being liable for damages.

Operation of law can include such things as the misrepresentation of material facts between the parties, a minor engaging in the transfer of real property, or fraud committed by one party.

Unfortunately, in some cases, a contract will terminate by breach by one party or the other. Generally, a breach occurs when a contractual promise is broken. To recover from breach of contract, a party must prove that the other party harmed them in some way. This is referred to as liquidated damages. Damages cover money lost but may include time lost as well. If the buyer is the one who defaults, the liquidated damages may be the earnest money, deposited by the buyer, paid to the seller, unless the contract stipulates the aggrieved can sue "to the fullest extent of the law," which could be the entire value the contract.

In some rare cases, if the seller has breached the agreement, the buyer may seek a suit for performance to force the sale of the property. In general, the breaching party also must pay for any expenses the other party incurred because of the violation.

Actual eviction, or a suit for possession, is the legal process of removing a tenant from the premises for some breach of the lease. Typical grounds for eviction include nonpayment of rent, unlawful use of the premises like conducting a business in a rental unit leased strictly for residential purposes, and noncompliance with health and safety codes.

Constructive eviction is conduct by the landlord that disturbs or impairs a tenant's enjoyment of the leased premises such that the tenant effectively evicts himself and terminates the lease without liability for any future rent. This concept is a product of modern property law, which now tends to place more emphasis on the quality of possession, or habitability, under a lease. Constructive eviction might occur if the landlord of a multistory apartment failed to maintain elevator service or repair the furnace in a timely manner. There can be no constructive eviction without the tenant's vacating the premises within a reasonable time of the landlord's act. The tenant's duty to pay rent is not terminated if the tenant remains in possession.

Common Contracts Used in Real Estate

Many contracts are used in real estate. Some examples include listing agreements, buyer's agency agreements, purchase agreements, leases, options, and property management agreements.

Remember that unless you are a licensed practicing attorney, you cannot write contracts. Furthermore, most states require that you use the state REALTOR forms if you are member of the local or state association. There is legal precedence that says when you're filling in blanks on a preprinted agreement such as those provided by the state association, you're not writing a contract per se and, therefore, not practicing law. So use those forms!

Parties to any contract, even those in real estate, should have their attorney review the contract before signing to make sure that it is accurate and that it reflects their intention.

Listing and Buyer Agency Agreements

Listing agreements and buyer agency agreements are contracts that employ the agent and bind him to the client. These contracts are required and must be signed by all parties to the contract, including the managing, or principal, broker.

These contracts define the rights, obligations, and duties of both parties during the time frame of agency. Under the statute of frauds, they must be in writing to be in force.

Purchase Contracts

The purchase contract is the backbone of the real estate sale. It, too, must be in writing and signed by all buyers and sellers of the property to be enforceable in a court of law.

Some of the clauses incorporated in the purchase agreement are these:

- The offer, such as the offer price
- The property identification
- The terms of financing
- The earnest money deposited, if any
- Any special instruction regarding personal property that may be annexed into the sale
- The time frame to close the contract, or the closing date
- The time frame for the seller to respond or make counteroffers
- The signatures of the buyers

Another potential item in the purchase agreement is any contingencies or special circumstances that must be met to bring about the full force of the contract. The clause that states the contingencies requires three other factors:

- The timeframe to complete the contingency
- The actions to complete, or clear, the contingency
- The party responsible for that action

A contingency can be anything that both parties agree to during the negotiation of the contract. Inherently, most purchase agreements have some built-in contingencies within the purchase agreement itself, like the home appraising for the agreed sales price, the home passing the suitable home inspection, or the buyer being able to get appropriate financing. A buyer could add other contingencies at his discretion, as long as the seller agrees to them.

HELPFUL HINT

Several years ago, when the market was hot and properties were selling quickly, I had a client make an offer subject to his wife's approval within 48 hours. His wife was out of town and unable to sign the initial offer immediately. The other party accepted the offer with the contingency, which we cleared the next afternoon when his wife returned home from her business trip.

Leases

A lease is a contract used between the lessor/landlord and the lessee/tenant. The lease is a temporary transfer of rights from a landlord to a tenant for an agreed amount of compensation, called the lease rate.

In most states, a lease is not a boilerplate contract that's provided by the state agency, and it must be written by a licensed attorney to be enforceable in a court of law. As a real estate professional, you should guide your client to a real estate attorney for help in this respect. If the other party to the lease has had one written by his attorney, your client should have his attorney review the lease prior to accepting it.

Options

An option is the only unilateral contract used in real estate. The option is the right of the optionee, the buyer, to buy a property from the optionor, the seller, at a predetermined price, called the strike price, at or before the end of the option period. In most cases, option consideration is given at the time the parties execute the option agreement.

The consideration for the option is most often included as part of the strike price, if the option is exercised by the optionee. In rare cases, it may not be.

An option is typically used in conjunction with a lease to give the tenant the option to buy the property at or before the end of the lease period.

Speculative investors often use options as a tool to gain control of property by tying up the seller to act if exercised. This technique is very powerful for the investor because it allows him to limit his downside on the investment. For example, suppose an investor has heard rumors that a big-box store is coming to the area and seeking ground to build. He may option some land, for an option consideration, from an owner at a strike price that's agreeable to both. If the big-box store then decides to buy the land from the investor at a price above his strike price, he would exercise his option from the landowner and resell the land to the big-box store for a profit. If, however, the big-box store decides not to buy the land, the investor doesn't have to exercise his option because the option is a unilateral contract. His only loss would be the nominal amount he gave as the option consideration.

Land Contracts

A land contract, sometime called owner financing, installment sale, or contract for deed, is an often-confused method of financing between a buyer and a seller. In the land contract, the owner of the property, the vendor, retains actual, legal title to the property while the buyer, the vendee, acquires *equitable title,* or equitable interest in the property.

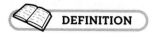 **DEFINITION**

Equitable title is an interest gained by a vendee based on the amount of equity he has paid toward the sales price of the property. This allows the vendee to acquire the property over a time period rather than be vested in the entire property instantly, as in a traditional purchase agreement.

In most cases, the vendee agrees to pay the homeowners' insurance as well as the real estate taxes. In most states, the vendee is allowed to claim the homeowner's exemption on his or her real estate taxes as well.

When the vendee has acquired enough equity in the property, he may seek traditional financing and gain the property via a traditional sale. Sometimes, the vendee may choose to let the vendor carry the entire amount of sales price. When the vendee pays off the entire amount, the vendor can quitclaim the deed of the property to the vendee, who then would own the property free and clear.

Other Types of Contracts

Many more contracts can be utilized in real estate, including earnest money contracts, power of attorney contracts, mutual releases from purchase agreements, and commercial lease agreements. Other custom contracts can be used as well.

In general, any time there's an agreement between the parties involved in a real estate transaction, a contract should be memorialized stating each party's intention.

The Least You Need to Know

- A contract is a legally binding or valid agreement between two parties.
- Contracts can be express or implied, bilateral or unilateral.
- Contracts can be valid, void, voidable, or unenforceable.
- A novation changes the contract but leaves the party intact, whereas an assignment changes the parties but leaves the contract intact.
- Breach of a contract occurs when a party fails to uphold his or her end of the contract.
- An option is the only unilateral contract used in real estate.

Leasing Versus Renting

Contrary to popular belief, leasing is not the same as renting. Renting is a broader term meaning the use of, or a license to use, property belonging to another in exchange for payment or other valuable consideration. In this case, consideration might mean a tenant improves the property while living there, which has value to the owner of the property. Renting does not necessarily require the parties to enter into a lease agreement. Leasing means the rental of property under a lease, or rental agreement, or when any lease agreement is signed as evidence of the rental of something of value. Leasing is a form of renting. You can rent something without leasing it, but you can't lease something without renting it.

In this chapter, we will discuss leases. We will explain the requirements needed to create a valid lease and how each paragraph within a lease transfers rights and responsibilities to the lessor, or tenant. We will discuss the different types of leases used in the residential world as well as talk about some key differences between the commercial and residential lease agreements.

In This Chapter

- Comparing lease agreements and rental agreements
- Defining leases and common lease clauses
- Types of leases used in real estate
- A look at evictions

The Differences Between Leasing and Renting in Real Estate

In real estate, a lease gives a tenant the right to live in a property for a fixed period—typically 1 year for residential leases, but it could be any length of time agreed on by the landlord and tenant.

Through a lease, the landlord and tenant mutually agree to a contract with fixed terms and conditions, such as the rental rate, rules regarding pets, duration of the agreement, etc. Neither party can change the agreement without written consent from the other.

When a lease expires, it usually does not automatically renew itself. A tenant who stays on with the landlord's consent after a lease ends becomes a month-to-month tenant, subject to the rental terms in the lease.

The lease is mutually beneficial to both parties. A tenant can't stop paying rent or vacate the property during the lease term without possibly being liable and in violation of the agreement. Likewise, the landlord can't arbitrarily force the tenant to move or increase the rental rate.

A rental agreement, by contrast, is a month-to-month agreement. At the end of each 30-day period, the landlord and tenant are both free to change the terms.

Leasehold Versus Freehold Estate

As covered earlier in the book, a freehold estate is for an indeterminable amount of time whereas a leasehold estate is for a determinable amount of time, called the lease period. A leasehold interest is created when a fee simple owner, called the landlord or lessor, enters into an agreement, or rental contract, with a tenant, or lessee. The lessee gives compensation to the lessor for the rights of use and enjoyment of the land, much as when one buys fee simple rights. However, the leasehold interest differs from the fee simple interest in several important respects:

- The holder of a leasehold estate does not own the land. He or she only has a right to use the land for a predetermined amount of time.

- If the leasehold estate is transferred to a new owner, use of the property is limited to the remaining time covered by the original lease.

- At the end of the predetermined time period, the property, along with all the rights, reverts to the lessor. This is called reversionary rights or a reversionary interest. Depending on the provisions of any surrender clause within the lease, the property and other improvements on the land also may revert to the lessor.

- The use, maintenance, and alteration of the leased property are subject to any restrictions contained in the lease.

There are four types of leasehold estates: estate for years, estate from period to period, estate at will, and estate at sufferance.

An estate for years, sometimes called a tenancy for years, lasts for a fixed period of time, such as a week, a year, or more. The duration of the lease period is known, as is the date of expiration of the lease. The tenant must do nothing for the tenancy to expire. If the lease continues for more than a year, the lease should be executed in writing to satisfy the statute of frauds.

A tenancy for years may be terminated any time with agreement between the landlord and the tenant. The termination is known as *surrender of the lease.* If the term remaining on the lease at the time of surrender exceeds a year, the surrender must be executed in writing. The landlord may accept the surrender of the lease agreement from the tenant, but this may not relieve the tenant from possibly being liable for damages to the landlord. Furthermore, any of the tenant's personal property not removed by the date within the surrender of the lease clause may become property of the landlord through constructive annexation.

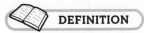 **DEFINITION**

> **Surrender of the lease** is when a tenant agrees to give up his legal rights and returns possession of the property with the landlord's consent. This terminates the lease agreement and ends the landlord-tenant relationship.

An estate from period to period, sometimes called a tenancy for period to period, has a duration from some time period to some time period, such as week to week, month to month, or year to year. In the lease, this tenancy has a defined beginning date but no defined end date. At the end of the defined time period, the lease automatically renews itself for another similar time period. To terminate this tenancy, a written notice, given by either party, must be submitted at least one time period in advance, notifying the intention to terminate the lease. An unusual law allows the landlord to terminate a year-to-year tenancy with only a 6 months' notice in writing to terminate.

An estate at will, sometimes called a tenancy at will, has no defined beginning date nor defined end date, but rather allows either the landlord or the tenant to terminate the tenancy at any time without notice, hence the phrase *at will.* This occurs mostly in the absence of a lease. But in the majority of residential tenancies, the landlord may not terminate the tenancy except for some cause, even though there's no written lease. By law, the tenancy existing at the will of the landlord only grants a similar right to the tenant. But a lease existing at the will of the tenant does not give similar right to the landlord.

Tenancy at will is terminated by the operation of law if …

- The tenant commits waste against his property.

- The tenant makes an assignment of his tenancy.

- The landlord transfers his interest in the property.

- The landlord leases the property to another tenant.

- The tenant or the landlord passes away.

An estate at sufferance, sometimes called a tenancy at sufferance, exists when a tenant possesses the property even after the lease has expired, creating a *holdover tenant.* The tenancy lasts until the landlord evicts the tenant from the property by a court proceeding. The tenant, however, should pay rent until the landlord forces him to move out at any time without prior notice.

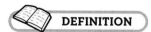

DEFINITION

> A **holdover tenant** is a tenant whose lease has expired but who continues to occupy the premises without the landlord's consent.

A landlord may unilaterally elect to hold a tenant to a new term—in effect renewing the lease under the old contract. When this decision is made, it can't be changed. If the landlord accepts any money from the tenant, in the form of a rent check, after the expiration of the lease, that may automatically renew the lease for a new term. The election to hold the tenant to a new term must be made within a reasonable time or the right is lost.

Common Lease Clauses

Most leases must be in writing; however, a lease less than 1 year in length may be oral under the statute of frauds. This "1-year" rule states that contracts that cannot be completed within a year must be written down. The 1-year rule does not mean a contract needs to be completed within the year; it only requires that it can be completed within a single year.

A lease is a contract, and as such, it must meet all the requirements for a valid contract. (See Chapter 6 for a review on contracts.)

HELPFUL HINT

> Remember, a lease is a contract, so real estate professionals, unless they're also attorneys, cannot legally draft leases for a client. A competent real estate attorney should be used instead.

In addition to the major rights and responsibilities of the landlord and the tenant, residential leases address other matters of concern to the parties. The following clauses typically appear in a residential lease to resolve matters of common concern:

Fixtures clause   The purpose of the fixtures clause in a residential lease is to obtain an understanding at the beginning of the lease that items of personal property belonging to the tenant will not become the landlord's property at the expiration of the lease. If the residential tenant chooses to attach his personal property to the improvement owned by the landlord, that property would ordinarily become the landlord's property after the expiration of the lease. On the other hand, these items could remain the tenant's fixtures or more specifically, the tenant's domestic fixtures, depending on the lease. The parties should provide for the disposition of these fixtures.

Entry clause   The landlord does not have the right to enter the property without notice unless the lease has callouts for specific instances. The landlord may enter the property to collect the rent, stop waste against the property, or in cases of emergency, typically denoted as cries for help, fire, or the sound of free-flowing water. Due to this prohibition on their right to enter, landlords typically insert a clause in the lease that gives them some rights to "enter with a 24-hour notice" or to show the property to a new tenant before the original lease expires.

Renewal clause   A common provision within the lease landlords desire is the requirement that the tenant provide written notice of his or her intention to renew the lease. The clause typically states that the tenant must inform the landlord within some given period before the expiration of the current lease of his intention to renew the lease. The clause typically asks for a written notice from the tenant that the lease will be renewed.

Insurance clause   The landlord needs adequate insurance coverage against hazards, such as fire, earth-quakes, and windstorms, to protect the investment in the rental property. The landlord can insert a clause in the lease requiring the tenant to carry such insurance and provide adequate proof of the coverage. Some landlords require the tenant to be name the landlord as "also insured" on the policy. If damage occurs due to the negligence of a tenant or the negligence of a visitor to the property, the landlord typically is not responsible. Consequently, the landlord will not have to compensate the tenant for losses of any personal property.

Security deposits clause   Security deposits are a major consideration in leases. The landlord wants to collect an adequate amount of money that may have to cover any physical damage beyond normal wear and tear the tenant causes. The security deposit also can be used to defer losses if the tenant breaches the lease. In some states, security deposits are not required to follow the "no commingling of funds" rule earnest money must adhere to.

Maintenance and repair clause   In most residential leases, maintenance and repairs, also called improvements, are completed by the landlord to avoid the tenant potentially causing serious damages. However, in commercial leases, these items may be absorbed into the tenant's responsibilities, often called tenant's improvements.

> **HELPFUL HINT**
>
> Maintenance of leased property is the first place agents see a drastic difference between the residential and commercial world. In the residential world, the landlord will make all repairs while in the commercial world, the tenant is responsible for the maintenance and repair of the lease property.

Miscellaneous rules and regulations clause   In addition to the preceding specific clauses, the typical lease contains a section stating various rules and regulations the landlord wishes to impose. For example, this section of the residential lease might contain the following statements:

- No pets allowed on the premises.

- Tenants must throw trash into specifically designated containers.

- Tenants will refrain from playing stereos, radios, or TVs in a loud manner after 10 P.M.

- The laundry room is for laundry purposes only and is open only from 9 A.M. to 9 P.M.

- Each tenant must park in his or her assigned parking space for the apartment.

- Vehicles other than the residents' cars are not permitted on the property.

These rules and regulations specify the landlord's preferences about the behavior of the individual tenants in an apartment building. The landlord's concern is to establish a code of behavior that maximizes the benefits for all individuals living in the building.

Consequently, everyone may have to avoid some activities at certain times they find beneficial or enjoyable. For example, one tenant may prefer to do laundry at 2 A.M. but doing so would disturb other tenants. Therefore, the rule covering the use of the laundry room facilities benefits the community at some small cost to individual preferences.

Please be careful when creating miscellaneous rules and regulations that you do not cross into gray areas or violations of the fair housing act. Seek legal advice when creating leases if you're not an attorney.

The Right to Assign

In an ideal situation for the tenant, the landlord allows them to move out before their lease ends without being liable for some sort of damages. If the tenant intends to leave permanently, the easiest, smartest, and quickest option is for the landlord to cancel the original lease, find a new tenant under a new lease, and weigh his options on whether to take the tenant to court for damages. However, in markets where a surplus of rental properties exists, a landlord might not be so kind to even consider this avenue. In that case, a tenant might consider whether a lease assignment or sublease is an option.

A lease assignment is a process by which the original tenant transfers his unexpired rights in the lease-hold estate to a new tenant. The new tenant takes over the role of the original tenant. In other words, the new tenant who receives the property through an assignment assumes the rights to the provisions and the responsibilities for the obligations specified in the original lease.

Under the provisions of the lease, the landlord can obligate the new tenant to pay the rent. Furthermore, he can allow the new tenant the use of property as specified in the lease and require him to conform to all other stipulations in the lease. The landlord and tenant are contractually bound to each other through the assignment clause, so if the new tenant does not make the rent payment, the landlord can force the payment or seek court remedies.

Typically, an assignment of leased property does not automatically release the original tenant from the contractual duties imposed in the lease. A *release from obligation*, sometimes called a mutual release from obligation, could be granted to the original tenant at the time of signing the assignment with the new tenant. However, it is not in the best interest of the landlord to do so, or even to suggest it for that matter.

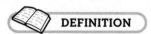 **DEFINITION**

A **release from obligation** is used when one party, such as a landlord, releases another party, such as a tenant, from contractual liability.

The Right to Sublease

A sublease is the process by which the original tenant enters into a separate and distinct lease arrangement with a new tenant. This lease agreement between the original tenant and the new tenant does not involve the landlord.

A sublease is a transfer of the original tenant's rights in the leased property. A sublease presupposes that the original tenant maintains some portion of the property, either physical or temporal. The original tenant subleases all or some part of the original leased space, or the original tenant subleases some portion of the time remaining in the original lease. For example, the original tenant could sublease one of the bedrooms in a two-bedroom apartment to a friend while retaining possession of the other bedroom, or the original tenant could sublease the entire apartment to a friend for 3 months of a 1-year lease. The process of subleasing involves a transfer of only a portion of the original tenant's leased property. However, the new sublease does not contain a provision by which the new tenant has any contractual obligation to the landlord.

The major distinction between an assignment and a sublease is that an assignment creates a contractual obligation between the new tenant and the landlord while a sublease does not. This is important in the landlord's right to seek legal remedies in case of a tenant breach.

With an assigned lease, the landlord must first attempt to obtain payment from the new tenant. Only after failing with the new tenant can the landlord sue the original tenant for payment if he or she was not released via a release of obligation. However, in the case of a sublease, the original tenant still is liable for the rent payment without any interruption in the contractual obligation. If the new tenant, the sublessee, fails to make a rent payment, the landlord must sue the original tenant directly because there's no contractual obligation between the landlord and sublessee.

Although the landlord has legal recourse against the original tenant under both the assignment (unless released) and the sublease, the landlord typically limits a tenant's right to sublease or assign the property. A clause within a lease usually accomplishes this purpose by stating that "assignments and subleasing are forbidden without the express written consent of the landlord" or similar wording. This clause gives the landlord the opportunity to check the new tenant's creditworthiness and decide what's best for him.

Residential Versus Commercial Leases

In the world of real estate leasing, residential and commercial leasing are as far apart as east is from west. Residential leases and commercial leases share many similarities, but they also have many differences.

Residential leases are designed for properties in neighborhoods where residential building codes apply. Maintenance, upkeep, and appearance of the residence are just a few items to contend with in residential properties. However, commercial leases are for properties zoned for commercial use, where typically different, more stringent, codes apply, such as environmental, zoning, and greenspace issues.

A residential lease may be less detailed to ensure the owner follows the applicable codes. Maintaining a livable, clean, and safe property is priority number one because it's assumed that the properties will be used as residential dwellings. Commercial leases generally go into more specific detail about the permitted uses of the property because commercial properties can encompass a wide range of uses.

Residential and commercial leases also differ in that residential leases typically assume the property to be an individual house, duplex, or apartment whereas a commercial lease is for a building in an area with multiple tenants operating as multiple different uses. The commercial lease must be more specific about what exact portions of the premises are being leased and what activities are allowed in there.

A final major difference between residential and commercial leases is the inclusion of clauses regarding owner improvements versus tenant improvements. Most residential real estate is rented as-is, with the assumption that the owner will fix or maintain the property and that the tenant must ask before making changes. Commercial properties often need to be changed to suit individual tenants, so there may be more shared responsibility in making property changes in a commercial lease.

 REALTOR WARNING

Agents beware, residential and commercial leasing are vast worlds apart. Each requires a special skill set that the other may not need or warrant. I suggest you seek advice when switching from commercial to residential leasing or vice versa.

Gross Leases

The gross lease can be used in a commercial lease or residential lease. In a residential lease, it's sometimes called a flat-rate lease or a fixed-rate lease.

Under a gross lease arrangement, the tenant pays a fixed, or gross, amount of rent, whether in the residential or commercial market. The landlord is then responsible for all the expenses connected with the leased property. The payment can be a flat, or fixed, amount per month or a price per unit, such as per square foot. The tenant is typically responsible for their own utilities connected with the leased space, such as cable, security monitoring, and utility payments.

Net Leases

The net lease breaks the rent payment into components: a fixed component and a variable component. In this arrangement, the tenant promises to pay the landlord a fixed sum periodically plus some or all of the expenses the landlord incurs in operating the property. The most typical expenses paid by the tenant under a net lease arrangement are the real property taxes and the property insurance premiums.

A net lease may provide that the tenant promise to pay either a flat fee plus the real property taxes, a flat fee plus the hazard insurance premiums, or a flat fee plus the real estate taxes and the hazard insurance premiums.

If the tenant pays the flat fee plus one expense, it's said to be a *single-net lease*. This type of lease is rarely used due to a majority of the expenses being placed on the landlord. Typically, a single-net lease pays the flat fee, or rent, plus the real estate taxes.

If the tenant pays two expense items, the parties consider it a net-net, or *double-net lease*. In this lease, the tenant might pay a flat fee plus property taxes and insurance.

The lease can require that in addition to paying a fixed amount, the tenant bears all the financial responsibility for maintaining and repairing the structure as well as all other costs of operating the property, such as the real estate taxes and the insurance premiums. This type of lease is a *triple-net lease*, or net-net-net lease. The triple-net lease is the "golden goose" of leases because it relieves the landlord of all variable costs. Furthermore, the landlord in a triple-net lease receives a fixed amount of rent, which assures his yield on the property as long as the tenant makes the payments.

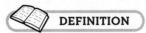
DEFINITION

> A **single-net lease** is a lease that requires a flat fee payment plus one of the landlord's expenses. A **double-net lease** requires a flat fee plus two of the landlord's expenses, typically taxes and insurance. A **triple-net lease** requires a flat fee plus all the landlord's major expenses, typically taxes, insurance, and maintenance of the property.

Graduated or Index Leases

A graduated lease initially allows for rent payments to be a fixed amount, either a flat rate or per unit. A graduated lease also contains an escalator clause that allows the rent to increase in the future based on anticipated increases due to inflation, an increase in the property's value, or a rise in the landlord's operating expenses. During the life of the lease and at set intervals specified in the lease, the payments increase accordingly. The lease agreement could state that rent increases at each interval by a predetermined percentage of the landlord's operating expenses or an increase per some financial index, sometimes called an *index lease*.

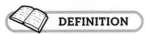
DEFINITION

> An **index lease** is one in which the base rent, or an increase in rent, is tied to a financial index or financial market in some manner, such as the consumer price index.

Furthermore, it could be stipulated that the tenant pays some flat-fee increase, such as $500 per month for the first year of operation, $750 per month in the second and third years of the lease, and $1,000 per month in the remaining years of the lease. This graduated lease agreement remains in force for the entirety of the lease.

If the rent increase is based on the value of the property increases, called a step-up lease, the increases might come at specified intervals or after periodic events, such as an appraisal of the property.

If the rent increase is based on percentage increases of the landlord's operating expenses, it might stipulate that the landlord is responsible for providing each tenant with an audited statement of the operating expenses incurred by the property as proof of the increase.

The graduated lease can be an advantage to both the tenant and the landlord. It allows newer tenants to get established without incurring large rental expenses in the beginning, and it may let a landlord fill a vacancy he might not otherwise fill at a higher rate. It's also an effective marketing tool for the landlord while providing a hedge against inflation.

Percentage Leases

In a percentage lease, which is typically used in retail and restaurants, the landlord and the tenant agree that the rent payment includes a specific percentage of the gross sales or gross revenues the tenant brings in.

The landlord and tenant define gross revenue, or gross sales, as a clause in the lease. For example, a grocery store might have sales of groceries off the shelf and also sales of food from the deli department. The landlord and tenant may agree on a percentage of the sale of groceries to determine the rent, which may not include the sales of premade sandwiches and such from the deli department. Furthermore, items like floral, magazines, lottery tickets, alcohol, etc., may not count as groceries. The definition of gross sales is important because it directly affects the tenant's rent payment and, therefore, the landlord's actual gross income from the property.

In addition, the tenant may have a policy of selling merchandise to employees at cost or a substantial discount. The tenant wants these sales excluded from the calculation of gross sales because the tenant makes little or no profit on them. If the landlord agrees, the lease may exclude these sales.

The commercial establishment's gross sales are probably related to the hours and the days the store is open, so the tenant and the landlord might agree to a schedule of dates and times during which the tenant will conduct business. In seasonal businesses, the landlord and the tenant could agree to special rent payment provisions that would apply while the business is closed or during the slow time of year. The agreement might provide for a small fixed sum to defray expenses when the business is not in operation yet the tenant still occupies the property.

Under a percentage lease, the landlord shares in both the good times and the bad times of the tenant's business. Consequently, some provisions, with some variations, may appear in a percentage lease to protect the landlord from the bad times. One provision may be requiring the tenant to pay a guaranteed fixed minimum rent, called a base. This protects the landlord from collecting no rental income due to a tenant having minimal or no sales. In effect, this protects the landlord's downside in a percentage lease.

In addition to that provision for a base, another provision might require the tenant to pay a "base plus a percentage of the sales." Due to the inclusion of a base amount of rent, there's typically a floor below which no percentage is due to the landlord. The base would presumably be the portion that would be covering the amount below the floor but is always required, even in years of slow sales.

A third version of this provision might be a "base or a percentage, whichever is the greater of the two." This would allow for no floor, but rather pay a percentage of all sales applicable to the lease definition.

For example, a tenant signs a lease for a commercial space under a percentage lease that states a base of $5,000 per month plus 4 percent of sales over $1 million (the floor) in gross revenue. If the sales were $1.7 million that year, the rent would be calculated as follows: The sales, $1,700,000, minus the floor, $1,000,000, would equal $700,000, called the overage. The percentage would be 4 percent of the overage, or $28,000. This is an annual rent; therefore, that would be equal to approximately $2,333 per month. Add that to the base, $5,000 per month, and you arrive at a $7,333 per month rent.

Using the same info as in the preceding example, now let's assume the lease states "a base of $5,000 per month or 4 percent of gross revenue." In this variation, there's no floor and a percentage is calculated on all sales. Of course, only the sales that count and are memorialized in the lease are applicable. The percentage portion would be calculated as 4 percent of the total $1,700,000, or $68,000 annual rent, which is $5,666 per month. Because the percentage is greater than the base, the monthly rent would be $5,666, not $5,000.

Another provision in the percentage lease is called the recapture clause. This enables the landlord to regain the property and find another tenant whose business may be more successful if, for example, the original tenant has paid only the minimum rent for a predetermined amount of time such as 2 consecutive years. The exact percentage applied to the tenant's gross sales to calculate that part of the rent is a point of negotiation, with the tenant desiring the lowest possible rate and the landlord wanting the highest rate.

REALTOR WARNING

In some states, Indiana for example, licensed agents work under a unified license. This means the same license that allows for brokerage activities, i.e. buying and selling, also grants permission to lease property for clients. In other states, a special license may be required to lease property.

Other Types of Leases

Unlimited lease combinations can be used between a landlord and a tenant. If the lease follows all the required rules of a contract and both parties agree, anything could be within the realm of possibility. The landlord and tenant could split bills in some manner, for example, or the landlord could pay a fixed amount of the bills, such as the first $500, and any amount over is paid by the tenant.

Or a tenant may be required to pay a portion of the landlord's bills in pro rata fashion to the amount of space he uses compared to other tenants. In another case, one tenant may be exempt from a bill, while other tenants may be required to pay for it. For example, the maintenance of an elevator may exclude all tenants on the first floor.

Evictions

A state's legal eviction procedures apply regardless of what a tenant has done or how a tenant behaves. Even if the tenant has not paid rent, has destroyed property, or has violated a term in the lease or rental agreement, a landlord may only legally remove the tenant by following state eviction procedures.

A self-help, or *distraint,* eviction occurs when a landlord retakes possession of a property without using the eviction process. The use of self-help may amount to landlord harassment. Nearly every state prohibits a landlord from using self-help to evict a tenant.

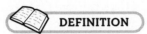

DEFINITION

Distraint is the seizure of someone's property to obtain payment of rent or other money owed.

Instead of using landlord harassment and other illegal means to force a tenant to vacate a rental property, a landlord must follow applicable state laws when evicting a tenant. Although it may take longer and cost more money, it could protect a landlord from hefty fines.

Eviction Notice Requirements

The initial step for eviction is a landlord serving an eviction notice to the tenant. An eviction notice is not the eviction itself. When a tenant is served with an eviction notice, he or she still has rights and options. An eviction notice is meant to inform the tenant that a legal process of eviction is about to begin if the landlord grievance cannot be resolved.

If the eviction is not based on a grievance, there's generally a much longer deadline to respond. In some states it could be up to 30 to 60 days versus 3 to 5 days for an issue-specific notice, like nonpayment of rent. In some cases, if the grievance is satisfied, such as paying the back rent, the landlord can stay, or stop, the eviction process immediately.

In any state, to be considered valid, an eviction notice must provide all the information a tenant may need to understand the landlord's reason for eviction, along with all the information needed to respond within the required time frame. Legal eviction processes begin only if a tenant doesn't use that information and respond appropriately before the deadline. The state courts determine what kind of information is necessary and how it must be presented.

A landlord's exact grievance must be stated on the eviction notice itself, along with instructions on how to fix the problem within the time limit. Often, landlord's issues involve accusations of a tenant breaking terms of the lease, such as failing to pay rent, disturbing neighbors, engaging in illegal activity, etc.

A notice of eviction is much like any other notice. If it or its method of delivery is invalid or defective in any way, it must be filed again by the landlord. At a minimum, this can provide the tenant with another week or two to work through a solution.

 HELPFUL HINT

Constructive eviction is a process by which the tenant evicts themselves due to a landlord failing to make a major repair to the property. However, the key to constructive eviction is the property must become uninhabitable due to the failure to repair it.

The typical 10-day eviction notice, as the name indicates, requires a response within 10 days of receiving it. It will indicate, at the beginning of the notice, the exact time frames and deadlines to respond and will never be upheld in court if a notice did not clearly communicate them to the tenant.

Types of Eviction Notices

It's important to note that the following types of notices are reasons for receiving a notice, not reasons for being evicted:

Notice to pay rent or quit   If a tenant doesn't pay rent when it's due, a landlord can serve a notice, giving the tenant some time, typically 3 to 5 days, to pay the amount owed plus any associated late fees, or move out.

Notice to correct a violation of the lease or quit   In most states, a landlord can give a tenant a notice to fix some violation of their rental agreement, such as a violation of zoning laws, an illegal pet, etc.

Notice to quit   In some states, a landlord may give a notice for a tenant to move without any possibility of correcting something. For example, a tenant is who is repeatedly late with the rent, causes damage to the rental property, threatens the health or safety of the property or other tenants, sells drugs on the property, etc., might warrant a notice to quit.

30-day or 60-day notices   In most states, a landlord can give an eviction notice for a tenant to move without giving any reason. The time allowed under most state laws for such a notice is usually 30 or 60 days, but it may be as short as 20 days or as long as 90 days. The landlord can't give such a notice for reasons of discrimination or as retaliation against a tenant.

If the tenant fails to cure the violation or refuses to vacate the premises within the specified time, the landlord must file an unlawful detainer action to have the tenant lawfully removed. The landlord must file a "complaint" with the small claims court in the county or township the property is located within. A complaint contains the facts that justify the eviction and may contain a request for back rent and damages. The landlord must serve the tenant with the complaint, along with a summons, which is the document informing the tenant of the lawsuit.

HELPFUL HINT

Many leases favor the landlord rather than the tenant because a landlord is in the business of renting property over a span of years, while most tenants only rent either sporadically or for a few times in their life. Therefore, many states have adopted the Uniform Residential Landlord and Tenant Act (URLTA) to help guard tenants against unlawful, irregular, or abusive practices. ULTRA was created in 1972 by the National Conference of Commissioners on Uniform State Laws in the United States to govern residential landlord and tenant interactions.

If the tenant does not respond to the complaint, a default judgment is issued for the landlord. If the tenant does respond with an answer but the court rules in favor of the landlord, that judgment entitles the landlord to possession of the property. A writ for possession will be served to the tenant.

Even though the landlord is entitled to repossess the property, the landlord cannot remove the tenant without the assistance of a law enforcement officer. When an officer, typically a marshal or a sheriff, receives the judgment and a fee, he or she will notify the tenant of the lawful eviction and the number of days the tenant has to move. If the tenant fails to vacate the property within the time specified, the law enforcement official may physically remove the tenant.

The Least You Need to Know

- Although leasing and renting are different concepts, leasing is a form of a rental agreement.
- A leasehold estate is for a determinable amount of time.
- A lease is comprised of many separate lease clauses that define the tenant's right of control.
- An assignment and sublease are different in respect to the contractual obligations between the parties.
- Commercial leases have many variations, including gross leases, net leases, percentage leases, and graduated leases.
- Eviction of a tenant must be handled through the court system and not via self-help by the landlord.

Land Use Regulations

Land use controls have been a part of Western civilization since 450 B.C.E., when the Roman Empire promulgated regulations concerning setback lines of buildings from boundaries and distances between trees and boundaries.

In this chapter, we will discuss the role the government has in the control of land owners' property and why they need that control. The history of the rules and regulations to maintain that control will also be covered in this chapter. The world is comprised of billions of acres of land. The environment surrounding that land is crucial to the balance of our ecosystem; we will discuss the laws to preserve our environment and how the government plays a role in maintaining it as well.

In This Chapter

- Governmental rules and regulations in real estate
- Environmental issues in residential real estate
- A look at homeowner associations

Government Rules and Regulations

Regulations on the use of land existed in colonial America, but the demand for public regulation of real estate development did not become significant until the twentieth century. As the United States shifted from a rural to an urban society, city governments sought to gain control over the location of industry, commerce, and housing. New York City adopted the first comprehensive zoning ordinance in 1916. By the 1930s zoning laws had been adopted in most urban areas.

The development of master plans and zoning regulations have become an accepted part of urban life. Following World War II, housing patterns shifted from the inner city to suburbia. The suburbanization of the United States led to the creation of discrete housing developments. Growing suburban communities began imposing regulations on the amount and type of housing that would be allowed within their municipal boundaries. Beginning in the 1970s, as urban sprawl created problems that crossed municipal borders, attention turned to regional planning. Concerns about the environment and historic preservation led to further regulation of land use. Federal, state, and local governments, to varying degrees, regulate growth and development through statutory law.

Nevertheless, many controls on land stem from actions of private developers and government units. The use of land can be affected by judicial determinations that frequently arise in either suits brought by one neighbor against another, suits brought by a public official against a neighboring landowner on behalf of the public at large, or suits involving individuals who share ownership of a parcel of land.

Comprehensive Plans

Usage regulation begins with a planning process that ultimately results in a master plan, called a *comprehensive plan*. The comprehensive plan is not a regulatory document or law, but rather a guide to direct the future growth of a town or municipality. The planning commission is the governing body of the master plan as well as the creator. However, the city government, most often a city council, must approve the plan and will call for regular revisions, updates, and reviews for efficacy.

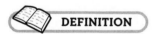 **DEFINITION**

> A **comprehensive plan** is a general guide to the location, character, and extent of proposed or anticipated land use, including public facilities. It provides guidance for land use development.

The comprehensive plan controls the following elements:

Housing   To promote an adequate housing supply that meets existing and forecasted housing demand at local levels.

Transportation   To promote the future development of various modes of transportation, including highways, transit, transportation systems, railroads, air transportation, trucking, water transportation, etc.

Utilities   To promote the future development of utilities and community facilities in the local governmental unit, such as sanitary sewer service, recycling facilities, parks, police, fire and rescue facilities, libraries, schools, and other governmental facilities.

Natural resources   To promote the conservation and promotion of effective management of natural resources such as groundwater, forests, productive agricultural areas, environmentally sensitive areas, etc.

Economic development   To promote the stabilization, retention, or expansion of the economic base and quality employment opportunities.

Land use   To promote the future development and redevelopment of public and private property.

Implementation   To promote that a compilation of programs and specific actions be completed in a stated sequence, including proposed changes to any applicable zoning ordinances, official maps, or subdivision ordinances, to implement official objectives, policies, plans, and programs.

These ordinances involve the exercise of the municipality's police power through zoning, regulation of subdivision developments, street plans, plans for public facilities, and building regulations.

Subdivision Plans

Land developers must create a subdivision plan in accordance with the comprehensive plan. The subdivision plan considers the location and type of activities occurring on the land along with the design and type of physical structures and facilities serving these activities.

Long-range projections of population and employment trends are considered, and the planning process is designed to enable a locality to plan for the construction of schools, streets, water and sewage facilities, fire and police protection, and other public amenities. The private use of land is controlled by zoning and subdivision ordinances enacted in compliance with the plan.

Regional Plans

Since the 1970s, more emphasis has been placed on regional and statewide planning. These planning initiatives often have been based on environmental concerns.

Regional planning has become attractive to urban areas that cross state lines as well. Instead of dealing with two or three competing and conflicting local plans, neighboring municipalities can refer to a regional plan that offers one comprehensive vision and one set of regulations.

Environmental Rules in Real Estate

Whether buying or selling residential or commercial real estate, all parties involved need to be aware of potential environmental issues. Environmental problems with real estate can greatly reduce the value or even render a property completely worthless. Also, if contaminated property is purchased, the buyer may be liable for cleanup costs that adhere to stringent governmental rules and regulations, even though he didn't cause or contribute to the problem.

Before making an offer on real estate, a potential buyer should ask the seller as well as any real estate professionals involved whether they are aware of environmental problems on the property. A buyer could ask the seller for a completed environmental study of the property for sale, called a phase I. A phase I is a desk audit of the property checking the property's historical uses. At the conclusion of the phase I, the company that completed the study either may seek a phase II, which is an invasive, in-ground drilling for contamination, or waive the requirement for a phase II.

A seller may not be under any obligation to volunteer information about environmental problems but, if asked, he is required to answer truthfully. If the seller does not answer truthfully and a problem is found, he can be charged with fraud. As a real estate professional, you can be liable as well and potentially charged with *negligent misrepresentation.*

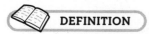 **DEFINITION**

> **Negligent misrepresentation** generally occurs when someone, such as a real estate professional, makes a statement they "should have known" was not true.

If the answer is "yes" to the environmental problems question, the buyer should seek further outside professionals to asses any environmental issues. Even if the seller has no knowledge of any issues, there may still be problems that he is unaware of, so additional precautions should be taken.

Lead-Based Paint

Lead-based paints were commonly used in the United States until the 1970s, when the lead in the paint was discovered to pose serious health risks. As of the writing of this book (late 2016), lead-based paint remains in about 24 million housing units, according to the Centers for Disease Control and Prevention. In 1977, the Consumer Product Safety Commission banned the use of lead in paint. Because of this, all residential properties built before 1978 require a Lead Based Paint Disclosure mandated by the federal government.

The lead in lead-based paint is highly toxic and has been found to cause many health issues, especially in children. When ingested or absorbed into the body, lead exposure can cause brain damage as well as kidney, nerve, and blood issues. Lead also is linked to behavioral problems, learning disabilities, seizures, and death in children and infants. You can learn more about both the dangers of lead as well as ways you can help protect your family from lead in the informational brochure, "Protect Your Family from Lead in Your Home," available at fsa.usda.gov/Internet/FSA_File/pfflinyhbrochure.pdf.

As required by federal law and all states, the form all real estate professionals use to require sellers to disclose any knowledge or records regarding lead-based paint in the property is called Disclosure of Information on Lead-Based Paint and/or Lead-Based Paint Hazards. Most people simply call it the Lead-Based Paint Disclosure. It's available at epa.gov/sites/production/files/documents/lesr_eng.pdf.

Basically, this form explains the seller's knowledge, or absence of knowledge, about lead paint in the house. Furthermore, the seller must submit any records they have of lead-based paint in their possession.

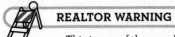

REALTOR WARNING

This is one of the very few forms where agents will actually sign their names stating that they did explain the responsibilities to their client.

The Lead-Based Paint Disclosure form is rather simple but carries with it a lot of weight and responsibility. Failure to properly disclose lead-based paint hazards can come at a hefty price because it's a federal law and required on most real estate transactions.

There are only a few times when this form is not required:

- With housing units constructed after 1978.

- When emergency repairs to the property are being performed to safeguard against imminent danger to human life, health, or safety, or to protect the property from further structural damage due to natural disaster, fire, or structural collapse. The exemption applies only to repairs necessary to respond to the emergency.

- When the property won't be used for human residential habitation. This doesn't apply to common areas such as hallways and stairways of residential and mixed-use properties.

- In housing exclusively for the elderly or persons with disabilities, with the provision that children younger than 6 years of age won't reside in the dwelling unit.

- When an inspection performed per the U.S. Department of Housing and Urban Development (HUD) standards finds the property contains no lead-based paint.

- When, based on documented methodologies, lead-based paint has been identified and removed and the property has achieved clearance.

- When the rehabilitation won't disturb any painted surfaces.

- When the property has no bedrooms.

- When the property is currently vacant and will remain vacant until demolition.

If you're buying or selling a home built before 1978, you need to utilize this form and be sure you disclose any knowledge you might have about lead-based paint or lead-based paint hazards in the home.

You may need to inspect a house for possible lead-based paint contamination. There are two acceptable methods: paint examination, in which you take samples of paint chips from each room and have them tested by a certified environmental laboratory, and risk assessment, in which you identify any suspect areas where paint is peeling or chipping away or lead dust may have accumulated. If found, assume the worst and remediate appropriately.

If a house has been determined to contain lead-based paint. Complete *encapsulation* is the preferred method of remediation. The removal via scraping is not a suggested nor encouraged method because the debris and air particles the activity may create. In encapsulation, a barrier is formed using a liquid-applied coating, called an encapsulant, or an adhesively bonded covering material. The encapsulant also may be attached to a surface using mechanical fasteners, the primary means of attachment for an encapsulant is bonding the product to the surface, either by itself or using an adhesive.

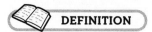 **DEFINITION**

> **Encapsulation** is the process that makes lead-based paint inaccessible by providing a barrier between the lead-based paint and the environment.

Asbestos

Asbestos is a mineral fiber that can be positively identified only with a special type of microscope. Several types of asbestos fibers exist.

Houses built before 1975 often contain asbestos insulation around heating systems, in ceilings, and in many other areas. Until 1981, asbestos was used in many other building materials, such as vinyl floors and tile, to strengthen them and provide heat insulation and fire resistance. Asbestos as a building material made sense before it was discovered to cause health problems. It was heat and fire resistant, and the glues that contained asbestos worked exceptionally well.

When buying or selling a home, people frequently have questions regarding asbestos containing materials (ACMs) that may present within their home or one they may buy. Currently, there are no federal disclosures regarding asbestos and, therefore, no prohibition on the sale of a property that contains asbestos.

If you own a home or are buying one you believe has ACMs and some of the ACMs are damaged, or if you plan on removing the ACMs during renovation, please seek professional help or guidance. Asbestos building materials may be considered damaged if they are worn, peeling, cracking, crumbling, or in an otherwise deteriorated condition. *Friable* ACMs are of greater exposure risk than nonfriable ACMs.

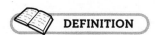 **DEFINITION**

> **Friable** is any material that, when dry, can be crumbled, pulverized, or reduced to powder by hand pressure.

Exposure to asbestos has been clearly linked to an increased risk of cancer, particularly for workers in the asbestos manufacturing industry or in construction jobs. Recognizing the health dangers of asbestos, the U.S. Occupational Safety and Health Administration (OSHA) sets standards for the testing, maintenance, and disclosure of asbestos in the workplace. These regulations do not cover residential homes, but many states require that sellers disclose information on asbestos on the disclosure forms they provide buyers about other potential issues, like leaky roofs, heating problems, and environmental hazards like lead or mold.

HELPFUL HINT

There is no federal requirement for disclosure of asbestos. However, some states have added a specific asbestos disclosure for real estate transactions. All states use some form of property hazard disclosure, which would inherently require the disclosure of asbestos.

If a state requires disclosure of asbestos within a property and the seller or his agent knows about the ACM but doesn't disclose that information, they could be liable to the buyer for damages suffered, such as lung and other health-related problems due to asbestos fiber inhalation.

If there is concern that a property has ACM that is, or may become, airborne for any reason, a trained and accredited asbestos professional should be hired to assess the situation. Encapsulation is the recommended method to reduce or eliminate exposure to asbestos fibers. If removal is necessary, only trained asbestos removal specialists should be involved. They'll ensure the debris is legally disposed of in approved hazardous waste disposal sites.

If you are planning any house remodeling in an area you suspect contains asbestos material, be sure to find out if that's the case before you start the demolition process. If you come across undamaged material that you know or suspect contains asbestos, it's best to leave it alone and monitor it for signs of damage that may release asbestos fibers. Also, limit access, especially by children, to that area.

HELPFUL HINT

Like lead-based paint, encapsulation, is the preferred method to remediate asbestos. Simply applying a new covering over the old without moving the original asbestos is accepted as common practice in today's safety-conscious world.

Water

The Safe Drinking Water Act (SDWA) of 1974 and its amendments have established a basic framework for protecting the drinking water used by public water systems in the United States. This law contains requirements for ensuring the safety of the nation's public drinking water supplies, which include water systems that regularly serve 25 or more people per day or that have at least 15 service connections.

The U.S. Environmental Protection Agency (EPA) sets national standards for drinking water to protect against health risks, considering available technology and cost. Each standard also includes monitoring and reporting requirements.

Other environmental laws help protect drinking water, including the Clean Water Act (CWA). The CWA recommends states designate surface waters used for drinking water and develop water quality standards for those waters. The act also establishes programs to prevent the release of pollution to these waters.

Hazardous Substances

Laws regulating the use, transport, storage, release, and generation of hazardous waste include the Comprehensive Environmental Response, Compensation, and Liability Act of 1980 (CERCLA), or commonly known as Superfund; the Superfund Amendments and Reauthorization Act (SARA); and the Resource Conservation and Recovery Act (RCRA).

CERCLA was enacted in response to concerns about the release of hazardous substances, except oil and gas, from abandoned waste sites. It requires the potential responsible parties (PRPs) to pay for or conduct cleanup and remediation at the sites. CERCLA created three liabilities to help identify the PRPs:

Strict   This idea is that if you owned the land, you caused the problem.

Joint and severable   This basically states that the government can bring court action against one party or all parties to recover damages.

Retroactive   This says liability can be determined historically. If you ever owned the property, you can be named as a PRP.

CERCLA was amended by SARA in 1986. SARA contributed $8.5 billion to Superfund. However, during the reauthorization process, SARA required one stipulation be added to the CERCLA liabilities clause. SARA created the innocent landowner defense, which provides a defense against liability of hazardous contamination an innocent landowner did not know or had no reason to know about before purchasing the property. It was modified by the 2002 amendments. Eligible landowners have the burden of proof for the innocent landowner defenses.

Homeowner Associations (HOAs)

Almost 12 percent of the U.S. population lives in planned communities, including townhouses, condominiums, co-ops, and entire real estate developments containing single-family homes. A common feature of all planned communities is a homeowner association (HOA), which oversees the maintenance and administration of the real estate, especially the common areas shared by all owners. A board of directors of the association, elected by the property owners, enforces the community's rules.

Planned communities often impose many restrictions on their members. These are typically contained in the real estate deed, which becomes a contract between the property buyer and the community. Purchasers are bound by these restrictions whether or not they read or understand them.

The restrictions may cover a wide range of architectural and aesthetic limitations and are believed to increase the value of property in the community. Unwary residents may find the limitations extreme. Residents of planned communities have faced limitations on things such as paint colors, pets, sports and sporting equipment, and outdoor decorations. Under such restrictions, homeowners have been threatened with fines, taken to court, and prohibited from activities.

Association dues can be used to pay for a lawsuit enforcing a restriction, and some bylaws require the defendant homeowner to reimburse the association's legal fees.

The more people live in neighborhoods with HOAs, the more likely they will encounter some disputes between the HOA and individual homeowners. For example, HOAs are required to keep a certain amount of cash in reserves for unexpected expenditures. If an HOA's cash balance falls below a certain level, it may raise the monthly HOA dues to cover the shortfall. But homeowners may balk at the rate hike, blaming the HOA for mismanaging the funds.

Most disputes between homeowners and their associations are simple misunderstandings cleared up easily and within a short period of time. However, some situations are considerably more serious and prove to be a battle between the two sides. Residents even have been sued by their HOAs for building the wrong type of fence, allowing on-street parking overnight, or even the wrong colored front door.

HOAs have broad powers, the main source of which derives from the community's covenants, conditions, and restrictions (CCRs). The community bylaws, architectural rules, and other community rules adopted by the board of directors are other sources of power. HOAs can restrict land usage through architectural guidelines, impose fines for violations, record liens on members' homes for unpaid assessments, and sue members to enforce rules.

Lawsuits against an HOA should be viewed only as a homeowners' final option if all other efforts have failed. The best method for avoiding HOA lawsuits is usually for the opposing parties to simply meet face to face and attempt to work out a compromise. Sometimes it may be in the homeowner's best interest to comply with an unreasonable HOA demand. If all other efforts fail, a lawsuit may become the best option; however, a homeowner should meet with a licensed attorney experienced in HOA disputes to discuss all available options.

 HELPFUL HINT

As mentioned earlier, the doctrine of laches is an equitable defense that seeks to prevent a party from ambushing someone else by failing to make a legal claim in a timely manner. For example, if a homeowner builds a deck without the permission of the HOA, it's assumed to violate the rules. After a prescribed amount of time—in most cases 3 to 5 years—the HOA has lost the right to file a suit, issue a grievance, or asses a fine to you under the doctrine of laches.

The Least You Need to Know

- The comprehensive plan is the guide to aid in a city's growth and controls how a city uses its natural resources, land, and people to achieve its goals.
- Every house bought, sold, or built before 1978 must be accompanied by the Disclosure of Information on Lead-Based Paint and/or Lead-Based Paint Hazards.
- CERCLA was created to handle hazardous waste issues in abandoned industrial sites.
- HOAs have the power to fine homeowners as well as levy liens for violation of the rules and regulations.

Evaluation and Financing

Understanding financing and being able to explain it to your client in simple, easy-to-understand language will gain you a client for life. Many people fail to understand financing and look to you as their advisers to explain the types of loans and the nuances associated with each one.

Guiding your client to the right loan product may mean the difference in being able to buy or not. It is a paramount issue for you as a real estate professional to keep current on changes and modifications to loan products and new loans that may be available.

Appraisals

Prior to the 1990s, no commonly accepted standards existed for either appraisal quality or appraiser licensure. In the 1980s, an ad hoc committee representing various professional appraisal organizations in the United States and Canada met to codify the best practices into what became known as the Uniform Standards of Professional Appraisal Practice (USPAP). As a result, all real estate appraisers must be state-licensed and certified today.

The Financial Institutions Reform, Recovery, and Enforcement Act of 1989 (FIRREA) demanded all states develop a system for licensing and certifying real estate appraisers. The practice of appraising is regulated by each state, but the federal government regulates appraisers indirectly. Should it find that a state's appraiser regulation and certification program is inadequate, then under federal regulations, all appraisers in that state would no longer be eligible to conduct appraisals for federally chartered banks. Also, all state and federal courts have adopted USPAP for real estate litigation.

In this chapter, we will cover the methodology of how an appraiser completes an appraisal and the techniques used to arrive at a value. We will talk about the three types of appraisals and when to use each one based upon the property type. We'll discuss the difference between the REALTOR's competitive market analysis and the appraisal. Finally, we will explain the mathematical process used by appraisers to arrive at a property's value.

In This Chapter

- A look at appraisers and appraisals
- The different types of appraisals and when they're used
- Understanding the competitive market analysis
- How appraisers determine value
- Mathematical concepts used in appraisals

The Importance of Real Estate Appraisals

Before you buy real estate, it's important to get an *appraisal* of the property. This evaluation verifies, to you and your lender, that the property is worth at least the amount that you want to borrow to pay for it. A real estate appraisal is an expert opinion put together by an educated and qualified person, an *appraiser,* trained in the methods of determining the value of real estate.

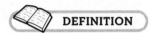 **DEFINITION**

An **appraisal** is a valuation of real property. An **appraiser** is a person trained in the techniques used to determine the appraisal.

The appraisal process is a series of steps that must be followed to ensure the correct answer is determined. The appraiser uses various types of data in these steps. Most commonly the data is of two types: general and specific. General data regards the neighborhood, the market in general, crime statistics, and overall information regarding the property's surroundings. Specific data focuses on the subject property, the house being evaluated, and all the specific information about the target property used to determine its value.

Every property differs in location, size, shape, use, etc.; however, all appraisals are performed in the same manner—through the systematic application of the valuation process. In the valuation process, the problem is identified; the work necessary to solve the problem is planned; and relevant data is collected, verified, and analyzed to form an opinion of value.

The steps in the valuation process could depend on the nature of the appraisal and the data available. But in all cases, the same basic steps are followed:

1. Identify the problem

2. Determine the scope of the work

3. Collect the necessary data and property description

4. Analyze the data

5. Determine a site value opinion

6. Apply the approaches to value

7. Reconcile the value

8. Report the defined value

The first step in the valuation process is to identify the problem. In this step the appraiser identifies the following:

• The client

• The intended users of the appraisal

• The intended use of the appraisal

- The purpose of the assignment

- The effective date of the opinion

- The relevant property characteristics

- The assignment conditions

Next the appraiser determines the amount and type of information he or she will need to research and analyze for the assignment. The scope of work must be clearly disclosed in the appraisal report.

From there, the appraiser gathers data. He or she collects general data related to property values in an area and specific data about the property being appraised, the subject property, and the data of the comparable properties that have been sold or leased in the local market.

The general data is then evaluated regarding the national, regional, and local trends. Supply and demand data is studied to understand the competitive position of the property. Data analysis of specific data, such as properties similar to the subject property, helps the appraiser find sale prices, incomes and expenses, capitalization rates, construction costs, economic life, and rates of depreciation. These figures are used in the calculations that result in the valuation of the subject property.

Highest and best use is a critical step in the development of a market value opinion. In highest and best use analysis, the appraiser considers the use of the land as though it were vacant and the use of the property as it is improved. The highest and best use must satisfy four criteria: it must be legally permissible, such as zoning laws; it must be physically possible, such as lot dimensions; it must be financially feasible, such as cost to build in the area; and it must be maximally productive and make sense in an area. A market analysis provides the basis for an appraiser's decisions about the highest and best use of a subject property.

 **DEFINITION**

Highest and best use is the most reasonable, probable, and legal use of a piece of improved or unimproved real property possible.

A site value opinion is determined by a variety of methods derived from the three approaches to value: a sales comparison, or a value based on the sales of other homes; a cost approach, or a value based on the cost to build other homes; and an income approach, or a value based on the income the property generates. (These are discussed in depth later in the chapter.)

Next, the appraiser begins to apply one or more of the three approaches to value and form an opinion of property value. The method used to create this opinion depends on the type of property as well as the intended use of the appraisal and the quality and quantity of the data available.

During the reconciliation of value step, the appraiser analyzes alternative answers and chooses a final opinion based on the values from among two or more indications of value. After making a thorough review of the entire valuation process, he or she makes a *reconciliation* of the results. The appraiser draws on his or her experience, expertise, and professional judgment to resolve differences among the values derived from each of three approaches.

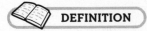 **DEFINITION**

Reconciliation is the process by which the appraiser evaluates, chooses, and selects from among alternative results to reach a final value estimate.

The appraiser determines a weight, or probability, of each answer as to the possibility of use based on the data collected. For example, when appraising a single-family home, the appraiser may calculate the values using all three methods, but during the reconciliation process, he or she may determine the probability of the income approach to be low because the property won't be used as a rental property.

An appraisal assignment is not completed until the conclusions and findings have been stated in a report and communicated to the client. The report of defined value will vary in type, format, length, and contents depending on the client's requirements and the scope of work criteria.

The USPAP has specific requirements for appraisal reports, which may be presented in one of three written formats: self-contained reports, summary reports, and restricted-use reports. A self-contained report fully describes the data and analyses used in the assignment as well as the comprehensive information contained within the report itself. A summary appraisal report summarizes the data used in the assignment. A restricted-use appraisal report only states the conclusions of the appraisal. This type of report may be provided when the client is the sole user of the report.

When circumstances permit, the appraisal also may be communicated by means of an oral report.

Who Do Appraisers Work For?

Many people believe the appraiser works for the buyer, but that's a misconception. Actually, the appraiser is hired by the lending institution to protect its interest in the real property. The lending institution hires the appraiser to determine a value of the real property to verify that it will be sufficient collateral for the loan it's being asked to make to the borrower.

Think of it like this: if you, the lender, were asked to loan a friend $10 to buy something, you might ask for some collateral to secure that loan. If your friend offered a pencil for collateral, you would hire a pencil expert—in this analogy the appraiser—to tell you the value of the pencil. If that expert determines the value of the pencil to be $10, or hopefully greater, you would make the loan to your friend and accept the pencil as collateral. If the value of the pencil is less than the amount your friend is requesting, you'd put yourself at risk loaning him the money due to insufficient collateral.

This is exactly how the lender protects himself when hiring an appraiser to determine the value of real property when the borrower requests a loan.

Determining Value

Value of real property is very subjective and is influenced by factors like demand, scarcity, utility, and transferability.

The demand for a property can drive its value upward compared to a property that has little or no demand. Scarcity also can tie into this definition because it can be similar in nature to demand when it comes to determining the value.

Imagine a piece of real property on an exclusive, high-end lake going for sale—say one of the 50 lakefront lots around the lake. The demand for that property will affect the value, and it will sell for a premium. The fact that there are a very limited number of parcels on that lake, or scarcity, ensures the property commands a premium. Contrast that with millions of acres of farmland, which are neither scarce nor in high demand (relatively speaking) and, therefore, won't command the same value per acre as the lakefront property.

Utility, or the manner in which the property could be used, is another factor that creates or drives value in a property. If a residential property is listed for sale but can be converted to commercial due to its location and surrounding growth of the city, it potentially will have more buyers and create more value to the owner when selling.

Finally, if a property can be transferred easily between buyer and seller, the value can be increased. For example, a property that's *free and clear* can be transferred easier than a property that has a mortgage. Likewise, a commercial piece of real estate that has some environmental issues with cleanup costs in the millions of dollars may have no value at all.

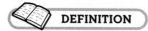 **DEFINITION**

> A **free-and-clear** property is one with no money encumbrances, or liens, placed on it.

Understanding Market Value

Market value is the most common value appraisers estimate; at least 90 percent of all appraisals address market value. Although the exact definition of market value has changed over the years, it has become more standardized recently.

The most widely accepted definition of market value is from USPAP: "The most probable price which a property should bring in a competitive and open market using cash, or its equivalent, in an arm's length transaction between a knowledgeable buyer and seller, each acting prudently, and assuming the price is not affected by undue pressure." In some states, the definition of market value may vary slightly from USPAP's. In these instances, the appraiser should state his version of the definition and be sure his value is consistent with the definition he defined in his report.

 HELPFUL HINT

> Market price is what the property actually sells for and is determined by negotiation between the seller and buyer. If an agent can get market value to equal market price, it is called a sale.

There are many ways in which to express value.

The principle of anticipation states that value is simply a function of the present worth of future benefits—that is, people are paying current dollars for future benefits. The principle of anticipation is the basis for the income approach. Under this principle, the past values are only important because they tend to predict future values. A buyer for a home might look at current house values of a neighborhood, and through the principle of anticipation, he may determine the future value of the property. Furthermore, using this past information gives the buyer insight as to what to pay for the property today.

The principle of balance relates one property to the other properties in the neighborhood. For example, if a builder builds houses in a neighborhood of 1,500- to 2,000-square-foot homes priced from $100,000 to $120,000, then using the principle of balance, the builder would expect to receive a higher value for a larger home.

The principle of change claims that as time and market conditions change, so do supply and demand for real estate, and so does the value of real estate. Under the principle of change, value changes as surrounding factors change, either up or down.

The principle of conformity, like the principle of balance, relates to real estate characteristics and the surrounding properties. It holds that maximum value is achieved and maintained when there's reasonable conformity among properties. Basically, the more a property conforms to the surrounding properties, the more value can be expected. Under the principle of conformity, a residential house that does not conform to the surrounding commercial neighborhood is worth less due because it doesn't conform.

The principle of contribution is based on the fact that the value of a component is a function of its contribution to the whole rather than as a separate component. This means the cost of an item does not necessarily equal a contribution to value. For example, the cost of a swimming pool might not add an equal amount to the value of the overall property. Perhaps it might even detract from the cost, as an above-ground swimming pool would. In other instances, the value of an additional feature might exceed the cost of that feature. For example, energy-conserving appliances, like a water heater or solar panels.

The principle of competition holds that profits tend to spur competition. The more profitable a venture may appear, the more competition is created. Under the principle of competition, a company moving into a market increases nearby land values simply due to the fact that others will want to compete with it.

The principle of external forces states that four major forces external to the property influence value: social, economic, physical, and governmental:

Social   This includes the number of elderly people, which can cause an increase in demand for more retirement communities.

Economic   Interest rates, employee wages, financing, etc., drive the demand to live in an area.

Physical   Buyers are not willing to buy a property in poor condition when they can buy a property in good condition for the same price.

Governmental   Local and state income taxes and property taxes affect the value of real estate as do the quality of the local schools, police and fire protection, and the availability of health care.

Because value is so subjective, individual buyers' and sellers' value can be influenced by forces outside the property.

The principle of highest and best use is defined as the most suitable use that will yield the best value to the owner over a sustained period of time. Simply put, it's the most valuable use. The four standard tests for highest and best use relate to the use that is physically possible, legally permitted, financially feasible, and maximally productive.

 HELPFUL HINT

Properties are normally appraised at their highest and best use.

The principle of increasing and decreasing returns relates to the principles of balance and contribution. The concept is that too much is too much, and there's a point at which adding more has no net increase in the value. For example, adding one or maybe two yard ornaments to a yard might make the yard look nice, but adding 72 ornaments may be detrimental. At some point, "too much became too much" and the value decreased rather than increased.

The law of increasing and decreasing returns also applies to an office building placed on a parcel of land. Adding stories to the building may increase the property value … until it's tall enough that an elevator must be added. From this point, the added cost may not result in added value equal with the cost of the improvements.

The principle of opportunity costs says that money allocated to one use cannot be used for another use. For example, if a rental property earns 6 percent return, but at some later time, a better house that's earning 8 percent return is found, the opportunity cost is 2 percent, or the difference between what a person is currently earning and what the opportunity could have earned with a different allocation of funds. Typically, the risks of the different opportunities are assumed to be equal to consider a true opportunity cost. It would be difficult to measure opportunity cost between a 5 percent government-insured bond and 6 percent return generated by a 30-unit apartment building, for example.

The principle of substitution is the basis for sales comparison approach and should be used in every appraisal and every appraiser's thought process. The principle of substitution says that houses that have sold can substitute for a house currently listed if the size, location, age, and other characteristics are substantially similar. A smart buyer would pay no more for a home than it would cost him to buy another one that would substitute for it. Substitution keeps the market in balance.

Appraisal Methods

Appraisers commonly think of value in three ways:

- **The substitution method**   The value based on recent sales of comparable properties in the market.

- **The cost approach method**   The current cost of building a reproduction, or replica, property.

- **The income method**   The value based on the property's earning power in an open market.

These different viewpoints form the basis of the three approaches appraisers use to value property. One or more of these approaches may not be useful in an assignment or may be less probable due to the lack of data available.

HELPFUL HINT

Typically, an appraiser will complete all three methods of valuation and then use the answers to mathematically determine a value using reconciliation (discussed later in the chapter).

The Substitution Method

The sales comparison approach is best used for homes with a history or that can be tracked in a local multiple listing service (MLS). Furthermore, this approach is most useful when several similar properties recently have been sold in the subject property's area.

Using this approach, an appraiser develops a value by comparing the subject property with similar target properties, sometimes called comparables or comps. The sale prices of comps give the appraiser a range to base the value of the subject property on.

The appraiser estimates the degree of similarity or difference between the subject property and the comparable sales by considering various elements:

- **Location**   Geographic location: rural, urban, etc.

- **Physical characteristics**   Size, acreage, age, etc.

- **Use/zoning**   Residential versus commercial sales

- **Property rights conveyed**   Fee simple, life estate, etc.

- **Financing terms**   Cash, financing, land contract, etc.

- **Market conditions**   REO driven, crime rates, etc.

- **Seller concessions, if any**   Closing cost assistance

- **Personal property conveyed, if any**   Washer/dryer, or other

Dollar amount adjustments, either up or down, may be applied to the known sale price of each comparable property to get a range of value indications for the subject property.

Through this comparative procedure, the appraiser ultimately arrives at an opinion of value. For example, a subject property may have three bedrooms and two baths, but all the comps have 2½ bathrooms. The appraiser may shift his or her sales price downward by the value of a half bath (in this example $5,000), from $150,000 to $145,000 or whatever value he determines a half bath is worth in that specific market.

HELPFUL HINT

Knowing the market is crucial for appraisers and REALTORS alike.

The Cost Approach Method

The cost approach method is best used for new-build homes or homes that have no history in a local MLS. The cost approach is based on the understanding that value can be related to the cost to build a home. In the cost approach, the value of the land is separated from the cost of the physical structure.

There are three commonly accepted practices to determine the value of a property using the cost approach:

The square-foot method   This is the easiest of the three methods to calculate and is based on the theory that each square foot is equally responsible for the cost of the build. For example, a 1,500-square-foot house that costs $150,000 to build has a $100/square foot cost. Using that rate, the value of a similar property that's 1,200 square feet would have a value of $120,000. This method is great for production builders whose cost per square foot is virtually the same across all the properties.

The unit-in-place method   This method takes a closer look at the property and determines that the overall subject property is a group of units that can be evaluated individually against the same units in target property. For example, suppose a subject property can be broken into a group of units or subcomponents: roofing unit, flooring unit, HVAC unit, etc. A comparison then can be made between each unit of the target property to get a monetary adjustment per unit. Using the preceding example, let's say the HVAC unit is +$5,000 better, but the roofing unit is worse by $10,000. The net would be −$5,000; therefore, the property value would be $115,000 ($120,000 − $5,000). This method is good for homes where similar style and construction techniques were used, much like comparing one production builder to another.

The quantity survey method   This is the most comprehensive and complete method of estimating building costs. Using this approach, the appraiser estimates all the material costs, labor costs, overhead costs, administrative costs, and more, as well as the builder's profit, and then totals these figures to arrive at the value much the same way as in the unit-in-place method. But instead of comparing units, the appraiser compares everything used in the construction. This method requires the blueprints to complete correctly so each part can be evaluated separately, even down to the number of nails, wood framing supports, roof decking sheets, etc. This method is best used for custom home builders when it's hard to find a house within the area similar to the subject property.

The index method   The index approach is used in circumstances when the original construction cost of the existing improvements is already known. It's most frequently used in the case of unique or unusual buildings. This approach simply updates the original construction costs to today's costs using published construction cost indexes. Many companies publish this data to help appraisers and builders. To use this method, the appraiser needs to know the original construction costs of the building and the year in which it was completed. The appraiser then looks up the index value in the year of completion and at the current time. This method is best used for historic or unique buildings. For example, an appraiser is assigned a job to appraise a building built in 1950 at a cost of $50,000. Using a published index of 500 for 1950 and the current index of 2100, here are his calculations:

Original cost × $\dfrac{\text{current index}}{\text{historic index}}$ = current cost

$50,000 × $\dfrac{2,100}{500}$ = $210,000

Depreciation to the structure must be taken into account in the cost approach. Depreciation is any loss in the value of a property over time. Tax laws allow investors to depreciate the value of the improvements. This depreciation reduces their taxable income and is usually figured using the straight-line method, which assumes depreciation occurs at an even rate over the structure's economic life.

Economic life is the length of time during which a piece of property may be used, usually less than its physical life. The *effective age* is the age of a property based on its condition, not its actual age.

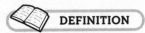 **DEFINITION**

Depreciation is a property's loss in value for any reason. The **economic life** is the lifespan a property can be used for its intended purpose. The **effective age** incorporates maintenance, or lack thereof, to make a property appear younger or older than its actual age.

For example, a property with a value of $265,000 and an economic life of 26½ years has a depreciation of $10,000 per year. The straight-line depreciation would be as follows:

$\dfrac{\text{Value}}{\text{economic life}}$ = depreciation rate

$\dfrac{\$265,000}{26.5 \text{ years}}$ = $10,000/year in depreciation

So, after 10 years (10 years × $10,000/year), the total depreciation would be $100,000 ($265,000 - $100,000 = $165,000), or the value would be $165,000.

Depreciation comes in three different types:

Physical deterioration   This is an impairment of condition and a loss in value inherent in property brought about by wear and tear, disintegration, use, and actions of the elements. It's either curable or incurable.

Functional obsolescence   This is where the property has lost value due to the reduction in functionality. For example, a house has become condemned due to disrepair over the years.

External obsolescence   This type of obsolescence occurs when some outside force affects the property. For example, if the neighborhood around the property goes downhill, the value of the property goes downhill as well.

Land value is estimated separately in the cost approach. This approach is particularly useful in valuing new or nearly new improvements and properties that are not frequently exchanged in the market.

The Income Method

In the income capitalization approach, value is measured as the present value of the property's future earning power. Income-producing properties, including residential rentals and commercial properties, are typically purchased as investments so the earning power is a critical element affecting property value.

There are two methods of valuation by using income: net income capitalization rate and some type of multiplier.

In the net income capitalization rate valuation method, the relationship between annual net income and value is reflected by a capitalization rate. The capitalization, or cap, rate is expressed as a percentage and is like a rate of return (ROR) for any investment vehicle. For example, if you bought a certificate of deposit (CD) from a bank paying 4 percent interest, the 4 percent interest paid on the investment would be a very similar analogy to a cap rate. The ratio of the net income to the cap rate determines the value of a property. Here's the equation used:

$$\frac{\text{Net income}}{\text{cap rate}} = \text{value}$$

Gross operating income (GOI) is all the income that can be generated from an investment, or income, property such as rent, late fees, parking fees, clubhouse rental, laundry machine income, etc. Sometimes, accounts may want to remove a loss and vacancy factor, typically a percentage of the GOI. For example, 5 percent loss and vacancy factor may be used when determining the true gross operating income.

Expenses are the bills that are required to operate an income property, such as payroll, lawn care, advertising, taxes, etc. Typically, this category does not include the mortgage payment. The mortgage payment, called debt service, is subtracted from the net operating income to give the cash flow of a property. Of course, this is before income taxes.

Net operating income (NOI) is the remaining money left over after expenses are removed from the GOI.

Remember these equations:

Gross operating income – expenses = net operating income

Net operating income – debt service = cash flow

Another type of valuation model is the multiplier model. This uses either the gross rents multiplier (GRM) or the gross income multiplier (GIM). The difference between the two would be the gross income number calculated to represent the income being used. GRM would solely use the rents collected from an investment property whereas the GIM would use the entire gross income—rents plus all other sources of income—as the income for the model.

Which should the appraiser use? Good question. Typically, the cap rate valuation is used in retail and office income-generating properties; however, both the GRM and GIM would be used for apartment complexes.

Making Comparisons with Comps

A comparative market analysis (CMA) or comp is prepared by a real estate broker and used to help evaluate how a seller's home compares against the other homes in the area that are or were recently on the market. The CMA takes an in-depth look at the other homes to determine the best price that will make the seller's home competitive.

The CMA includes a fact-based report of a home, including information such as square footage, number of bedrooms, number of full and half baths, size of major rooms, age of the home, property taxes, and desirable amenities.

The CMA also looks at the length of time, called *days on market,* the property has been/was on the market to help determine value.

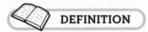 **DEFINITION**

Days on market is the total number of days a property has been listed on the MLS.

Depending on the market, a CMA covers a specific geographic range around the home, from one or two streets up to a mile away in some areas and possibly farther if the home is in a rural area. The CMA also takes into consideration a time frame, such as year.

The CMA is best described as an art and not a science. In many cases, one method is acceptable in one scenario but not in another. For example, in one situation, a property may be in a great area among similar properties, which allows for comps to be used for five or six blocks away. However, another property could be bounded in one direction by an area that may be very undesirable or crime-ridden, not allowing for any comps to be used in that direction.

Some Appraisals Math

Appraisers are often seen as the smarter big brother in the real estate world, due to the fact they do many different and varied mathematical calculations. Let's look at some appraisals math now.

Calculating Acreage and Square Footage

Many times, an appraiser must calculate the acreage of a property based on the lot size or dimensions.

Example 1: The basic area calculation is length times width. A simple lot of 210 feet by 100 feet equals an area of 21,000 square feet. Given the fact that 1 acre is 43,560 square feet (a good number to memorize given the business you're going into) this lot would contain 21,000 ÷ 43,560 or 0.48 acres of land.

Example 2: How many square feet are in 3.4 acres of land? 3.4 acres × 43,560 square feet per acre is 148,104 square feet.

Example 3: A farmer wants to sell his land for $35,000 per acre. He has it surveyed, and the land measures 1,100 feet by 5,000 feet. For how much will he list the property? 1,100 feet × 5,000 feet = 5,500,000 square feet. 5,500,000 square feet ÷ 43,500 square feet per acre = 126.262 acres of land. At $35,000 per acre, his listing price would be 126.262 acres × $35,000 per acre or $4,419,170 (rounded to nearest dollar).

Example 4: Sometimes commercial property is sold based on the front foot, which is a measure of exposure to the main road the property sits on. If a 2.75-acre property is 475 feet deep and is listed for sale at $10,000 per front foot, what's the listing price? 2.75 acres × 43,560 square feet per acre = 119,790 square feet of land. If the lot is 475 feet deep, the measure of the front foot can be determined by knowing the area of a rectangle is front foot × the depth of the property or front foot = the area ÷ depth of the property. 119,791 square feet ÷ 475 feet depth equals 252.2 front feet (rounded). If the property is listed for $10,000 per front foot × 252.2 front feet, it would be listed at $2,520,000.

Calculating Value Using Capitalization Rate

Remember, cap rate is a measure of the net income to the value of a property. With some math manipulation, you can see that value equals the cap rate ÷ net income of the property.

$$\frac{\text{Net income}}{\text{cap rate}} = \text{value}$$

Or:

$$\frac{\text{Net income}}{\text{value}} = \text{cap rate}$$

Or:

$$\text{Cap rate} \times \text{value} = \text{net income}$$

Example 1: Determine the value of a 5-unit strip center if the appraiser knows the follow facts:

Annual rents = $500 per month per unit

Annual expenses = $10,000

Cap rate = 8 percent

First, determine the annual net income of the property:

5 units × $500/unit/month × 12 months = $30,000 gross income

Net income = gross income − expenses, so $30,000 − $10,000 = $20,000 in annual net income.

$$\frac{\$20,000}{0.08} = \$250,000 \text{ value}$$

Example 2: If a property has an annual net income of $35,500 and the appraiser determines its value to be $200,000, what is the cap rate he used in the calculation?

$$\frac{\text{Net income}}{\text{value}} = \text{cap rate}$$

So:

$$\frac{\$35,500}{\$200,000} = 0.1775 \text{ or } 17.75 \text{ percent}$$

Calculating Value Using Gross Rent and Income Multipliers

Often agents will represent apartment owners as investor clients. Calculating value for apartments uses a slightly different methodology than strip malls or office buildings. Apartment value is based upon the total rent earned by each unit rather than per square foot as we discussed earlier. The gross rent multiplier (GRM) and gross income multiplier (GIM) are common measurements of value for apartments or apartment complexes.

Example 1: Using the information provided, calculate the value of the property. A 30-unit apartment complex earns monthly rental income of $450 per unit. It generates $500 in both laundry and soft drink sales per year as well as $4,500 annual income from the rental of the common area clubhouse. The appraiser knows the GRM is 75 and GIM is 65. Using each method, determine the value of the apartment complex.

GRM: 30 units × $450/unit/month × 12 months = $162,000 in gross rents per year. Using the GRM of 75, the value would be $162,000 × 75 or $12,150,000.

GIM: Gross income would equal rents plus all other income, on an annual basis. $162,000 (rental income) + $6,000 (laundry) + $6,000 (soft drinks) + $4,500 (clubhouse rental) = $178,500 annual gross income. Using a GIM of 65, the value would be $178,500 × 65 or $11,602,500.

Reconciliation

Reconciliation is the process by which an appraiser uses the probability of each type of valuation in the overall determination of the single final value.

Example 1: If an appraiser is hired to appraise a residential home in a residential neighborhood for a lender, he would complete the assignment by doing all three valuation types:

Method	Valuation
Sales comparison approach	$120,000
Cost approach	$115,000
Income approach	$125,000

Using his expertise and knowledge, the appraiser reconciles the values by assigning a probability for each occurrence:

Method	Probability
Sales comparison approach	75 percent
Cost approach	25 percent
Income approach	0 percent (not commercially zoned)

Therefore:

Method	Probability
Sales comparison approach	$120,000 × 75 percent = $90,000
Cost approach	$115,000 × 25 percent = $28,750
Income approach	$125,000 × 0 percent = $0

Using the weight, or probability, of each occurrence determines the value to be $118,750 ($90,000+$28,750+$0=$118750).

The Least You Need to Know

- A real estate appraisal is an opinion by an educated and qualified person.
- An appraiser is hired by the lending institution to protect its interest in a real estate transaction.
- Appraisers must be licensed per the FIRREA and follow best practices methodology set forth by the USPAP.
- Value of a property can be controlled by demand, utility, scarcity, and transferability of property.
- Appraisers determine the market value of property, while market price is determined by negotiation.
- An appraiser can use three different methodologies based on the property type: substitution, cost, or income.
- A CMA is not an appraisal, but rather a range of values generated by a real estate broker, usually free of charge to the client.

Financing and Mortgages

Financing a home purchase is a daunting task, full of mortgage brokers, lenders, down payments, points, etc. Understanding the lending process—and better yet, being able to explain the process to someone else—is a great way for any real estate professional to help their client through the financing maze.

In this chapter, we will cover the basics of mortgages: what they are, how they are created, who they serve, and what happens if you fail to make your mortgage payments. We will discuss the many different types of mortgages and when they are used. We will also discuss foreclosures.

In This Chapter

- Promissory notes and why they're used
- A look at mortgages and deeds of trust
- How buyers take title when using a mortgage
- The primary and secondary mortgage markets
- Types of financing
- The foreclosure process and ways to avoid it

Promissory Notes

A promissory note, sometimes called a financing instrument or financing vehicle, is basically an IOU. It's a written, signed, unconditional promise to pay a specific amount of money on demand at a specified time and is often used to borrow money or take out a loan for a specific purchase. Along with repaying the note, the borrower promises to pay *interest* as well.

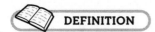

DEFINITION

Interest is the amount of money you pay to borrow someone else's money.

Promissory Note Terms

When someone decides to borrow money from a lending institution, he seeks out the most favorable financing terms he can find, such as low interest rate, low down payment requirements, credit score flexibility, etc. The note outlines key terms both parties must agree upon, such as the amount borrowed; the interest rate; the prepayment penalties, if any; and the repayment period. The amount borrowed is called the principal of the loan and is based on the borrower's needs, wants, and desires. The ratio of loan amount to the value of the collateral is called the loan-to-value (LTV) ratio. The higher the LTV, or the more money that's loaned in relation to the value of the property, the higher the interest rate required. The theory is that at higher LTVs, a lender is taking more risk and, therefore, should be compensated better for that risk.

HELPFUL HINT

When determining the LTV of a loan, the bank will determine the value to be the lower of either the purchase price or the appraised amount.

Equity is the amount of the loan the borrower has paid off, either as an initial down payment at the closing or the accrual of principal after each payment. A conventional loan is considered the most secure loan due to the low LTV, typically 80 percent or less. Overall, the determining factors that drive the LTV and down payment are the ability of the borrower to repay the loan and the appraisal of the property being purchased. The borrower's ability to repay the loan is usually based on such factors as job status, credit score, and current income earned. These will be checked and verified during the application process through tax returns, bank status, credit reports, pay stubs, etc. In some cases, the borrower may require a higher LTV due to lower cash reserves for a down payment; however, the bank might seek an insurance policy, known as *private mortgage insurance (PMI)*, to protect itself should the borrower default on the loan. It covers the top 20 to 30 percent of the loan against the default of the borrower and allows lenders to make riskier loans than they may otherwise be comfortable making. When the borrower has accrued enough equity—typically 20 to 22 percent—the lender releases the PMI.

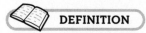

DEFINITION

Private mortgage insurance (PMI) is an insurance policy designed to protect the lender should the borrower default on the loan. Typically, the monthly premiums are paid by the borrower and added to the monthly note payments.

The Interest Rate

Interest is the charge a person pays to use another person's money expressed as a percentage of the outstanding loan balance. Interest can be paid at the beginning of the payment period, called in advance, or at the end of the payment period, called in arrears. Whether paid at the end or the beginning of each payment only matters when a property is sold and the loan is paid off prior to its maturity date. *Usury* is the illegal activity of charging an interest rate higher than allowed by state law. As of March 1981, Title V of the Depository Institutions Deregulation and Monetary Control Act of 1980 exempts from the usury laws *federally related* loans made after that date for residential one-to-four-family first-lien loans.

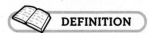

DEFINITION

Usury laws regulate the maximum interest rates that can be set for loans to protect borrowers. A **federally related loan** is a loan made by a federally chartered bank, lending institution, or agency of the federal government.

The loan origination fee is what the lender charges the borrower for making the loan. The fee is expressed in terms of a point, or 1 percent of the loan amount. A discount point is a type of prepaid interest or fee mortgage borrowers can purchase that lowers the amount of interest they pay on each payment. The discount point is expressed as a point, or 1 percent of the total loan amount.

The Prepayment Penalty

A prepayment penalty is a clause in a loan stating that a penalty will be assessed if the loan is paid off within a certain time period. Typically, the penalty is based on a percentage of the remaining mortgage balance and has a short life span, ranging from 1 to 5 years. Loans with a prepayment penalty typically have a ¼ to ½ percent interest rate reduction, due to the fact the lenders know the borrower is locked in for at least a given period of time.

The Repayment Period

There's a set time frame during which a borrower is obligated to repay the total amount of the principal plus the interest for a loan. The common residential loan is paid back in a 30-year term. However, other terms are available, such as 10, 15, and 20 years. The effect of the repayment period determines the monthly payment, so a longer repayment schedule lowers every month's total payment.

Mortgages and Deeds of Trust

A mortgage is a legal contract that conveys an interest or right of ownership on a piece of real property by its owner, the mortgagor, to a lender, the mortgagee, as security for a loan. The lender's security interest is recorded as a matter of public record and is released when the loan is repaid in full, called a satisfaction of lien. The borrower then enters the satisfaction of lien into the public records to show full ownership of the property.

HELPFUL HINT

When a borrower needs money, they ask a bank for a loan, or IOU. You offer collateral to the bank for the IOU. The mortgage is the document that promises you'll give them the collateral if you fail to make good on the IOU. Therefore, the borrower becomes the **mortgagor**. The bank, or lender, accepts the mortgage and becomes the **mortgagee**.

A deed of trust, although like a mortgage, is another method of achieving the same concept of home ownership. Sometimes called trust deed, a deed of trust is a deed wherein legal title to real property is transferred to a trustee, who holds it as security for a loan. The equitable title remains with the borrower. The borrower is referred to as the trustor, while the lender is referred to as the beneficiary. When the trustor pays off the loan amount, the trustee deeds the property back to the trustor, or the borrower, by a reconveyance deed. The borrower then enters the deed in the public records to show full ownership of the property.

The Lien Theory Versus Title Theory System

A main difference between the mortgage and deed of trust systems is the way they're secured. The mortgage creates a lien that's placed against the property in the public records naming the lender as the lien holder. The other method transfers ownership of the property to the trustee, as owner of the property via a deed of trust. Within the mortgage or deed of trust is a clause called the *defeasance clause*. This requires the trustee to transfer the property back to the original trustor upon fulfillment of the payment obligations required in the original loan.

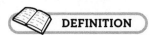

DEFINITION

A **defeasance clause** is a provision included in a mortgage agreement that the borrower will be given the title to the property after all mortgage terms are met. The buyer has no right to the title until all principal and interest payments have been made.

Many obligations are required of the borrower, either as the mortgagor or trustor, in the document, such as:

- He must maintain the property.

- He must make the payments per the requirements of the note.

- He must make the real estate tax payments.

- He must maintain the homeowners' insurance.

- He must not let the property fall into disrepair.

- He must contact the lender should improvements, or alterations, be needed.

The Default of Mortgage, or Deed of Trust, Clause

Default is defined within the mortgage, or deed of trust, and is typically 60 to 90 days without a payment. Once default occurs, other clauses can be activated as well. Should the borrower fail to pay real estate taxes, acquire or maintain homeowners' insurance, or make necessary repairs on the property, the lender has the right to keep the property, which is the security of the loan, safe and viable.

The Acceleration Clause

The acceleration clause states that the lender has the right to call the loan due immediately. The amount called due can be the entire amount of the outstanding principal balance of the loan and not the sum of the remaining payments. This clause is to help protect the lender during the foreclosure process. Without the acceleration clause, the lender would have to sue the borrower after each missed payment.

The Assignment Clause

This clause allows the lender to assign the mortgage to another person. In this case, the loan is sold because it has value, while the mortgage that covers the loan is assigned. The mortgage is said to *back the loan*.

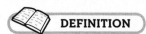

DEFINITION

Back the loan is a phrase that means "protect the loan by giving the lender a piece of collateral." Sometimes it's called a *mortgage-backed security*. This loan is the security backed by the mortgage as collateral.

Another clause within the mortgage is the alienation clause, or the due on sale clause. This clause protects the lender by requiring the borrower to pay the outstanding balance of the loan upon loss of beneficial interest, such as through a sale or gift. It also can be activated upon a land contract that transfers the beneficial interest to the vendee during the period of the land contract

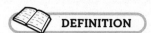

DEFINITION

To **record** is to enter something into the public records to reflect the true nature, or intent, of the document being recorded.

The Tax and Insurance Reserves Clause

If the lender requires the borrower to escrow the real estate taxes and the homeowner's insurance, this clause gives that power to the lender. Furthermore, the lender might require flood insurance reserves based on the location of the property. Loans and mortgages are placed in the public record by the date they were created. The first one created, or recorded, gets first priority. However, in some cases, a clause called a *subordination clause* allows recorded documents to switch priorities even though one may be younger than the other.

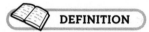 **DEFINITION**

A **subordination clause** allows two documents to switch priorities, regardless of the dates they entered the public records.

The Primary Mortgage Market

The primary mortgage market brings borrowers together with lenders, be they individuals, entities, or institutions, that have money to lend for real estate. The borrowers include individuals seeking funds to buy a new or existing home, investors seeking funds to buy investment properties, and businesses seeking funds to buy property.

Secondary Markets

The secondary mortgage market is a provider of funds to the primary mortgage market. The secondary market *pools,* or *blocks,* together loans to make packages of loans sold to an investor to generate income to replenish the primary market funds.

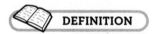 **DEFINITION**

A **pool** or **block** is when a maker of mortgages combines individual mortgages of similar interest rates and terms to form a bigger group to attract an investor. This group of loans is then packaged as a mortgage-backed security (MBS).

The three largest investors of the primary mortgage market are the Federal Home Loan Mortgage Corporation (Freddie Mac), the Federal National Mortgage Association (Fannie Mae), and the Government National Mortgage Association (GNMA).

Freddie Mac was created by Congress in 1970 and purchases single-family, multifamily, and home-improvement conventional mortgage loans. It also purchases conventional single-family mortgages under optional delivery programs.

Fannie Mae was created by Congress in 1938 as a wholly owned governmental corporation. Fannie Mae purchases single-family, multifamily, FHA, VA, and conventional mortgages.

GNMA has authority to purchase subsidized and unsubsidized single-family, multifamily, FHA, and VA mortgages and, at times, conventional mortgages. GNMA guaranties *pass-through certificates* as well. The securities are issued by mortgagees approved by the U.S. Department of Housing and Urban Development (HUD) and guaranteed by GNMA.

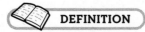 **DEFINITION**

> A **pass-through certificate** is a type of investment issued by the GNMA that earns income from the interest and principal payments made on mortgages by mortgage holders and passed through to the investor.

While making risky loans is more profitable, a severe problem occurred when the subprime mortgage crisis exploded. As housing prices fell in 2006, the value of their loans dropped tremendously. If they hadn't been nationalized, there essentially would have been no housing market whatsoever because banks just stopped lending without government guarantees.

 HELPFUL HINT

> In 2006, the U.S. government bought all the stock of FNMA and FHLMC entities and nationalized them for the good of the people. GNMA has always been wholly owned by the government.

Common Financing Types

Many different types of mortgages are available to home buyers. The loan type can depend on many factors, such as property type, price range, location, and more. Figuring out what kind of mortgage works best for each individual requires research.

Fixed-Rate Loans

A fixed-rate loan is the most common loan. The distinguishing factor of a fixed-rate mortgage is that the interest rate over every time period of the mortgage is known at the time the mortgage is originated. The fixed-rate loan is usually *amortized* over some time period.

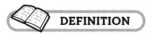 **DEFINITION**

> **Amortization** is the reduction of debt by regular payments of interest and principal sufficient to pay off a loan by maturity.

Adjustable-Rate Loans

An adjustable-rate loan has some features that must be understood, including the index rate, the margin or spread, the interest rate caps, and the conversion. The index rate is the financial vehicle the loan is based on. Lenders base adjustable-rate loan rates on a variety of indices, the most common being rates on 1-, 3-, or 5-year Treasury securities. The margin, or spread, is the number of percentage points lenders add to the index rate to determine the borrower's ultimate interest rate. Interest rate caps are the limits on how much the interest rate payment can change over the life and each single change of the index. Conversion is a clause that allows the buyer to convert the adjustable-rate loan to a fixed-rate mortgage at some designated time.

Private Loans

Many people believe a bank is the only place to get a home loan, but that's not true. Anyone can make a loan. The good thing about private loans is that they can take the form of any of the other loans: fixed-rate, adjustable-rate, conventional, etc.

Other Financing Types

I previously discussed the common types of home loans and accounted for a majority of all loans made. However, many other loans can be used for other specific situations.

Blanket Loans

A blanket loan is secured by multiple properties as collateral for the loan. This is a great loan for investors who may be buying several properties at once, or it can be used to consolidate several loans into one loan. A *partial release of lien* is required if you need to sell or refinance one specific property; you can get the lien released from that property with a substantial pay down of the outstanding principal due.

Construction Loans

A construction loan is a short-term, high-interest-rate loan designed to pay for the construction of a new home. It may be offered for a set term, usually 1 year at maximum, to allow you the time to build your home. At the end of the construction process, when the house is done, you need to get a new loan to pay off the construction loan. This is called a permanent loan or take-out loan.

Home-Equity Loans

Home-equity loans allow you to borrow against the equity accrued in your property. These loans appeal to borrowers because they can borrow relatively large amounts of money in a shorter time period. They're also easier to qualify for than other types of loans because they're secured by an asset you already own, such as your primary residence. A home-equity loan acts like a second-lien mortgage.

Open-End Loans or Home-Equity Lines of Credit

If you don't need all the money at once, you can consider a home equity line of credit (HELOC), or open-end loan. This option provides a pool of money you can draw from if and when you need it. You only pay interest on the principal money you've actually borrowed and not the entire amount that was approved.

Package Loans

A real estate loan is used to finance the purchase of both real property and personal property, such as a new home plus carpeting, window coverings, and major appliances. Typically, real property is sold via a mortgage, and the personal property is sold via a *bill of sale*. A package loan allows a borrower to mortgage personal and real property.

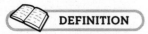 **DEFINITION**

A **bill of sale** is a document that details, in writing, a sale of goods transferred from one party to another. A typical retail purchase receipt can be considered a bill of sale because it details the specific goods sold to the buyer and the specific price paid.

Purchase Money Mortgages

A purchase money mortgage (PMM) is a mortgage made at the closing table by the seller to help bridge the gap between the total money the seller can bring to the table and a loan acquired from another source. The PMM acts like a second mortgage for the seller and requires the same documents as the primary loan.

Reverse Mortgages

A reverse mortgage is a loan available to homeowners 62 years or older that allows them to convert part of the equity in their homes into cash. The loan is called a *reverse* mortgage because instead of making monthly payments to a lender, as with a traditional mortgage, the lender makes payments to the borrower. The borrower is not required to pay back the loan until the home is sold, typically upon the death of the owner, or otherwise vacated. The borrower must remain current on property taxes, homeowners' insurance, and homeowner association dues.

Wraparound Loans

With a wraparound loan, a borrower takes out a second mortgage without paying off the original mortgage. The borrower makes payments on both mortgages to the new lender, called the wraparound lender. The wraparound lender then makes the payments to the original mortgage lender.

Governmental Loans

In most cases, the U.S. government does not actually lend money. Instead, loans are offered by traditional lenders and backed, or insured, by the government. That guarantee reduces the risk for the lenders and makes them more willing to lend at attractive rates and in situations when a borrower might not qualify for a loan otherwise.

Federal Housing Administration Loans

The Federal Housing Administration (FHA), which is part of HUD, doesn't actually make the loan but rather insures the loan. The typical down payment required is considerably lower than conventional lending practices—currently 3.5 percent. Also, an FHA-insured loan is prohibited from having a prepayment penalty. However, because of the high LTV of the loan, the lender charges a mortgage insurance premium (MIP) that must be paid up front or rolled into the loan. Lenders are allowed to charge origination and discount points to the borrower for the loan as well. If the borrower chooses to use an FHA loan, the house he or she is getting the loan on must be appraised by an FHA-approved appraiser, and the borrower must meet certain credit qualifications set forth by the FHA.

Veterans Affairs Loans

The U.S. Department of Veterans Affairs (VA) is authorized to guarantee loans for eligible individuals. VA home loans are provided by private lenders, such as banks and mortgage companies. The VA guarantees a portion of the loan, enabling the lender to provide more favorable terms. The VA does not require a minimum credit score for a loan, but lenders generally have their own internal requirements. Borrowers must show sufficient income to repay the loan and shouldn't have excessive debt, but the guidelines are usually more flexible than for conventional loans. A positive feature is that the VA guidelines allow veterans to use their home-loan benefits a year or two after bankruptcy or foreclosure. A VA loan is available only to finance a primary home and cannot be used to purchase or refinance vacation and investment homes. Lenders are required to get proof of a veteran's service during the VA loan process. The *Certificate of Eligibility* serves as that proof and tells a lender that an applicant has officially met the minimum service requirements.

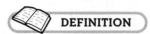 **DEFINITION**

> A **Certificate of Eligibility** certifies that a veteran qualifies for a VA loan by meeting one of these requirements: 181 days of service during peacetime, 90 days of service during war time, or 6 years of service in the Reserves or National Guard. Some surviving spouses of veterans killed in the line of duty are eligible as well.

When a borrower makes an offer on a property using a VA loan, the lender has the property appraised according to their standards. The VA seeks a certificate of reasonable value (CRV) in addition to the bank's appraisal.

U.S. Department of Agriculture or Rural Loans

U.S. Department of Agriculture (USDA) loans, sometimes called Farmer MAC loans, are mortgages backed by the USDA as part of its USDA Rural Development Guaranteed Housing Loan program. USDA loans are available to home buyers with below-average credit. To qualify for the USDA's Rural Housing Program, the home must be in a rural area. However, the USDA's definition of *rural* is liberal. The two areas where USDA loans are different are with respect to the loan type and down payment amount. With a USDA loan, you don't have to make a down payment, and you're required to take a fixed-rate loan. Adjustable-rate mortgages aren't available via the USDA rural loan program. However, USDA loans require PMI.

Financing Legislation

The federal government regulates financing and lending practices of mortgage lenders through the Truth in Lending Act (TILA), Real Estate Settlement Procedures Act (RESPA), Equal Credit Opportunity Act (ECOA), and the Community Reinvestment Act of 1977 (CRA).

Truth in Lending and Regulation Z

TILA is a federal law designed to promote the informed use of consumer credit by requiring disclosures about its terms and costs to the borrower. The regulations implementing the laws are known as Regulation Z. Effective July 21, 2011, TILA's general rule-making authority was transferred to the Consumer Financial Protection Bureau (CFPB), whose authority was established pursuant to provisions enacted by the passage of the Dodd-Frank Wall Street Reform and Consumer Protection Act (Dodd-Frank) in July 2010. Under TILA, a borrower must be fully informed of all the charges necessary to finance a loan as well as the true costs associated with the loan before closing. In the case of a lender making a mortgage to finance the purchase of a home, the *annual percentage rate* (*APR*) must be disclosed as well.

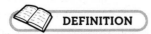 **DEFINITION**

> **Annual percentage rate (APR)** is the interest rate of the loan if you include the cost of the loan as part of the calculation.

Regulation Z, or Reg Z, provides for strict regulation of advertising in all media, specifically when pertaining to home loans. General terms may be used, such as *terms available;* however, if any details are given in the ad, the ad must be complied with in its entirety. Using trigger terms like *down payment, financing charges, monthly payment, loan term,* or *interest rate* requires the advertisement to disclose the following as well:

- The total of all payments made for the life of the loan

- The down payment requirement

- The cash price

- The number, amounts, and due dates of all payments

- The APR

Creditors and Requirements

TILA applies to each individual or business that offers or extends credit when four conditions are met:

- The credit is offered or extended to consumers.

- The credit is extended more than 25 times per year or more than 5 times for transactions secured by real property.

- The credit is subject to a finance charge or is payable by written agreement in more than four installments.

- The credit is primarily for personal, family, or household purposes.

Credit Fraud and Protection

The Federal Trade Commission (FTC) prohibits credit discrimination based on race, color, religion, national origin, sex, marital status, age, or dependence on public assistance. Creditors may ask you for one or all of these pieces of information, but they may not use it when deciding whether to give you credit, nor can they use it for discrimination when setting the terms of your credit.

Consumer Finance Protection Bureau (CFPB)

In 2014, Congress established the Consumer Financial Protection Bureau (CFPB) through the Dodd-Frank act. The CFPB requires mortgage lenders to provide all borrowers with a pamphlet that explains the information they are required to provide along with their contact information. The pamphlet also must include information on how to initiate a complaint should the lender not be following the rules laid out by the CFPB. The lender must:

- Provide billing information to the borrower in writing

- Give the borrower a 2-month notice of their ARM rate change

- Promptly credit the borrower's payments

- Respond quickly about loan pay-off statements

- Not overcharge for forced-placed insurance or charge for any insurance not needed

- Quickly resolve all disputes and complaints

- Follow good customer service policies and procedures

- Work with the borrower if they are having trouble paying the mortgage, even before the foreclosure process

- Allow the borrower to seek review of any decision regarding a loan workout request

The *Closing Disclosure* and *Loan Estimate* forms are the result of the new requirements for disclosure, called TILA-RESPA Integrated Disclosure (TRID), also known as the Know Before You Owe (KBYO) mortgage initiative. The new KBYO, or TRID, rules and forms took effect on October 3, 2015.

 HELPFUL HINT

The **Closing Disclosure** form replaces the settlement statement required by RESPA, while the **Loan Estimate** form takes the place of the truth-in-lending disclosure and good faith estimate.

Foreclosures

A foreclosure is the legal right of a mortgage holder or other third-party lien holder to gain ownership of the property, sell the property, and use the proceeds to pay off the mortgage if the mortgage or lien is in default. Foreclosure proceedings typically start with a formal demand for payment, which is usually a letter issued from the lender. This letter of notice is referred to as a notice of default (NOD).

Types of Foreclosures

The mortgage or lien holder can usually initiate foreclosure any time after a default has been declared by the lending institution. There are several types of foreclosure, including foreclosure by judicial sale, foreclosure by power of sale, and strict foreclosure. The most important type is foreclosure by judicial sale. It involves the sale of the mortgaged property done under the guidance of a court. Non-judicial foreclosure, called foreclosure by power of sale involves the sale of the property by the mortgage holder without the guidance or supervision of a court. Strict foreclosure in another type of foreclosure and is only available in limited states. Under strict foreclosure, when a mortgagor defaults, a court orders the mortgagor to pay the mortgage within a certain time period. If the mortgagor fails to pay, the mortgage holder automatically gains title, with no obligation to sell the property.

Short Sales

A *short sale* is an option some homeowners use when their mortgage lender provides them with the option of selling their home to a third party at a price that's much lower than the remaining principal on the loan. Homeowners who are trying to avoid getting caught up in a foreclosure proceeding often opt for short sales.

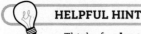

HELPFUL HINT

Think of a **short sale** as selling the property short of the outstanding balance owed to the lender.

Two major facets must be considered when a short sale is granted by the lender: deficiency judgment or waiver of deficiency judgment. With deficiency judgment, the homeowner is held liable to pay whatever the difference, called the deficiency, between the short sale amount received and the amount owed on the loan. The waiver of deficiency judgment is the most popular choice among homeowners but it's the least popular for the lender. The mortgagor isn't liable for any deficiency created due to the short sale. This means they are free and clear of obligations after their property sells.

The Least You Need to Know

- A note is a financing instrument for real property; while the mortgage is the document pledging the collateral for the note.
- Interest is the money you pay to borrow money and usury is an illegal activity charging too much interest.
- The primary mortgage market provides the bulk of the money used in consumer mortgages, while the secondary mortgage market buys loans in pools from the primary mortgage market.
- FHA, VA, and USDA are not lenders, but rather are guarantors or insurers of loans made by lenders.
- Regulation Z, of the truth in lending law, requires lenders to be honest and fair in their advertisements.
- Foreclosure is the process by which a lender sues to obtain their outstanding loan balance or regain control of a property.

CHAPTER 19

Taxes and Assessments

One of the powers conferred by governmental powers is the right to tax, or taxation. This power grants the government the right to collect taxes in many ways, including sales tax, income tax, and of course real estate taxes.

In this chapter, we will discuss real estate taxes: how they are calculated, assessed, and collected. Understanding the way real estate gets assessed is a key factor in being able to determine the cost of taxes on real estate. Within the real estate taxing process, there are several exemptions a homeowner can claim. We will cover the different types, their values, and how they protect a homeowner.

In This Chapter

- Real estate taxes and how they're assessed
- Real estate tax calculations
- The differences in tax exemptions available
- Tax lien sales and how they work

Taxes and Real Estate

The right to tax real estate enables the government to impose and collect taxes on real property. There are typically two types of real estate taxes: ad valorem taxes and special assessment taxes.

Real estate taxes are assessed on most privately owned properties. Some communities, such as parts of Alaska, do not impose taxes on real property. The revenue generated from real estate taxes are used to help pay for local services like road maintenance, snow removal, public schools, and the operation of local government offices. Real estate taxes are calculated as a percentage of a property's tax value.

Taxes levied against real property have a high degree of certainty of collection so tax liens are very rarely, if ever, recorded.

How Taxes Are Levied

A property tax is a levy an owner is required to pay on real property. The tax is imposed, or levied, by the governing authority that holds jurisdiction over the area where the property resides. Property taxes may be paid to a federal government agency, a state government agency, a county government agency, or a municipality. In some cases, multiple government agencies may tax the same property.

There are four broad types of property: land, improvements to land such as buildings, personal property, and intangible property. *Real property* refers to the land and all the naturally occurring elements plus any manmade improvements on it. Under a property tax system, the government requires and performs an appraisal of the value of each property, and tax is assessed in proportion to that value, called the *assessed value.*

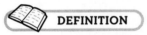 **DEFINITION**

The **assessed value** is the value determined by the government and is the basis upon which taxes are calculated.

Different forms of property tax are used among state, local and municipalities, while real property is often taxed based on its classification. Classification is the grouping of properties based on similar use. Properties in different classes are taxed at different rates. Examples of different classes of property are residential, commercial, industrial, special use, and vacant real property.

A special assessment tax is sometimes confused with property tax. These are two distinct forms of taxation: ad valorem tax, which relies on the assessed value of the property being taxed, and special assessment tax, which relies on a special enhancement called a benefit to the property and its owner.

The property *tax rate* is often given as a percentage. In some cases, it also may be expressed as a *mill*, or a millage rate. A mill is $\frac{1}{1,000}$ of \$1, or \$0.001. For example, 40 mills would be $\frac{40}{1,000}$ of \$1, or \$0.040, or 4 percent. This would mean the tax rate would be \$40 for every \$1,000 in value.

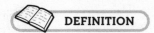 **DEFINITION**

> The **tax rate** is the amount at which real property is taxed and is established by most state taxing authorities. A **mill** is $1/1,000$ of $1, or $0.001. Tax rates are typically set by statute in each state.

How Taxes Are Collected

After the taxes have been levied against a piece of real property, the next step is the collection of the taxes. A property's tax bill is calculated by multiplying the tax rate and the assessed value along with an equalization factor.

The date taxes are due, called the penalty date, is typically set by state statute. Property taxes are payable in two semiannual payments, four quarterly payments, or twelve monthly payments. Some states pay taxes at the beginning of the tax year, called prepaid; others pay at the end of the tax year, called arrears. Furthermore, some states pay taxes a full year in arrears—that is, they pay last year's taxes in this year's calendar year. States that offer monthly payments also may offer a discount if the taxes are paid in full.

All states charge a penalty in the form of interest on taxes not paid by the penalty date. Should the taxes go unpaid for an extended period, most states offer the property at a tax sale (discussed later in this chapter).

How Taxes Are Calculated

Ad valorem and special assessment taxes are calculated in different ways, but they may be paid as one bill in most states.

The ad valorem (Latin for "according to value") tax is a simple calculation that requires the knowledge of the tax rate, *equalization factor,* and assessed value. Typically, the ad valorem tax is an annual value levied against property. For example, a house with an assessed value of $100,000 is in an area with a tax rate of 23 mills. The house has an equalization factor of 0.80. What are the monthly taxes?

Ad valorem = tax rate × assessed value × equalization factor

So:

Ad valorem = 0.023 × $100,000 × 0.80 = $1,840 per annum

The monthly tax rate is $1,840 ÷ 12 or $153.33 per month.

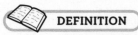 **DEFINITION**

> The **equalization factor** is a number, or factor, by which the assessed value of a property is multiplied to arrive at a value for the property that's in line with statewide tax assessments. If an equalization factor is not mentioned or present, it's assumed to be equal (i.e., 1).

A special assessment tax is levied to cover the costs of improvements that will benefit everyone who is taxed. The proceeds of a special assessment tax could be used for new sidewalks in a community, new streets to gain access to a housing addition, or sewer lines to replace the old septic tanks in an area.

A special assessment tax can be assessed in any manner the taxing authority determines equitable. The two most common methods are pro rate and equal fashion. For example, a neighborhood of 10 houses, under a special assessment tax, is required to pay for a new road, costing $50,000, and sidewalks, costing $15,000. The road should provide equal benefit to all houses so the $50,000 is divided equally between the 10 houses, giving a tax levy of $5,000 per house. The sidewalks may benefit some houses more due to them having a larger yard than others. Suppose of the 10 houses, 5 had double lots and 5 had single lots. The five with double lots might pay double the tax the other five pay. Therefore, five houses would be levied $2,000 while the others only $1,000.

If the amount of the special assessment tax is too large, some states allow for equal payments to made along with the ad valorem tax, rather than one lump sum.

Exemptions for Real Estate Owners

Although all property is assessed, not all of it is taxable. Some properties, such as those owned by religious organizations or governments, are completely exempt from paying property taxes. Others are partially exempt, such as veterans who qualify for an exemption on part of their homes. Most exemptions are offered by the local taxing authority, such as a municipality, a county, or a school district.

Other forms of exemptions exist for property belonging to the United States, property belonging to the state, property belonging to the municipality, reservation land, university and college property, property held for cemetery use, hospitals and sanatoriums, airport improvements, Public Service Railroads, and anyone who asks and is granted an exemption. Some taxing authorities also grant special exemptions to large industries that employee many workers or sports teams they determine to be important to the economic benefit of the area. Check with your local assessor to determine what exemptions are available in your community.

In general, exemptions, no matter the type, work by reducing the overall assessed value of the real property, thus reducing the tax burden levied on a property owner. For example, if a property has an assessed value of $100,000 with no exemptions, it would be taxed at the full value. However, if the property has a $45,000 exemption, such as Indiana's homestead exemption, the property would be effectively taxed as if the value was $55,000 ($100,000 − $45,000). This new effective value would reduce the homeowner's overall property taxes. Furthermore, if a property has been granted multiple exemptions, they would be cumulative in nature. The total amount would be deducted from the assessed value, as before.

Types of Exemptions

Several different types of exemptions can be granted to private property. Typically, they're only partial exemptions rather than full exemptions.

> **HELPFUL HINT**
>
> In most states, the property owner is the only person who can file for a real estate tax exemption. Furthermore, most states have a statute of limitations date by which they must file for an exemption for it to be eligible in that year.

Depending on the state, numerous exemptions are available for property owners. All real property owners have the right to apply for any exemption for which they qualify, including, but not limited to homestead, mortgage, senior citizen, disabled citizen, widow/widower of veteran, historic property, or home improvement.

A homestead exemption provides for the exemption in assessed value from the property tax assessment of any real property owned and occupied as a principal place of residence.

Different states provide different degrees of protection under the homestead exemption laws. Some states protect property by dollar value, some on acreage limitations, and others use both. If a person's debt exceeds the limits of protection granted by the state taxing authority, creditors may force the sale to satisfy the outstanding debt.

Let's look at some examples of exemptions. California protects up to $75,000 for single people, $100,000 for married couples, and $175,000 for people over 65 or legally disabled. Texas's homestead exemption has no dollar value limit and a 10-acre exemption limit for homesteads inside urban areas and 100 acres for those in rural areas outside the city. Both the Kansas and Oklahoma exemptions protect 160 acres of land, of any value, in rural areas while only exempting 1 acre in the city. Indiana has a $45,000 exemption. New Mexico has a $60,000 exemption. Alaska has a $54,000 exemption. Colorado has a $60,000 exemption, or $90,000 for people who are over 60 or disabled. In most states, the real dollar value of protection provided by these laws has diminished over the years because exemption dollar amounts are seldom adjusted for inflation. Therefore, this protective intent of exemptions has been eroded in most states.

In a few states, real property that has a lien and mortgage recorded against it also will be able to seek a mortgage exemption. The value of the exemption differs in every state. Indiana's, for example, is $2,000.

Most if not all states have an exemption for senior citizens to help reduce their taxes. Every state differs in the exact requirements, so check with your taxing authority to find the exact rules for your state, if any. Most states have an age requirement, typically between ages 62 and 65, while other states have added a household low-income component.

Most states have a disabled citizen exemption. To qualify, the taxpayer must be "unable to engage in any substantial gainful activity because of a physical or medical impairment ...." In all states that grant this exemption, proof requirements must be met in advance before applying for the exemption.

In some states, any widow or widower of a veteran may claim this exemption. If the widow or widower remarries, they would no longer be eligible for the exemption. If a husband and wife were divorced before either of their deaths, they are not considered a widow or widower and not allowed the exemption. When filing for the first time, a death certificate may be required.

To qualify for the historic exemption, properties may be residential or commercial and must be either individually listed in the National Register of Historic Places, a contributing building in a National Register District, or designated as historic under the provisions of a local preservation ordinance.

To qualify for a home improvement exemption, the residential property must be occupied by the owner and be bettered in value due to an addition or improvement to the property. Most states have a maximum value that can be exempted regardless of the increase in the value added. For example, in Illinois, the maximum amount of exemption is $25,000, even if you improved the value more than that. Furthermore, some states only grant the exemption for a time period, and at the end of it, the value would level up. So the $25,000 exemption may be for only the first 4 years after the improvement happened, for example.

These are just a few examples of exemptions granted in various states. Some states may have more opportunities for exemptions, while others may not offer any of these at all, except for the homestead. Check in your state to see exactly what exemptions may be available.

Full Versus Partial Exemptions

HELPFUL HINT

All states offer a homestead exemption in some manner. In some states they offer a full exemption—an exemption for the full value of the property—while other states only offer a partial exemption—only a portion of the value of the property.

Exemptions can range from full to partial relief of a homeowner's tax liability. One authority may provide a full exemption for real property, like Texas, whereas another authority may provide only a partial exemption for these types of property. The limitations can be expressed in terms of dollar amounts or by a percentage of value.

Full exemptions typically defer the entire amount of the property tax burden. This type of exemption can be granted only by a taxing authority with the approval of the controlling government entity, such as the state, local, or municipality. Typically, full exemptions are reserved for large companies that can bring a large impact to a city. The foregoing of property tax gained by the city is offset by the influx of workers who would stimulate the city's economy.

Partial exemptions only reduce, not eliminate, the tax burden a property owner could be levied based on each exemption's value. Partial exemptions are primarily given to private individuals as a benefit to reduce their overall real estate taxes.

Tax Lien Sales

A tax sale is the forced sale of real property by a governmental entity due to the property owner failing to pay taxes. Depending on the state, the sale may be a tax deed sale, where the actual property is sold at the sale, or a tax lien sale, where a lien on the property is sold. With the tax lien sale, the buyer is merely buying the lien on the property rather than the property itself. Basically, the buyer is taking out the taxing authority by buying their place in line.

Before either of these situations can happen, the tax must be on a charged property, applied equitably to all properties and for a legal purpose. This makes the real estate taxes valid and enforceable by the taxing authority. After some statutory period of nonpayment of real estate taxes, typically 1 or 2 years, the taxing authority offers the property at auction. The date, time, and location must be disclosed to all parties in a public newspaper as well as in a certified letter to the property owner.

Because the outstanding balance of taxes owed is known, the minimum bid must be at least equal to that outstanding balance. The auction's highest bidder is given a certificate of sale when the bidder pays the cash to the taxing authority. In some states the holder of the certificate may take possession of the property immediately, while in others, there is a statutory period of redemption for the owner losing the property (more on this in upcoming "Statutory Right of Redemption" section).

Equitable Right of Redemption

All states allow for the equitable right of redemption, or the paying of past-due real estate taxes. Once the property owner has been notified that his property will be included in a tax sale, he has the right to bring the balance current by making a payment before the sale date.

In most states, he must bring the entire balance due—late taxes plus any accrued penalties and interest. Some states go one step further and require the payment of the next installment of taxes as well.

Statutory Right of Redemption

The statutory right of redemption is a state law used by some states to allow a property owner to reclaim his property even after the tax sale has occurred.

Most states are categorized as either tax lien or tax deed states. In tax deed states, buyers purchase the tax deeds to own the properties immediately, thus with no statutory right of redemption. However, purchasers of tax lien certificates do not immediately own the properties upon purchasing said certificates. They may not acquire possession of the properties or evict property owners. The homeowners may remain on the properties during the redemption period set by state statutes.

To regain their property during the statutory right of redemption period, a property owner must pay the entire sum of back taxes plus interest, mandated by each state (usually 4 to 18 percent), to the tax lien holder. The timeframe for the redemption period varies from state to state; it may be anywhere from 6 months to 4 years.

Tax lien states are Alabama, Arizona, Colorado, Florida, Illinois, Indiana, Iowa, Kentucky, Maryland, Mississippi, Missouri, Montana, Nebraska, New Jersey, North Dakota, Ohio, Oklahoma, South Carolina, South Dakota, Vermont, West Virginia, and Wyoming. The District of Columbia is a tax lien jurisdiction as well.

The Least You Need to Know

- Taxes are paid on real property based on the assessed value.
- Taxes are based on ad valorem or special assessment.
- Tax rates are expressed in mills or $1/1{,}000$ of $1.
- Property owners can be granted exemptions for many different issues to reduce the overall burden of taxes on real property.
- Properties can be sold at a tax sale for unpaid real estate taxes.
- Some states allow property owners to reclaim a property sold at a tax lien sale, even after the sale is completed.

Real Estate Investing

Historically, real estate investments perform better than other kinds of assets, and investing in real estate has become a popular way of building an investment portfolio. Although the real estate market has plenty of opportunities for making big gains, buying and owning real estate is a lot more complicated than investing in stocks and bonds.

Real estate investors are attracted to this type of investing because the potential for profit is tremendous. However, the possibility of losing it all always lurks, too, because as with any investment, risk is involved. Successful real estate investing is achievable at any point in time, despite the economic conditions. Although change is inevitable, the risk involved is manageable, if the investor continues to follow a few basic principles.

In This Chapter

- The advantages and disadvantages of investing in real estate
- Buy-and-hold investing versus buy-and-sell
- The different kinds of investing structures
- How technology helps real estate investing
- Understanding capital gains
- How to exchange properties without paying taxes

Getting Started Investing

There are only two reasons to invest in real estate: money now, or the buy-and-sell strategy, and money later, or the buy-and-hold strategy. That's it. Nothing complicated or hard to understand.

It's also essential that all aspiring real estate investors determine an exit strategy for every investment they make.

Money Now Strategy

The money now strategy is a simple method of buying a property and reselling it, often called flipping. This is the glamorous life portrayed on all the reality television shows, where an investor buys a rundown piece of real estate and then rehabs the property. After the rehab is completed, the investor places the property back up for sale—through a local REALTOR hopefully—to make a profit.

Everything is not wine and roses, however, especially for the novice investor; problems often occur. Price overruns, delays in the rehab timetable, over-rehabbing, and more can waylay the inexperienced. Lack of construction know-how, no knowledge of the local market, or not understanding what a buyer wants in décor and more can cause a rehab to spiral out of control very quickly.

Money Later Strategy

Holding an asset, be it art, gold, comic books, or real estate, creates true wealth. Holding is the key. Plus, in real estate, during the holding period, you can make money in the present in the form of rent.

Think about this: where else can you buy an asset (real estate) using someone else's money (a bank's), have another person (a tenant) repay your monthly debt on that asset (rent) plus some extra (cash flow), and you get all the credit (mortgage buy down) for it? It's brilliant!

Exit Strategies

You must have an exit strategy for each property. Both the buy-and-hold and buy-and-sell strategies have their place and purpose. The key is knowing which property fits which strategy before you even buy the property so you can exit the investment in a timely and profitable manner.

You also must know how you'll exit the property. Will you sell using a REALTOR? Sell on owner financing? Or keep it in your own personal portfolio and will it to your family when you die? These methods of exiting an investment come at a price; you should know exactly what price and if you're prepared to pay it.

More Considerations

It's also important to consider how you're going to acquire the property. Are you getting a loan? Are you paying cash? Are you buying on contract? Lease-option? Other *creative financing?*

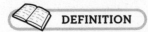 **DEFINITION**

Creative financing is a term real estate investors use that implies some financing technique other than a standard mortgage from a traditional lending institution.

One of the first activities that a novice real estate investor should undertake is an honest self-evaluation of your strengths and weaknesses. This will help determine if you'll be successful in real estate investing. Here are some questions you should ask yourself and answer truthfully:

- Do I know what I'm really getting into?

- Do I have access to capital?

- Do I want to be an active or passive investor?

- Do I know how to rehab a property, really?

- Can I count on the support of my spouse or family?

- Do I have access to property information?

Be sure you know the answer to all the questions before the situation arises.

The Pros and Cons of Investing

Investing in real estate comes with plenty of pros as well as cons. Understanding these ups and downs can get you out ahead of potential danger or put you in a position to capitalize on an investment.

Investing Advantages

The internet abounds with articles on the number of millionaires who credit real estate investing as the vehicle that made them rich. Why? Because the upside is astounding: the better-than-average returns, the greater control over your investments, the use of *leverage* to buy property, the tax benefits, the lower long-term volatility, the insulation from outside market influences, and the government protection.

 **DEFINITION**

Leverage is the use of other people's money.

In the decades since World War II, real estate has produced greater than average returns on investments than most stocks or bonds. In some real estate markets around the country, impressive returns on investment are almost immediate. California, Florida, and some parts of the East Coast can produce huge returns in a short period, assuring the investor an almost certain profit on the real estate when sold.

Every real estate investment you buy gives you ultimate control. You can make improvements, refinance the property, raise the rents, find better tenants, and sell at your discretion. You may be at the mercy of the economic cycle, but you have much more control in making and timing of those decisions.

Leverage in a rising market is a great benefit to real estate investors. Being able to borrow 80 percent, or in some cases 100 percent, of the cost of an investment from someone else is genius in its simplicity. For example, a 3 percent increase on a property where you put 20 percent down is a 15 percent cash-on-cash return. In 5 years, your equity will double, even if the appreciation only equals the inflation rate. Not only can you deduct the interest on an up to $1 million mortgage on your primary home, you also can sell your owner-occupied home for tax-free profits, called capital gains, on up to the first $250,000 for singles and $500,000 for married couples, as long as you live in the home for the 2 of the last 5 years. Furthermore, all expenses associated with managing your rental properties are deductible against your rental income.

Real estate will always be worth more in the future. So even if your property loses a little value in the short run, earning a profit is only a matter of time. Real estate will never become worthless on the open market, and we all know that companies, even huge companies can go bankrupt and be gone tomorrow, but not real estate. Because real estate is local, you'll be more insulated from the national and global economy issues.

Not only do you get tax deductions for expenses and limited taxes on profits, you also can get government bailouts if you can't pay your mortgage. The government is aggressively going after banks to force them to extend loan modifications to people in trouble. Programs such as Home Affordable Refinance Program, known as HARP 1.0 and HARP 2.0, are making it easier for less-qualified buyers to buy or refinance their homes. Plenty of nonrecourse states such as California and Nevada don't go after other assets if you declare bankruptcy and stop making payments.

Investing Disadvantages

Investing in real estate is not all upsides. In fact, there are some significant downsides to investing in real estate, including the liquidity; the steep learning curve; the active, hands-on management; and the significant liabilities.

Unlike the stock market, real estate investing deals with an asset that cannot be bought and sold quickly. If you, as an investor, owned a property and wanted to sell it quickly, you'd find that liquidity, or the measure of the ability of something to be sold on command, is the number-one problem. For example, suppose an investor wants to sell a property for only $10. He would have many offers immediately, but to close the property correctly through an insured closing may take days, weeks, or even months. In the grand scheme of life, that's not long, but suppose the investor needed the $10 for lunch that day.

In real estate, you are responsible for many different facets, so you must be knowledgeable in many different arenas, and you must have experience in the real estate field. You must have the capability to learn quickly, gain insight, learn on the move, and overcome many of the little problems that arise in the course of your investing career. Generally, knowledge and expertise are required in many areas of real estate investing, such as mortgages, titles, insurance, construction, negotiations, market familiarity, appreciation potential, income potential, etc. Mastering them all can take time, and you're bound to have missteps along the way. Some of them might be quite expensive in terms of money or time.

Combine today's litigious world and the perils of real estate investing, and you can become a target for lawsuits. You'll need strong representation from an attorney to guide you through this venture. You'll also need insurance to protect yourself from the accidents that may occur to your tenants, their friends, or the public on or around your properties. The unforeseen issues of insurance claims and legal attacks can drive many beginning investors out of investing altogether.

Working with Real Estate Investors

This biggest factor that can help a REALTOR work with an investor is to think like an investor. Investors are not like mom-and-pop clients. Most agents get used to helping their mom-and-pop buyers by thinking in terms of how they might view a property: Is the house in a good school district? Is the house large enough for our family? Does the kitchen have granite countertops?

But investors probably don't look at a property the same way. They have a much different perspective than your other clients. They tend to ask themselves these types of questions: Can I get owner financing? What's the rent in the neighborhood for this size of house? How much rehab will I have to do to resell this house?

Many investors don't know or understand the benefits of working with a qualified broker. Furthermore, the work and red tape agents need to navigate around the buying and selling process is an unknown factor for most investors. Some investors want a broker to work 100 percent for them and continually have them writing lowball offers, that will never be accepted, for little or no compensation to the broker. Some investors don't understand what an agent does or the benefit they provide. They mistakenly think there's no reason to list or buy with them.

For an agent, the benefits of working with an investor are many. Due to the better-than-average return on investment, a large number of investors are actively buying and selling all types of real estate. This increases the pool of potential clients for an agent to dive into to gain work. Also, active investors tend to do more deals than buyers, or sellers, of owner-occupied properties. Studies show that a homeowner moves every 7 to 11 years; therefore, your owner-occupied client won't need your service again for a long while. The investor-client may have one to five or more transactions per year, so working with an investor means an increase in your deal flow.

Agents who work with investors can put in place systems that are repeatable for an investor or many investors, such as detailed searches within the MLS that automatically find properties that fit what an investor wants. Standing orders at a title company that deal with specific investors, a streamlined application process for financing, and a trained home inspector aware of the investors particular quirks are other items that can be standardized when dealing with an investor who is buying or selling many properties per year.

Investors tend to hang around other investors. A great agent can get referrals, even from one investor to another. That investor referral may lead to other multiple investor deals, too.

During the process of helping an investor, an agent is bound to learn about investing as well. This is a great source of real-life education—and it's typically free.

These are just a few of the advantages of dealing with investors that may outweigh any negatives that come with working for them.

Types of Investing Structures

When treated like a business, investing in real estate can be very lucrative and exciting. The key is to understand that it's a business. Most investors who treat it like a hobby, or only do it for a quick buck, tend to fall victim to bad deals, costly mistakes, or even lengthy lawsuits. Dedicating sufficient time, energy, capital, and effort requires some knowledge of the business world. Therefore, an investor should understand how to invest and the different types of vehicles available.

Sole Investing

Many investors take the approach of being the sole investor in a property. There are many upsides to this: only one decision-maker, no profit splitting, more control, etc.

However, sole investing can be fraught with problems: no one to gain knowledge from, the entire investment is all on your shoulders, etc. It can be scary if you have no experience.

Partnerships

A partnership is a legal entity in which two or more parties agree to come together as a business and operate as one entity. Of course, profits are split in some manner, but the division of labor, knowledge, and experience far outweighs that issue.

Another type of investing vehicle is a *joint venture (JV)*. Many people think partnerships and JVs are the same, but not quite. The JV allows for two or more people to join forces on one specific project, such as the purchase and rehab of a house. This allows for one person, for example, to be skilled at finance and acquisition while another is skilled at the rehab process. This marriage of skills increases the odds of success by allowing each party to do the portion of the project that best suits their specific skill set. At the end of the project, each person goes their separate ways.

The biggest difference is how they're taxed for income. In a partnership, the partnership is taxed accordingly. In a JV, the income is taxed as each person's income earned.

 **DEFINITION**

> A **joint venture (JV)** is a contractual arrangement between two parties that aims to undertake a specific task.

Real Estate Syndicates

In its simplest form, a real estate syndicate is the pooling of money from numerous investors and organizing the funds to buy real estate projects. The pooled money can be used as cash to invest in a real estate project or as a down payment to secure a mortgage or trust deed to fund the bulk of the cost and development of the project. Common examples include buying and rehabbing houses or purchasing land to develop an apartment complex, an office building, or an industrial park.

Another type of syndicate is called a real estate mortgage investment conduit (REMIC). The rules of a REMIC are very complex and should be investigated carefully before anyone invests. Basically, in this form of investing, the pool of money from the investors is used to fund other investors' purchases. The investor becomes the bank and makes loans from the money pool to other buyers. The interest those borrowers pay is returned to the investors of the REMIC.

> **HELPFUL HINT**
>
> In some cases, real estate professionals can become members of syndicates by using their skills to find suitable properties. I know of an agent in Louisville, Kentucky, who helps investors acquire malls and retains 1 percent of the ownership as part of his commission. He has gained a great passive income over the years.

Real Estate Investment Trusts

A real estate investment trust (REIT) is another vehicle for investing in real estate. In an REIT, you become a passive investor. You don't actively manage the property; that's what the REIT does.

Most REITs are public companies that are openly traded on the stock market. As of this writing in late 2016, Simon Properties Group is the largest mall REIT in United States. It sell shares of the company to investors who are seeking a highly secure return. For example, if you buy a $100,000 house with cash and collect $8,000 annual rent, your return is 8 percent. Of course, no other factors are added for this example. But what if you don't have $100,000 nor access to get it? You can buy a share of an REIT for $100, and at the end of the year, when the REIT disperses dividends of $8 per share, your return is still 8 percent without any of the hassle of the property management, time required dealing with tenants, collecting rent, etc.

> **REALTOR WARNING**
>
> As a real estate professional, you cannot sell shares of REITs. They are considered a security and, therefore, must be sold by a qualified securities broker dealer. The REIT business is primarily vested in real estate, but the shares sold are of the business and not the real estate itself. Check with your state for more information.

Technology Helpful with Real Estate Investing

Technology has increased the number of investors and the success of those investors across the board. Access to information such as financing options, market information, properties for sale, and much more is now available at your fingertips, thanks the advent of the World Wide Web. Furthermore, technology has increased the ways data can be analyzed and accessed—and the speed as well—allowing investors to act quicker and with more certainty.

Financial Analysis Software

One major aspect of investing is the analysis of the financial data that drives an investor's decision to buy or sell. Many financial software packages are available that can determine the timing, method, and type of financing available as well as if the purchase should be made in the first place.

Financial analysis software can be used to determine the initial cost of a project plus the cost of rehab in advance with a high degree of certainty, informing the investors whether to buy or not. The software can calculate an investor's tax burdens and profit margins given specific situations or allow an investor to run multiple scenarios that help determine which investment would give the best return.

Property Management Software

Property management software (PMS) helps landlords—those investors using the buy-and-hold strategy—be more successful with less effort. In the first evolution of the PMS, the program resided on the investor's computer in the office or at home. Today, most PMS platforms have online or cloud-based platforms, allowing the investor mobility.

Most PMSs have great marketing features that help a landlord fill vacancies quickly and effectively. Helpful software should be able to post "for lease" listings on a variety of local and national rental websites. Using an online application process can simplify the process by helping an investor narrow the list of prospective tenants and reducing routine paperwork. Good tenant management software allows your residents to pay rent online, view lease documents, and submit maintenance requests, too. Property managers also benefit from tenant management software with the ability to view tenant statistics and histories instantly. Tenants and managers alike should be able to submit and view work orders via email or through the online property management software. The software also should allow managers to solicit bids, and track and pay vendors electronically.

The PMS accounting features are the core benefit. They enable an investor to view income and expenses, create detailed reports, and make payments when necessary. The PMS should create income tax statements for the investor, determine 1099 tax forms for independent contractors and W-2s for employees, as well as balance the general ledgers.

Taxes for the Investor

The successful investor will generate income from his real estate investments. That means taxes.

First, let's discuss the two types of investors: active and passive. If you are an active investor, based on the definition from the Internal Revenue Service (IRS), the taxation rules that apply to you are different from the rules that apply if you are a passive investor.

The Tax Reform Act of 1986 states that, in general, all real estate investment transactions are considered passive investments. The act introduced what are now referred to as passive activity rules. Losses arising from those passive investment activities can no longer be deducted from active income earned, such as salaries, wages, dividends, etc. The tax reform was enacted to deal with what was considered widespread abuse of tax shelters at the time. Understandably, the real estate investment industry was hit hard, with many investors going bankrupt. Some examples of passive real estate investments might be REITs, partnerships or JVs depending on your level of activity, REMICs, and so forth.

In the Revenue Reconciliation Act of 1993, Congress relaxed the rules somewhat for the active real estate investor. The act allowed taxpayers who met the necessary requirements to be considered real estate professionals (not to be confused with the term I've been using in this book to mean a licensed real estate professional) to bypass the passive activity rules for real estate investments in which they materially participated. In other words, an active real estate investor could apply unlimited losses from their real estate activities against any other earned income.

The IRS defines a real estate professional as a taxpayer who performs more than 750 hours of personal services during the tax year in real property trades and businesses or someone who had more than half of his or her personal services performed during the year in real property trades and businesses. The IRS also stipulates that the taxpayer must meet both requirements to be considered active.

When you start your real estate investing career, you most likely won't be considered an active real estate investor per the IRS definition. If this is true, you may still be able to qualify for some limited deductions of your real estate losses against your active income under the IRS's $25,000 exemption rule. The rule states that if you participate in passive rental real estate activity, you can deduct up to $25,000 of the loss of the activity from your nonpassive income. The key determination as to if you qualify for this exemption is whether or not you actively participated in the real estate activity. For more information or to see if you qualify, check with a real estate accountant to determine if your specific situation warrants deductions or not.

Capital Gains

You can claim many deductions when you become a real estate investor. Basically, every cost you incur to run, operate, or maintain the property can be a deduction against the income you earn.

Unfortunately, when you sell the property for a gain, you must share your profits with Uncle Sam in the form of taxes. Unlike an owner-occupied home that gets tax breaks on the profit of a sale up to a certain amount, investment property does not have the same luck. When you sell an investment property, you pay tax on every dollar of profit earned, or the *capital gains*.

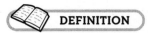 **DEFINITION**

> **Capital gains** is an increase in the value of a capital asset, such as real estate, that gives it a higher worth than the purchase price. A capital gain is not realized until the real estate is sold and can considered short or long term. With a short-term capital gain, you own the property for 1 year or less and it's taxed as ordinary income per your tax bracket when the property is sold. With a long-term capital gain, you own the property for more than 1 year and it's taxed by statute. As of this writing, it's currently a flat rate of 15 percent.

When an investor buys a house to be held for investment purposes, the purchase price of the house becomes the tax basis of the property. The adjusted tax basis can be determined by adding the cost of any improvements to the property less any depreciation that has been taken during the ownership. So:

Adjusted tax basis = tax basis + improvements − depreciation

The capital gain can be calculated by subtracting the property's adjusted tax basis from the actual sales price.

Capital gain = sales price − adjusted tax basis

For example: If an investor buys a $50,000 property and adds $10,000 in improvements during the rehab, his basis would be $60,000. If he sells the property in the same tax year for $100,000, his capital gain would be $100,000 − $60,000 or $40,000. Because he held this property for less than 1 year, it would be a short-term capital gain and taxed at his tax bracket.

Many others items can be calculated into the adjusted tax basis and capital gain equations, such as fees, taxes, loan points, etc. Seek outside counsel for each situation.

Depreciation Recapture

When an investor purchases an investment property for use over several years, the investor can deduct a percentage of the asset's value from his or her yearly taxable income over the economic life of the asset. Remember, the straight-line depreciation discussed in a previous chapter? The IRS publishes specific depreciation schedules for different classes of real estate that tell taxpayers what percentage of an asset's value may be deducted each year and the number of years in which the deductions may be taken. The values of these deductions are used to determine the asset's recomputed basis at the time the taxpayer sells the asset. As of 2016, residential real estate, per the IRS, has an economic life of 27½ years, while a commercial piece of real estate has 39 years.

For example, if a taxpayer purchased a home with a $100,000 tax basis, then deducts $3,636.36 ($100,000 ÷ 27.5) from his ordinary income each year for the house's depreciation, after 4 years, the house's adjusted tax basis would be $85,454.56.

When an investor sells that house for a gain after taking deductions for depreciation, depreciation recapture is used to tax the gain. Because the investor received a deduction from ordinary income for the depreciation of the house, any gain he receives, up to the depreciation amount, must be included as ordinary income to offset the earlier deduction.

Using the preceding example again, the investor sells the house for $120,000 in the fifth year. He has taken 4 years of depreciation and must recapture that amount, or $14,545.45. So the $14,545.54 is taxed as ordinary income, while the $20,000, the amount over the tax basis, is taxed as a capital gain. In this case, it's a long-term capital gain at a flat rate of 15 percent.

IRS Code Section 1031: Tax-Deferred Exchanges

In a normal scenario, an investor would sell his property, pay the taxes required on the capital gain, and move on to his next purchase. However, anyone can see that losing a portion of profit greatly inhibits the purchase price of the next property, assuming some leverage is involved.

For example, an investor sells a property and creates a capital gain of $60,000. His tax, at a minimum, assuming long-term holding, will be 15 percent × $60,000 or $9,000. That leaves the investor with just $51,000. Assuming he can leverage the next property and use the $51,000 for his down payment, at an 80 percent leverage, the biggest property he could buy would be $255,000. However, what if he could use all the profit he earned? The property price could then be $300,000, an increase of $45,000 or 17 percent in buying power.

The IRS tax code section 1031, tax-deferred exchange, allows for just that. In this case, the investor does not pay taxes on the capital gain but rather rolls the profit into the next purchase of a *like-kind* property and uses it as the down payment.

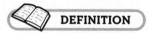 **DEFINITION**

A **like-kind** property is one held for the same purpose—that is investment in the case of real estate. An investor with a residential duplex can exchange for a multitenant strip center because they both are investment properties. You cannot exchange an investment property for a vacation house you intend to use in the summer, though.

To be a true tax-deferred exchange, the investor must use the entire amount of money from the previous sale, or more. There's a saying in the tax-deferred world: "Even or up" will ensure a fully tax-deferred situation. If not, the investor risks paying a capital gains tax on the unused portion.

In some cases, during the exchange an investor must add boot to get the value of the two properties to balance. Boot is any item, typically cash, used to balance the difference between exchanged properties. Boot is taxed as ordinary income to the party receiving it.

 REALTOR WARNING

The 1031 tax-deferred exchange is a very complicated process and must be followed to the letter to be successful. As a real estate professional, you should not try to execute one without the aid of an attorney or accountant. Many rules, deadlines, disclosures, etc., must be considered.

The Least You Need to Know

- Real estate investing is a very lucrative business Either through buy-and-hold or buy-and-sell strategies.
- Investors look at property differently than the average owner-occupied house buyer or seller.
- Brokers can make great partners for an investor because an investor may provide a broker with multiple deals a year versus other owner-occupied clients
- REITs and REMICs can provide a passive investor with high-security investments without any of the hassles that come with investing.
- Technology has increased the success of real estate investors.
- You can avoid paying some capital gain taxes using a tax-deferred exchange.

Mathematics in Real Estate

Real estate professionals perform many different types of calculations. Real estate math is more arithmetic than mathematics, although you can expect a bit of geometry when dealing with square feet of sites or structures.

In this chapter, we review some of the mathematics you can expect to perform as a real estate professional.

In This Chapter

- General mathematical concepts used in real estate
- The theory of unit analysis
- Real estate commission calculations
- The math of appraisals
- Calculating area, depreciation, taxes, and more

General Math Concepts

In general, real estate calculations using arithmetic consist of commission calculations, appreciation and depreciation calculations, area and perimeter measurements, loan-to-value ratios, simple interest payments, discount points and origination fees, proration of bills, real estate taxes, transfer taxes, and sales-to-list price ratios.

 HELPFUL HINT

This chapter was written with the presumption that you have a basic understanding of decimals and fractions and their manipulations. If you need a refresher on some of these topics, myriad resources are available online, including examples and practice problems.

Unit Analysis for Real Estate

Unit analysis, or dimensional analysis, is perhaps the coolest and most useful math trick you'll ever learn. Understanding unit analysis is much easier than learning algebra formulas—and it's a lot more useful as well. Unit analysis is simply converting one thing to another.

Let's first agree that everything in the world has a number, or unit, of measure when we talk about it. A unit could be dollars, feet, miles, acres, etc. The best way to explain it is to show you an easy example.

Example 1: Five days is how many hours?

First, read the problem and then ask yourself, "*What units will the answer be in?*" The answer is hours. You now can rearrange the question to what you know:

$$1 \text{ day} = 24 \text{ hours or } \frac{24 \text{ hours}}{1 \text{ day}}$$

So the question is: 5 days is how many hours:

$$\frac{24 \text{ hours}}{1 \text{ day}} \times 5 \text{ days}$$

See the units that can cross out because there's one in the numerator (the top number) and one in the denominator (the bottom number)? Mentally get rid of those.

$$\frac{24 \text{ hours}}{1 \text{ day}} \times 5 \text{ days}$$

Now the only unit left is hours, which is the unit you want the answer to be. So now you can do the math:

$$\frac{24 \text{ hours}}{1 \text{ day}} \times 5 \text{ days} = 120 \text{ hours}$$

Therefore, 5 days is 120 hours.

Example 2: How many seconds is 3 weeks?

$$\frac{60 \text{ seconds}}{1 \text{ minute}} \times \frac{60 \text{ minutes}}{1 \text{ hour}} \times \frac{24 \text{ hours}}{1 \text{ day}} \times \frac{7 \text{ days}}{1 \text{ week}} \times 3 \text{ weeks}$$

This is the basic setup. Please note, plural units don't matter. *Day* and *days* are the same unit, just plural.

$$\frac{60 \text{ seconds}}{1 \text{ minute}} \times \frac{60 \text{ minutes}}{1 \text{ hour}} \times \frac{24 \text{ hours}}{1 \text{ day}} \times \frac{7 \text{ days}}{1 \text{ week}} \times 3 \text{ weeks}$$

Again, the units can cross each other out, one on top and one on bottom. So now just do the numerical calculation:

$$60 \times 60 \times 24 \times 7 \times 3 = 1{,}814{,}400 \text{ seconds}$$

Therefore, 3 weeks = 1,814,400 seconds.

With a little practice, you'll be able to use unit analysis like a pro.

Real Estate Math

Real estate is really a set of simple arithmetic calculations that, once learned and understood, will serve you well in your career. I'm going to cover these basic operations in example form for the best illustration.

 HELPFUL HINT

Most calculations in the real estate world, once learned, are used in many scenarios. Learning the basics will allow you to apply the same technique in many different situations.

Commission Calculations

Commissions are negotiated between the listing broker and the seller of the property. The listing broker has the right to make his commission anything he wants, but of course the market must be willing to pay it. Commissions are expressed in terms of a percent, or a portion of the final agreed-upon sales price between the seller and the buyer.

For example, what is the commission on a sales price of $247,500 if the listing broker charges 6 percent commission?

$$\$247{,}500 \times 0.06 = \$14{,}850$$

That's an easy one to get you started. Let's continue.

Appreciation and Depreciation Calculation

Appreciation is an increase in the value of a property over time.

Example 1: Ten years ago, a property was worth $100,000. In today's market, the value is $150,000. The property has appreciated $50,000. This is a 50 percent increase, or appreciation, over the 10-year period, which is also a 5 percent annual increase.

$150,000 − $100,000 = $50,000 in appreciation

$50,000 ÷ $100,000 = 50% over the 10-year period is 5%/year

Appreciation can be used most often to forecast values of a property by using today's value and historical data.

Example 2: In a market with 3 percent appreciation, what would be the value of a property in 20 years if the value is $300,000 today?

20 years x 3%/year = 60%

Therefore, $300,000 × 0.60 = $180,000 projected appreciation, so the value in 20 years would be $480,000.

Now let's look at some depreciation calculations. Remember, depreciation is a decrease in the value of a property for any reason.

Example 3: Two years ago, a property was worth $110,000. In today's market, the value is $100,000. Therefore, the property has depreciated $10,000. This is a 9 percent decrease, or depreciation, over the 2-year period, which is also a 4.5 percent annual decrease.

$110,000 − $100,000 = $10,000 in depreciation

$10,000 ÷ $110,000 = 9% over the 2-year period is 4.5%/year

HELPFUL HINT

Please note this is assuming simple appreciation and depreciation rather than compound appreciation and depreciation. That's a more difficult calculation beyond the scope of this book. If you want to learn this method, hop online and look for tutorials.

Area and Perimeter Measurements

Land area and perimeter measurements require knowledge of basic geometry and shapes. In most cases, rectangles and triangles are used singularly or in combination to determine an area or perimeter.

Example 1: How many acres in a piece of land that measures 250 feet long by 350 feet wide?

Area of rectangle is L × W, or 250 feet × 350 feet = 87,500 square feet

An acre is 43,560 square feet, so there are 2.01 acres in the subject property.

Oftentimes, commercial developers are more interested in the frontage along the road to allow access of traffic into their development. This is called the front foot.

Example 2: What is the cost of a 2-acre property that has a depth of 250 feet if the seller wants to get $10,000 per front foot?

The first step is to determine the land's square footage:

2 acres × $\frac{43,560 \text{ square feet}}{1 \text{ acre}}$ = 87,120 square feet

Area = L × W, so we can see this:

W = $\frac{\text{area}}{\text{length}}$

So, the width, or front footage, is 87,120 ÷ 250 feet = 348.48 feet front footage.

Further, we can see that 348.48 front foot × $10,000/front foot is a sales price of $3,484,800.

Another common area calculation would be irregularly shaped properties, such a lot on a cul-de-sac. The best way to calculate the area of such shapes is to consider the parcel a combination of simple geometric shapes, such as a rectangle added to a triangle.

 HELPFUL HINT

The area of a rectangle is length multiplied by width and the area of a triangle is ½ the area of a rectangle.

You can see that this shape is really a rectangle 300 feet × 50 feet and a triangle of 300 feet × 150 feet. Therefore, the area would be 300 feet × 50 feet = 15,000 square feet for the rectangle plus the area of the triangle (area = ½ base × height) or ½ × 150 feet × 300 feet = 22,500 square feet. The total area would be the addition of the two areas:

15,000 square feet + 22,500 square feet = 37,500 square feet or 0.86 acres

Oftentimes, the perimeter of the parcel may be needed, such as when your client wants to build a fence. The perimeter is the distance around the border of the property.

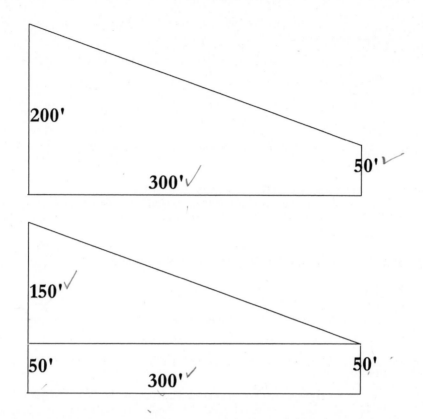

When faced with an irregular shape (top), rethink it as a combination of familiar shapes, such as a triangle and a rectangle (bottom).

Example 3: A client wants to build a fence around his 150 feet × 300 feet lot. How many feet of fence is required to build the fence?

A simple addition of the distance around the property is needed:

150 feet + 300 feet + 150 feet + 300 feet = 900 feet of fence

Loan-to-Value Ratios

The loan-to-value (LTV) ratio compares the loan amount to the *value* of the property. Lenders use this to determine the risk undertaken when making a loan. Typically, a lender's risk is higher with higher LTV ratios than with lower LTV ratios. Additionally, a loan with a high LTV ratio might require the borrower to purchase private mortgage insurance (PMI) to offset the risk. A higher LTV ratio loan might incur a higher interest rate on the loan, too.

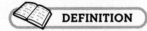

DEFINITION

The **value** is defined as the purchase price or the appraised amount, whichever is the lower of the two.

Example 1: A borrower needs a loan in the amount of $130,000 for the purchase of a $150,000 house. What is the LTV ratio of the loan?

$$\frac{\$130,000}{\$150,000} = 86.67\% \text{ LTV}$$

Example 2: A buyer makes an offer on a $220,000 house, and it's accepted. The house appraises for $220,000. If the buyer wants to get a conventional loan with an 80 percent loan amount, how much is the down payment required?

$220,000 \times 0.80\ (80\%) = \$176,000$ loan made by the lender

So:

$220,000 - \$176,000 = \$44,000$ down payment needed

HELPFUL HINT

The LTV ratio is a common calculation used by mortgage brokers as well as the real estate brokers. Speaking the common language of others in the industry will increase your success at you own profession.

Simple Interest

Interest is the money you pay to borrow someone else's money. Simple interest payments are calculated as the amount of the loan multiplied by the interest rate on that loan.

Example 1: If a borrower borrows $250,000 at an interest rate of 3.5 percent per year, what's the simple interest for the first year of the loan?

Loan amount $\times$ interest rate = interest payment

$205,000 \times 0.035 = \$7,175$

A client may not know, or have forgotten, their interest rate; however, it's possible to determine the rate based on the annual interest paid and the initial loan amount received.

Example 2: Your client has paid $5,500 in interest this year on his purchase of $150,000. However, he got an 80 percent loan with his 20 percent down payment at closing. What was the interest rate of the loan?

Loan amount = purchase price × LTV or $120,000

His interest rate can be determined by this equation:

$$\frac{\text{Interest paid}}{\text{loan amount}} = \text{interest rate}$$

Or:

$$\frac{\$5,500}{\$120,000} = 4.58\%$$

Discount Points and Origination Fees

Discount points and origination fees are front-end charges the lender might impose when making a loan. Both are calculated as a percentage of the loan amount and expressed as 1 percent, called a *point*. The loan documents the borrower signs will expressly state the loan origination fees and discount points.

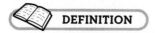 **DEFINITION**

A **point** is 1 percent of the loan amount taken by the borrower.

The lender charges loan origination fees to cover the costs associated with processing the borrower's application, examining his or her credit, and performing other administrative functions for the loan.

Example 1: A lender makes a loan to a borrower of $150,000 at 3.875 percent interest plus 2 points loan origination fee. How much does the borrower pay in fees?

$150,000 × 0.02 (2%) = $3,000 in fees

The lender uses discount points to increase his rate of return on the loan without raising the interest of the loan. This would raise the monthly payment for the borrower.

Example 2: A lender makes a loan to a borrower of $150,000 at 3.875 percent interest plus 2 discount points. How much does the borrower pay in fees?

$150,000 × 0.02 (2%) = $3,000 in fees

You can see that loan origination fees and discount points are calculated in the same manner. Therefore, a borrower could add the two to determine the overall cost of the loan. (Understand that there is actually a difference between the two technically.)

Example 3: A lender makes a loan to a borrower of $150,000 at 3.875 percent interest plus 2 discount points and 1 point for origination. How much does the borrower pay in fees?

$150,000 × 0.03 (2 + 1 = 3%) = $4,500 in fees

Proration of Bills

During the closing process, expenses and sometimes income must be divided between the seller and buyer so each pays only for the expenses used during their respective ownership periods. Some of these expenses and income include real estate property taxes, rents on income property, homeowner association (HOA) fees, insurance, etc.

Proration deals with dividing these expenses or income between the buyer and the seller in some fashion. An important element of this division of expense is whether the items are *prepaid* or *in arrears*.

 **DEFINITION**

A **prepaid** expense is one that's paid prior to the use of the item, such as HOA fees. Expenses paid after the use of the items are called **in arrears.** In many states, real estate taxes are paid in arrears.

Example 1: Assume property tax payments are due on December 31 of each year—that is, in arrears. The annual property taxes are $5,000. The property is sold on June 30. What is the proration?

The seller owned the property for 181 days, and the buyer will own it for the remainder of the year, or 184 days. The buyer will be liable for the tax bill that comes due on December 31, so the seller needs to compensate the buyer for the period he owned the property, or 181 days.

$5,000 ÷ 365 days = $13.70 per day or $2,479.70 (181 × $13.70) is due to the buyer from the seller at closing

In the situation of a prepaid bill, the seller pays the bill first and then seeks money from the buyer for the unused portion during the period the buyer will own the property.

Example 2: Assume HOA fees are due on January 1 of each year, or prepaid. The fees are $300 annually. The property is sold on June 30. What is the proration?

The seller owned the property for 181 days, and the buyer will own it for the remainder of the year, or 184 days. Because the seller was liable for the HOA fees in January, the buyer will reimburse the seller for the days the buyer will own the property—that is, the days the seller won't be using the item he already paid for.

$300 ÷ 365 days = $0.82 per day

Therefore, the buyer must reimburse the seller:

184 days × $0.82 per day = $150.88

Real Estate Taxes

In some states, real estate taxes are based on the assessed value of the property as determined by the taxing authority located in the state, county, or municipality where the property exists. In some states, the assessed value of the property may be presumed to be the sales price of the property. Other states may use a fixed percentage of the market value of the real estate as the assessed value. Check your local area to see what the taxing authority uses for your specific tax calculation.

Other items that must be known are the tax rate used by each taxing authority, usually express in mills, and the equalization factor used in many states to balance the properties in a neighborhood (see Chapter 19).

Example 1: A property valued at $145,000 has an assessed value of 75 percent of the market value and a tax rate of 45 mills. How much are the annual taxes?

$145,000 × 0.75 (75%) = $108,750 assessed value

Therefore:

$108,750 × $0.045 (45 mills) = $4,893.75 annual taxes

Example 2: A property valued at $175,000 has an assessed value of $150,000, an equalization factor of 0.8, and a tax rate of 12 mills. How much are the annual taxes?

$150,000 × 0.8 × $0.012 (12 mills) = $1,440 annual taxes

Transfer Tax

At the closing, the property transfers from the seller to the buyer—that is, from the grantor to the grantee. In 37 states and the District of Columbia, taxes are imposed by states, counties, and municipalities on the transfer of the title of real property within the jurisdiction. The seller pays the tax. However, if the seller doesn't pay the tax, or is exempt from it, the buyer must pay it.

The tax is expressed in one of two ways: a flat percentage of the sales price, such as 1 percent of the sales price, or a dollar rate per unit of money, such as $2 per $1,000 of the sales price. Most states use the second method. An important factor to understand when using this method is that there can be no fractional units.

HELPFUL HINT

Think of a taxing unit as a car. If a car only holds four people, but five people are going to dinner, how many cars would you need to drive? You can't take 1¼ cars; you'd have to take 2. Furthermore, you could add a sixth, seventh, and eighth person and still have the same number of cars going to dinner.

Example 1: If a state charges $1 per $1,000, or any fractional portion thereof, on $145,900 sales price, how much tax is paid?

First, figure the number of taxing units:

$145,900 ÷ $1,000 is 145.9 units

However, you can't have a fraction of the taxing unit, so you must round up to 146 units. Therefore:

146 units × $1 per unit = $146 transfer tax

You can see that a sales price of $145,001 up to and including $145,999 has the same number of taxing units and the same transfer tax.

Example 2: What is the transfer tax collected on a property sold for $225,000 in a state that has a 1.5 percent transfer tax rate?

$225,000 × 0.015 (1.5%) = $3,375 transfer tax

Sales-to-List-Price Ratios

Brokers and sales associates who list a property with a seller price the property so that the property sells within a reasonable time in an open market with good market exposure. This is traditionally done using a comparative market analysis (CMA).

Another factor agents use to determine the strength of a market is the ratio of what a property sells for compared to the original price it was listed.

For example, if a property was originally listed at $190,000 but finally sold for $179,000, the ratio of sales-to-list price was 94.2 percent. While there is no magic ratio number, agents can use the ratio of similar homes in an area to estimate the approximate starting list price.

$$\frac{\text{Sales price}}{\text{List price}} = \text{Sales to list price ratio.}$$

$$\frac{\$179,000}{\$190,000} = 0.942 \text{ or } 94.2 \text{ percent}$$

Example 1: If a seller wants or needs to get a sale price of $125,000 from the sale of their home and the REALTOR knows, on average, the sales to list ratio is 91 percent, he can estimate a good starting list price of $137,362:

$$\frac{\$125,000}{0.91} = \$137,362 \text{ list price}$$

Most probably, the agent would suggest a starting list price of $132,500 to fit conventional pricing strategy.

The Least You Need to Know

- Mathematics is an integral part of being a licensed real estate professional.
- You can use many different calculations to help your clients with their real estate needs.
- LTV ratio is a great number to understand as it describes the amount of indebtedness your client has incurred with his loan.
- In states that use the transfer tax, you must be able to calculate the tax as well as remember to explain to your client this added closing cost he may incur.
- During the closing of a property, there are numerous bills that will get prorated between the parties. Being able to understand and verify these amounts is paramount for your client.
- Understanding the sales-to-list price ratio in a neighborhood will provide you with some great statistics when setting your list price with your client.

Practice Exams and Solutions

In this section, we will cover many practice questions and solutions to very common real-life examples. You can use this section as a test of your knowledge, or you can use this section as a very important study guide to understand the reason why an answer is the best one (or the correct one).

Complete each chapter quiz, grade the quiz, and assess your knowledge. The solutions have been given to help you understand the basic reasons, laws, or rules that you would need to know in your daily practice of real estate to provide your client with the correct answer to their issues.

Test 1: Rights, Interest and Estates, Ownership

1. When demand for a commodity decreases and supply remains the same:

    A. Price tends to rise.

    B. Price tends to fall.

    C. Price is not affected.

    D. The market becomes stagnant.

Answer: B. Price and demand work in concert when holding supply constant; however, price and supply work in contrast when holding demand constant. For example, if I have 10 apples and 10 buyers, and I raise the number of apples to 100 (supply) but still have 10 buyers (demand), the price would fall. But if I have 10 buyers (demand) and only 1 apple (supply), the price would raise.

2. A licensed real estate professional acting as a point of contact between a buyer and a seller in the sale, rental, or purchase of a property is known as:

    A. A sales affiliate

    B. A broker

    C. A property manager

    D. An appraiser

Answer: B. A broker brings together a buyer and a seller.

3. Which of the following would affect the supply of real estate?

    A. Population

    B. Demographics

    C. Interest rates

    D. Wage levels

Answer: C. Issues or items that can be defined as usage of real property, would be considered demand, such as population, demographics (the study of population), and their wage levels. Supply are the things that would affect the creation of real property, such as the interest rates.

4. All the following would affect supply except:

    A. Population

    B. Construction costs

    C. Interest rates

    D. The labor force

Answer: A. Supply includes the things that would affect the creation of real property, like construction costs, the number of people in the labor force, and interest rates. The things that can be defined as usage of real property, is the demand, such as population.

5. All the following are categories of the uses of real property except:

   A. Residential

   B. Developmental

   C. Agricultural

   D. Industrial

Answer: B. Developmental is not a use of property but rather a type of property. Residential, ag, and industrial are ways to use property.

6. A professional who performs a visual survey of a property's structure and systems and prepares to generate an opinion of value is:

   A. An educator

   B. An appraiser

   C. A property manager

   D. A home inspector

Answer: B. An appraiser is a person who uses his education, expertise, and knowledge of the real estate market to generate an opinion of value in a formal report called an appraisal.

7. When supply equals demand in an open, fair market, it is known as:

   A. Equity

   B. Equilibrium

   C. Covenant of seisen

   D. Appurtenant value

Answer: B. The economic term given to a fair and open market when supply and demand are equal is equilibrium.

8. When responsible for preserving a client's property and maximizing a return on a client's investment, a broker is serving as:

   A. A rental agent

   B. A building maintenance specialist

   C. A property manager

   D. An investment counselor

Answer: C. Property managers are responsible for achieving a client's needs, preserving the property, and generating a return on a client's investment.

9. Detailed information about the age, education, behavior, and other characteristics of members of a population group is called:

   A. Population

   B. Demographics

   C. Family lifestyles

   D. Households

Answer: B. Demographics is the study of a population.

10. Efforts to increase home ownership include all the following except:

   A. Requiring lower down payments

   B. Offering adjustable-rate mortgages

   C. Penalizing first-time homebuyers for using funds from IRAs

   D. Lowering closing costs for first-time homebuyers

Answer: C. If you hamper people's access to money, it would not be in their best interest to use the money to buy a home.

11. The real cost of owning a home includes certain costs/expenses that many people overlook. Which of the following is not such a cost/expense of home ownership?

    A. Income lost on cash invested in the home

    B. Interest paid on borrowed capital

    C. Maintenance and repair expenses

    D. Personal property taxes

Answer: D. Personal property taxes would be considered relevant when discussing real property issues.

12. That portion of the value of an owner's property that exceeds the amount of their mortgage debt is called:

    A. Equality

    B. Escrow

    C. Surplus

    D. Equity

Answer: D. The difference between the value of a property and the loan amount is called equity. For example, if I have a house worth $100,000 but owe only $75,000, I have $25,000 in equity.

13. Homeowners may deduct all the following expenses when preparing their income tax return except:

    A. Real estate taxes

    B. Mortgage interest on a first home

    C. Mortgage interest on a second home

    D. Mortgage interest on a third home

Answer: D. A homeowner's third home is not subject to any benefits from the tax laws. Note, that is a third home owned concurrently, not consecutively. For example, I own homes in Indiana, Florida, and California at the same time (concurrently) so the third home gets no tax "breaks." But if I owned a home in Indiana, sold it, bought a home in Florida, sold it, then bought a third home in California, it would be eligible for a tax break because I did not own them all at the same time.

14. Federal income tax law excludes gains realized on the sale of a primary residence for individuals filing separately and for couples filing jointly. The amount of this exclusion is (separately/jointly):

    A. $100,000/$200,000

    B. $250,000/$250,000

    C. $300,000/$500,000

    D. $250,000/$500,000

Answer: D. By definition from the IRS tax code. Think of $250,000 for a tax break per person. Therefore, $250,000 for one and $500,000 for two.

15. Damage from which of the following is not covered in a basic homeowners' policy?

    A. Fire and lightning

    B. Explosion

    C. Windstorm and hail

    D. Flood

Answer: D. Flood insurance is a separate insurance policy and is not part of a standard homeowners' insurance policy.

16. Federal income tax regulations allow homeowners to reduce their taxable income by amounts paid for:

    A. Repairs and maintenance

    B. Hazard insurance premiums

    C. Real estate taxes

    D. Principal and interest

Answer: C. Real estate taxes are a tax deduction on all residential owner-occupied houses, but not on investment or rental properties.

17. Which type of development combines office space, stores, and residential units in a single, vertical community?

    A. Planned unit development

    B. Manufactured housing park

    C. Mixed-use development

    D. Timeshare community

Answer: C. Whenever you mix distinct zoning types, you have a mixed-use property.

18. Three years ago, a couple moved from the house they had lived in for 20 years but did not sell it. They decided to travel and bought a mobile home to live in. They now want to sell the house. How much of their capital gain on the house is taxable?

    A. 15 percent, depending on their tax bracket

    B. 28 percent, depending on their tax bracket

    C. All of it, if it is more than $500,000

    D. None of it, if it is less than $500,000

Answer: D. The deduction for a married couple, living in a property for 2 out of 5 years (they need not be consecutive years) is $500,000. If the capital gains earned is over the diminimus value, they would pay only on the portion over the amount, not on the entire amount. In this example, the couple earned less than the diminimus level so no taxes are due.

19. A woman held fee simple title to a vacant lot adjacent to a business and was persuaded to make the lot available to the business. She had her attorney prepare a deed that conveyed ownership of the lot to the business "… as long as it is used for commercial purposes." After the completion of the gift, the business will own a:

    A. Life estate

    B. Tenancy for years

    C. Determinable fee estate

    D. Periodic tenancy

Answer: C. Because she added a stipulation to the title, as is her right, she has created a title with a determinable condition. In this scenario, if the business quit using the property for its intended use, she would gain control of the property with no court action required. She also could will or gift this right away to her heirs or successors.

20. A person who has complete control of a parcel of real estate is said to own a:

    A. Leasehold estate

    B. Fee simple estate

    C. Life estate

    D. Defeasible fee estate

Answer: B. Fee simple is the highest form of ownership with all the rights and benefits intact.

21. A man owned 2 acres of land. He sells 1 acre to a neighbor and reserves for himself an appurtenant easement over his neighbor's land for ingress and egress. The man's land:

    A. Is the servient tenement

    B. Is the dominant tenement

    C. Can be cleared of the easement when the man sells the withheld acre to a third party

    D. Is subject to an easement in gross

Answer: B. He is the one taking the use of another property; therefore, he is dominant over that party.

22. If the owner of the dominant tenement becomes the owner of the servient tenement and merges the two properties:

    A. The easement becomes dormant.

    B. The easement is unaffected.

    C. The easement is terminated.

    D. The properties retain their former status.

Answer: C. Once an easement is no longer needed because one owner now owns both parcels, the easement may be terminated.

23. A portion of a building is inadvertently built on someone else's land. This causes an:

    A. Accretion

    B. Avulsion

    C. Encroachment

    D. Easement

Answer: C. A physical portion of a building, fence, shed, etc., on another person's property is an encroachment. This may include encroachment of airspace as well, such as a tree limb hanging over the property line.

24. A homeowner acquires ownership of land that was deposited by a river running through his property by:

    A. Reliction

    B. Succession

    C. Avulsion

    D. Accretion

Answer: D. Accretion is the act of depositing soil along a bank line, creating more land for the owner.

25. A homestead exemption protects against judgments:

    A. Of unsecured creditors

    B. That result from unpaid taxes

    C. That result from foreclosure of a mortgage

    D. That result from the costs of improvements

Answer: A. The homestead act is one of the legal life estates, along with dowry and curtesy, that protect the residence against unsecured creditors, such as a credit card. However, it does not protect against secured creditors, like a mortgage company, that hold a secured lien against the property.

26. A life estate conveys to the life tenant:

    A. A leasehold for life

    B. A reversionary interest

    C. A legal life estate

    D. Ownership for life

Answer: D. The ownership is only guaranteed for the life of the owner. Upon his death, the property transfers to whomever is the recipient of the life estate.

27. The owner of a secluded area adjacent to an ocean has noticed that people from town walk along the shore in front of his property. The owner also has learned that the local citizens have been walking along this beach for several years. He goes to court to try to stop people from walking along the water's edge in front of his property. The owner is likely to be:

    A. Unsuccessful because the local citizens have been doing this for years and, thus, have an easement

    B. Unsuccessful because the owner's property extends only to the high-water mark, and the public may use the land beyond this point

    C. Successful because the owner's property extends to the low-water mark

    D. Successful because the owner can control access to his own property

Answer: B. Littoral rights of an owner adjacent to a lake allow for control and rights only to the high-water mark. Courts have determined that below this mark is for public use and enjoyment.

28. Which of the following is an example of a legal life estate?

    A. A wife's interest in her deceased husband's property

    B. Estate conveyed by one party to a second party for the life of the second party

    C. Estate created by a will

    D. Estate conveyed to a second party subject to a condition

Answer: A. There are three legal life estates: dowry, curtesy, and homestead. Dowry is the wife's interest in the husband's property, curtesy is the husband's interest in the wife's property, and homestead is the family's interest in the owner-occupied real property against unsecured creditors.

29. The phrase "bundle of legal rights" is properly included in:

    A. The definition of real property

    B. A legal description

    C. Real estate transactions

    D. Leases for less than 1 year

Answer: A. The definition of title and, therefore, real property is called the bundle of legal rights.

30. All the following are included in the right to control one's property except the right to:

    A. Sell the property to a neighbor

    B. Exclude the utilities meter reader

    C. Erect "no trespassing" signs

    D. Enjoy profits from its ownership

Answer: B. When you exclude any party from entrance to your property, you are exercising your right of exclusion, not control.

31. According to law, unless negotiated otherwise, a trade fixture is usually treated as:

    A. A fixture

    B. An easement

    C. Chattel

    D. A license

Answer: C. Chattel is considered personal property. A trade fixture only becomes real property if the tenant fails to remove their personal property before the end of the lease.

32. A potential buyer is interested in a house that fits most of her needs, but it's in a busy area where she's not sure she wants to live. Her concern about the property's location is called:

A. Physical deterioration

B. Area preference

C. Permanence of investment

D. Immobility

Answer: B. When a buyer is concerned with a physical location rather than a right or benefit, it is a concern over area, or location.

33. Which of the following is considered personal property?

A. Wood-burning fireplace

B. Awnings

C. Bathtubs

D. Patio furniture

Answer: D. If a piece of personal property is affixed in a manner to become permanent, it becomes a fixture and not personal property. Use the movability rule of thumb: If it can be moved easily, it's personal property; if it requires work to move, as in a fireplace, bathtub, or an awning, it would be treated as real property.

34. Real property can become personal property by:

A. Severance

B. Purchase

C. Hypothecation

D. Attachment

Answer: A. Severance means "to sever from" or make real property become personal property. Annexation, meaning "to join," would make personal property become real property.

35. All the following are physical characteristics of land except:

A. Indestructibility

B. Uniqueness

C. Immobility

D. Scarcity

Answer: D. Scarcity is an economic factor dealing with value, whereas the other three are physical characteristics of real property.

36. A licensee shows an owner-occupied property that has window screens, custom blinds, and a Murphy bed to a buyer whose offer is then accepted by the owner. Before the close of escrow, the seller may remove:

A. All the items because they are trade fixtures

B. Only the blinds as personal property

C. Only the Murphy bed because it is real property

D. None of the identified items

Answer: D. None of the items mentioned are movable; they are attached in such a manner as to be permanent.

37. Land is considered:

A. Indestructible

B. A wasting asset

C. Immune to the forces of supply and demand

D. Subject to personal property rights

Answer: A. You cannot destroy land.

38. The type of housing that can become permanent if affixed to the land is called:

    A. On-site built

    B. Semidetached single family

    C. Manufactured

    D. Multifamily

Answer: C. If a property is built off-site but affixed to a permanent foundation, it's a manufactured home.

39. All the following are treated as personal property except:

    A. Chattels

    B. Trade fixtures

    C. Emblements

    D. Fructus naturales

Answer: D. Fructus naturales are the naturally occurring fruits, such as trees, shrubs, and flowers. They are treated as real property in the sale of a home and not specifically called out in the purchase agreement.

40. Fixtures are:

    A. Treated as real property

    B. Considered chattels

    C. Removable by a tenant before the expiration of the lease

    D. Removable by a tenant after the expiration of the lease

Answer: A. A fixture once was personal property but now is attached in such a manner as to be permanent; therefore, it's treated as real property.

41. All the following are economic characteristics of land except:

    A. Scarcity

    B. Permanence of investment

    C. Uniqueness

    D. Area preference

Answer: C. No two properties are alike. They differ in location, size, composition, etc., which are some physical characteristics of property.

42. Generally, personal property can be distinguished from real property by its:

    A. Greater variety

    B. Mobility

    C. Cost

    D. Multiplicity of use

Answer: B. The test to distinguish between real and personal property is, "Can it be moved?" If so, it's personal property.

43. An important characteristic of land is that it may be modified or improved at some point in time. Depending on its type, an improvement may increase the value of real estate greatly. All the following are considered to be improvements except:

    A. Sewers

    B. Crops

    C. Buildings

    D. Roads

Answer: B. An improvement is a manmade item or structure. Sewers, roads, buildings, etc., are considered improvements, but crops, called emblements, are treated as personal property.

44. Rights or privileges that are connected with real property are:

 A. Improvements

 B. Appurtenances

 C. Not conveyed with the real estate

 D. Restricted to air and water rights

Answer: B. Appurtenances are things that belong to and go with real property, the appurtenance being less significant than what it belongs to. For example, the backyard of a house or an assigned parking spot with a condo is an appurtenance.

45. The term improvements, when referring to real estate, include:

 A. Shrubbery

 B. Trees

 C. Sidewalks

 D. Lawns

Answer: C. Any manmade items, such as a sidewalk, are improvements to a property.

46. Which of the following is not a test to identify a fixture?

 A. Intent of the parties

 B. Size of the item

 C. Method of attachment of the item

 D. Adaptation of the item to the real estate

Answer: B. The size of an item has no consideration in the determination of a fixture, only the intent of the parties, the method of attachment, and how it's used in a system, or adaption.

47. The owner of a house wants to fence the yard for her dog. When the fence is erected, the fencing materials are converted to real estate by:

 A. Severance

 B. Annexation

 C. Immobility

 D. Indestructibility

Answer: B. Annexation means "to join or include." The fence, once installed, becomes real property via annexation.

48. The uniqueness of land and its inability to be substituted is known as:

 A. Nonhomogenity

 B. Scarcity

 C. Permanence of investment

 D. Nonheterogenity

Answer: A. Unique means "sufficiently different from others." The prefix non- means "not," while homo- means "same." Therefore, "not the same" or unique.

49. The rights of ownership of real property include all the following except the right of:

 A. Disposition

 B. Exclusion

 C. Control

 D. Compatibility

Answer: D. The legal bundle of rights includes control, disposition, exclusion, enjoyment, and possession.

50. A bill of sale is used to transfer the ownership of:

    A. Real property

    B. Fixtures

    C. Personal property

    D. Appurtenances

Answer: C. A mortgage is used in real property, whereas a bill of sale is used for personal property, such as a bike, refrigerator, etc.

Test 2: Encumbrances, Liens, Title Transfers, Leasing

1. The current market value of a property is $35,000. For tax purposes, it is assessed at 40 percent of market value. The tax rate is $4 per $100 of assessed value. What is the amount of the tax due?

    A. $560

    B. $625

    C. $705

    D. $740

Answer: A. The assessed value would be $0.40 \times \$35,000$ or $14,000. If the tax rate is $4 per $100, then $14,000 \div \$100 =$ 14 units of value at $4 each, $14 \times \$4$ is $560.

2. When a company furnishes materials for the construction of a house and is subsequently not paid, it may file:

    A. A deficiency judgment

    B. A lis pendens

    C. An estoppel certificate

    D. A mechanic's lien

Answer: D. A contractor can file for nonpayment of items or services it provides a homeowner.

3. A mechanic's lien is properly classified as:

    A. An equitable lien

    B. A voluntary lien

    C. A general lien

    D. A specific lien

Answer: D. Because it is filed against the property where the work took place, it must be specific. A general lien attaches to personal property as well, and that is not true.

4. What is the difference between a general lien and a specific lien?

    A. A general lien cannot be enforced in court, while a specific lien can be enforced.

    B. A specific lien is held by one person, while a general lien is held by at least two persons.

    C. A general lien affects all of a debtor's property, while a specific lien affects only a certain piece of property.

    D. A specific lien covers real estate, while a general lien covers only personal property.

Answer: C. Specific liens attach to only the specific piece of real property, whereas general liens attach to both real and personal property.

5. Which of the following is a lien on real estate?

    A. Easement

    B. Recorded mortgage

    C. Encroachment

    D. Restrictive covenant

Answer: B. All may be encumbrances, but liens are monetary in nature. The others are a limitation of one of the legal bundle of rights.

6. Real estate taxes are also known as:

    A. Special assessments

    B. Ad valorem taxes

    C. Appropriation funds

    D. General, voluntary liens

Answer: B. Real estate taxes are based on a value of the home, called the assessed value. Ad valorem, meaning "at value," taxes are for real estate taxes.

7. Normally, the priority of general liens is determined by the:

    A. Order in which they are filed or recorded

    B. Order in which the cause of action arose

    C. Size of the claim

    D. Court

Answer: A. The priority of a lien is generally assigned by the date recorded. First one in gets first priority, hence the name "first lien" for the mortgage that gets recorded first.

8. After real estate has been sold by the state or county to satisfy a delinquent tax lien, the defaulted owner usually has a right to:

    A. Have the sale canceled by paying the back taxes and penalties

    B. Pay his or her creditors directly and have their liens removed

    C. Redeem the property within the time specified by law

    D. Record a notice of nonresponsibility for the unpaid taxes

Answer: C. After the sale of real property for delinquent taxes, there is a state law, or statutory right, to redeem the property within the prescribed period of time allotted. Answer A would be the definition of the equitable right of redemption.

9. John is involved in a lawsuit. He owns a rental home that's free of any mortgage. What can a creditor obtain to prevent John from selling the rental home before the lawsuit is settled?

A. Judgment

B. Foreclosure notice

C. Seizure notice

D. Writ of attachment

Answer: D. After being found liable in a lawsuit, real property can be "attached" to keep a person from selling the property without the requirement to pay his court obligations.

10. In which of the following situations could a quitclaim deed not be used?

A. To convey title

B. To release a nominal real estate interest

C. To remove a cloud on title

D. To warrant that a title is valid

Answer: D. A quitclaim deed offers no warranties at all, but rather transfers the interest, whatever it is, to the person accepting the quitclaim deed.

11. A valid will devises a decedent's real estate after payment of all debts, claims, inheritance taxes, and expenses through the:

A. Administrator of the estate

B. Law of testate succession

C. Granting clause established in the will

D. Court action known as probate

Answer: D. To validate a will by selling off assets to pay outstanding bills of the deceased is called probate.

12. Real estate that's inherited from a person who died testate is referred to as a:

A. Legacy

B. Bequest

C. Devise

D. Demise

Answer: C. The legal term used for real property in a will is a devise. It goes to the devisee by transference from the will.

13. Which of the following is an example of involuntary alienation?

A. Selling a property to pay off debts

B. Giving a piece of land to the zoo

C. Having a piece of land sold for delinquent taxes

D. Letting another person plant crops on your land

Answer: C. If a property is used, sold, or given away under the power of the owner, it is voluntary. If it's taken by another party through adverse possession, foreclosure, eminent domain, or escheat, it's involuntary.

14. The reversion of real estate to the state because of the lack of heirs or other people legally entitled to own the property is called:

A. Eminent domain

B. Escheat

C. Attachment

D. Estoppel

Answer: B. If a person dies with no will leaving his or her property to someone or has no legal heirs, the state acquires the property via escheat.

15. The seller conveyed a quitclaim deed to the buyer. Upon receipt of the deed, the buyer may be certain that:

    A. The seller owned the property.

    B. There are no encumbrances against the property.

    C. The buyer now owns the property subject to certain claims of the seller.

    D. All the seller's interests in the property belong to the buyer.

Answer: D. A quitclaim only transfers the grantor's rights to the grantee. There is warranty, or guarantee, of ownership, quiet enjoyment, etc.

16. A man owns a one-quarter undivided interest in a parcel of land. While he's still living, he wants his interest transferred to his sister. Generally, which of the following actions will transfer the man's undivided interest out of his name?

    A. Redemption from foreclosure sale

    B. Making and signing a will

    C. Delivery and acceptance of a deed

    D. Signed acceptance of offer to purchase

Answer: C. A sale or gift can transfer property between parties. The sale would use a deed to transfer ownership.

17. A special warranty deed differs from a general warranty deed in that the grantor's covenant in the special warranty deed:

    A. Applies only to a definite limited time

    B. Covers the time back to the original title

    C. Is implied and not written in full

    D. Protects all subsequent owners of the property

Answer: A. A special warranty deed gives no warranties regarding any historical transactions prior to the current owner. It only applies to the time in which the current owner had possession and ownership of the property.

18. The type of deed in which the grantor defends the title back to its beginning is a:

    A. Trustee's deed

    B. Quitclaim deed

    C. Special warranty deed

    D. General warranty deed

Answer: D. A general warranty deed has the covenant of warranty forever. However, a special warranty deed has no warranties except during the period they owned the property. Quitclaim and trustee's deeds have no warranties at all.

19. A deed must be signed by the:

    A. Grantor

    B. Grantee

    C. Grantor and grantee

    D. Grantee and two witnesses

Answer: A. Only the grantor, or seller, need sign the deed.

20. All the following are required for a deed to be valid except:

    A. Date

    B. Legal description

    C. Name of the grantee

    D. Signature of the grantee

Answer: D. The buyer, or grantee, does not sign the deed. He is only named in the deed.

21. The recording of a warranty deed:

    A. Gives actual notice of the grantee's rights

    B. Gives constructive notice of an individual's interest

    C. Prevents claims of parties in possession

    D. Provides defense against adverse possession

Answer: B. Recording a document in the public record provides for constructive notice. Actual notice can be accomplished to everyone regarding his new ownership.

22. The history of all owners of a specific parcel of real estate is the property's:

    A. Chain of title

    B. Certificate of title

    C. Title insurance policy

    D. Abstract of title

Answer: A. A chain of title is the history of ownership in a specific parcel of real property.

23. The best reason for a buyer to obtain title insurance is:

    A. That the mortgage lender requires it

    B. To ensure that the seller can deliver marketable title

    C. To ensure that the abstractor has prepared a complete summary of title

    D. To pay future liens that may be filed

Answer: B. Title insurance, like any other insurance, is a protection against harm, defects, or mistakes. Furthermore, title insurance can guarantee the owner can make good if he has problems with the transfer of the real property.

24. A written summary of the history of all conveyances and legal proceedings affecting a specific parcel of real estate is called:

    A. An affidavit of title

    B. A certificate of title

    C. An abstract of title

    D. A title insurance policy

Answer: C. A chain records the ownership interests, but an abstract of title records all legal action taken against a property.

25. The type of title insurance that protects the owner in a sale is:

    A. A lender's policy

    B. An owner's policy

    C. A leasehold policy

    D. A certificate of sale policy

Answer: B. The portion of the title work designed to cover the seller, or owner, is called the owner's policy; the lender's policy is designed to protect the buyer's lender and his interest.

26. The mortgagee receives a title insurance policy on the property a buyer is pledging as security for the mortgage loan. Which of the following is true?

    A. The policy is issued for the benefit of the buyer.

    B. The policy guarantees the equity will be protected.

    C. The amount of coverage is equal to the loan amount.

    D. The amount of coverage increases as the equity increases.

Answer: C. The title insurance policy is designed to make the lender whole, in the worst-case scenario, and is only equal to the amount borrowed from the lender.

27. All the following liens need to be recorded to be valid except:

    A. Mortgage lien

    B. Real estate tax lien

    C. Judgment lien

    D. Mechanic's lien

Answer: B. Real estate tax liens are not recorded.

28. A family's apartment lease has expired, but their landlord has indicated that they may remain on the premises until a sale of the building is closed. They will be charged their normal monthly rental during this period. The right held by the family is called:

    A. A year-to-year holdover

    B. An estate for term

    C. An estate at sufferance

    D. Tenancy at will

Answer: D. A lease that can end without any date or notice is defined as tenancy at will. The phrase at will loosely means "whenever."

29. Generally, an oral lease for 5 years is:

    A. Illegal

    B. Unenforceable

    C. A short-term lease

    D. Renewable only in writing

Answer: B. Only leases less than 1 year in length can be verbal. Under the statute of frauds, leases longer than 1 year must be in writing.

30. The lessor and lessee have agreed to a lease term of 5 years. To ensure that the rental income during the term is reflective of market conditions, the lessor could:

    A. Negotiate a new lease each year

    B. Collect an additional security deposit each year

    C. Negotiate an index lease

    D. Negotiate a gross lease

Answer: C. An index lease is one tied to, or reflective of, some financial index and can adjust accordingly if that index adjusts.

31. The tenant leases a heated apartment, but the landlord fails to provide heat because of a defective central heating plant. The tenant vacates the premises and refuses to pay any rent. This is an example of:

    A. Abandonment

    B. Actual eviction

    C. Constructive eviction

    D. Lessor negligence

Answer: C. The tenant, in essence, evicted themselves due to unlivable conditions.

32. A tenant's lease has expired, but the tenant has not vacated the premises or negotiated a renewal lease. The landlord has declared that the tenant is not to remain in the building. This situation is an example of:

    A. An estate for years

    B. An estate from year to year

    C. Tenancy at will

    D. Tenancy at sufferance

Answer: D. The tenant is a holdover tenant because he's unlawfully occupying the property after his lease has expired. With no new creation of a lease, the landlord will have a tenancy at sufferance.

33. A lessee who pays some or all the lessor's property expenses has a:

    A. Gross lease

    B. Net lease

    C. Percentage lease

    D. Sublease

Answer: B. The landlord receives the net amount of money due to the tenant paying some or all of his bills.

34. The principal difference between an estate for years and an estate from year to year is that:

    A. An estate for years is a life estate.

    B. An estate for years cannot be terminated.

    C. An estate from year to year must be in writing.

    D. An estate from year to year has no expiration date.

Answer: D. A period-to-period tenancy has no defined end and renews at the end of each period. A period-to-period tenancy must be terminated in writing by either party to end.

35. The covenant implied in a lease that ensures the landlord will not interfere in the tenant's possession or use of the property is the covenant:

    A. Of seisin

    B. Of quiet enjoyment

    C. Of warranty forever

    D. Against encumbrances

Answer: B. Quiet enjoyment means free of any outside interference in the right to enjoy the property.

36. A tenant has an estate for years. Per the written 1-year lease, the tenancy expires on May 1. To obtain possession as of that date, the landlord:

    A. Must give the tenant 30 days' notice

    B. Must give the tenant 60 days' notice

    C. Must give the tenant notice before April 15

    D. Is not required to give the tenant any notice

Answer: D. An estate for years has a defined ending, and no notice of termination is needed by either party.

37. The owner of real estate who leases it to another is called the:

    A. Vendor

    B. Lessor

    C. Grantor

    D. Trustor

Answer: B. The one doing the action is always signified by the suffix -or. So the landlord is the lessor, and the tenant is the lessee.

38. A lease that terminates within 1 year of its inception:

    A. Is invalid

    B. Violates the provisions of the statute of frauds

    C. Must be in writing

    D. May be oral

Answer: D. Under the 1-year rule, a contract that can be complete within 1 year need not be in writing.

39. Which of the following is the best definition of actual eviction?

    A. Right of a landlord to use the rental premises

    B. Enforcement of a court order to remove a lessor

    C. Landlord's reversionary right in the rental premises

    D. Enforcement of a court order to remove a lessee

Answer: D. The landlord evicts the tenant for a violation of clause contained within the lease, typically nonpayment of rent, violation of zoning rules, having pets, etc.

40. When a tenant holds possession of a landlord's property without a definite lease term but with the consent of the landlord, this is called:

  A. Tenancy in common

  B. Tenancy at sufferance

  C. Tenancy at will

  D. Trespassing

Answer: C. At will means "whenever," or that no definite expiration terms are in place. The tenant would still pay rent, however.

41. In the event that it is necessary for a landlord to remove a tenant from the premises, he or she does it by:

  A. Refunding any rents paid

  B. Refunding any security or other deposits paid

  C. Filing a suit for possession

  D. Using the minimum amount of physical force necessary

Answer: C. Distraint of a tenant is not allowed; that is, no self-help when it comes to removing a tenant. A landlord must use the court system to enact an eviction. The first step is to be awarded a suit for possession to regain the property from the tenant.

42. The purpose of a security deposit is to:

  A. Provide additional revenue for the landlord

  B. Repair damage to the property caused by the tenant

  C. Pay for the last month's rent

  D. Ensure that the lease is valid

Answer: B. A security deposit ensures that the tenant returns the property in substantially the same condition he or she received it.

43. With a tenancy for years:

  A. The term of the lease must be for at least 1 year.

  B. No notice is required to terminate the lease.

  C. A 30-day notice is required to terminate the lease.

  D. The lessee has a freehold estate.

Answer: B. In a tenancy for years, the beginning date and end date are known and agreed upon at the onset of the lease. It requires no notice of termination for this reason.

44. Under a percentage lease, a commercial lessee may agree to pay:

  A. Maintenance

  B. Real estate taxes

  C. Insurance

  D. A percentage of sales

Answer: D. A percentage lease, as the name implies, pays a portion of the sales as rent.

45. A lessee is in possession of property under a tenancy at will. Which of the following is true?

  A. The lessee has not received the consent of the landlord to possess the property.

  B. The tenancy will terminate if the lessee dies.

  C. The tenancy was created by the death of the lessor.

  D. The tenancy has a definite termination date.

Answer: B. At will tenancy can be terminated by death of either party or at will of either party.

46. A tenant's lease does not terminate for 5 more years. The premises, however, have become too small to accommodate the tenant's growing business. Another business owner is interested in leasing the premises from the tenant for 3 years. Which of the following would the parties use for the tenant to lease the space to the business owner?

    A. Assignment

    B. Novation

    C. Sublease

    D. Tenancy at sufferance

Answer: C. Although not the preferred method, a sublease allows a tenant to find another tenant and replace them in the property.

47. An individual rents an apartment for 1 year. The landlord sells the building during the 1-year lease term. What effect does the sale have on the lease?

    A. The sale does not affect the lease.

    B. The lease is automatically terminated.

    C. The new landlord will decide whether to honor the existing lease.

    D. The lease is terminated after 60 days' notice from the new owner.

Answer: A. In most states, properties sell with tenants' rights, meaning any lease in place with the old owner is in place with the new owner unless there's a specific clause addressing a sale of the property contained within the lease itself.

48. A tenant agrees to rent on a month-to-month basis after the termination of the original lease. This is known as an:

    A. Estate for years

    B. Estate from period to period

    C. Estate at will

    D. Estate at sufferance

Answer: B. A periodic tenancy is defined as one that automatically renews itself and never expires, unless by written request by either party.

49. When does a deed pass from seller to buyer?

    A. Upon recording of the deed

    B. Upon the money being transferred

    C. After the buyer and seller agree to sell the property

    D. Upon delivery and acceptance of the deed

Answer: D. Deed transfers when the buyer takes possession of the deed.

50. A percentage lease calls for a base rent of $6,000 per month plus an additional 5 percent on all gross sales. If the company has annual sales of $550,000, what is the amount of the annual rent?

    A. $27,500

    B. $99,500

    C. $72,000

    D. $34,500

Answer: B. The overage would be 5 percent of $550,000, or $27,500 per year. The annual rent would be $6,000 × 12, or $72,000 per year. Therefore, the total rent would be the base + the overage, or $72,000 + $27,500 = $99,500.

Test 3: Land Use, Legal Land Descriptions, Contract Law

1. All the following are designated uses by zoning ordinances except:

   A. Industrial

   B. Commercial

   C. Residential

   D. Rental

Answer: D. A rental is a type of property rather than a zoning classification.

2. The purpose of building permits is to:

   A. Generate revenue

   B. Control building inspectors

   C. Ensure compliance with building codes

   D. Prevent encroachments

Answer: C. Building permits ensure builders follow set guidelines for public health and safety.

3. Which is not a method of creating a deed restriction?

   A. Deed

   B. Statute

   C. Written agreement

   D. General plan of a subdivision

Answer: B. Deed restrictions are not created by state laws.

4. A variance is defined as a:

   A. Zoning ordinance exception

   B. Court order prohibiting certain types of properties

   C. Revocation of ownership

   D. Termination of an easement

Answer: A. A variance is an exception to allow for other uses.

5. The plat for a proposed subdivision is submitted for approval to:

   A. A developer

   B. The state department of builders

   C. A municipality

   D. The new property owners

Answer: C. Local municipalities approve subdivision plans and use them to guide their comprehensive plan.

6. A municipality establishes development goals in its:

   A. Public subdivision regulations

   B. Private restrictive covenants

   C. Statewide environmental regulations

   D. Local comprehensive plan

Answer: D. A municipality's long-range plan to grow is based on its resources.

7. Bulk zoning's main purpose is to:

    A. Ensure that certain kinds of properties get built

    B. Specify certain styles for new buildings

    C. Control density and population of an area

    D. Set development goals for the community

Answer: C. Bulk zoning is used to define the allowable structures per acres, thus controlling population.

8. The construction of additional rooms has been completed on the owner's home. Before use of the new rooms can occur:

    A. The state must issue a building permit.

    B. The rooms must be inspected by a home inspector.

    C. The municipality must issue an occupancy permit.

    D. The municipality must issue a nonconforming use permit.

Answer: C. After it gets inspected but before being occupied by people, a structure must possess an occupancy permit.

9. Restrictive covenants:

    A. Are no longer effective when the property is sold

    B. Apply only until the developer has finished the addition

    C. Can be removed by a court

    D. Apply to and bind successive owners of the property

Answer: D. Restrictive covenants are passed to the new owner upon each successive sale of the property.

10. The taking of private property for public use is allowed under the state's right of:

    A. Police power

    B. Escheat

    C. Confiscation

    D. Eminent domain

Answer: D. Eminent domain is one of the governmental powers.

11. Deed restrictions may legally control or limit:

    A. The sizes and types of structures to be built

    B. The potential future owners of the properties

    C. The race of future owners and occupants of a property

    D. The exterior finish and decoration of the yard and adjoining land

Answer: A. Disallowing a certain ethnicity to buy property is the central theme of the fair housing laws. Furthermore, a yard can be decorated as the owner decides.

12. If a buyer builds an outbuilding that violates his CCRs, he:

    A. May forfeit the title to the property immediately

    B. May be sued and required to alter the structure or remove it

    C. May be sued and required to pay damages to the other residents

    D. Is safe from legal actions taken by other residents in the area about this matter

Answer: B. Violating CCRs is grounds for removal of any outbuildings.

13. When land is taken for public use:

    A. The owner must receive just compensation.

    B. The health, safety, and welfare of the government must be the reason.

    C. The local use will benefit the residents in the immediate area.

    D. The property is then established as a fee simple estate for a particular use.

Answer: A. Under the takings clause, a homeowner must be compensated if their property is taken.

14. A man applies to the municipality for permission to open a business in his residential neighborhood. He may be granted:

    A. A variance

    B. A nonconforming use permit

    C. An amendment to the zoning ordinance

    D. A conditional use permit

Answer: D. A conditional use permit allows for an activity that otherwise would not be allowed in an area.

15. Control by zoning ordinances regulates the following, except:

    A. The height of buildings in an area

    B. The density of population

    C. The use of the property

    D. The price of the property

Answer: D. The price is determined by the buyer and the seller through negotiations and not statute.

16. A wooded area is situated between a commercial area and a residential area. This area is considered:

    A. A special use under federal guidelines

    B. A variance to the existing zoning

    C. A utility easement

    D. A buffer zone

Answer: D. A buffer zone is used to separate zoning classifications.

17. Which is not a method of identifying a legal description?

    A. Lot and block

    B. Metes and bounds

    C. Arc and string

    D. Rectangular survey

Answer: C. Method C is not a method of legal description.

18. The primary survey line running north and south in any area described by the rectangular survey system is its:

    A. Township line

    B. Base line

    C. Range line

    D. Principal meridian

Answer: D. A principal meridian is the basis or the rectangular survey method. It runs north and south.

19. The intersection of a range and a tier is called:

    A. An acre

    B. A plot

    C. A section

    D. A township

Answer: D. A geographic township is the overlapping of a specific tier and range. It's identified as a combination of the each, such as 2RW,2TN.

20. A standard rectangular survey system section contains:

    A. 36 townships

    B. 160 government lots

    C. 160 acres

    D. 640 acres

Answer: D. 640 acres by definition of a section, or 1 square mile.

21. A township contains:

    A. 6 square miles

    B. 640 acres

    C. 23,040 square feet

    D. 36 sections

Answer: D. A township is 6 miles square, or 36 square miles. It contains 23,040 acres.

22. The primary survey line running east and west in the rectangular survey system is the:

    A. Township line

    B. Baseline

    C. Range line

    D. Principal meridian

Answer: B. Several baselines throughout the United States run east to west and are used in rectangular survey systems.

23. The survey lines running north and south and parallel to the principal meridian are called:

    A. Prime meridians

    B. Baselines

    C. Range lines

    D. Principal meridians

Answer: C. A range of land is 6 miles wide and bounded on each side by a range line.

24. The legal description system that defines a parcel of land by defining its perimeter is the:

    A. Geodetic survey

    B. Rectangular survey

    C. Lot and block system

    D. Metes and bounds system

Answer: D. The metes and bounds system is defined as a distance and direction to define the exterior perimeter of a property.

25. The owner has a large parcel of land. He then files a subdivision plat. He's using which method of legal description?

    A. Street address

    B. Government survey

    C. Metes and bounds

    D. Lot and block

Answer: D. A subdivision uses the lot and block method to divide property smaller than 10 acres.

26. Strips of land 6 miles wide that run north and south are called:

    A. Tiers

    B. Ranges

    C. Latitudes

    D. Longitudes

Answer: B. A range runs north and south.

27. Strips of land 6 miles wide that run east and west are called:

    A. Tiers

    B. Ranges

    C. Latitudes

    D. Longitudes

Answer: A. A tier runs east and west.

28. A metes and bounds legal description must end:

A. At a manmade monument

B. Within 50 feet of the beginning

C. At the point of beginning

D. At a monument, nearest to the beginning

Answer: C. The metes and bounds must end with the statement "back to the POB" to ensure the boundary is closed.

29. The following legal description contains how many acres: the N½ of the SE¼ of the NW¼ of Section 26 of principal meridian #2?

A. 2½

B. 5

C. 10

D. 20

Answer: D. To solve, use the denominators given in the problem and the empirical math formula 2 × 4 × 4 = 32. There are 640 acres in a section; therefore, 640 ÷ 32 = 20 acres.

30. How many acres are in a parcel described as, "The SE¼ of the SE¼ and the S½ of the SW¼ of the NE¼ of Section 6 principal meridian #3"?

A. 40

B. 50

C. 60

D. 80

Answer: C. See question 29. There are two parcels in this question: (1) 4 × 4 = 16 .640 ÷ 16 = 40 acres, and (2) 2 × 4 × 4 = 32.640 ÷ 32 = 20 acres. Therefore, 40 + 20 = 60 acres.

31. The method of describing land that can allow for the use of angles and the phrase "more or less" is known as the:

A. Angular system

B. Metes and bounds system

C. Rectangular survey system

D. Lot and block system

Answer: B. The metes and bounds system is the only legal method of description that allows for these two special issues.

32. The school section in the rectangular survey system is:

A. Section 12

B. Section 16

C. Section 20

D. Section 36

Answer: B. By definition.

33. The height of a property can be defined by:

A. A monument

B. A benchmark

C. An elevation detector

D. An azimuth

Answer: B. Height is based on the datum point or a benchmark relative to the datum point.

34. A township contains how many sections?

A. 12

B. 16

C. 20

D. 36

Answer: D. A township is 36 square miles and contains 36 sections. Each section is 1 square mile.

35. Which of the following gives the best evidence of the buyer's intention to carry out the terms of the real estate purchase contract?

    A. "Subject to" clause

    B. Agreement to seek mortgage financing

    C. Earnest money deposit

    D. Provision that "time is of the essence"

Answer: C. While a buyer is seeking to get financed in most deals, remember, cash could be used. Therefore, earnest money is the best act that shows a buyer is dedicated to buying a piece of property.

36. Money compensating a seller when a buyer defaults on a contract is known as:

    A. Actual damages

    B. Liquidated damages

    C. Escrow funds

    D. Earnest money

Answer: B. Liquidated damages, not earnest money, are awarded by the court. Typically, they are numerically equivalent.

37. Which is not a requirement for a valid contract?

    A. Offer and acceptance

    B. Signatures of both parties

    C. Competent parties

    D. Consideration

Answer: B. Contracts, in general, can be oral; therefore, signatures are not required to make a contract valid.

38. A bilateral contract is:

    A. One in which only one party is required to act

    B. One in which the action of both parties is required

    C. A clause that's completed in one part

    D. A restriction placed on a party to limit their performance

Answer: B. Bilateral means both parties must act.

39. On day 1, the seller offers to sell his vacant lot to the buyer. On day 2, the buyer counteroffers. On day 3, the buyer withdraws the counteroffer and accepts the original offer. What is the outcome?

    A. There is a valid agreement.

    B. There is not a valid agreement because the buyer's counteroffer was a rejection of the seller's offer, and once it was rejected, it cannot be accepted later.

    C. There is a valid agreement because the buyer accepted before the seller advised the buyer the offer was withdrawn.

    D. There is not a valid agreement because the seller's offer was not accepted within 3 business days.

Answer: B. Once an offer has been countered, it's considered legally rejected and, therefore, no longer binding on the offeror.

40. A void contract is one that:

    A. Is not in writing

    B. Is rescindable by agreement

    C. Is missing an essential element

    D. Contains an element defective in nature

Answer: C. A void contract is completely missing a required element. A voidable contract appears valid, but one or more of the clauses is defective.

41. The mixing of earnest money with a broker's company account is:

A. Conversion

B. Commingling

C. Legal in most states

D. Permitted in offices with fewer than three agents

Answer: B. A broker cannot place earnest money into a private or company account. Similarly, a broker cannot place private money into an earnest money account except to maintain, or start, the account.

42. The use of earnest money by a broker for company expenses is:

A. Conversion

B. Commingling

C. Legal in most states

D. Permitted in offices with fewer than three agents

Answer: A. Once commingling has occurred, if a broker writes a check out of that account—because you cannot determine which dollars went out, you have converted that earnest money for private use.

43. A seller grants a potential buyer the right to purchase the property within a period of time for a predetermined price. This is called:

A. An option

B. A purchase agreement

C. A land contract with owner financing

D. An installment agreement

Answer: A. This is the definition of an option used in real estate.

44. An option:

A. Requires the optionee to complete the purchase

B. Gives the optionee an easement on the property

C. Requires option consideration

D. Makes the seller liable for a commission

Answer: C. For the contract to be valid, it must have consideration in the form of option consideration.

45. All the following are true regarding contingencies except:

A. Common contingencies could include mortgage and inspection contingencies.

B. They must specify what's required to satisfy the contingency.

C. They must specify the payor of the costs.

D. They must be "cleared" for the purchase agreement to be in effect.

Answer: A. Common contingencies include financing and inspection. They could include others as agreed upon by negotiations between the buyer and seller.

46. In the presence of the broker, a third-party individual persistently urges the seller to accept a low offer. If the seller accepts the buyer's offer against their will, the seller may later claim that:

A. It was the broker's fault for the buyer's low offer. The contract is valid.

B. He can sue the buyer due to the low offer. The contract may be voided.

C. He did not enter the contract freely, but under duress from another individual. The contract may be voidable.

D. His rights were abused by the broker and the buyer. The contract may be void.

Answer: C. Mutual ascension is a required element in a valid contract. Coercing someone by force, verbally or by threat of violence, is not allowed.

47. A lease agreement is signed by a lessee who is an underage minor. Which of the following is true?

A. The lease agreement is void.

B. The lease agreement is voidable.

C. The lease agreement is valid.

D. A minor cannot sign a lease.

Answer: B. A voidable contract appears to be valid, but upon inspection, one element is defective, such as whether the signer is legally competent.

48. When a land contract is signed and agreed upon by both parties:

A. The buyer may not take possession of the real estate until the contract is paid in full.

B. The seller only grants the buyer the right of disposition.

C. The buyer receives legal title to the property.

D. The buyer receives equitable title to the property.

Answer: D. In a land contract, called owner financing, the owner maintains legal title while the vendee (buyer) receives equitable title to the property.

49. What action returns a contract's parties to their positions before the contract as if it never happened?

A. Cancellation

B. Rescission

C. Substitution

D. Subordination

Answer: B. A rescission returns all parties to the state they were in before the contract as if it never happened because there never was a contract in place. This is opposed to a mutual release of a contract, which signifies there was a contract in place and now is not. Therefore, one party may be liable to another.

50. If the seller breaches a purchase agreement, the buyer may do all the following except:

A. Sue the seller for specific performance

B. Recover the earnest money

C. Sue the seller for damages

D. Sue the broker for specific performance

Answer: D. In a contract between the buyer and seller, a real estate broker is not liable for the performance of either party.

Test 4: Agency and Listing Agreements

1. A real estate licensee acting as the agent of the seller:

  A. Must promote and safeguard the seller's best interests

  B. Can disclose the seller's minimum price

  C. Should present to the seller only the highest offer for the property

  D. Can accept an offer on behalf of the seller

Answer: A. An agent's primary role is to safeguard his or her client's best interest and ensure they don't get harmed.

2. A licensee's responsibility to keep the principal informed of all the facts that could affect a transaction is the duty of:

  A. Care

  B. Disclosure

  C. Obedience

  D. Accounting

Answer: B. An agent must keep his or her client informed of all facts.

3. A licensee is helping a buyer and seller fill out a sales contract but is not representing either party. The licensee is:

  A. A transactional broker

  B. An unlicensed broker

  C. A traditional broker

  D. A designated broker

Answer: A. An agent with no clients in a transaction is serving as a transactional agent. He or she has no fiduciary responsibilities to either party under this arrangement.

4. If a seller and a buyer agree to change the closing date, the seller will most likely have his broker complete an:

  A. Amendment

  B. Addendum

  C. Assignment

  D. Assumption

Answer: A. An amendment is most often used to change terms within a contract that has already been established.

5. In designated agency, all the following apply except:

    A. The licensee could be a dual agent.

    B. The same licensee may represent both the buyer and the seller at the same time.

    C. The licensee can choose an agent in the office to represent the seller.

    D. The licensee may appoint an agent to negotiate for the buyer.

Answer: B. This is the definition of a dual or limited agent.

6. Two salespeople working for the same broker obtain offers on a property listed with their firm. The first offer is obtained early in the day. A second offer for a higher purchase price is obtained later in the afternoon. The broker presents the first offer to the seller that evening. The broker does not inform the seller about the second offer so the seller could make an informed decision about the first offer. Which of the following is true?

    A. The broker's actions are permissible provided the commission is split between the two salespeople.

    B. After the first offer was received, the broker should have told the salespeople that no additional offers would be accepted until the seller decided on the offer.

    C. The broker has no authority to withhold any offers from the seller.

    D. The broker was smart to protect the seller from getting into a negotiating battle over two offers.

Answer: C. An agent must disclose all information to his client, including all offers received.

7. The relationship of a licensee to his or her client is that of:

    A. A trustee

    B. A subagent

    C. A fiduciary

    D. An attorney-in-fact

Answer: C. An agent acts for his client in their best interest and represents them to other parties throughout the transaction.

8. Which of the following best defines the law of agency?

    A. Selling of another's property by a properly licensed brokerage company

    B. Rules of law that apply to the responsibilities of a person who acts as agent for another

    C. Principles that govern conduct in business

    D. Rules and regulations of the state's licensing agency

Answer: B. By definition.

9. The changing of a contract is called:

    A. An assumption

    B. An addendum

    C. An assignment

    D. A novation

Answer: D. A novation is a legal changing of contract as long as both parties agree to do so.

10. When a principal tells her licensee not to advertise her property in a certain newspaper that's out of the area, the licensee complies because he:

    A. Has never advertised in that newspaper anyway

    B. Must obey the lawful instructions of his principal

    C. Is not intending to advertise the property at all

    D. Is allowed to advertise only in local newspapers

Answer: B. An agent must follow all legal commands of his or her client.

11. Which of the following is considered dual agency?

    A. A licensee acting for both the buyer and the seller in the same transaction

    B. Two brokerage companies cooperating with each other

    C. A licensee representing more than one principal

    D. A licensee listing and then selling the same property

Answer: A. A dual agent represents both clients on the same property at the same transaction. If he represents one client as a buyer's agent and then lists the property for the same client later, is not dual agency due to different transactions.

12. A client fails to sign any paperwork with his agent; however, if the agent continues to help the buyer find a suitable property to buy, what type of agency is the agent is working under?

    A. Express agency

    B. Implied agency

    C. Dedicated agency

    D. Oral agency

Answer: B. An implied agency is created in the absence of an express agency.

13. The law that states documents must be writing is called:

    A. Statute of writing

    B. Statute of agency

    C. Statute of frauds

    D. Statute of required consent

Answer: C. By definition.

14. An unlicensed assistant may:

    A. Show property

    B. Negotiate listing commissions

    C. Make telemarketing calls to gain listing appointments

    D. Disclose the price of a house

Answer: D. Unlicensed assistants may disclose customer-level information, including price, location, and directions to properties.

15. An agent working under a dual agency must:

    A. Get written permission from both clients

    B. Pass one client to another agent

    C. Get approval from his broker

    D. Disclose the agency to the title company

Answer: A. Failure to get written permission from both parties during dual agency is a violation of ethics.

16. When an agent of a broker has the seller and another agent of the same broker has the listing, this is known as:

    A. Limited agency

    B. Dual agency

    C. Designated agency

    D. Separate agency

Answer: C. When a broker uses two agents within the same office to represent different sides, that's defined as designated agency.

17. Ensuring your client has the correct listing price is included in which fiduciary responsibility:

    A. Accounting

    B. Disclosure

    C. Care

    D. Obedience

Answer: C. An agent's job is to ensure his or her client doesn't get harmed, such as listing a property below its true market value.

18. A gratuitous agency:

    A. Is not allowed by the National Association of REALTORS

    B. Works for free

    C. Is only used when the seller has no money

    D. Can be approved only by your local association

Answer: B. The compensation does not create the agency; therefore, a broker can offer his services free of charge at his discretion.

19. When a property has a material defect, it falls under which fiduciary responsibility?

    A. Accounting

    B. Disclosure

    C. Care

    D. Obedience

Answer: B. An agent must disclose all material defects to the buyer.

20. After agency has been terminated, which fiduciary responsibility remains in place?

    A. Accounting

    B. Disclosure

    C. Care

    D. Obedience

Answer: A. Accounting and confidentiality fiduciary responsibilities are maintained even after termination of agency, for any reason.

21. Which listing agreement affords the most protection to the listing broker?

    A. Exclusive-agency

    B. Exclusive-agency buyer agency

    C. Open

    D. Exclusive-right-to-sell

Answer: D. An agent earns a commission in any situation under an exclusive-right-to-sell, thereby giving the broker the best protection and guarantee of getting paid.

22. Agent A, working for a buyer, brings him an investment property on which he subsequently makes an offer that gets accepted. However, agent B also is working for the buyer but receives no commission on the purchase. The buyer most likely is working under what type of agency?

    A. Exclusive agency

    B. Exclusive-agency buyer agency

    C. Open

    D. Exclusive right to sell

Answer: C. In an open agency, only the agent who brings the deal earns the commission. Any other agent receives no commission.

23. Which activity is most likely to cause an agency to terminate?

    A. Death of the sales agent

    B. Expiration of the listing agreement

    C. The seller disagreeing with the marketing of his property

    D. The broker wishing to gain more commission

Answer: B. All listing contracts must have an expiration. The death of a sales agent does not cause termination. To terminate agency, it must be the death of the broker or principal.

24. A licensee has an exclusive-right-to-sell listing on a building. The owner is out of town when the licensee gets an offer from a buyer to purchase the building providing the seller agrees to take a purchase-money mortgage. The buyer must have a commitment from the seller before the seller is scheduled to return to the city. Under these circumstances:

    A. The licensee may form a binding agreement on behalf of the seller.

    B. The licensee may collect a commission even if the transaction falls through because of the seller's absence from the city.

    C. The buyer is obligated to keep the offer open until the seller returns.

    D. The licensee must obtain the signature of the seller to affect a contract.

Answer: D. The agent cannot enter into contracts for their clients. They must have the written agreement, usually by a signature, of their principal to accept the offer.

25. The relationship between a broker and a salesperson typically is:

    A. Employee and employer

    B. Independent contractors

    C. Neither; they are not bound by any agreement

    D. Coworkers

Answer: B. By IRS rules, agents are independent contractors of real estate brokers, unless there is a specific contract stating otherwise.

26. A broker places a client's earnest money into his business account for safekeeping until the closing. This activity is:

    A. Considered common practice to hold the earnest money in that account

    B. Wrong because the broker has committed commingling of monies

    C. The right thing to do for safety purposes

    D. Not right because it must go to the title company for safekeeping

Answer: B. Commingling is the act of placing other person's earnest money into a personal or business account.

27. A property owner lists his property for sale with a licensee. During the listing negotiations, he tells the licensee he wants $150,000 for the property and anything above that amount the licensee can keep as a commission. This listing is known as:

    A. A gross listing

    B. A net listing

    C. An open listing

    D. A nonexclusive listing

Answer: B. A net listing is when a client gets a net amount and the broker's commission is anything over and above that net amount. In essence, the commission is variable based on the final sales price accepted. Net listing may be illegal in some states.

28. The type of listing agreement that provides a commission to the broker when the owner makes the sale himself is called an:

    A. Exclusive-right-to-sell listing

    B. Open listing

    C. Exclusive-agency listing

    D. Option listing

Answer: A. An exclusive-right-to-sell listing affords the listing broker a commission regardless of who brings the buyer.

29. If a seller needs to pay off his $100,000 mortgage after the sale, what's the minimum amount the seller can accept as the sales prince of the house if the seller's closing costs include a 7 percent commission and $1,500 in other expenses?

    A. $107,500

    B. $108,500

    C. $109,140

    D. $110,633

Answer: C. The seller needs $101,500 to pay his closing costs and pay off his mortgage. He receives 93 percent of the final sales price, and the agent charges 7 percent commission: $101,500 ÷ 0.93 = $109,139.79 or $109,140.

30. The seller wants to earn $165,000 on the sale of his house after paying the licensee a fee of 6 percent. How much must the gross selling price be?

    A. $175,532

    B. $176,093

    C. $177,035

    D. $166,091

Answer: A. $165,000 ÷ 0.94 or = $175,532.

31. Under which listing agreement can owners of listed property sell the property on their own without having to pay the listing licensee a commission?

    A. Exclusive-right-to-sell listing

    B. Open listing

    C. Exclusive-agency listing

    D. Exclusive-right-to-buy listing

Answer: B. An open listing allows the seller to find a buyer and owe no commission to the listing agent.

32. Which of the following is not a type of listing contract?

A. Open

B. Exclusive-agency

C. Exclusive-right-to-sell

D. MLS

Answer: D. The MLS is a database agents use to list properties for their sellers and find properties for their buyers.

33. All the following reasons are a valid basis for terminating a listing agreement except:

A. Sale of the property

B. Death of the salesperson

C. Agreement of the parties

D. Destruction of the premises

Answer: B. The death of a sales agent does not terminate an agency.

34. A licensee signs a listing agreement with a seller under which the seller receives the proceeds from the sale of a lot and the licensee receives 7 percent commission on the sale. This type of listing is:

A. A gross listing

B. A guaranteed listing agreement

C. An exclusive-right-to-sell agency

D. A net listing

Answer: C. The agreement provides for the listing agent to get a commission.

35. A listing contract in which only the licensee producing a buyer is granted a limited agency is called:

A. An open listing

B. A net listing

C. An exclusive-right-to-sell listing

D. An exclusive-agency listing

Answer: A. In an open listing, the agent who brings the buyer also gets the listing, creating a dual agency. All other agents receive no commission at all. A seller can form as many open agencies as he wishes.

36. By executing a listing agreement with a seller, a real estate licensee becomes:

A. A partner to the sale

B. Obligated to open a special trust account

C. The agent of the seller

D. Responsible for sharing commissions

Answer: C. The listing agency confers agency from the seller to the agent.

37. A property owner signs an exclusive-right-to-sell listing agreement with a licensee. During the time the contract is in force, the owner dies. Now the listing is:

A. Binding on the owner's spouse

B. Still in effect because the owner's intention was clearly defined

C. Terminated within 60 days after the death of a principal

D. Terminated automatically due to death of the principal

Answer: D. The death of a principal to a listing terminates an agency.

38. An agent performs a comparative market analysis for a client and finds comps in the area between $140,000 and $145,000. The final decision of a listing price should be:

    A. By negotiation with the owner

    B. Decided by the owner

    C. The average of the sales comparables

    D. Determined by the highest property sold in the area within the last 6 months

Answer: B. An agent should never decide the listing price, but merely help the client arrive at a suitable number.

39. A broker lists a property for $535,000 for 5.5 percent on an exclusive-right-to-sell listing agreement. The buyer offers $499,000, and the offer is accepted. If seller found the buyer, the broker is due:

    A. $0 because the seller found the buyer himself

    B. $29,425

    C. $27,445

    D. $31,455

Answer: C. The commission is based on the sales price and not the listing price. Therefore, the commission earned is $0.055 \times \$499,000 = \$27,445$.

40. A broker lists a property for $535,000 for 5.5 percent on an exclusive-agency listing agreement. The buyer offers full price, and the offer is accepted. If the seller found the buyer, the broker is due:

    A. $0 because the seller found the buyer himself

    B. $29,425

    C. $27,445

    D. $31,455

Answer: B. The commission is based on the sales price and not the listing price. However, in this example, the sales price and listing price are the same. Therefore, the commission earned is $0.055 \times \$535,000 = \$29,425$.

41. A broker lists a bank-owned property for 7 percent commission. One of his agents brings in the buyer for the property. The agent receives 60 percent of the commission, $3,550. How much is the house's selling price?

    A. $83,333

    B. $84,524

    C. $85,244

    D. $86,410

Answer: A. $3,500 \div 0.60 = \$5,833.33$ total commission earned by the listing broker. So $5,833.33 \div 0.07 = \$83,333$ sales price.

42. The doctrine of laches states:

    A. It is a failure not to bring a legal claim within a reasonable time.

    B. No homeowner association (HOA) can approve repairs to a property.

    C. A neighbor may sue based on a violation of HOA rules.

    D. When seeking a new mortgage, the HOA must approve the lender providing the funds.

Answer: A. If an HOA waits too long to bring a lawsuit against a homeowner for a violation of the rules, it may lose its right under the doctrine of laches.

43. When a broker uses earnest money to satisfy company bills such as rent, he may be guilty of:

    A. Commingling

    B. Conversion

    C. Contempt

    D. Contrition

Answer: B. If a broker uses others' money to pay a bill or any purpose other than earnest money, he could be in violation and charged with conversion.

44. A seller brings the buyer to his home; however, the seller still owes the broker a commission. This listing type is:

    A. An open listing

    B. A net listing

    C. An exclusive-right-to-sell listing

    D. An exclusive-agency listing

Answer: C. An exclusive-right-to-sell listing causes the listing broker to be a procuring cause and, therefore, is due a commission upon the sale of the property.

45. An escrow account, held by a broker, may:

    A. Accrue interest

    B. Not accrue interest

    C. Be accessible to all the agents for when they close their deals

    D. Be emptied every year on December 31 and started over again at $0 balance

Answer: A. In general, an escrow account can earn interest; however, that interest must be returned to the client as proceeds. In some states, interest on earnest money must be earned and paid; other states may make it illegal to even earn the interest. Check with your local state commission for the rules regarding earning interest on earnest money accounts in your state.

46. If a seller wishes to terminate his listing agreement with his broker, he may:

    A. Immediately demand a release

    B. Ask his agent for a personal release

    C. Seek a mutual release from the broker

    D. Stop showing the property

Answer: C. A seller may ask for, and be granted, a mutual release by a listing broker. However, the seller is under contract that he must abide by should the listing broker not grant the request.

47. An agent for broker A lists a property for $500,000 at 6 percent commission. Then broker A decides to offer 50 percent of the commission to the selling broker who brings in a buyer. An agent for broker A signs an independent contractor agreement stating he shall receive 70 percent of the commission earned by broker A. Broker B brings in a buyer who offers $475,000, which the seller accepts. The listing agent's portion of the commission is:

 A. $10,500

 B. $12,250

 C. $9,975

 D. $4,275

Answer: C. The commission earned is $475,000 × 0.06 = $28,500. Half of that commission, or $14,250, is paid to the selling broker. The agent for the broker will be paid by the broker 70 percent of the commission, or $14,250 × 0.70 (70%) = $9,975.

48. An FSBO seller finally agrees to sign a listing with a broker but retains the right to find a buyer without paying the agent a commission. This type of listing is most probably:

 A. An open listing

 B. A net listing

 C. An exclusive-right-to-sell listing

 D. An exclusive-agency listing

Answer: D. An exclusive-agency listing allows a seller to owe no commission to the listing broker should the seller bring the buyer himself.

49. A seller pays his broker $7,500 in commission on the sale of $125,000 house. The broker's commission rate is:

 A. 6 percent

 B. 6.5 percent

 C. 7 percent

 D. 7.5 percent

Answer: A. $7,500 ÷ $125,000 = 0.06 or 6 percent commission rate charged by the listing broker.

50. A salesperson who is employed by a broker tells a prospective buyer the house she was looking at is "the best house in the area." Because of this statement:

 A. The salesperson was guilty of fraud.

 B. The broker was guilty of fraud because the employing broker is responsible for the actions of the salesperson.

 C. The salesperson was practicing puffing.

 D. The salesperson would be guilty of fraud only if the buyer purchased the house.

Answer: C. Puffing is the exaggeration of facts regarding the house or its surroundings.

Test 5: Sales Contracts, Brokerages Business, Fair Housing

1. The landmark Supreme Court case that created the slogan "separate but equal" is:

    A. *Brown* v. *Board of Education*

    B. *Plessy* v. *Ferguson*

    C. *Jones* v. *Mayer*

    D. *Roe* v. *Wade*

Answer: B. *Plessy* v. *Ferguson* established separate but equal, which was virtually overturned by *Brown* v. *Board of Education*.

2. A sales agent of a broker did an outstanding job on a specific sale. He can legally receive a performance bonus from:

    A. The seller

    B. The buyer

    C. No one

    D. The broker

Answer: D. Only a broker can pay a sales agent a commission, even in the form of a bonus.

3. Which discrimination suit would be filed in a federal court?

    A. A racial discrimination lawsuit

    B. A sexual orientation discrimination lawsuit

    C. An age discrimination lawsuit

    D. A religious discrimination lawsuit

Answer: A. Discrimination based on race, disallowed by the Civil Rights Act of 1866, is automatically filed in federal court.

4. The listing and the selling broker agree to split a 7 percent commission 50/50 on a $200,000 sale. The listing broker gives the listing salesperson 60 percent of his commission, and the selling broker gives the selling salesperson 65 percent of his commission. How much does the selling salesperson earn from the sale?

    A. $4,800

    B. $4,100

    C. $4,200

    D. $4,550

Answer: D. $200,000 \times 0.07 \times 0.50 \times 0.65 = \$4,550$.

5. The National Do Not Call Registry provides that:

    A. Licensees may never contact consumers without written authorization.

    B. Consumers with whom a licensee has had a business relationship can be contacted for up to 18 months after the purchase.

    C. Licensees may not contact a previous customer if included in the registry.

    D. Consumers who have made an inquiry to a licensee may be contacted up to 6 months later.

Answer: B. You can call a client for 18 months and anyone who sought out you for information for 3 months, even if they are on the Do Not Call list.

6. A licensee is accused of violating antitrust laws. Of the following, she is most likely accused of:

    A. Violating equal housing opportunity laws

    B. Undisclosed limited agencies

    C. Group boycotting

    D. Dealing in unlicensed securities

Answer: C. Only group boycotting is a violation among the choices available.

7. The federal Fair Housing Act does not prohibit:

    A. Blockbusting

    B. Panic selling

    C. Discriminating based on marital status

    D. Redlining

Answer: C. Marital status is not a protected class under the Fair Housing Act.

8. A licensee asks if they could sell an owner's vacant residential lot. After procuring a buyer for the lot, the owner refuses to pay a brokerage commission. The licensee may:

    A. File a complaint against the landowner with the real estate licensing authorities

    B. File a lien against the owner's properties

    C. Sue the landowner in civil court

    D. Do nothing, as there was not a valid contract in place

Answer: D. There is no contractual obligation to pay a commission. The agent merely was asking if he or she could sell a lot.

9. A real estate licensee is responsible for initial action that resulted in the sale of a property. This is known as the:

    A. Pro forma

    B. Proffered offer

    C. Private offering

    D. Procuring cause

Answer: D. By definition.

10. A broker lists a property for sale at $150,000 with a 5 percent commission, and he later obtains an oral offer from a prospective buyer to purchase the property. A day later, the buyer rescinds the offer. The broker is entitled to a:

    A. Full commission

    B. Partial commission

    C. No commission

    D. Statutory rate of commission

Answer: C. Under the statute of frauds, an offer must be in writing to be valid. Because the offer was oral, not written, no commission can be earned.

11. Unless some other written agreement has been made, a licensee has earned a brokerage commission when:

- A. The purchaser takes possession of the property.
- B. The seller lists the property with the broker.
- C. The transaction is closed.
- D. The seller accepts an offer procured from a ready, willing, and able buyer.

Answer: D. The commission is earned upon the formation of a purchase contract. It may not be paid out until the closing, however.

12. Multiple brokerage companies list a property for a seller under an open listing agreement. The broker who is entitled to the commission is the one who:

- A. Listed the property first
- B. Advertised the property the best
- C. Brought the first offer
- D. Was the procuring cause of the sale

Answer: D. In an open listing, the listing is awarded to the agent who brings the buyer, thus creating a dual agency as well.

13. A void contract:

- A. Is an oral contract
- B. Is never legally enforceable
- C. Is rescindable by the parties
- D. Can be undone by one of the parties

Answer: B. A void contract is missing an essential element and, therefore, is not legally enforceable.

14. In real estate, fee for service is best described as:

- A. Offering real estate services in a cafeteria-style arrangement, allowing the customer to choose from options
- B. Allowing unlicensed persons to conduct real estate transactions if no licensed agents are available
- C. An agency that specifically works only with FSBOs
- D. Providing consumers all the limited services at a discounted price

Answer: A. A fee for service brokerage allows a client to pick and choose the services they want to receive, much like a cafeteria that allows a consumer to pick and choose the food they want.

15. To be considered valid, in general, a contract must:

- A. Contain some consideration
- B. Be witnessed
- C. Contain signatures of the parties
- D. Be written by a practicing attorney

Answer: A. Consideration is an essential element within a contract. It must be present for the contract to be valid.

16. The elements of a contract include all the following, except:

- A. offer and acceptance
- B. Acknowledgment
- C. Competent parties
- D. Consideration

Answer: B. An acknowledgment is not necessary for a contract to be enforceable in a court of law.

17. A bilateral contract differs from a unilateral contract in what way?

    A. Something is to be done by one party only.

    B. Both parties must act per the negotiated contract.

    C. Only one of the parties is obligated to act.

    D. One party is limited to the performance by the other.

Answer: C. Bilateral is a contract that requires both parties to make promises that must be carried out under the weight of law.

18. Money that serves to compensate a seller should the buyer default on a contract is known as:

    A. Actual damages

    B. Liquidated damages

    C. Compensatory damages

    D. Earnest money damages

Answer: B. If a seller is harmed, he is awarded liquidated damages, typically in the amount of the earnest money. However, it could be more or it could be less.

19. In this series of events …Day 1: the seller lists his property for sale. Day 2: the buyer makes an offer to the seller. Day 3: the seller counteroffers. Day 4: the seller rescinds the counteroffer and decides to accept the original offer. The contract is:

    A. Not a valid agreement because the buyer's original offer was rejected by the seller's counteroffer, and once rejected, it cannot be accepted later

    B. Not a valid agreement because the buyer's offer was not accepted within the allotted timeframe

    C. A valid agreement because the buyer accepted before the seller advised the buyer that the offer was rescinded

    D. A valid agreement because the buyer accepted the seller's offer exactly as it was made

Answer: A. Once an offer is countered, it has been legally rejected and, therefore, is no longer binding on the original offeror.

20. The deposit of earnest money in a broker's personal account is:

    A. Conversion

    B. Permitted in most states

    C. Common practice by listing brokers

    D. Commingling

Answer: D. Commingling is the mixing of personal or business funds with earnest money.

21. When a seller grants a buyer the right to purchase the property by a certain date at a prenegotiated price, this is called a:

    A. Lease option

    B. Purchase option

    C. Right of first refusal

    D. Land contract

Answer: B. A purchase option is the right to buy property at a later date based on a price negotiated earlier.

22. In a purchase option, the optionor:

    A. Requires the optionee to purchase the property within a time period

    B. Gives the optionee an easement on the property prior to purchase

    C. Is required to pay the broker a commission

    D. Gives the optionee the right to buy the property within a specified time

Answer: D. A purchase option is the right of the optionee to buy property from the optionor at a later date based on a price negotiated earlier.

23. All the following are required in a contingency to make it valid except:

    A. It must state the broker's name and commission earned.

    B. It must state what's required to satisfy the contingency.

    C. It must state who will pay for any costs involved.

    D. It must state the timeframe to clear the contingency.

Answer: A. An optionee or optionor is not required to pay a broker a commission.

24. If one party states, "I will wash your car for $20 today" and another party accepts the offer, the contract:

    A. Is void because it's an oral agreement

    B. Is voidable because it's missing an essential element

    C. Is valid but may be unenforceable

    D. Is void because it wasn't witnessed by a third party

Answer: C. Oral contracts are valid, but they may be unenforceable or valid only between the parties.

25. The Civil Rights Act of 1866 prohibits discrimination solely based on:

    A. Handicap

    B. Race

    C. Religion

    D. Sex

Answer: B. The Civil Rights Act of 1866 is the original discrimination law that protects only race.

26. The Fair Housing Act is enforced by the:

    A. Department of Justice

    B. Federal Housing Administration

    C. Department of Veterans Affairs

    D. Department of Housing and Urban Development

Answer: D. The Fair Housing Act is administered by the Department of Housing and Urban Development (HUD).

27. A lending institution may not refuse to make a residential real estate loan solely because of the:

  A. Questionable economic situation of the applicant

  B. Neighborhood of the property

  C. Applicant not being of legal age

  D. Deteriorated condition of the premises

Answer: B. Redlining is a violation of the Fair Housing Act.

28. As of April 28, 2014, the maximum civil penalty for a first violation of the fair housing laws is:

  A. $55,000

  B. $75,000

  C. $100,000

  D. $175,000

Answer: B. By definition.

29. The clause in the purchase agreement that provides evidence of the buyer's intention to buy real property is the:

  A. Earnest money clause

  B. Financing clause

  C. Subject to clause

  D. Time is of essence clause

Answer: A. The earnest money deposit is the best evidence a buyer intends to buy a property because it requires the buyer to place money at risk.

30. Which of the following is considered legal?

  A. Charging a security deposit based on the number of children

  B. Charging more security deposit for a person in a wheelchair

  C. Picturing only white people in a brochure

  D. Charging more security deposit to a person with a mental illness

Answer: B. You can charge more security deposit for any modifications that need to made above and beyond what a landlord has already made to suit a disabled tenant.

31. The Fair Housing Act of 1968 is known as:

  A. Title XIII of the Civil Rights Act of 1968

  B. Title VIII of the Civil Rights Act of 1866

  C. Title VIII of the Civil Rights Act of 1968

  D. Title VIII of the Civil Rights Act of 1988

Answer: C. Title VIII of the Civil Rights Act of 1968 by definition.

32. If a handicapped tenant cannot access the bathroom facilities in his wheelchair due to the narrow door width, which of the following is true?

  A. The landlord is required to make the adjustments for a person in a wheelchair.

  B. The tenant cannot make any changes due to his lease agreement.

  C. The tenant is entitled to make the necessary alterations.

  D. The landlord should not have rented this apartment to the tenant.

Answer: C. The tenant can make alterations as long as he returns the house to the original condition at the end of the lease. Failure to do so may make him liable for damages.

33. Which act provides protection from threats or acts of violence against those who assist and encourage open housing rights?

   A. Civil Rights Act of 1866

   B. Civil Rights Act of 1968

   C. Fair Housing Act of 1964

   D. Fair Housing Amendments Act of 1988

Answer: B. Civil Rights Act of 1968 by statute.

34. The federal Fair Housing Act is enforceable:

   A. Only in those states that do not have specific state fair housing laws

   B. Only in those states that have ratified the act

   C. Only in those states that do not have substantially equivalent laws

   D. In all states

Answer: D. The federal Fair Housing Act is enforceable in all states.

35. The practice of guiding families who speak the same language toward or away from homes in certain areas is:

   A. Considered common practice

   B. A form of blockbusting

   C. A basis for redlining

   D. Illegal discrimination

Answer: D. Steering is the act of guiding a person toward or away from an area based on one of the protected classes.

36. Discrimination based on familial status was prohibited with the passage of the:

   A. Civil Rights Act of 1866

   B. Civil Rights Act of 1964

   C. Fair Housing Act of 1968

   D. Fair Housing Amendments Act of 1988

Answer: D. The Fair Housing Amendments Act of 1988 added disability and familial status as protected classes.

37. A woman makes an application for an apartment in a community for older people. She is the legal guardian for her granddaughter. Her application is rejected because the community does not allow anyone under the age of 18. Is this permissible?

   A. Yes, if the policy is consistently applied to all tenants with children.

   B. No, because familial status is always a protected class in all housing.

   C. No, if fewer than 10 percent of the occupants are over age 55.

   D. Yes, if the housing complies with all the regulations for elderly housing.

Answer: D. HOPA allows for communities to not allow people under age 55.

38. Exemptions exist for all the protected classes to fair housing law except:

   A. Racial considerations

   B. Private membership clubs

   C. Handicapped individuals

   D. Religious organizations

Answer: A. There is never an exemption for race.

39. A woman owns a four-unit building and she lives in one. Her most recent ad reads, "One bedroom, one bath available. No pets. Adults only." Which of the following is true?

    A. She is not required to comply with the familial status requirement but must allow service animals.

    B. She is exempt from the Fair Housing Act because she lives in one of the units.

    C. She may not exclude children from her rentals.

    D. She may not publish discriminatory advertisements.

Answer: D. At no time is advertising allowed for any of the exemptions.

40. The Fair Housing Act makes it illegal to discriminate:

    A. Against a person who has a history of dangerous behavior

    B. Because of a person's marital status

    C. Due to a person being convicted of distributing a controlled substance

    D. Should a person have HIV

Answer: D. HIV is considered a disability and is protected under the Fair Housing Act.

41. A prospective buyer with a physical disability relies on an animal to assist him in his day-to-day activities. If he makes an application at a condominium that prohibits pets, which of the following is true?

    A. This restriction applies to a person who uses an animal for disability-related assistance.

    B. This restriction does not apply to a person who uses an animal for disability-related assistance of any kind.

    C. This restriction applies to a person who uses an animal for disability-related visual impairments.

    D. The condominium can waive the enforcement of the covenant only if there are not suitable accommodations anywhere else within the complex.

Answer: B. A helping animal, by definition, is not a pet and not subject to pet rules.

42. Title I of the Americans with Disabilities Act requires:

    A. All real estate to be free of barriers to people with disabilities

    B. All employers to adopt nondiscriminatory employment practices

    C. That employers make reasonable accommodations for employees with disabilities

    D. That existing premises be remodeled for people with disabilities regardless of the cost involved

Answer: C. Title I of the ADA requires employers to make reasonable accommodations for employees with disabilities.

43. When a broker tells a homeowner that minorities are moving into the area and will lower the value of their home so they should move now to get the best price, that's considered:

   A. Blockbusting

   B. Power selling

   C. Discriminatory advertising

   D. Legal if it's true

Answer: A. Also known as panic selling, the act of creating a fear, or panic, by threatening the loss of value is illegal under the Fair Housing Act.

44. A person who thinks they have been discriminated against under the fair housing laws must file a complaint within:

   A. 6 months

   B. 12 months

   C. 18 months

   D. 24 months

Answer: B. You must file a complaint within 1 year of the aggrieved incident under the Fair Housing Act.

45. If HUD seeks reconciliation between the parties, it is:

   A. Seeking an amicable resolution

   B. Filing a grievance in federal court

   C. Asking for a judge to find fault in a court case

   D. Determining the guilty party's punishment

Answer: A. A reconciliation is the amicable settling of a disagreement.

46. With respect to the fair housing laws:

   A. A state can be less restrictive if it has had no issues in the past 10 years.

   B. A person is not required to follow the rules if he or she is in the military.

   C. A state can be more restrictive than federal laws.

   D. Houses less than 2 years old may be exempt if the builder only builds within one state.

Answer: C. States can be more restrictive than the federal laws but not less.

47. An agent makes a comment, and his client feels it is racially disparaging. The client files charges against the agent. The agent may:

   A. Be guilty, because intent is not required to be guilty of a violation of the fair housing laws

   B. Not be guilty, because intent is required to be guilty of a violation of the fair housing laws

   C. Not be guilty, because a client cannot file charges against his or her own agent

   D. Be guilty, because an agent cannot speak to his client in that manner

Answer: A. The Fair Housing Act is not an intent law, but rather an effects law, meaning there's no intent needed to make a person feel discriminated against. The result only needs to be that the effect makes the person feel that way.

48. A contract that requires only one party to act is called a:

    A. Unified contract

    B. Unitary contract

    C. Unilateral contract

    D. Uniform contract

Answer: C. A contract that requires only one party to act is called a unilateral contract. The prefix uni- means "one" (think unicycle, or "one wheel").

49. A salesperson working for broker A sells a $150,000 home listed with another brokerage. The listing commission is 6.5 percent of the selling price. Of this amount, 40 percent goes to the listing broker, and 60 percent belongs to the selling broker. Broker A and the salesperson agreed she would receive 60 percent of any commission generated for their office. Under this agreement, she is entitled to receive:

    A. $2,632.50

    B. $3,510.00

    C. $3,412.50

    D. $5,850.00

Answer: B. $150,000 \times 0.065 \times 0.60 \times 0.60 = \$3,510$.

Test 6: Economics, Appraisals

1. The two forces that affect value the most are:

   A. Interest rates and wage levels

   B. Supply and demand

   C. Population and demographics

   D. External and internal forces

Answer: B. The two biggest forces that affect value are supply and demand.

2. An appraiser determining value using the cost approach, most probably uses:

   A. The estimated replacement cost of the building

   B. The owner's purchase price of the building

   C. The sales prices of comparable buildings

   D. The assessed value of the structure less the value of the land

Answer: A. The cost approach deals with the value if you were to replace the building.

3. Johnny's Market sells 10 apples for $10. The customers love the apples and Johnny continually sells out of stock. However, the supply of his apples has become increasingly harder to get due to a labor strike. Which is the most probable price for his apples next week?

   A. $11 for 10 apples

   B. $8 for 10 apples

   C. No change at all

   D. $10 for 5 apples

Answer: D. A price increase is for sure due to the lower supply, and D represents the most probable increase. Notice he has lowered the number of apples in the bundle, in effect doubling the price.

4. Depreciation means:

   A. The value of real estate at the end of its economic life

   B. The loss of value for any reason

   C. The cost to renovate a building back to full utilization

   D. The capitalized value of gross income

Answer: B. By definition.

5. Which of the following is considered general data?

    A. Dimensions of the subject property

    B. Employment opportunities in the area

    C. Sales data for comparable properties

    D. Gross rent multipliers for the area

Answer: B. General data deals with information about the neighborhood and surrounding area.

6. David's hardware store bought 100,000 nails on sale from his wholesaler, but the demand during the winter has gone down due to the snow and cold. What would happen to the price of the nails during the winter months?

    A. It will drop.

    B. It will rise.

    C. It won't change.

    D. It won't be affected at all by supply and demand.

Answer: A. If supply is stable and demand lowers, the price lowers as well.

7. All the following affect demand except:

    A. Population

    B. Demographics

    C. Wage levels

    D. Uniqueness

Answer: D. Uniqueness is a factor of supply and demand.

8. Depreciation is generally divided into three categories. Normal wear and tear on a property would be considered:

    A. External depreciation

    B. Physical deterioration

    C. Functional obsolescence

    D. Economic deterioration

Answer: B. Wear and tear are physical aspects that can be curable or incurable.

9. A homebuilder must borrow money to build a custom home for a client. Which characteristic would he be most affected by?

    A. Governmental controls and monetary policies

    B. Population

    C. Demographics

    D. Wage levels

Answer: A. The interest rate would be an influential factor on a builder who needs to borrow money to buy materials.

10. The study of population is known as:

    A. Demographics

    B. Populatics

    C. Demonstrative

    D. Informatics

Answer: A. By definition.

11. The appraisal is created to:

    A. Set the amount of consideration the seller should accept from a purchaser

    B. Set the market price of a property

    C. Determine the projected income of a property

    D. Estimate the value of a property

Answer: D. An appraiser estimates the value through his expertise and knowledge.

12. When the supply equals demand, it's called:

    A. Equality

    B. Equilibrium

    C. Evenness

    D. Even keel

Answer: B. When supply and demand are equal, it's known as equilibrium.

13. Higher wage levels are considered within what characteristic of value?

    A. Supply

    B. Neither supply or demand

    C. Demand

    D. Both supply and demand

Answer: C. If people get paid more, they spend more, creating a larger demand for products and services.

14. If the annual incomes from a rental property are:

Gross potential rent: $40,000
Laundry facilities: $350
Garage rental: $350
Vacancy and loss factor: 5 percent

What is the effective gross income?

    A. $38,000

    B. $39,000

    C. $40,000

    D. $41,000

Answer: A. Effective gross income is the actual income received after a property owner figures vacancy and nonpaying tenants: $40,000 × 0.05 = $2,000, so $40,000 − $2,000 = $38,000.

15. Which of the following are not considered when calculating the net operating income when an appraiser uses the income method to determine the value?

    A. Real estate taxes

    B. Management fees

    C. Debt service

    D. Utilities

Answer: C. Debt service, or mortgage payments, are not an expense. They would be subtracted from the net income to give the cash flow of the property, however.

16. When the supply of a commodity decreases while demand remains the same:

    A. Price tends to rise.

    B. Price tends to drop.

    C. Demand tends to rise.

    D. Demand tends to drop.

Answer: A. If there are fewer widgets to buy but the same number of people want to buy them, the price rises.

17. A large local employer has left the city and left more than half the town unemployed. What is most likely to happen to prices within the city?

    A. They will drop.

    B. They will rise.

    C. They won't change.

    D. They won't be affected at all by supply and demand.

Answer: A. If there's less money to spend but the supply stays the same, the prices will drop.

18. Reconciliation is:

    A. Selecting the highest value given by the three approaches to value

    B. Comparing comparable properties and identifying their amenities

    C. Determining the probability of the three methodologies used to determine the value

    D. Determining the final value by selecting one value from those

Answer: C. The weighing of probability for each valuation method of a property.

19. In the valuation of an investment property, which of the following approaches to value is most likely to be used?

    A. Cost approach

    B. Sales comparison approach

    C. Income approach

    D. All approaches equally weighted

Answer: C. The income approach is the most common method of valuation in any investment property.

20. Using the income approach, an appraiser will most likely use the:

    A. Reproduction cost

    B. Capitalization rate

    C. Depreciation schedules

    D. Replacement cost

Answer: B. Income property valuation is the idea that a property's value is based on the income it can generate. Therefore, the cap rate is a measure of the value based on the net income by the property.

21. A statewide frost has killed most of the orange crop in Florida. What is most likely happen to the price of oranges?

    A. It will drop.

    B. It will rise.

    C. It won't change.

    D. It won't be affected at all by supply and demand.

Answer: B. If there's less product but the demand stays the same, prices will rise.

22. In the valuation of a property, which of the following approaches to value will an appraiser consider depreciation?

    A. Sales comparison approach to value

    B. Income approach to value

    C. Cost approach to value

    D. Gross rent multipliers

Answer: C. Depreciation is used when figuring the cost of building a structure.

23. The market price is defined as:

    A. The price it sold for

    B. The price it should have sold for

    C. The price that was asked for it

    D. The assessed value

Answer: A. What the house actually sells for is determined by the buyer.

24. The tomato crop has had an exceptional year, with production double what was expected. What is most likely happen to the price of tomatoes?

    A. It will drop.

    B. It will rise.

    C. It won't change.

    D. It won't be affected at all by supply and demand.

Answer: A. If there are more of a product and demand stays equal, the price drops.

25. Which of the following is considered external depreciation?

    A. An outdated roof that needs to be completely replaced

    B. Convenient access to shopping malls

    C. A poorly designed floor plan that could be modified

    D. Run-down properties in the neighborhood

Answer: D. External depreciation is any factor outside the control of the homeowner. It's almost always considered incurable.

26. All the following affect demand except:

    A. Population

    B. Demographics

    C. Wage levels

    D. Fiscal policy

Answer: D. Fiscal policy, or interest rates, affects the supply while the others are all characteristics of demand.

27. When estimating the value of property using the cost approach, an appraiser considers all the following except:

    A. Cost of permits to build the property

    B. Loss due to an outdated heating system

    C. Loss due to poor workmanship

    D. Loss due to uncollected rent

Answer: D. Income generated, collected or uncollected, by a property is not a factor used in the valuation of a building when using the cost approach.

28. All the following affects supply except:

    A. Population

    B. Construction costs

    C. Governmental controls

    D. The labor force

Answer: A. Population is a characteristic of demand—more people, more demand.

29. The time over which any improvement remains useful is called:

    A. Amortized life

    B. Chronological life

    C. Economic life

    D. Actual life

Answer: C. The economic life is the useful life of an improvement.

30. Which of the following least affects demand?

 A. Fiscal policy

 B. Demographics

 C. Wage levels

 D. Population

Answer: A. The cost of money, i.e., interest, is a supply issue. The others are demand issues.

31. When demand for a commodity decreases and supply remains the same:

 A. Price tends to rise.

 B. Price tends to fall.

 C. Price is not affected.

 D. The market becomes stagnant.

Answer: B. If fewer people want a widget but the same number of widgets are still available, the price lowers. This is the general concept of any retail item going on sale. It's to get rid of the product.

32. To find the net operating income of a property using the income approach to value, if the value and the capitalization rate were known, the appraiser would:

 A. Multiply the value by the capitalization rate

 B. Multiply the effective gross income by the capitalization rate

 C. Divide the net operating income by the capitalization rate

 D. Divide the capitalization rate by the net operating income

Answer: A. Net income = value × capitalization rate.

33. The cost comparison approach to value is most important when estimating the value of:

 A. An existing residence

 B. An apartment building

 C. A retail location

 D. A new residence

Answer: D. Cost is used to find the value of a newly built property because there are no, or few, other sales in the area to use the sales comparison approach.

34. Which of the following least affects supply?

 A. Fiscal policy

 B. Demographics

 C. Wage levels

 D. Population

Answer: D. More people create more demand, not supply.

35. In the appraisal of a commercial building, external depreciation is considered:

 A. Termite damage to the wood structure

 B. Poor design by the architect

 C. Lack of a sufficient number of bathrooms within the building

 D. Retrofitted aluminum wiring under a new law

Answer: D. New rules and regulations that were not created by the property owner are considered external.

36. The income approach is most used by appraisers during the valuation of:

A. A condominium

B. A residence

C. An office building

D. A residential lot

Answer: C. Income approach is used by investment properties.

37. A huge company enters a small town and employees many workers. As a real estate professional, you determine the house prices will most likely:

A. Drop

B. Rise

C. Not change

D. Not be affected at all by supply and demand

Answer: B. More people employed creates more demand with the supply constant. Prices will rise.

38. A residential property with its child's game room next to the master bedroom is considered:

A. Physically incurable

B. Economically obsolete

C. Functionally obsolete

D. An appropriate design

Answer: C. This is a concept of bad design and isn't seen as favorable by the public; therefore, the functionality is hindered.

39. An appraiser's job can be described as:

A. Estimating value

B. Computing value

C. Determining value

D. Finding value

Answer: A. The opinion of the appraiser causes an estimate of the value.

40. The gross rent multiplier (GRM) is used to estimate the value based on the:

A. Ratio of the gross rents to the net rent

B. Relationship of value to the income

C. Capitalization of the net rental income

D. Ratio of rent due to the rent collected

Answer: B. Value = gross rents × GRM. Therefore, the GRM is a measure, or multiple, of the gross income to the value.

41. A building is valued at $400,000 and contains six apartments that rent for $500 each per month. The owner estimates that the expenses are 40 percent of the gross rental receipts. What is the capitalization rate?

A. 3.5 percent

B. 7.8 percent

C. 4.5 percent

D. 6.4 percent

Answer: C. The gross rents are 6 × $500/month × 12 months = $30,000. The expenses are $12,000 ($30,000 × 0.4). Therefore, the net income is $18,000. Cap rate = net income ÷ value = $18,000 ÷ $400,000 = 0.045 or 4.5 percent.

42. The income approach uses:

A. Depreciation rate

B. Equalization factor

C. Appreciation multiplier

D. Capitalization rate

Answer: D. The cap rate is the only factor, from the choices available, used in income property valuation. Other potential factors could be the GRM or the gross income multiplier (GIM).

43. Tom has a home-repair business. During the busy months of the summer, his prices will most likely:

A. Rise, to get the best value for his time

B. Drop, to accommodate more business

C. Rise, to limit the amount of time he works

D. Drop, to ensure he can pay his employees

Answer: A. Tom raises his prices to get the most value for his time spent working.

44. A student has completed a report about the area, including a section on education levels, age of the residents, and other important characteristics. He has completed a study in:

A. Population

B. Demographics

C. Fiscal policies

D. Political factors

Answer: B. The study of a population is an area is called demographics. The study could include data such as age, pay rate, racial components, etc.

45. A house with a one-car garage most likely is considered:

A. External depreciation

B. Physically deteriorated

C. External deterioration

D. Functionally obsolete

Answer: D. The current population would see a one-car garage as unfavorable by today's standards. So it is functionally obsolete.

46. Which of the following is not a characteristic of value?

A. Scarcity

B. Utility

C. Functionality

D. Transferability

Answer: C. Functionality is not a direct component of value.

47. Using which of the following requires the value of the land to be subtracted out from the value of the structure?

A. Cost approach

B. Income approach

C. Sales comparison approach

D. Gross rent multiplier

Answer: A. During the use of the cost approach, the appraiser only determines the value of the structure less the land. When his calculation is complete, he adds the value of the land back into the value of the structure.

48. In the sales comparison approach, an appraiser uses which of the following?

    A. Sales prices of similar properties

    B. Owner's original cost of construction

    C. Estimate of the building's replacement cost

    D. Property's depreciated value as used for income tax purposes

Answer: A. The principle of substitution considers homes of similar style, structure, and design to determine the value of the subject property.

49. Which of the following steps are not in the appraisal process?

    A. Gathering specific data on the target, or subject, property

    B. Gathering general data for the neighborhood

    C. Applying the three approaches to value to the collected data

    D. Collecting the seller's estimate of the property's value

Answer: D. The seller's opinion is not considered during the appraisal process.

50. In a steady market of home sales per month, a REALTOR notices the average sales price has dropped. He can conclude:

    A. Fewer homes are on the market.

    B. More homes are on the market.

    C. The number of homes doesn't affect the sales price.

    D. He can conclude nothing from this information.

Answer: B. If the average price is lower but the supply is steady, he can conclude there must be more properties for sale in the market.

Test 7: Finance

1. A woman has just made the final payment on her loan. The lender then calls the trustee, who issues:

    A. A satisfaction of mortgage

    B. A reconveyance of mortgage

    C. An alienation of mortgage

    D. A reversion of mortgage

Answer: B. A reconveyance deed is used to transfer a deed initially placed in a trust.

2. If a buyer obtains a $150,000 mortgage with 2½ points, how much will the lender charge at closing?

    A. $6,400

    B. $3,700

    C. $3,750

    D. $4,000

Answer: C. $0.025 \times \$150,000 = \$3,750$.

3. If a lender charges more interest than is allowed by the state, it is known as:

    A. Usury

    B. Excessive

    C. Deficiency

    D. Estoppel

Answer: A. By definition.

4. The fee a lender charges to cover the administrative costs of making a loan is:

    A. A prepayment penalty

    B. An advance interest payment

    C. A prepayment of mortgage insurance

    D. A loan origination fee

Answer: D. The lender charges a loan origination fee to cover its costs associated with making the loan to a borrower.

5. The pledging of an asset, typically real estate, as security for a loan is known as:

    A. Hypothecation

    B. Loan to value

    C. Subrogation

    D. Subordination

Answer: A. The collateral for a loan is pledged, or hypothecated.

6. The right a mortgagor has to regain the property by paying the debt after a foreclosure sale is called:

    A. Equitable right of redemption

    B. Statutory right of redemption

    C. Inalienable right of reversion

    D. Statutory right of recapture

Answer: B. After the sale, a law, or statutory regulation, allows the mortgagor to regain the property.

7. A mortgagor is also known as the:

    A. Borrower

    B. Lender

    C. Provider of mortgage funds

    D. One who institutes the foreclosure

Answer: A. A borrower offers the mortgage to the lender as collateral for a loan. Therefore, a borrower is the mortgagor and a bank is the mortgagee.

8. After paying off his loan, the lender files what to release the lien?

    A. Reversion of mortgage

    B. Reconveyance of mortgage

    C. Alienation of mortgage

    D. Satisfaction of mortgage

Answer: D. The lien remains present until the lender files a release or satisfaction of lien. In some cases, the lender sends the release to the mortgagor who is responsible for placing it in the public records.

9. The mortgage having first priority is typically the one:

    A. With the highest face value

    B. That was signed first

    C. With the oldest date on it

    D. The buyer notified first

Answer: C. FIFO—first in, first out. Unless a subordination agreement has been exercised between two lien holders, the first one recorded has first priority.

10. The right a mortgagor has to regain the property by paying the debt before a tax lien sale is called:

    A. Equitable right of redemption

    B. Statutory right of redemption

    C. Inalienable right of reversion

    D. Statutory right of recapture

Answer: A. Before the sale, a person has the right to pay what's owed, or what's fair, hence the words equity or equitable right of redemption.

11. The buyer is unable to qualify for a traditional lender's loan. However, the seller and the buyer form a land contract. The buyer's interest in the property is known as:

    A. Joint title

    B. Legal title

    C. Equitable title

    D. Naked title

Answer: C. The vendee has equitable title while the vendor retains the legal title.

12. Under a contract for deed, the legal title to the property is held by the:

    A. Trustor

    B. Vendee

    C. Vendor

    D. Trustee

Answer: C. The vendor has legal title while the vendee retains the equitable title.

13. Sometimes called a friendly foreclosure, what is used to avoid any court proceedings?

    A. Reconveyance deed

    B. Deed in lieu of foreclosure

    C. Special warranty deed

    D. Assumption

Answer: B. A deed in lieu executed by a quitclaim deed is used to transfer property to the lender and avoid any further court proceedings.

14. A promissory note:

    A. Is a promise by a government agency, such as the Federal Housing Administration

    B. Is always sold on the secondary market

    C. Creates a contract for personal liability by the borrower

    D. Is always executed in connection with a real estate transfer

Answer: C. A promissory note is a legal contract that binds the borrower to the debt.

15. A mortgage broker generally offers which of the following services except:

    A. Handling the loan escrow procedures

    B. Bringing together the buyer and the seller

    C. Providing credit qualification and evaluation reports

    D. Granting real estate loans using investor funds

Answer: B. Bringing together the buyer and the seller is a real estate professional's job.

16. If a property sold at a mortgage foreclosure does not bring an amount sufficient to satisfy the outstanding mortgage debt, the mortgagor may be responsible for a:

    A. Default judgment

    B. Punitive judgment

    C. Summary judgement

    D. Deficiency judgment

Answer: D. The difference between the outstanding balance on the loan and the amount collected by the lender is a deficiency and is due to the lender from the borrower.

17. A loan that only pays the portion to cover the rent of the money borrowed is known as:

    A. An amortized loan

    B. An adjustable rate loan

    C. A straight loan

    D. An interest-only loan

Answer: D. An interest-only loan pays only the interest accrued during the loan. The principal balance is due in full at the end of the loan.

18. The result of increasing the amount of time required to pay back a loan has what effect on the monthly payments?

    A. Higher monthly payments

    B. Higher escrow requirements

    C. Lower monthly payments

    D. Lower escrow requirements

Answer: A. Given the same principle amount, more time results in lower monthly payments. However, it results in more interest paid over the time frame.

19. Fannie Mae, Ginnie Mae, and Freddie Mac all:

A. Originate residential mortgage loans

B. Primarily insure residential mortgage loans

C. Guarantee existing mortgage loans

D. Are secondary buyers of residential mortgage loans

Answer: D. All are secondary buyers of residential mortgage loans.

20. A Federal Housing Administration–insured loan is originated by:

A. A lending institution insured by the Federal Housing Administration

B. A Department of Housing and Urban Development–approved lender

C. A lending institution approved by the Federal Housing Administration

D. The Federal Housing Administration itself

Answer: C. The Federal Housing Administration only insures loans made by approved lenders. It does not actually loan money.

21. Per the Truth in Lending Act (TILA), a creditor is someone who extends commercial credit more than how many times, or how many if secured by a first lien position?

A. 20/10

B. 25/10

C. 25/5

D. 25/25

Answer: C. Per the rules of TILA, more than 25 times a year for consumer credit or more than 5 if the loan is secured by a residential lien.

22. Which of the following is considered a trigger item under Regulation Z?

A. Easy terms available

B. Conventional financing available

C. Zero down

D. Listed at $130,000

Answer: C. You can't mention a trigger term such as a down payment amount without mentioning all the terms of the loan.

23. All the statements are true about mortgages guaranteed through the Department of Veterans Affairs (VA) except:

A. Discount points may be paid by the seller.

B. The borrower cannot have a prepayment penalty.

C. Funding fee amounts are negotiable.

D. The borrower must apply for a certificate of eligibility.

Answer: C. The funding fees are set by the lender.

24. A borrower obtained a loan for the purchase of an investment property. After the final scheduled payment was made, a balance remained on the original loan amount. What type of loan is this?

A. Fully amortized loan

B. Partially amortized loan

C. Interest-only loan

D. Accelerated loan

Answer: B. After the regularly scheduled payments come to an end and a balance remains, the loan is only partially amortized rather than fully amortized, which has $0 balance at the end.

25. A short-term high-interest-rate loan designed to be taken over by a take-out, or permeant, loan is most likely called:

    A. A construction loan

    B. A pass-through loan

    C. An amortized loan

    D. A home equity line of credit (HELOC)

Answer: A. By definition of a construction loan.

26. The Federal Reserve System controls the flow of money through which of the following?

    A. Reserve requirements

    B. The Department of Housing and Urban Development (HUD)

    C. Real estate investment trusts (REITs)

    D. The Federal Housing Administration

Answer: A. The Federal Reserve System controls the flow of money in two ways: the discount rate and reserve requirements.

27. An investor has three residential rental properties for sale. He is offered a deal for only one property and accepts the offer knowing he can release one property per the terms of his loan agreement without paying off the entire loan amount. What type of loan did the developer have?

    A. HELOC

    B. Blanket mortgage

    C. Amortized mortgage

    D. Open-end mortgage

Answer: B. A blanket loan allows for a partial release providing a substantial payment is paid toward the outstanding balance of the loan.

28. The type of mortgage loan that uses both real and personal property as security is:

    A. An open-end loan

    B. A blanket loan

    C. A package loan

    D. A construction loan

Answer: C. By definition of a package loan.

29. The principal distinction between the primary and secondary mortgage market is:

    A. The primary market makes loans; the secondary insures loans.

    B. The primary market makes loans; the secondary buys loans.

    C. The primary market insures loans; the secondary buys loans.

    D. The primary market insures loans; the secondary makes loans.

Answer: B. The primary market is made of those who put their hand in their pocket and make loans; the secondary market buys the notes created by the borrowers for those loans.

30. If a borrower is making a PITI payment to the lender every month, his payments are said to be "escrowed," meaning the lender creates special escrow amounts for:

    A. Taxes and insurance

    B. Taxes and interest

    C. Total investment

    D. Total amount of insurance

Answer: A. PITI stands for principle, interest, taxes, and insurance.

31. A lender ensures the real estate taxes will be paid by requiring the borrower to:

   A. Obtain private mortgage insurance

   B. Prepay the tax bill at closing

   C. Sign a promissory note

   D. Create an escrow account

Answer: D. Lenders will require a borrower to create escrow accounts that are paid into each month from the borrower's house payment.

32. The amount borrowed is called the:

   A. Interest amount

   B. Principal amount

   C. Escrow amount

   D. Income amount

Answer: B. The amount of the loan borrowed from a lender is called the principal loan amount.

33. The amount of the value above the outstanding loan amount is called the:

   A. Loan-to-value ratio

   B. Amount of the loan

   C. Equity

   D. Outstanding balance on the loan

Answer: C. The difference between the loan amount and the value represents the equity gained by the owner of the property.

34. The appraiser is hired by:

   A. The lender

   B. The mortgagor

   C. The buyer

   D. The seller

Answer: A. An appraiser is hired by a lender to protect its interest in the loan to ensure the collateral offered for the loan is of sufficient value to cover the loan amount should the borrower default.

35. One of the factors of a Federal Housing Administration–insured loan is the:

   A. High loan-to-value ratio

   B. Speed to get the loan

   C. Prepayment penalty

   D. Restrictions on what areas of the country are eligible

Answer: A. Federal Housing Administration loans only require a 3.5 percent down payment.

36. With a VA guarantee, the lender does an appraisal on the property; however, the VA also performs a:

   A. Certificate of reasonable value

   B. Certificate of eligibility

   C. Certificate of deposit

   D. Certificate against encumbrances

Answer: A. The VA has certificate of reasonable value performed on a property to protect its interest by having one of their own value the property.

37. The last year Federal Housing Administration-insured loans were freely assumable was:

A. 1989.
B. 1986.
C. 1998.
D. They still are freely assumable.

Answer: B. The last year Federal Housing Administration-insured loans were freely assumable was 1986. Between then and 1989, they were partially assumable, and since 1989, you just fully qualify to assume a loan.

38. Which of these is not a secondary buyer?

A. Insurance companies
B. Credit unions
C. Pension companies
D. REITs

Answer: D. A REIT is an investment company and does not buy loans from the primary market.

39. Mr. Johnson hired a broker to find him a 100+-unit apartment complex for sale. Upon finding one, he made an offer for $1.5 million to include all the personal property as well. Mr. Johnson may have to seek a special loan, called:

A. An amortized loan
B. A balloon loan
C. A package loan
D. An interest-only loan

Answer: C. The property includes a large amount of personal property, which would require a package loan.

40. A really great mortgage broker, when asked what the current interest rate is, should say "What do you want it to be?" He is most likely referring to:

A. An interest buydown
B. A balloon loan
C. A reverse mortgage
D. Puffing

Answer: A. A buydown is a temporary or permanent prepayment of the interest on a loan.

41. A loan you get approved for based on the equity of your home, but on which you make no payments until you draw the money out of the bank, and only pay interest on the money you use is called:

A. A HELOC
B. An open-end loan
C. A construction loan
D. A wrap loan

Answer: B. An open-end loan means you have been approved for the ability to use the money. If you don't, there are no payments, and you only pay the interest on the money you borrow.

42. The alienation clause is most often called the:

A. Assignment clause
B. Due on sale clause
C. Habendum clause
D. Acceleration clause

Answer: B. Due on sale. When you lose control of the collateral, i.e., sell it, the lender wants its money back.

43. A clause in a document that allows two lien holders to switch priorities in the public records is known as:

    A. A convent of seisin

    B. A subordination clause

    C. A subrogation clause

    D. An alienation clause

Answer: B. By definition of subordination clause.

44. Which system is also known as the two-party system?

    A. Lien theory

    B. Deed of trust theory

    C. Title theory

    D. Trustee theory

Answer: A. The lien theory system, the mortgage system, and the two-party system all mean the same thing.

45. If the loan, at 4 percent interest, has semiannual interest payments of $2,600, the principal amount of the loan is:

    A. $100,000

    B. $110,000

    C. $130,000

    D. $120,000

Answer: C. $2,600 × 2 = $5,200 ÷ 0.04 = $130,000.

46. If a lender makes a loan higher than it normal feels comfortable making to a borrower, it may seek further assurance by means of:

    A. Extra collateral

    B. Private mortgage insurance (PMI)

    C. A lower credit rating by the borrower

    D. Extra monthly payments to principal

Answer: B. PMI is an insurance policy to cover the lender should the borrower default on the loan.

47. If a lender accepts less money than is owned by the mortgagor, this is known as a:

    A. Delinquent loan

    B. Subordinate loan

    C. Short sale

    D. Short of the market

Answer: C. The lender is accepting "short" payoff; therefore, it is called a short sale.

48. If the amount of a loan is $130,500 and the interest rate is 6.5 percent, what's the amount of the annual interest payment?

    A. $8,082.50

    B. $8,482.50

    C. $9,482.50

    D. $8,786.50

Answer: B. $130,500 × 0.065 = $8,482.50.

49. If the amount of a loan is $12,500 and the interest payment is $430, what's the amount of the annual interest rate?

    A. 3.20 percent

    B. 3.32 percent

    C. 3.44 percent

    D. 3.53 percent

Answer: C. $430 ÷ $12,500 = 0.0344 or 3.44 percent.

50. If a loan contained a clause that states there is a 5/3/1 prepayment penalty and the borrower borrowed $87,500, what would be the penalty if he repaid the loan within the first year?

    A. $2,375

    B. $4,875

    C. $5,375

    D. $4,375

Answer: D. on a 5/3/1 prepayment penalty loan, the penalty would be 5 percent the first year, 3 percent the second year, and 1 percent the third year. So the total penalty would be $87,500 × 0.05 = $4,375.

Test 8: Investments, Taxes, Ethics

1. A house is listed at $180,000, the agreed-upon sale price is $175,900. If the buyer wanted to be fully leveraged in the deal, how much did he borrow?

A. $4,100

B. $175,000

C. $175,900

D. $180,000

Answer: C. Leverage is the use of a loan in a purchase. Therefore, fully leveraged means the use of all of the loan and no equity, or 100 percent loan to value (LTV).

2. An advantage of investing in real estate is:

A. The possibility of a tax-deferred exchange

B. The liquidity

C. The use of leverage to increase rates of return

D. Tax deductions

Answer: C. The ability to increase your rate of return by using other people's money.

3. The term depreciation is the same as which of the following?

A. Appreciation

B. Cost recovery

C. Recapitalization

D. Capitalization

Answer: C. Depreciation is the loss in value for any reason, and it must be recapitalized when a property is sold for a gain.

4. One of the methods a real estate investor may use to defer capital gains tax is to:

A. Sell the property for cash only

B. Reduce the leverage over time

C. Use a legal 1031 exchange

D. Buy another property within 30 days of the sale

Answer: C. A 1031 tax-deferred exchange allows an investor to pay no capital gain tax when executed properly.

5. If, as part of a 1031 exchange, an investor has to give something to balance the values, this is called:

A. Leverage

B. Like kind

C. Collateral

D. Boot

Answer: D. Boot is the equalization of value and can be anything the two parties agree on, such as cash, a vintage car, etc.

6. An investor bought a double for $65,000 using all cash. He later sold the property for $78,000 to a buyer using an 80 percent LTV loan. The profit he earned is called:

A. Capital profit

B. Capital gain

C. Adjusted basis

D. Basis

Answer: B. Profit is synonymous with capital gain.

7. Which is the highest leverage?

    A. 50 percent LTV

    B. Using more of your own funds than what you borrow

    C. All cash with no loan at all

    D. 100 percent LTV

Answer: D. Leverage is the use of a loan in a purchase. Fully leveraged means the use of all of the loan and no equity, or 100 percent LTV.

8. Per IRS rules, which of the following investments cannot be depreciated?

    A. an investor's duplex

    B. an investor's vacant residential lot

    C. an owner-occupied duplex

    D. an investor's vacant strip center

Answer: B. Vacant land cannot be depreciated, regardless of the ownership entity.

9. An investor looking to invest in relatively safe real estate with a high return would probably invest in a:

    A. Real estate investment trust (REIT)

    B. Limited partnership

    C. General partnership

    D. Corporation

Answer: A. REITs are publicly traded companies that invest in real estate and offer a stable return with a relative degree of safety.

10. Net income refers to the:

    A. Amount of money flowing into and out of a property

    B. Bookkeeping function that accounts for the cash each day

    C. Taxes, operating expenses, and loan payments on the property

    D. Gross amount of income after all expenses have been paid

Answer: D. The gross income less expenses is defined as net income.

11. When an investor uses the equity of the first property as a down payment to buy a second property while maintaining ownership of the first property, it's most likely called:

    A. Investing the equity

    B. Pyramiding through sale

    C. Pyramiding through refinance

    D. 1031 exchange

Answer: C. Because he maintained ownership, he refinanced the property to use the equity. Pyramiding through sale is selling a property and using the cash to buy a bigger property.

12. The type of real estate investment that's required by federal law to distribute 95 percent of its income to its shareholders is:

    A. General partnership

    B. Limited partnership

    C. REIT

    D. Timeshare estate

Answer: C. By definition, a REIT must distribute 95 percent of its earnings to investors in the company.

13. Expenses that affect net income include all the following except:

    A. Payroll of the property manager

    B. Real estate taxes

    C. Maintenance and repairs

    D. Mortgage payments

Answer: D. A mortgage payment, sometimes called debt service, is not an expense. Net income less debt service is defined as cash flow.

14. All the following are advantages of investing in real estate except:

    A. Better-than-average returns

    B. The use of leverage to buy property

    C. Tax benefits to the investor

    D. Less control than other investments

Answer: D. A high degree of control is a hallmark advantage of investing in real estate.

15. Leverage is defined as:

    A. The amount of down payment brought to the table

    B. The use of other people's money

    C. The sum of the loan plus the equity

    D. The difference between the appraised value and sale price

Answer: B. The use of a loan from a lender, which is other people's money (OPM).

16. If an investor borrows $125,000 to buy a property and was 75 percent leveraged, what was the sales price of the property?

    A. $165,000

    B. $166,333

    C. $167,000

    D. $167,666

Answer: D. 75 percent leveraged means a 75 percent loan: $125,000 \div 0.75 = $166,666.

17. The single biggest downside to investing in real estate is:

    A. Leverage

    B. Liquidity

    C. Proration

    D. Pyramiding

Answer: B. Being able to divest yourself of real estate through a sale is often the hardest and longest process. Therefore, liquidity is a huge downside to investing in real estate.

18. When two or more people work together on a single project, it's a:

    A. Partnership

    B. Joint venture

    C. Corporation

    D. Limited liability company (LLC)

Answer: B. The fact that they're working on a single project and not joined together for a business venture makes it a joint venture.

19. A legal entity that pools money for the purpose of investing in real estate, is called a:

    A. REMIC

    B. JV

    C. REIT

    D. FDIC

Answer: C. REITs are publicly traded companies that invest in real estate and offer a stable return with a relative degree of safety.

20. The biggest aid from technology in the property management field is:

    A. Cloud-based software

    B. The deadbolt locking system

    C. Buyer's agents who bring tenants to property managers

    D. The control of locking mechanisms

Answer: A. Cloud-based technology has progressed property management by leaps and bounds.

21. Capital gains is basically:

    A. The loan amount of property

    B. The amount of taxes saved by investing

    C. The difference between the loan amount and sales price

    D. The profit on a deal

Answer: D. Profit and capital gain are synonymous terms.

22. The basis for an investment property is defined as:

    A. The amount paid for the property

    B. The amount leveraged on a property

    C. The amount assessed on the property

    D. The difference between the loan and appraised value

Answer: A. The actual price paid for a piece of real property is the basis. You can adjust the basis by adding the improvements made less the depreciation (cost recovery) you have taken over the life of ownership.

23. The adjusted basis is defined as:

    A. The improvements on a property

    B. The improvements on a property less the depreciation already taken property

    C. The purchase prices less the depreciation already taken on a property

    D. The basis plus the improvements less depreciation already taken on a property

Answer: D. The actual price paid for a piece of real property is the basis. You can adjust the basis by adding the improvements made less the depreciation (cost recovery) you have taken over the life of ownership.

24. To avoid paying taxes on the capital gain tax of a sale of investment property, the investor would use:

    A. 1330 tax-deferred exchange

    B. 1031 tax-free exchange

    C. 1033 tax-deferred exchange

    D. 1031 tax-deferred exchange

Answer: D. The 1031 tax-deferred exchange was created to help investors buy other like-kind properties without having to pay the capital gain on the property they're selling.

25. A REALTOR is best described as a:

    A. Person who brings together a buyer and seller

    B. Member of the National Association of REALTORS (NAR)

    C. Person who gets paid based on commission

    D. Person who works for the broker

Answer: B. A member of the NAR. A person can be a licensed real estate professional and earn a commission without being a member of the NAR.

26. The agreement that binds a salesperson to a broker is most likely:

    A. A listing agreement

    B. A buyer-agency agreement

    C. An independent contractor agreement

    D. A noncompete agreement

Answer: C. A managing broker signs an independent contractor agreement with every salesperson under them.

27. A broker can get paid in all ways except:

    A. Hourly

    B. Flat fee

    C. A percentage of listing amount

    D. A commission amount

Answer: C. You don't get paid from the listing amount.

28. A commission fee can be:

    A. Negotiated on every deal

    B. Always the same

    C. Based on the price

    D. Level for all customers

Answer: A. A commission set by the broker can be different in all cases if he chooses.

29. All the following are components of the Sherman Antitrust Act except:

    A. Price fixing

    B. Tie-in agreement

    C. Collusion document

    D. Group boycotting

Answer: C. There's no such thing as a collusion document in real estate.

30. A victim of the Sherman Antitrust Act can receive:

    A. An immediate apology

    B. Triple damages plus court costs

    C. $10,000 per violation

    D. 1 year in prison

Answer: B. Victims can receive triple their damages plus their court costs.

31. The major difference between a broker's customer and a broker's client is:

    A. The spelling of the words

    B. The agency between them

    C. The price of the commission charged

    D. There is no difference between these two people and they're treated in the same manner

Answer: B. A customer is someone with whom you have no agency responsibilities; a client is someone with whom you have agency.

32. The process of a seller accepting the buyer's offer is called:

    A. Forming a contract

    B. Finishing a contract

    C. Basing a contract

    D. Delegating a contract

Answer: A. A contract is said to be formed when both parties agree to the terms.

33. When two or more sales agents work together to increase their productivity, it's most likely:

    A. A group

    B. A brokerage

    C. A team

    D. An oligarchy

Answer: C. A team works as a one group and usually under one name to exponentially expand their deal flow.

34. Some states use the salesperson/broker model for their licensee, in that state the principal broker can best be described as:

    A. The one with the most sales in each year

    B. The boss who is responsible for the salespersons under them

    C. The one who has the single largest listing in each year

    D. The one who started the business

Answer: B. The managing broker, or principal broker, is the person responsible for the actions of the all the agents underneath them and is often thought of as the boss.

35. Laws that are borne out of a judge's decision and can change over the years are best described as:

    A. Common law

    B. Statutory law

    C. Administrative law

    D. Criminal law

Answer: A. Common law can change over the years; agency works under common law. In fact, it's often called the common law of agency.

36. A written system of standards by the NAR is best described as:

    A. The Rules of Agency

    B. The Laws of Decent

    C. The Code of Regulations

    D. The Code of Ethics

Answer: D. The Code of Ethics is the NAR's written system of conduct for all REALTORS to follow.

37. An ad valorem tax is based on:

    A. The loan amount

    B. The appraised mount

    C. The sales price

    D. The assessed value

Answer: D. The ad valorem tax is based on an assessed value of the real property. That value can be determined in many ways, but it's still the value used for taxing purposes.

38. All the following are taxable except:

    A. A farmer's 80-acre parcel of land

    B. A washer and dryer bought via a bill of sale

    C. Improvements to land, such as buildings

    D. Loss in value of a building that uses straight-line depreciation

Answer: D. A loss is never taxed.

39. Failure to pay your real estate taxes could result in:

    A. Foreclosure by your mortgage company

    B. The state auctioning your property at a tax sale

    C. The state absorbing your property via escheat

    D. Your lender exercising its power of sale clause

Answer: B. Failure to pay real estate taxes could lead to the state selling your property at auction for the outstanding amount due.

40. John paid his current year's taxes based on the value of his home. This type of tax is known as:

    A. Ad valorem tax

    B. Special assessment tax

    C. Personal income tax

    D. Usage tax

Answer: A. Ad valorem tax is based on a valuation of the property.

41. A tax collected to pay for a new sewer in a housing addition is most likely:

    A. An ad valorem tax

    B. A special assessment tax

    C. A personal income tax

    D. A usage tax

Answer: B. A special assessment tax is issued on improvements made out of the ordinary or for a one-time event.

42. An owner buys a house for $125,000 that is assessed at 80 percent of the value. If the tax rate is 40 mills, what are the monthly taxes?

    A. $4,000

    B. $333.33

    C. $2,533

    D. $5,100

Answer: B. The assessed value is $125,000 × 0.80 = $100,000. The millage, or tax rate, is 40 mills, which is 0.040. Therefore, the taxes would be $100,000 × 0.040 = $4,000 per year. The question asked for monthly taxes, so $4,000 ÷ 12 = $333.33 per month.

43. If a tax rate is 125 mills, that's equal to:

    A. 0.0125

    B. 12.5 percent

    C. 1.25 percent

    D. 0.125 percent

Answer: B. 125 mills is 0.125 or 12.5 percent.

44. All the following are typically exempt from real estate taxes except:

    A. The airport authority

    B. A parcel of municipal property

    C. A community soccer field

    D. A public service railroad

Answer: C. A community piece of real estate is a taxable parcel of land.

45. In some states, an owner's residence is most protected from seizure from an unsecured creditor by:

A. Homestead exemption

B. Mortgage exemption

C. Tenants by the entirety

D. Right of search and seizure

Answer: A. The homestead exemption varies in many states; however, the premise is still to protect the primary residence against unsecured creditors.

46. Who establishes the tax rate of real property?

A. The state

B. The seller's personal income tax rate

C. The buyer's personal income tax rate

D. The volume of property sold in an area divided by the number of homes sold in the same area

Answer: A. The state establishes the tax rate. Other entities, such as parks, water districts, libraries, etc., may add to the tax rate.

47. The right of redemption prior to the tax sale is known as:

A. Statutory right of redemption

B. Unified right of redemption

C. Equitable right of redemption

D. Mandatory right of redemption

Answer: C. The right before the sale is known as equitable. Think of paying the money you owe. Money is equity and, therefore, equitable. The right after the tax sale is a law, or statutory.

48. A mill is best described as:

A. 1/100 dollar

B. 1/10 dollar

C. 1 percent

D. 1/1,000 dollar

Answer: D. A mill is 1/1,000 dollar or $0.001.

49. If owner A and owner B are assessed a special assessment tax for new sidewalks, and owner A's property is three times wider than owner B's property, what's the most probable outcome?

A. Owner B's tax is equal to owner A's tax.

B. Owner B's tax is double owner A's tax.

C. Owner B's tax is less than owner A's tax.

D. Owner B's tax is three times more than owner A's tax.

Answer: D. The benefit to owner A is three times larger due to the exposure of his property to the sidewalk.

50. The investor who sells property on a land contract, or owner financing:

A. Is taxed on the entire gain in the year the property is sold

B. Is taxed on the gain equally over a 10-year period

C. Is taxed on the gain received in each year

D. Is taxed on the entire gain in the year the property is paid off

Answer: C. Under Internal Revenue Service rules, capital gain is only taxed in the year you actually receive it.

Test 9: Closings, Risk, and Property Management

1. The deed recording is typically a:

    A. Seller debit

    B. Buyer debit

    C. Seller credit

    D. Buyer credit

Answer: B. The buyer pays for this to ensure the transfer of title is recorded.

2. Truth in Lending; Real Estate Settlement Procedure Integrated Disclosure (TRID) applies to the activities of:

    A. Licensed real estate brokers

    B. Licensed securities salespeople

    C. Lenders making residential loans on real property

    D. Secondary markets purchasing residential mortgages

Answer: C. TRID is deigned to make the lending process more transparent for the borrower when buying a residential property.

3. The details of a closing are always governed by the:

    A. Seller

    B. Buyer

    C. Agreed-upon purchase contract

    D. Title company during the closing process

Answer: C. The closing is guided by a properly executed and legal purchase contract for real property.

4. The real estate broker's commission generally appears as a:

    A. Credit to the seller

    B. Credit to the buyer

    C. Debit to the seller

    D. Debit to the buyer

Answer: C. The seller pays the commission.

5. TRID provides that:

    A. Buyers must receive their closing disclosure statement at least 72 hours in advance.

    B. Advertisements must include the annual percentage rate (APR).

    C. Buyers must be given a loan estimate form prior to closing.

    D. Real estate syndicates must comply with the disclosures required by blue-sky laws.

Answer: C. A loan estimate form must be given to a borrower making application to inform him of all the costs associated with getting the loan.

6. The division of expenses so the buyer and the seller pay their respective portion is called:

    A. Assessment

    B. Proration

    C. Balancing

    D. Reconciliation

Answer: B. By definition, the proration is the splitting of a bill so each person pays for his or her own portion of the use of that bill.

7. All the following items are usually prorated between the buyer and the seller at closing except:

    A. Recording charges

    B. Real estate taxes

    C. Rents

    D. Utility bills

Answer: A. The recording charges are paid by each person for the cost of recording their own specific documents.

8. At the closing, which one of the following cannot be any more than quoted on the loan estimate form:

    A. Loan origination fee

    B. Title fee

    C. Homeowners' insurance

    D. Commission

Answer: A. The origination fee is an example of a zero-tolerance fee—that is, one that cannot be increased in any amount above the fee quoted at the time of application.

9. The principal balance on an assumed mortgage loan is entered on the closing statement as a:

    A. Credit to the seller and a debit to the buyer

    B. Debit to the seller and a credit to the buyer

    C. Credit to both the seller and the buyer

    D. Debit to both the seller and the buyer

Answer: B. On an assumed loan, the buyer gets all the credit for payment already made by the seller.

10. TRID is a federal statute administered by the:

    A. Department of Housing and Urban Development (HUD)

    B. Securities and Exchange Commission (SEC)

    C. Consumer Financial Protection Bureau (CFPB)

    D. Federal Housing Administration

Answer: C. TRID is governed by the CFPB.

11. The closing statement involves debits and credits to the parties in the transaction. A debit is:

    A. A bill already paid

    B. A bill yet to be paid

    C. An adjustment for an expense paid outside of closing

    D. A proration

Answer: B. A debit is a charge of a bill that's already paid by either the seller or buyer.

12. TRID requires:

    A. The closing must be held within 90 days of the purchase contract.

    B. Lenders must keep a specified amount of money to seed escrow accounts.

    C. Lenders must disclose the ultimate holder of the promissory note.

    D. Buyers must know how much money is required to offset any proration amounts 72 hours prior to closing.

Answer: B. TRID requires lenders to maintain only a specified amount of money to seed an escrow account and cannot charge excess amounts at the closing table.

13. TRID rules states all the following except:

   A. A loan estimate form must be given to the borrower.

   B. A uniform settlement form must be used at loan closings.

   C. The borrower may cancel the loan transaction within 7 days before the closing.

   D. Lenders must provide borrowers with a closing estimate form.

Answer: C. TRID allows for a 3-day right of rescission on refinances.

14. Which of the following are prohibited under TRID:

   A. Mortgage brokers may pay a referral fee for a lead.

   B. Only borrowers may pay fees charged for the collateralized loan obligation (CLO) service.

   C. Brokers may charge whatever fees they determine are fair for the service.

   D. Brokers are required to disclose the existence of loan products other than those presented by their CLO.

Answer: A. A mortgage broker cannot pay a finder's fee, referral fee, or fee splitting of any kind.

15. Affiliated Business Arrangements (ABA) are permissible under the following condition:

   A. Consumers are unaware of ABA.

   B. Consumers are required to use the ABA.

   C. Consumers are aware and approve the ABA in advance.

   D. Companies pay referral fees between them.

Answer: C. ABA are legal as long as the client is aware of the arrangement and condones it.

16. If a bill is prepaid, the credit belongs to the:

   A. Buyer.

   B. Seller.

   C. There is no credit allowed.

   D. The buyer and seller split the credit.

Answer: B. A prepaid bill is paid prior to use; therefore, it must be paid by the seller.

17. If a bill is accrued, the credit belongs to the:

   A. Buyer.

   B. Seller.

   C. There is no credit allowed.

   D. The buyer and seller split the credit.

Answer: A. An accrued bill is paid after it is used; therefore, the new owner (buyer) pays it after the closing. He gets a credit for the portion used by the seller.

18. When determining the rent rate, a property manager considers the economic principle of:

   A. The supply and demand of the local market

   B. The style of the building

   C. The proximity to amenities

   D. The racial equality of the tenants

Answer: A. Supply and demand.

19. Risk management strategies include all the following except:

   A. Avoid

   B. Ignore

   C. Control

   D. Retain

Answer: B. The four methods to control the risk are: avoid, control, retain, and transfer. Never is ignoring a risk a wise idea in any profession.

20. Title passes from the seller to the buyer:

   A. When the deed gets recorded

   B. When the seller signs the deed

   C. When the deed is delivered and accepted

   D. When the seller accepts the money

Answer: C. The title passes upon delivery and acceptance of the deed.

21. Security deposits are a:

   A. Seller debit

   B. Buyer debit

   C. Seller credit

   D. Buyer credit

Answer: D. Security deposits must be transferred to the new owner, the buyer. They are a credit of the full amount of deposit.

22. A management agreement is most similar to:

   A. A listing agreement

   B. A purchase agreement

   C. A buyer's agreement

   D. An agency agreement

Answer: A. To a property manager, the management agreement is analogous to the listing agreement for a broker.

23. Under TRID rules, an annual percentage rate (APR) change greater than 0.125 percent requires the lender to extend the closing:

   A. 1 day

   B. 2 days

   C. 3 days

   D. 1 week

Answer: C. If the APR increases more than ⅛ percent, the lender must have 3 days to review the new document.

24. A clause in a commercial lease that allows the tenant to extend his expired lease for a new term is often called:

   A. A renewal clause

   B. A first-right clause

   C. An extension clause

   D. An entry clause

Answer: A. The renewal clause allows the tenant to extend the current lease under a new lease.

25. A licensed property manager:

   A. Must not profit from private contracts awarded to properties he or she manages

   B. May manage the client's property to their discretion

   C. Must offer maintenance at above-market rates

   D. Can benefit from interest earned on earnest money funds

Answer: A. A property manager cannot profit from a contract to repair a property he or she has a fiduciary responsibility to. For example, if an HVAC professional quotes $1,000 for repair of a unit, the property manager cannot charge the owner $1,100 and make a profit on the transaction.

26. Adaptations made by a tenant to fit a specific layout or configuration are called:

   A. Tax-related improvements

   B. Tenant improvements

   C. General improvements

   D. Ad hoc improvements

Answer: B. Tenant improvements are made by the tenant to the specific layout they may require.

27. All the following cause a low vacancy rate except:

  A. Properly run management companies

  B. Poor location

  C. Nearness to shopping centers and grocery stores

  D. Very desirable amenities

Answer: B. Low vacancy is equivalent to a high occupancy rate; therefore, poor location does not cause a high rental occupancy.

28. At a closing, an annual prepaid bill of $600 needs to be prorated between the buyer and seller. If the closing was on August 31, the bill is split:

  A. The seller is credited $400.

  B. The buyer is credited $400.

  C. The seller is credited $200.

  D. The buyer is credited $200.

Answer: C. Because it is a prepaid bill, the seller paid the $600; however, he used $400 worth of the bill. Therefore, he is owed the unused portion, or $200, at closing.

29. A property manager does all the following except:

  A. Pay the taxes on the income earned from rent

  B. Provide or oversee security for the property

  C. Satisfy the tenants to the best of his or her ability

  D. Provide or oversee maintenance of the property

Answer: A. A property manager does not pay the income tax earned from rent; the owner does.

30. At closing, an accrued bill of $150 must be prorated between the two parties. If the closing happened on July 15, how is the bill split:

  A. $81.25 credit to the seller

  B. $81.25 credit to the buyer

  C. $68.75 credit to seller

  D. $68.75 credit to buyer

Answer: B. An accrued bill is paid by the new owner, the buyer, when it comes due. The buyer uses 5½ months of the bill, or $68.75, so he or she needs to collect the used portion from the seller in the amount of $81.25.

31. The property manager's primary concern should be to:

  A. Achieve the owner's objective

  B. Preserve or increase the value of the property

  C. Generate income

  D. Provide a profitable return for the investor

Answer: B. In all cases, the property manager wants to ensure the property does not go into disrepair. He or she may not collect rent all the time, due to scheduled maintenance or property rehab between tenants.

32. The property manager's principle duties are to:

  A. The tenants

  B. The lender

  C. The local community

  D. The owner

Answer: D. The property manager is an agent for the owner and as such, his fiduciary duties are for the owner first.

33. All the following should be a consideration in selecting a tenant for the property except:

    A. Square footage of the apartment

    B. Tenant's ability to pay rent

    C. Tenant's credit history and score

    D. Tenant's religious heritage

Answer: D. Religion is a protected class under the Fair Housing Act.

34. The property manager is considered the agent of:

    A. The tenant

    B. The owner

    C. Neither the owner nor the tenants

    D. Both the owner and the lender

Answer: B. The property manager is an agent for the owner and as such, his fiduciary duties are for the owner first.

35. The property manager does all the following except:

    A. Verify tenant history and credit worthiness

    B. Provide the owner with a market study of local rent rates

    C. Provide the owner with current reports regarding the property

    D. Provide the tenant with help when moving in or out

Answer: D. The property manager is not required to help a tenant move.

36. The property manager needs to be familiar with laws concerning all the following except:

    A. Environmental laws

    B. Zoning laws

    C. Securities laws

    D. Fair housing laws

Answer: C. He has no dealings with the securities laws within the real estate realm.

37. A property manager does all the following except:

    A. Show rental space to tenants

    B. List vacant properties for rent

    C. Maintain accurate reports and rent rolls

    D. Maintain tenant personal property

Answer: D. A property manager has no dealings with tenants' personal property.

38. A warehouse rents for $19,000 per month and measures 112 × 150 feet. What is the rental rate?

    A. $10.75 per square foot

    B. $13.75 per square foot

    C. $13.57 per square foot

    D. $11.75 per square foot

Answer: C. 112 feet × 150 feet = 16,800 square feet; the annual rent would be $19,000 × 12 = $228,000. Therefore, $228,000 ÷ 16,800 = $13.57 per square foot.

39. An office suite rents for $900 per month and measures 50 feet × 20 feet. What is the rental rate?

    A. $10.80 per square foot

    B. $8.10 per square foot

    C. $11.25 per square foot

    D. $11.75 per square foot

Answer: A. 50 feet × 20 feet = 1,000 square feet; rent is $900 × 12 = $10,800. So the rental rate is $10,800 ÷ 1,000 = $10.80 per square foot.

40. If he finds a tenant, a property manager receives a leasing commission of 5 percent of the annual lease amount. If he leases out a flex space that measures 50 feet × 75 feet at $5.75 per square foot, what is the commission he earned?

    A. $100.50

    B. $310.50

    C. $512.50

    D. $862.50

Answer: D. 50 feet × 75 feet = 3,750 square feet; rent is 3,750 × $5.75 = $21,562.50. A commission of 4 percent leads to $21,562.50 × 0.04 = $862.50.

41. If a property manager generates a report for his client that itemizes all the costs associated with a rental property, it is most likely called:

    A. A gross income report

    B. A balance sheet

    C. A net income report

    D. An expense report

Answer: D. Expense reports itemize the costs incurred by a specific property.

42. When setting rental rates, which is not likely considered?

    A. It must be sufficient to cover the cost of the property.

    B. It must provide a return to the property owner.

    C. It must give the tenant adequate space to park a car.

    D. It must be in line with rental rates of surrounding properties.

Answer: C. The tenant's parking is not a concern when determining rental rates.

43. When dealing with tenants, which is the most detrimental to good relations?

    A. A good website that allows for maintenance requests

    B. An office with 24-hour emergency maintenance

    C. A pool and playground that are maintained daily

    D. An excessive late fee

Answer: D. An excessive late fee, which may be determined by the owner and only enforced by the property manager, does not make for good relations with tenants.

44. Which is not a type of maintenance provided by a property manager?

    A. Preventative

    B. Repair

    C. Routine

    D. Restrictive

Answer: D. There is no such thing as restrictive maintenance.

45. A successful property management company has an office with 17 employees and routinely gets visitors stopping by to see vacant units. The property manager is most concerned with which laws for his employees?

    A. Fair Housing Act

    B. Americans with Disability Act (ADA)

    C. The Freedom of Information Act (FOIA)

    D. The Constitution

Answer: B. The property manager has employees and should consider the ADA laws with addressing their needs.

46. The property manager should be concerned with all the following environmental concerns except:

    A. Trash removal

    B. Insect infestation

    C. Dirty laundry

    D. Sick building syndrome

Answer: C. Dirty laundry is a tenant issue.

47. The ADA requires employers, such as a property management company, to make reasonable modifications to accommodate handicapped employees. All the following are considered reasonable except:

    A. A ramp for wheelchair access

    B. Raised letters on elevator buttons

    C. Lowering of public telephones

    D. Building a new bathroom entirely handicapped accessible

Answer: D. Building an entirely new bathroom is considered an unreasonable accommodation.

48. In a closing statement, a prepaid item is:

    A. A debit charged to the buyer

    B. An item prepaid by the seller

    C. An item paid in advance by the buyer

    D. Is not considered in the closing because it has already been paid.

Answer: B. Prepaid means "paid before use"; therefore, it must have been paid prior to closing by the seller.

49. A commercial tenant finds himself in financial trouble and decides to rent some of his space to another tenant. This is most likely under what type of lease?

    A. New lease

    B. Gross lease

    C. Net lease

    D. Sublease

Answer: D. A sublease is one in which a tenant rents part of their rented space to another party.

50. Any accrued items are:

    A. Bills that already have been paid by the seller prior to closing

    B. The seller's total bills

    C. Bills that are due and must be settled at the time of the closing

    D. The buyer's total bills

Answer: C. Accrued items are bills that must be paid by the buyer when they come due at some later time. He must collect the portion due to him from the seller at the closing.

Test 10: Real Estate Math

1. A property measures 150 feet by 125 feet. The owner wants to add a 6-foot privacy fence around the entire property. A contractor says the cost is $1.25 per foot of fence plus $500 for the labor to install it. How much is the total quote from the contractor?

    A. $687.50

    B. $1,287.50

    C. $1,087.50

    D. $1,187.50

Answer: D. 550 feet × $1.25 = $687.50 for the fence plus $500 for the labor = $1,187.50. (The perimeter of the fence would be 150' + 125' + 150' + 125' = 550'.)

2. The paint for the fence in question 1 is $4.00/gallon and covers 300 square feet. How much did the owner spend on paint for the entire fence?

    A. $68.50

    B. $44.00

    C. $27.50

    D. $7.33

Answer: B. 550 feet × 6 feet = 3,300 square feet. 3,300 square feet ÷ 300 square feet = 11 gallons × $4/gallon = $4,400.

3. An agent lists a seller's house for 6 percent commission. The final agreed sales price is $234,500. How much commission did the seller pay?

    A. $14,070.00

    B. $14,770.00

    C. $1,477.00

    D. $1,477.50

Answer: A. $234,500 × 0.06 = $14,070.00.

4. The seller paid $23,500 in commission to his agent. His house sold for $457,900. How much was the commission rate the agent charged?

    A. 3.0 percent

    B. 6.0 percent

    C. 5.1 percent

    D. 4.875 percent

Answer: C. $23,500 ÷ $457,900 = 0.051 or 5.1 percent.

5. A broker charges 5.5 percent on his client's listing of $125,900. The selling agent's client offers $125,000, which the seller accepts. The listing broker offers 60 percent of the commission earned to the selling broker. How much does the listing broker earn?

    A. $4,125

    B. $2,750

    C. $2,000

    D. $4,750

Answer: B. $125,000 × 0.055 = $6,875 total commission. If selling broker gets 60 percent, then the listing broker gets 40 percent of the commission: $6,875 × 0.40 = $2,750.

6. The broker earns $22,050 for his portion of the commission on a limited agency transaction. The commission is 7 percent. How much did the house sell for?

    A. $314,125

    B. $315,000

    C. $315,125

    D. $316,000

Answer: B. $22,050 ÷ 0.07 = $315,000.

7. A lender charges 2 points origination fee on a home sale of $300,000 where the borrower uses a 90 percent loan to value (LTV) ratio. How much does the borrower pay for the loan?

    A. $4,125

    B. $5,000

    C. $5,400

    D. $6,000

Answer: C. Points are calculated based on loan amount, so in this case, the loan is $300,000 × 0.9 = $270,000. A point is 1 percent of the loan amount, so 2 points is 2 percent of the $270,000, or 0.02 × $270,000 = $5,400.

8. How many acres are in the NW¼ of the NW¼ of the NW¼ of Section 24 of 2RN, 2TN of principal meridian #2?

    A. 20

    B. 10

    C. 5

    D. 30

Answer: B. 4 × 4 × 4 = 64. There are 640 acres in a section; therefore, 640 ÷ 64 = 10 acres.

9. How many acres are in the NW¼ of the NW¼ of the NW¼ and the N½ of the NE¼ of the NW¼ of Section 24 of 2RN, 2TN of principal meridian #2?

    A. 20

    B. 10

    C. 5

    D. 30

Answer: D. There are two parcels of land here. One is 4 × 4 × 4 = 64. There are 640 acres in a section; therefore, 640 ÷ 64 = 10 acres. The second parcel is 2 × 4 × 4 = 32; 640 ÷ 32 = 20. So there are 10 + 20 acres, or 30 acres.

10. A seller asks his broker to list his farmland at $57,000 per acre. He describes the property as 500 feet along the road and 750 feet deep. What's the listing price?

    A. $475,000

    B. $480,300

    C. $490,700

    D. $497,500

Answer: C. 500 feet × 750 feet = 375,000 square feet ÷ 43,560 square feet per acre = 8.61 acres × $57,000/acre = $490,700.

11. A subdivider is required to have 2.25-acre lots at a minimum per the covenants, conditions, and restrictions (CCRs). How many lots can he have in a 76-acre parcel of farmland he just acquired?

   A. 33

   B. 34

   C. 35

   D. 36

Answer: A. 76 acres ÷ 2.25-acre minimum lot is 33.78 lots. Therefore, he can have 33 lots.

12. The transfer tax on a parcel of land is $1.25 per $500 of value. The property sold for $130,000. How much is the transfer tax?

   A. $305

   B. $325

   C. $350

   D. $320

Answer: B. $130,000 ÷ $500 = 260 units of taxable product. Each unit is taxed at $1.25; therefore, 260 × $1.25 = $325.

13. The transfer tax on a property is 30¢ per $250 of value. However, the first $10,000 of the sales price is exempt from taxes. The property sold for $80,000. How much is the transfer tax?

   A. $75

   B. $82

   C. $96

   D. $84

Answer: D. The sales price is $80,000; however, the effective sales price is only $70,000 due to the exemption. Therefore, there are $70,000 ÷ $250 = 280 taxing units at 30¢ per unit = $84 in transfer tax.

14. If the seller pays $150 in transfer tax on the sale of his property, and each unit is taxed at $1.25 per unit, how many taxing units does he have to pay?

   A. 110 units

   B. 115 units

   C. 120 units

   D. 125 units

Answer: C. If his tax bill is $150 and each unit is $1.25, he paid $150 ÷ $1.25 per unit or 120 units.

15. A borrower pays $750 per month on a $100,000 fully amortized 30-year fixed loan at 6 percent interest. After the first payment, what is the remaining balance on the principal amount of his loan?

   A. $99,000

   B. $99,850

   C. $99,750

   D. $98,000

Answer: C. The annual interest is $100,000 × 0.06 = $6,000 or $500 per month. If his payment is $750 and $500 is interest, then $250 is principal: $100,000 − $250 = $99,750.

16. Using the data from question 17, what's the principal after the second payment?

   A. $99,500.00

   B. $99,498.75

   C. $99,650.25

   D. $98,000.99

Answer: B. The loan amount is no longer $100,000 but rather $99,750. Therefore, the interest is now $99,750 × 0.06 = $5,985 annual interest ÷ 12 months = $498.75 per month. $750 − $498.75 = $251.25 to the principal, or $99,750 − $251.25 = $99,498.75 loan amount left on the principal.

17. A broker and a sales agent agree to a split of 75/25, with the larger portion going to the sales agent. The broker allows the sales agent to list a property for 6 percent. The house sells for $134,900. Assuming limited agency occurred, how much does the broker receive as his portion?

    A. $6,030

    B. $8,094

    C. $5,050

    D. $2,023.50

Answer: D. $134,900 × 0.06 = $8,094 total commission. The broker gets 25 percent, or 0.25 × $8,040 = $2,023.50.

18. A seller agrees with a broker to pay 5.5 percent commission plus an advertising fee of 0.5 percent. How much does the seller pay in commission on the sale of his $350,000 home?

    A. $16,030

    B. $18,000

    C. $15,000

    D. $17,000

Answer: B. In essence, the broker charges the seller 5.5 + 0.5 or 6 percent commission. $300,000 × 0.06 = $18,000. This type of agreement only dictates how much the broker must spend on advertising. So although he receives the $18,000 in commission, he pays $1,500 ($300,000 × 0.005) in advertising.

19. A property sells for $150,000 and appraises at $155,000. However, it's assessed at 90 percent of the sale price. The tax rate is 40 mills. What are the monthly taxes?

    A. $5,580

    B. $5,400

    C. $450

    D. $465

Answer: C. The assessed value is 0.90 × $150,000 = $135,000, and the tax rate is 0.040 (40 mills); therefore, 0.04 × $135,000 = $5,400 annual taxes. $5,400 ÷ 12 = $450 per month.

20. If a property's monthly tax bill is $250 on the assessed value of $180,000, what is the tax rate?

    A. 1.6 percent

    B. 20 mills

    C. 2.5 percent

    D. 31 mills

Answer: A. The monthly tax is $250, so the annual taxes are $3,000. $180,000 ÷ $3,000 = 0.016 or 1.6 percent. 16 mills also is an acceptable answer.

21. A commercial seller wants to list his 5.25-acre rectangular property for sale. He commands the broker to list it at $5,000 per front foot along the main highway. The seller tells the broker the property is 295 feet deep. The broker, following his command, lists the property at:

    A. $3,876,100

    B. $3,576,100

    C. $3,276,100

    D. $3,976,100

Answer: A. The 5.25 acres are 228,690 square feet (5.25 acres × 43,560 square feet/acre). The front foot is 228,690 square feet ÷ a depth of 295 feet, or 775.22 feet. Therefore, the list price is $5,000 × 775.22 feet, or $3,876,100.

22. The metes and bounds legal description of a property is this: starting at the POB, east 200 feet, south 300 feet, west 375 feet, and north 325 feet back to the POB. The parcel of land lists for $125,000 per acre. How much is the most probable list price?

    A. $250,000

    B. $249,700

    C. $247,500

    D. $244,600

Answer: C. This can be seen as two parcels added together: a rectangle 200 feet × 300 feet, and a triangle 300 feet × 175 feet (375 feet − 200 feet). The area of the rectangle is 60,000 square feet, and the area of the triangle is 26,250 square feet (½ × 300 feet × 175 feet). Therefore, the parcel is 86,250 square feet. $86,250 square feet ÷ 43,560 square feet/acre=1.98 acres × $125,000/acre, or $247,503.44 or approximately $247,500.

23. A borrower finds a loan with 80 percent loan to value (LTV) ratio for his $250,000 purchase. How much is down payment for the loan?

    A. $25,000

    B. $50,000

    C. $75,000

    D. Not enough information to calculate

Answer: B. If the loan is 80 percent, his down payment is 20 percent, or $250,000 × 0.20 = $50,000.

24. A borrower finds a loan with 80 percent LTV for his $250,000 purchase. How much is the loan amount?

    A. $225,000

    B. $200,000

    C. $275,000

    D. $150,000

Answer: B. 0.80 × $250,000 = $200,000.

25. Using the data from question 24, the borrower has to pay 2½ points to get the loan. How much money does he need to bring to closing, assuming no other fees?

    A. $50,000

    B. $20,000

    C. $7,000

    D. $55,000

Answer: D. A down payment of $50,000. If his LTV is 80%, then he must be bringing 20 percent of the purchase price for the down payment:

    0.025 (2.5 points) × $200,000 = $5,000 in loan fees

    $50,000 (down payment) + $5,000 (Loan fees) = $55,000

26. If a borrower pays 1 point origination fee and 2½ discount points for his 90 percent LTV on the purchase of $175,900, how much does the loan cost the borrower to acquire?

    A. $5,512.50

    B. $5,540.85

    C. $7,030.22

    D. $5,530.35

Answer: B. The fees are 3-½ percent (1 + 2-½) of the loan amount. $175,900 × .90 (90% LTV) = $158,310—the loan amount. $158,310 × 0.035 = $5,540.85.

27. A borrower gets a loan with no equity required and pays $3,050 for the loan on the purchase of a $95,000 house. How many points does he pay in fees?

    A. 4.21 points

    B. 3.18 points

    C. 3.68 points

    D. 4.00 points

Answer: C. The points are the fees divided by the loan amount. $3,050 ÷ $95,000 = 0.0368, or 3.68 percent, or 3.68 points.

28. A borrower qualifies for a 75 percent LTV; however, he only has $42,000 as a down payment. How much loan can he acquire from the lender?

    A. $150,000

    B. $165,000

    C. $168,000

    D. $175,000

Answer: C. His down payment portion has to be at least 25 percent because the biggest loan he can get is 75 percent LTV. If $42,000 is 25 percent of the loan amount, $42,000 ÷ 0.25 = $168,000 loan.

29. How much simple interest is paid on a loan amount of $150,000 at 4 percent interest?

    A. $4,000

    B. $5,000

    C. $6,000

    D. $7,000

Answer: C. $150,000 × 0.04 = $6,000.

30. A Federal Housing Administration-insured loan requires a 3.5 percent down payment. Your client finds a property for sale at $180,000. However, he successfully, with your help, negotiates a lower purchase price of $177,900. How much down payment is required for this deal?

    A. $6,300.00

    B. $6,226.50

    C. $6,000.25

    D. $5,998.75

Answer: B. The down payment is based on the sales price. Therefore, $177,900 × 0.035 = $6,226.50.

31. A sales agent does a study of the neighborhood and finds the average list price is $175,000 but the average sales price is $172,500. He can conclude:

    A. The sales price to list price ratio is 98.6 percent.

    B. The sales price to list price ratio is 97.5 percent.

    C. The sales price to list price ratio is 99.5 percent.

    D. The sales price to list price ratio is 98.1 percent.

Answer: A. The ratio is determined by the sales price and divided the list price. $172,500 ÷ $175,000 = 0.986 = 98.6 percent. This is often a measure of where to begin the listing price.

32. A client wants to sell his property for $150,000. After doing a thorough study of his neighborhood, the agent concludes that houses sell for, on average, 94 percent of the list price. What is a reasonable starting list price?

    A. $154,000

    B. $160,000

    C. $157,000

    D. $150,000

Answer: B. The sales price-to-list price ratio is used to determine a reasonable starting list price. So $150,000 ÷ 0.94 = $159,574 or $160,000.

33. Using a cap rate of 8 percent, what is the value of a building with a net income of $125,000?

    A. $1,362,500

    B. $1,400,750

    C. $1,521,300

    D. $1,562,500

Answer: D. The cap rate is the relationship between the value and the net income. Cap rate = net income ÷ value, or $125,000 ÷ 0.08 = $1,562,500.

34. An appraiser estimates the value of a commercial building to be $750,000 with a net income of $55,000. What cap rate did he use in his valuation process?

    A. 10.6 percent

    B. 9.6 percent

    C. 9.2 percent

    D. 7.3 percent

Answer: D. The cap rate is the ratio of the net income to the value. So $55,000 ÷ $750,000 = 0.073 or 7.3 percent.

35. A 45-unit retail shopping complex with all units rented at $350/month has expenses of 40 percent of the gross income. The appraiser uses a cap rate of 7.5 percent in his valuation process. What value does he estimate the building to be worth?

    A. $1,362,500

    B. $1,400,750

    C. $1,512,000

    D. $1,562,500

Answer: C. The gross rent is 45 × $350 × 12 = $189,000 per year. The expenses are $75,600 ($189,000 × 0.40); $189,000 - $75,600 = $113,400 (net income). Using a cap rate of 0.075, the value is net income ÷ cap rate = $113,400 ÷ 0.075 = $1,512,000.

36. An appraiser highly trained in appraising apartments in his area is assigned to appraise a 10-unit complex. He finds they are rented at $500 per month, and the expenses are $35,000 per year. He uses a gross rent multiplier (GRM) of 25, based on his knowledge and experience. What's the value of the apartment complex?

    A. $1,365,500

    B. $1,500,000

    C. $1,520,000

    D. $1,565,500

Answer: B. The gross rent is $500/month/unit × 10 units × 12 months = $60,000. The expenses play no part in this calculation because the GRM uses the gross rents, not the net. Therefore, $60,000 × 25 = $1,500,000.

37. A building has an economic life of 39 years. The value of the building is estimated to be $650,000. What is the annual depreciation amount?

    A. $15,000 per year

    B. $15,670 per year

    C. $16,150 per year

    D. $16,667 per year

Answer: D. Straight-line depreciation is determined by dividing the value of the building by its economic life: $650,000 ÷ 39 years = $16,667 per year.

38. A prepaid bill of $600 is prorated at closing. The closing date is November 15. How much is credited, or debited, to the seller, or buyer?

    A. Credit to seller; debit from buyer $525

    B. Credit to seller; debit from buyer $75

    C. Debit from seller; credit to buyer $525

    D. Debit from seller; credit to buyer $525

Answer: B. The closing date is 10½ months of a 12-month year, or 0.875. Because it's prepaid, the seller paid the amount and is due a credit from the buyer at closing. The seller uses $0.875 \times \$600 = \$525$ of the bill. Therefore, the buyer credits the difference back to the seller at closing, or $600 − $525 = $75. Another way to think of it is that because the seller used 0.875 of the bill, the buyer owes for the remaining 0.125 of the bill. So $600 × 0.125 = $75.

39. An accrued bill of $550 is settled at the closing on September 30. How much is credited, or debited, to the seller, or buyer?

    A. Credit to seller; debit from buyer $91.66

    B. Credit to seller; debit from buyer $458.33

    C. Debit from seller; credit to buyer $458.33

    D. Debit from seller; credit to buyer $91.66

Answer: C. The buyer pays the entire bill of $550 on December 31. However, the seller owes for the portion he has used but not paid for yet. Therefore, it's a credit to the buyer from the seller in the amount of $458.33 (10 months of the 12 month = 0.8333) × $550.

40. A tenant signs a commercial lease for $1,150 per month plus an additional 4 percent of sales over a minimum of $100,000. If the company has annual sales of $230,000, what is the monthly rent paid by the tenant.

    A. $1,150.00

    B. $1,250.33

    C. $1,916.66

    D. $1,583.33

Answer: D. The overage is 0.04 of the $130,000 ($230,000 − $100,000) or $0.04 \times \$130,000 = \$5,200$, or $433.33 per month in addition to the base rent of $1,150 = $1,583.33 per month.

41. A tenant signs a lease for $1,150 per month or 4 percent of sales, whichever is greater. If the company has annual sales of $230,000, what's the monthly rent paid by the tenant.

    A. $1,150.00

    B. $766.66

    C. $1,916.66

    D. $1,583.33

Answer: A. The annual sales is $230,000 at 4 percent, or $230,000 × 0.04 = $9,200 annual rent, or $766.67 per month. Because this is lower than the base, the tenant pays just the base.

42. A sales agent is paid a 4 percent commission on the total lease he brings to the landlord. If the tenant is leasing an industrial space that's 125 feet × 75 feet for 5 years at a rental rate of $3.50 per square foot, what's the agent's commission?

    A. $5,562.50

    B. $6,280.50

    C. $6,955.50

    D. $6,562.50

Answer: D. The value of the lease is 9,375 square feet (125 feet × 75 feet) × $3.50 per square foot × 5 years = $164,062.50. The agent earns 4 percent of that value, or 0.04 × $164,062.50 = $6,562.50.

43. A tenant is paying $1,250 per month rent for his commercial office space of 1,250 square feet. What's the rental rate of his lease?

    A. $9/square foot

    B. $10/square foot

    C. $11/square foot

    D. $12/square foot

Answer: D. The annual rent is $1,250 × 12 = $15,000. The rental rate is the annual rent divided by the area, or $15,000 ÷ 1,250 square feet, or $12.

44. A developer must maintain a minimum of ½-acre lots in his new development that's 53 acres. He also must dedicate at least 20 percent of the development to greenspace, such as parks, gardens, walking trails, etc. What's the maximum number of lots he can develop for building houses?

    A. 106

    B. 83

    C. 84

    D. 85

Answer: C. If the development is 53 acres but only 80 percent (100 percent − 20 percent for greenspace) can be developed for houses, that's only 42.4 acres. If the lots must be a minimum of ½ acre each, he can build 84 houses in the development.

45. At the closing, a buyer is debited $150 for a pre-paid bill. The closing is on March 31. How much is the bill the seller pays?

    A. $37.50

    B. $50.00

    C. $150.00

    D. $200.00

Answer: D. Because it's a prepaid bill, the seller pays it in full. However, he uses only ¼ (3 of the 12 months) of the bill. He should be credited the unused amount, or 75 percent of the bill. If the buyer credits him $150, the total bill is $150 ÷ 0.75 = $200.

46. The owner of an investment property buys a property for $137,500 and later sells it for $187,000. What's his return on his investment?

    A. 36.0 percent

    B. 33.3 percent

    C. 26.5 percent

    D. 23.8 percent

Answer: A. The profit is $49,500 ($187,000 – $137,500). That's a 36 percent increase of his investment. $49,500 ÷ $137,500 = 0.36 or 36 percent.

47. A buyer qualifies for an 80 percent LTV loan. He makes an offer of $189,000 on a house listed at $199,000 with an earnest money check of $1,500. The seller accepts his offer. How much money will the buyer bring to the closing, assuming no other fees?

    A. $36,800

    B. $37,800

    C. $36,300

    D. $37,300

Answer: C. The down payment is 20 percent of the sales price, $189,000, or $37,800. However, he's already placed $1,500 in earnest, so he will bring the difference, or $36,300.

48. If a property purchased 3 years ago for $130,000 has appreciated 15 percent, what's the value now?

    A. $19,500

    B. $137,500

    C. $149,500

    D. $154,500

Answer: C. The value 3 years ago was $130,000. Over the 3 years, its value has increase 15 percent, or 0.15 × $130,000 = $19,500. Therefore, the value now is $130,000 + $19,500 = $149,500.

49. Broker A offers 50 percent of the 7 percent commission on the sale of a $600,000 home to broker B for bringing in the buyer. The selling broker B's sales agent gets 70 percent of the commission. What's the selling sales agent's total commission?

    A. $14,700

    B. $21,000

    C. $6,300

    D. $11,750

Answer: A. The total commission is 0.07 (7 percent) × $600,000 = $42,000. The selling broker is paid 50 percent, or $21,000, of the total commission. The selling broker's sales agent is paid 0.70 (70 percent) × $21,000, or $14,700.

50. A property's tax rate is 45 mills, and the owner pays $325 in real estate taxes per month. What's the assessed value of his home?

    A. $83,333.33

    B. $85,666.67

    C. $86,000.00

    D. $86,666.67

Answer: D. His annual taxes are $325 × 12 = $3,900 per year. If his rate is 0.045 (45 mills), his assessed value is his annual taxes divided by the rate, or $3,900 ÷ 0.045 = $86,666.67.

Glossary

acknowledgment   An acknowledgment is a verification that the people signing the document are, in fact, who they say they are. An acknowledgment by a notary public is not a legal validation of the document and does not suppose any legal information at all.

adjustable rate loan   A loan that has a varying interest rate and payment based on an adjustment period. The adjustment depends on the variation in a benchmark index, usually the LIBOR or prime rate. Also called a variable rate mortgage.

administrator   *See* executor.

affidavit of one and the same   A legal contract that declares that a person is the same person using a different name, such as after a marriage, divorce, or legal name change.

air rights   The legal ability to use or control the space above a property. Air rights can be sold, rented, or leased to another party.

amortization   The reduction of debt by regular payments of interest and principal sufficient to pay off a loan by maturity.

annual percentage rate (APR)   The interest rate of the loan if you included the cost of the loan as part of the calculation.

appraisal   A valuation of real property.

appraiser   A person trained in the techniques used to determine the appraisal.

approval code   An approval code is issued to a real estate school when it gets approved by the state to teach real estate prelicensing or continuing education. In some states, this code may be called a school's license number or registration number.

assessed value   The value determined by the government that is the basis upon which taxes are calculated.

big-box brokerage   A national franchise company that brokers real estate throughout the United States and abroad.

bill of sale   A document that details, in writing, a sale of goods, usually personal property, transferred from one party to another.

block   *See* pool.

boutique brokerage   A small brokerage consisting of only a few agents.

capital gain   The seller's gain on an asset used in a trade or business or for investment, including real estate.

Certificate of Eligibility   Certifies that a veteran qualifies for a VA loan by meeting one of the requirements set forth by the VA.

certificate of occupancy   Evidence that the building or residence complies substantially with the plans and specifications that have been submitted to, and approved by, the local authority.

chain of title   A successive conveyance of title to a specific parcel of land.

cloud on the title   Any mistakes, misspellings, or irregularities in the chain of title that would give a reasonable person pause before accepting title.

Code of Ethics   A standard of conduct required by license laws and by the National Association of REALTORS.

commingling   The act of a broker placing a client's earnest money into a personal or business account, other than the earnest money account.

comparative market analysis (CMA) or comps   Data used in assessing or establishing the fair market value of a property.

comprehensive plan   A general guide to the location, character, and extent of proposed or anticipated land use, including public facilities.

conciliation   The process of adjusting or settling disputes in a friendly manner through extrajudicial means, by bringing together two opposing sides to reach a compromise in an attempt to avoid taking a case to court.

condemnation   The process used to exercise eminent domain, or the right of the government to seize private property.

consanguinity   The degree of relationship between people of the same kinship, blood, or common ancestry.

constructive annexation   An action whereby a landlord's property value is increased by labor, material, or items added to the property by a tenant.

constructive eviction   An eviction that results from some action or inaction by the landlord that renders the premises unsuitable for the use agreed to in a lease or other rental contract.

contract   A legally binding agreement between two parties. To have a valid contract of sale in real estate there must be an offer, an acceptance, competent parties, consideration, legal purpose, written documentation, description of the property, and signatures of the principals.

conversion   The act of a broker spending the client's earnest money for a bill, expense, or payment.

cooperating broker   An arrangement between two brokerage firms to share a commission; used when one broker is the seller's agent and the other broker represents the buyer.

covenant against encumbrances   A promise in a deed that the title does not cause encumbrances except those set forth in the deed.

covenant for further assurances   A promise in a deed that the grantor will execute further assurances that may be reasonable or necessary to perfect the title for the grantee.

covenant of quiet enjoyment   A promise in a deed or lease that the grantee or lessee won't be disturbed in the use of the property because of a defect in the grantor's or lessor's title or lease.

covenant of seisin   A promise in a deed ensuring the grantee that the grantor has the title being conveyed.

covenant of warranty   A promise in a deed that the grantor will defend the title against lawful claimants.

creative financing   A term real estate investors use that implies some financing technique other than a standard mortgage from a traditional lending institution.

days on market   The total number of days a property has been listed on the MLS.

deed   A written instrument transferring an interest in real property when delivered by the grantor and accepted by the grantee.

deed in lieu of foreclosure   The conveyance of title to the mortgagee by a mortgagor in default to avoid a record of foreclosure.

desk fee   A fixed fee the agent pays to the broker to cover a broker's fixed costs in exchange for a desk to work at within the office.

depreciation   The expensing of the original cost of an asset, plus any qualified improvements, over its scheduled life as defined by the Internal Revenue Service.

distraint   The seizure of someone's property to obtain payment of rent or other money owed.

doctrine of laches   A failure to bring a legal claim in the proper, or a reasonable, time.

dominant tenement   The party, or tenement, that is taking the use of the property.

double-net lease   Requires a flat fee plus two of the landlord's expenses, typically taxes and insurance.

dower   The part of or interest in the real estate of a deceased husband given by law to his widow during her life.

dual agent or limited agent   A broker or salesperson who represents both the buyer and seller in the same transaction.

economic life   The period of time during which property is financially beneficial to an owner.

effective age   The useful life of an item as determined by IRS statute.

eminent domain   The right of the government to take private land for the betterment of the public.

enabling acts   Laws passed by state legislatures authorizing cities and counties to regulate land use within their jurisdictions

encapsulation   The process that makes lead-based paint inaccessible by providing a barrier between the lead-based paint and the environment. Also used with asbestos.

equalization factor   The number, or factor, by which the assessed value of a property is multiplied to arrive at a value for the property that's in line with statewide tax assessments.

equitable title   An interest gained by a vendee based on the amount of equity he has paid toward the sales price of the property.

equity   The difference between what something is worth and any loan secured by the asset.

estate at sufferance   The continuation to occupy property after legal authorization has expired.

estate at will   A leasehold condition that may be terminated at any point by either party.

estate for life   The interest of real property that ends with the death of a person.

estate for years   A leasehold condition of definite duration.

estate in real property   An interest sufficient to provide the right to use, possession, and control of land. It also establishes the degree and duration of ownership.

exclusive-agency agreement (exclusive listing)   An agreement between a broker and a seller designating the broker as the seller's sole agent for the purpose of selling his or her property. This agreement does not preclude the owner from effectuating a sale on his own.

exclusive-buyer-agency agreement (exclusive listing)   An agreement between a broker and a seller designating the broker as the seller's sole agent for the purpose of selling his or her property.

exclusive-right-to-sell agreement   An agreement between a broker and a seller designating the broker as the seller's sole representative for the purpose of selling property. In contrast to an exclusive-agency agreement, under an exclusive-right-to-sell agreement, a commission is due to the broker even if the property is sold directly by the owner.

executor   The person who will oversee the probate of a will.

Fannie Mae   The nickname for the Federal National Mortgage Association (FNMA), a privately-owned corporation that purchases loans from the Federal Housing Administration (FHA) and Veteran Affairs (VA) as well as conventional mortgages.

Federal Housing Administration (FHA)   A federal agency that is part of the U.S. Department of Housing and Urban Development (HUD) that sets policy for mortgage underwriting and provides insurance for residential mortgages.

federally related loan   Any loan backed by the full faith of the government, such as FHA, VA or USDA.

findings of fact The term applied to the conclusion reached by a panel, arbitrators, or court. It's the determination of truth after consideration.

foreclosure An enforcement process in which the lender under a defaulted mortgage takes title to the property for the purposes of selling it to recoup moneys owed under the mortgage.

formed When one party makes an offer and another party accepts the offer, the contract is formed.

free and clear property One with no money encumbrances or liens placed on it.

freehold estate An estate in land for an indeterminable amount of time.

friable Any material that, when dry, can be crumbled, pulverized, or reduced to powder by hand pressure.

general warranty deed A deed denoting an unlimited guarantee of title.

Ginnie Mae The nickname for Government National Mortgage Association (GNMA), a U.S. government agency that purchases FHA and VA mortgages.

graduated lease A lease in which the rent changes from period to period over the lease term. This type of lease is usually used by a new business tenant whose income will increase over time.

gross lease A lease in which the lessor pays all costs of operating and maintaining the property, including the property taxes.

ground lease A long-term lease of unimproved land, usually for construction purposes.

hang To place a license with a broker.

highest and best use The most reasonable, probable, and legal use of a piece of improved or unimproved real property possible.

holdover tenant A tenant who once occupied a property legally under a lease but is now there illegally without permission from the landlord.

involuntary alienation The transfer of title to real property as a result of a lien foreclosure sale, adverse possession, filing a petition in bankruptcy, condemnation under power of eminent domain, or, upon the death of the titleholder, to the state if no heirs exist.

improvement Any permanent structure on real property, or any work on the property (such as planting trees) that can increase its value.

in arrears A bill paid after the usage of the item. Also called accrued.

independent brokerage A broker not affiliated with any brokerage and who works solely for themselves.

independent contractor agreement A legal contract entered into by the new licensee and her broker. This contract spells out many terms and conditions they both agree upon.

index lease One in which the base rent, or an increase in rent, is tied to a financial index or financial market in some manner, such as the consumer price index.

interest The amount of money you pay to borrow someone else's money.

intestate The condition of dying with no will in place.

joint venture A contractual arrangement between two parties that aims to undertake a specific task.

judicial foreclosure Requires a foreclosure to be processed through the state's courts.

land contract A form of ownership conveyance between a vendor, seller and vendee, buyer. With a land contract, land ownership is transferred based on the portion of equity earned through each payment from the vendee to the vendor, giving the vendee an interest in the property based on the equity earned, hence equitable title.

latent defect   An unforeseen or hidden defect in the property. Typically, latent defects cannot be determined by someone other than a professional specifically seeking that defect

leasehold estate   An estate land for a determinable amount of time.

lessee   A person, called a tenant, who leases the property from a lessor, called a landlord.

lessor   A person, called a landlord, who leases property to the lessee, called a tenant.

leverage   The use of other people's money.

like kind property   Property held for the same purpose—that is, investment in the case of real estate.

listing   The term used by brokers to market a property for sale or rent.

listing broker   The broker who represents the interests of the seller or landlord in the sale or rental of his or her property.

loan origination fee   The financing charge required by a lender.

loan-to-value ratio (LTV)   The mortgage amount divided by the lower of the purchase price or the appraised value of the property. This ratio is expressed as a percentage. A lender will use this ratio in determining the maximum mortgage loan it will make on the property.

mobile closing   A closing that takes place outside regularly accepted locations or timeframes by allowing a closing agent to travel and meet with the buyer and seller in a remote location.

mortgage   A pledge of real estate collateral to secure a debt. Also a legal document describing and defining the pledge.

mortgage-backed security   A loan that is secured by collateral, most often real property.

mortgage banker   An institution that performs services similar to those of a mortgage broker. However, a mortgage banker is also legally permitted to lend its own funds.

mortgage broker   A real estate professional who represents an array of banks seeking to issue mortgages. The mortgage broker meets with a customer, assists with the application, and facilitates the mortgage process on behalf of the borrower.

mortgage insurance   Insurance that protects the lender in case the home buyer does not make their mortgage payments.

mortgage note   A document signed at closing that states the borrower's promise to repay a sum of money along with an interest rate and a fixed period of time (term) for repayment.

mortgage satisfaction   The full payment of a mortgage loan.

mortgagee   The lender in a mortgage transaction.

mortgagor   The borrower in a mortgage transaction.

multiple listing service (MLS)   A central service for real estate listings available to member brokers.

National Association of REALTORS (NAR)   The largest and most prominent trade organization for real estate brokers and agents.

negligent misrepresentation   Generally occurs when someone, such as a real estate professional, makes a statement they "should have known" was not true.

net listing   A listing whereby the seller receives a net amount and the agent receives the balance of the sale price.

non-judicial foreclosure   Does not require the lender to go to court to force a foreclose on a home.

open buyer agency   An agency that allows for the seller to enter as many listing agreements as he deems fit. The agent bringing the buyer will also receive the listing portion of the commission paid.

open listing   A property for sale for which the owner has not signed an exclusive agreement with a real estate broker. Many brokers may represent the seller, or the seller can promote the property independently.

option   The right to buy property at a later date for a price agreed upon in the present time that's sealed by some option consideration.

partition   A court action that can be brought to divide the property into individual shares among the owners, allowing each owner to move forward with his or her share independently.

pass-through certificate   A type of investment issued by the Government National Mortgage Association (GNMA) that earns income from the interest and principal payments made on mortgages by mortgage holders and passed through to the investor.

percentage lease   A lease that has a rental amount that's a combination of a fixed amount plus a percentage of the lessee's gross sales.

point   1 percent of the loan amount taken by the borrower.

pool   When a maker of mortgages combines individual mortgages of similar interest rates and terms to form a bigger group to attract an investor.

premium   A monthly cost that a client pays to an insurance company to accept the risk of a given outcome for a given activity.

prepaid   An expense that's paid prior to the use of the item.

primary board   The board where you will do the majority, if not all, of your work.

priority of liens   A theory that states that liens gain priority, or preference, based upon the order they are recorded; therefore, the first lien recorded gets primary position, hence the name primary lien.

private mortgage insurance (PMI)   *See* mortgage insurance.

probate   The legal process whereby a will is proved factual, or validated, in a court and accepted as a valid public document that is the true last testament of the deceased.

procuring cause   A broker who, by their actions, brought about the sale of a property. For the listing agent, this might be simply getting the seller to sign the listing agreement. For the buyer's agent, it might be the agent who showed the property to a buyer who ultimately entered into a purchase agreement with the seller.

real estate broker   An individual employed on a fee or commission basis as an agent to bring buyers and sellers together and assist in negotiating real estate contracts between them.

real estate commission   A governing body of individuals appointed or elected in some states to administer, enforce, and uphold license law within their state.

real estate professional   Any person who practices real estate brokerage and is licensed under the laws of the state in which they practice. A *REALTOR* is a member of the National Association of REALTORS (NAR).

real estate team   A group of licensed REALTORS working together to increase their efficiency or flow as a whole.

real property   Includes real estate, and it adds a bundle of rights. This bundle of rights consists of the rights for property owners to use their property as they see fit.

reconciliation   The process by which the appraiser evaluates, chooses, and selects from among alternative results to reach a final value estimate.

redlining   The resistance of lending institutions to make loans for the purchase, construction, or repair of a dwelling due to the socioeconomic conditions of the property's location.

release from obligation   Used when one party, such as a landlord, releases another party, such as a tenant, from contractual liability.

rescind   To withdraw, or take back, an offer presented by the offeror to the offeree.

right of survivorship   The right of an owner to receive the title to a co-owner's share upon death of the co-owner, as in the case of joint tenancy and tenancy by the entirety.

sales comparison approach   An appraisal tool for estimating the value of a property with other similar properties that have sold recently.

servient tenement   The party, or tenement, that is giving up the use of the property.

single-net lease   A lease that requires a flat fee payment plus one of the landlord's expenses.

specific performance   Where one party or the other fails to complete a contract without cause.

statute of frauds   A law that requires that certain contracts be in writing, and that those contracts be signed by the parties who are to be bound by the contract.

subordination clause   Allows two documents to switch priorities, regardless of the dates they entered the public records.

successors in interest   The right of a party to acquire a usage or control of real property directly from a successive property owner through a voluntary sale or inheritance.

surrender of the lease   When a tenant agrees to give up his legal rights and returns possession of the property with the landlord's consent.

taking   Occurs when the government deprives a person of property or directly interferes with or substantially disturbs a person's use and enjoyment of his or her property.

tax rate   The amount at which real property is taxed and is established by most state taxing authorities. A mill is $\frac{1}{1,000}$ of $1, or $0.001. Tax rates are typically set by statute in each state.

tenants by the entirety   Refers to co-ownership limited to husband and wife, with the right to survivorship.

testate   When a person dies and leaves a last will and testament.

testator   The maker of a last will and testament.

title   The evidence or documentation that an owner is in lawful possession of the property, such as a property deed.

unity of interest   When co-owners all have the same percentage of ownership in a property.

unity of possession   When all co-owners have the right to possess any and all portions of the property owned, without physical division.

unity of time   When co-owners receive title at the same time in the same conveyance.

unity of title   When co-owners have the same type of ownership in a property.

VA guaranteed loan   A mortgage loan in which the loan payment is guaranteed to the lender by the U.S. Department of Veteran Affairs.

valid contract   One in which all elements are intact and enforceable in a court of law

value   The purchase price or the appraised amount, whichever is the lower of the two.

variance   A deviation from specific requirements of a zoning ordinance due to special conditions of the property.

vendee   The party who receives equitable title and gains possession of the property during a land contract.

vendor   The party who is passing equitable title and retains actual, or legal, title during a land contract.

void contract   A contract of no legal force because one or more elements are missing from the contract.

voidable contract   Appears to be valid on the surface, but after inspection, one element is defective.

zoning   The laws regulating land use.

zoning ordinance   A statement setting forth the type of use permitted under each zoning classification and specific requirements for compliance.

zoning overlay   An additional requirement designed to enhance, or curtail, above and beyond the current zoning classification.

National Sample Test and Answers

1. The idea that no two parcels of land are identical is called:

    A. Immobility

    B. Subdivision

    C. Uniqueness

    D. Location

2. When the supply of something decreases while demand remains the same, the price will tend to:

    A. Remain the same

    B. Increase

    C. Decrease by an undetermined value

    D. Decrease by a value equal to the price

3. The physical dirt and earth rights, mineral rights, and air rights in the land are included in the definition of:

    A. Attachments

    B. Real property

    C. Subsurface rights

    D. Improvements

4. Owners with littoral rights enjoy:

    A. Unrestricted use of available waters, but only to the high-water mark

    B. The right of disposition

    C. Unrestricted use of the surface of the earth

    D. Unrestricted rights to the use of fixtures

5. Growing trees, manmade fences, and buildings are all considered:

    A. Chattels

    B. Land

    C. Fixtures

    D. Real estate

6. A new owner received the right to use a parking space in the multiunit building where she purchased a condominium. This right is an example of:

    A. An improvement

    B. A fixture

    C. An appurtenance

    D. A chattel

7. Methods of annexation, adaptation, and agreement are the legal tests for determining whether an item is:

    A. A chattel or an emblement

    B. A fixture

    C. Land or real estate

    D. Fructus naturales or fructus industriales

8. An important characteristic of personal property is:

    A. Small enough to be carried by a person

    B. Movable

    C. Alive

    D. Less than 100 years old

9. A woman planted a rose bush on her property and plans to dig it up and take it with her when her house is sold. The sales contract explicitly excludes the rose bush from the sale. This provision is necessary because it would be normally considered:

    A. A trade fixture

    B. Personal property

    C. An emblement

    D. Real estate

10. If the dominant estate and the servient estate are joined into one parcel, which of these is true?

    A. The easement still exists for the entire parcel.

    B. The easement is suspended but cannot be terminated.

    C. The easement is terminated.

    D. The new owner must bring a suit seeking severance of the easement from the combined properties.

11. When a group of more than one individual decides to buy a property, it is considered:

    A. Cooperation

    B. Co-ownership

    C. Community effort

    D. Joint venture

12. If brothers bought an investment property together, and the deed listed only each of their names, what form of ownership are they presumed to have taken?

    A. Tenancy by the entireties

    B. Joint tenancy with right of survivorship

    C. Tenancy in common

    D. In severalty

13. What form of ownership requires one person transferring ownership to someone else to manage for a third-party person?

    A. Joint venture

    B. Joint tenancy

    C. Trust

    D. Severalty

14. A man owns a cottage in fee simple. He also owns an undivided percentage interest in all the common area located in the development. The man's ownership is probably best described as a:

    A. Time-share estate

    B. Time-share use

    C. Condominium

    D. Cooperative

15. Which is not a unity of joint tenancy?

    A. Unity of title

    B. Unity of ownership

    C. Unity of time

    D. Unity of possession

16. These are characteristics of a tenancy by the entirety except:

    A. The title may be conveyed only by a deed signed by both parties.

    B. The surviving spouse automatically becomes sole owner of the property upon the death of the other spouse.

    C. Each spouse owns an equal, undivided interest in the property as a single, indivisible unit.

    D. The surviving spouse automatically owns half of the property acquired during the marriage.

17. These systems are used to describe a legal description except:

    A. Lot and block

    B. Metes and bounds

    C. Rectangular survey

    D. Monuments

18. A man sells 4 acres of prime undeveloped property to a woman for $3.40 per square foot. How much did the woman pay?

    A. $466,560

    B. $592,416

    C. $612,360

    D. $733,860

19. A man is willing to pay $1,500 per acre. He is planning to buy the SE ¼ of the SE ¼ of the SE ¼ of Section 11. How much will he pay for the land?

    A. $3,000

    B. $15,000

    C. $6,000

    D. $24,000

20. A sale is closing on August 31. Real estate taxes, calculated on a calendar year basis, have not been paid for the current year. The tax is estimated to be $2,400. What amount of proration will be credited to the buyer?

    A. $1,100

    B. $1,600

    C. $1,485

    D. $1,500

21. A seller would be responsible for providing all these items except:

    A. Documents necessary to clear any clouds on the title

    B. Affidavits of title

    C. The deed

    D. Preparation of mortgage and note

22. A seller owns a fully occupied apartment building. If he sells the apartment building to a buyer, how will the tenants' security deposits be reflected on the closing statement?

    A. Credit seller, debit buyer

    B. Debit both seller and buyer

    C. Credit buyer, debit seller

    D. None of these

23. A buyer is purchasing a house from a seller. The single-family home is subject to an existing 30-year mortgage of $286,500 at a fixed rate of 6 percent. Under the terms of the sales contract, the buyer assumes the seller's mortgage at 6 percent interest and pays the federally insured lender's assumption fee of $100. In addition, the seller assists the buyer by taking back a purchase money mortgage in the amount of $25,000 at 8 percent interest. Is this transaction subject to RESPA?

    A. No, because this transaction involves a purchase money mortgage taken back by the seller.

    B. No, because the terms of the assumed loan were not changed.

    C. Yes, because the seller is taking back a purchase money mortgage at an interest rate higher than that charged for the assumed loan.

    D. Yes, because the lender's fee on the assumed loan is more than $50.

24. All these items are usually prorated at closing except:

    A. Prepaid general real estate taxes

    B. Interest on an assumed loan

    C. Appraisal fees

    D. Rents collected in advance

25. How is earnest money treated if the buyer does not default and shows up for closing?

    A. Credit seller

    B. Debit buyer

    C. Credit buyer

    D. Debit seller

26. A tenant makes a single payment each month to the landlord. The landlord then pays the taxes, insurance on the building, and maintenance. What type of lease is this?

    A. Net lease

    B. Gross lease

    C. Percentage lease

    D. Graduated lease

27. Some tenants want to buy the house they are renting but do not have enough money for the down payment. The landlord agrees to put part of the tenants' rent toward the purchase price. The landlord and tenants have agreed to:

    A. A lease purchase

    B. A sale leaseback

    C. A ground lease

    D. An option

28. A tenant lives in an apartment building owned by a landlord. Vandals break into the building and destroy the central air-conditioning system, making the tenant's apartment uncomfortably warm. The next day, the tenant sues the landlord for constructive eviction. In this situation, will the tenant win?

    A. Yes, if the tenant's lease promises that the apartment will be air conditioned.

    B. Yes, to claim constructive eviction, it is not necessary that the condition be the result of the landlord's personal actions.

    C. No, to claim constructive eviction, the tenant must prove that the premises are uninhabitable.

    D. No, the premises are not unusable, the condition was not due to the landlord's conscious neglect, and the tenant has not abandoned the apartment.

29. A lease that provides for rent increases at set future dates is called:

    A. An adjustable lease

    B. A graduated lease

    C. A percentage lease

    D. An interval lease

30. How many acres are contained in a parcel described as follows: the NE ¼ of the NW ¼ and the N ½ of the NW ¼, NE ¼, of Section 10?

    A. 40 acres

    B. 60 acres

    C. 70 acres

    D. 74 acres

31. The intersection of ranges and tiers in the rectangular survey system are called:

    A. Base lines

    B. Principal meridians

    C. Ranges

    D. Township squares

32. The end of a metes-and-bounds land description must always end at:

    A. A monument

    B. A benchmark

    C. The point of beginning

    D. A baseline

33. The grantor is conveying an interest that's less than fee simple absolute. This explanation of the extent of ownership will be found in the:

    A. Covenant of seisin clause

    B. Granting clause

    C. Habendum clause

    D. Exceptions and reservations

34. The document used to transfer any interest in a real property is called:

    A. Title

    B. Deed

    C. Attachment

    D. Mortgage

35. All these are necessary to a valid deed except:

    A. Consideration

    B. Words of conveyance

    C. The grantee's signature

    D. Delivery

36. The type of deed that imposes the least liability on the grantor is a:

    A. Special warranty deed

    B. Bargain and sale deed

    C. Quitclaim deed

    D. General warranty deed

37. Title is not considered transferred until the deed is:

    A. Signed by the grantor

    B. Accepted by the grantee

    C. Recorded in public records

    D. Released from escrow

38. All these are acceptable evidence of an owner's title except:

    A. A recorded deed

    B. An abstract of title and attorney's opinion

    C. A title insurance policy

    D. A certificate of title

39. To serve as public notice, a deed is recorded in the:

    A. City where the owner lives

    B. County where the property is located

    C. State capital

    D. Largest city in the state

40. Which of these laws extended housing discrimination protections to families with children and persons with disabilities?

    A. Civil Rights Act of 1866

    B. Fair Housing Amendments Act of 1988

    C. Housing and Community Development Act of 1974

    D. Civil Rights Act of 1968

41. The Fair Housing Act is administered by the:

    A. Office of Equal Opportunity

    B. Department of Housing and Urban Development

    C. Department of Justice

    D. Federal court system

42. One major provision of the Fair Housing Amendments Act of 1988 is:

    A. A repeal of the facilities and services requirements designed by HOPA

    B. The addition of sexual orientation to the list of protected classes

    C. A change that made the penalties for violations more severe and also included additional damages

    D. The addition of religion to the list of protected classes

43. These people are considered members of protected classes except:

    A. A member of Alcoholics Anonymous

    B. A person convicted of the manufacture of illegal drugs

    C. A person diagnosed with HIV

    D. A visually disabled person with a seeing eye dog

44. A seller states "Don't show my house to anybody not born in this country." In this circumstance, the real estate professional:

    A. Ignores the client and shows the house to anyone

    B. Must decline to take the listing with this restriction

    C. May take the listing and ignore the instruction

    D. May take the listing and hope no noncitizens ask to see the property

45. When an Indian couple came to a broker to look for a home to buy, he suggested they look at listings only in the neighborhood with a large Indian population. The broker violated the Fair Housing Act because his actions constitute:

    A. Stereotyping

    B. Blockbusting

    C. Redlining

    D. Steering

46. An elderly man left the family home to his second wife with the provision that when she dies, the home goes to his son by his first wife. The second wife owns a bundle of rights but does not own the right to:

    A. Sell, give, or will the property

    B. Mortgage the property

    C. Lease the property

    D. Decorate the property

47. A woman was given permission to park her car in the nearby parking garage. She then receives a notice that the garage will be replaced by a newer garage, but the owner won't offer her a spot to park. Can the owner do this?

    A. No, because she has been parking there; she has an easement by prescription.

    B. No, because she paid regularly and on time.

    C. Yes, because she only had a license.

    D. Yes, because she has nothing in writing.

48. A man conveyed a 1-acre parcel of land to a local school. In the deed, the man stated that the property was to be used only as a school and nothing else, and the man reserved a right of possible reentry. What kind of estate has the man granted?

    A. Leasehold

    B. Fee simple subject to a condition subsequent

    C. Fee simple absolute

    D. Curtesy

49. A man files a notice in the public record of "future lawsuit pending." This notice reflects which of these?

    A. Fee simple determinable

    B. Police power

    C. An encroachment

    D. A lis pendens

50. A key element of an agent's fiduciary responsibility of loyalty is to:

    A. Report the status of all funds received from or on behalf of the principal

    B. Avoid conflicts of interest

    C. Obey the principal's instructions in accordance with the contract

    D. Place the client's needs over his or her own

51. When a broker places trust funds of others into the company's operating account and then withdraws funds for the firm's use, what illegal practice has taken place?

    A. Escrowing

    B. DBA accounting

    C. Conversion

    D. Asset-liability management

52. In a buyer representation agreement, the broker acts as the agent of the buyer and must protect the buyer's interests:

    A. At all points in the transaction

    B. Only during property showings

    C. Until the representation agreement is signed

    D. Only when negotiating on behalf of the buyer

53. An owner listed her home for sale with a broker. When the owner sold the home, she did not owe anyone a commission. Based on these facts, what type of listing did the broker and the owner most likely sign?

    A. Exclusive-right-to-sell listing

    B. Net listing

    C. Multiple listing

    D. Exclusive-agency listing

54. All this information is generally included in a listing agreement except:

   A. Lot size

   B. Termination clause

   C. Client's requirements for a suitable property to buy

   D. Property condition disclosures

55. When may a broker's agreement to represent a buyer be terminated?

   A. The buyer dislikes the properties shown by the broker

   B. Only agreements between brokers and sellers can be terminated

   C. Under a mutual agreement to terminate the agency

   D. None of these

56. A listing agreement is:

   A. A contract between the buyer and the seller

   B. A contract to purchase real property

   C. An employment agreement between the broker and the sales associate

   D. An employment contract between the seller and the broker

57. After making an offer but prior to receiving any response from the seller, a buyer changed their mind about buying the property. In written form, their agent sends a form stating, "Withdraw my offer." This action is called a:

   A. Counteroffer

   B. Rejection

   C. Breach of contract

   D. Revocation

58. A real estate broker announces to the salespeople in her office that she will pay a $1,000 bonus to the top-selling salesperson each quarter. This contract is an:

   A. Implied bilateral contract

   B. Express unilateral contract

   C. Implied unilateral contract

   D. Express bilateral contract

59. A buyer makes an offer on a house, and the seller accepts in writing. What is the status of this relationship?

   A. The buyer and seller do not have a valid contract until the seller delivers title at closing.

   B. The buyer and seller have an express, bilateral executed contract.

   C. The buyer and seller have an express, bilateral executory contract.

   D. The buyer and seller have an implied, unilateral executory contract.

60. A woman offers to buy a man's house for the full $215,000 asking price. The offer contains this clause, "Possession of the premises on August 1." The man is delighted to accept the woman's offer and signs the contract. First, however, the man crosses out "August 1" and replaces it with "August 3" because he won't be back from vacation on the first of the month. He then begins scheduling movers. What is the status of this agreement?

    A. Because the man changed the date of possession rather than the amount, the man and woman have a valid contract.

    B. The man has accepted the woman's offer. Because the reason for the change was out of the man's control, the change is of no legal effect once he signed the contract.

    C. The man has rejected the woman's offer and made a counteroffer, which the woman is free to accept or reject.

    D. The man technically rejected the woman's offer, but his behavior in scheduling movers creates an implied contract between the parties.

61. All these are essential to a valid real estate sales contract except:

    A. Offer and acceptance

    B. Consideration

    C. An earnest money deposit, held in an escrow account

    D. Legally competent parties

62. The millage breakout for ad valorem taxes are library: 0.5; school: 1; school debt service: 0.5; community college: 1; vocational school: 0.5; and all others: 5. If the property is assessed at $165,000, how much is the tax bill?

    A. $1,200.25

    B. $1,402.50

    C. $1,405.75

    D. $1,800.50

63. Which of these characteristics apply to a real estate tax lien?

    A. Specific, involuntary lien

    B. Specific, voluntary lien

    C. General, involuntary lien

    D. General, voluntary lien

64. The market value of an undeveloped parcel is $40,000. Its assessed value is 40 percent of market value, and properties in its county are subject to an equalization factor of 3.00. If the tax rate is $2 per $100, what is the amount of the tax owed on the property?

    A. $480

    B. $960

    C. $1,080

    D. $1,800

65. To give notice of a potential claim against the property and establish priority, a creditor may file:

    A. A lis pendens

    B. An attachment

    C. A general lien

    D. A specific lien

66. A man and a woman are married, 65 years old, and retired. They have almost $800,000 in equity in their home, but they don't have enough cash to travel as they've always dreamed of doing. The couple should consider which of these financing alternatives?

A. Novation

B. An adjustable-rate mortgage

C. A reverse mortgage

D. A growing equity mortgage

67. A document that indicates a loan has been made is a:

A. Promissory note

B. Mortgage deed

C. Deed of trust

D. Satisfaction

68. A house is listed for $250,000. A man buys it for $230,000, with a 20 percent down payment. He borrows the balance on a fixed-rate mortgage at 6 percent. The lender charges 4 points. If there are no other closing costs involved, how much money does the man need at closing?

A. $7,360

B. $26,000

C. $46,000

D. $53,360

69. A deed of trust involves these terms, except:

A. Lender

B. Borrower

C. Trustee

D. Mortgagor

70. This month, a man made the last payment on a mortgage loan secured by a woman. The man's lender must execute a:

A. Release deed

B. Promissory note

C. Possessory note

D. Satisfaction of mortgage

71. These are roles of the Federal Reserve System except:

A. It counteracts inflationary trends.

B. It creates a favorable economic climate.

C. It maintains sound credit conditions.

D. It makes direct loans to buyers.

72. The primary mortgage market lenders that have most recently branched out into making mortgage loans are:

A. Credit unions

B. Endowment funds

C. Insurance companies

D. Savings associations

73. One way a borrower can obtain a mortgage loan with less than 20 percent down payment is by:

A. Obtaining a package loan

B. Obtaining a blanket loan

C. Obtaining private mortgage insurance

D. Obtaining permission from the FDIC

74. A package loan includes:

A. Real and personal property

B. Private mortgage insurance

C. Multiple parcels or lots

D. Cash for the construction of improvement on real estate

75. To qualify for most conventional loans, the borrower's monthly housing expenses and total other monthly obligations cannot exceed what percent of the total gross monthly income?

    A. 28 percent

    B. 36 percent

    C. 41 percent

    D. 45 percent

76. A property is listed for sale at $235,000. A buyer's offer of $220,000 is rejected by the seller. Six months later, the seller reduces the price to $225,000. Another buyer offers $210,000, and the seller accepts because the seller has found another house to buy and needs to close quickly. The property is subsequently appraised at $215,000. Which of these figures most accurately represents the property's market value?

    A. $210,000

    B. $215,000

    C. $225,000

    D. $235,000

77. When appraising a newly built home, an appraiser likely uses the:

    A. Sales comparison approach

    B. Income approach

    C. Cost approach

    D. GRM

78. Buyer A purchases a small house in a highly desirable neighborhood consisting of much larger and more expensive homes. Buyer B buys a nearly identical house in a neighborhood of homes of similar size and market value. What economic principle best describes the reason why buyer A paid more than buyer B?

    A. Plottage

    B. Substitution

    C. Regression

    D. Progression

79. The land on which a house was built is worth $50,000. The house was constructed in 1990 at a cost of $265,000 and was expected to last 50 years. Using the straight-line method, determine how much the house has depreciated by 2014.

    A. $28,600

    B. $96,600

    C. $127,200

    D. $145,200

80. A complete history of property's legal activities, including liens and encumbrances, would be:

    A. A title insurance policy

    B. Unrecorded documents

    C. A chain of title

    D. An abstract

81. Which of these would be covered in a standard title insurance policy?

    A. Defects discoverable by physical inspection

    B. Unrecorded liens

    C. Forged documents

    D. Easements and restrictive covenants

82. In real estate, a sales associate is typically:

    A. An independent contractor

    B. An employee of a licensed broker

    C. A licensee who performs real estate activities on behalf of a broker

    D. A combination office manager, marketer, and organizer with a fundamental understanding of the real estate industry who may or may not be licensed

83. A real estate broker had a listing agreement with a seller that specified a 6 percent commission. The broker showed the home to a prospective buyer, and the next day, the buyer called the seller directly and offered to buy the house for 5 percent less than the asking price. The seller agreed to the price and informed the broker in writing that no further brokerage services would be required. The sale went to closing 6 weeks later. Based on these facts, which of these statements is true?

    A. The broker was the procuring cause of the sale, but the seller properly canceled the contract; without a valid employment agreement in force at the time of closing, the broker is not entitled to a commission.

    B. The broker is entitled to a partial commission, and the buyer is obligated to pay it.

    C. Under the facts as stated, the broker is not the procuring cause of this sale but is still entitled to a commission.

    D. The broker was the procuring cause of the sale and is entitled to the full 6 percent commission.

84. A seller listed and sold her property for $325,000. She agreed to pay the listing broker a 6 percent commission. The listing broker offered a listing 40/60 selling split to any cooperating broker who sold the property. How much did the seller pay in total commission fees?

    A. $9,100

    B. $11,375

    C. $13,650

    D. $19,500

85. A broker listed a seller's home for $425,000 with a 4 percent commission, plus $2,500 for advertising costs. The buyer offered $380,000 and, after several counteroffers, finally agreed to $400,000. What was the total cost to the seller?

    A. $16,000

    B. $18,500

    C. $19,000

    D. $20,000

86. An individual who is authorized and consents to represent the interests of another person is:

    A. A customer

    B. A principal

    C. An agent

    D. A facilitator

87. A broker has an agency agreement to represent a seller in the sale of a house. The agreement's expiration date is June 10. On May 5, the house is struck by lightning and burns to the ground. The seller, overwhelmed by grief, dies. Based on these facts, which of these is true?

A. The agency agreement was terminated by the fire, although the seller's death also would have done so.

B. The agency agreement was not terminated until the seller's death.

C. If the house had not been destroyed by the fire, the seller's death would not have terminated the agreement; the broker would become the broker for the seller's estate.

D. Only the mutual agreement of the parties can terminate a valid agency agreement before its expiration date.

88. A broker was hired to represent a seller to market a property and to solicit offers to purchase. The broker is called a:

A. General agent
B. Special agent
C. Facilitator
D. Nonagent

89. All these will terminate an agency relationship except:

A. The death of either party
B. The destruction of the property
C. An offer made on the property
D. An expiration of the agreement

90. A property manager's first responsibility to the owner should be to:

A. Keep the building's occupancy rate at 100 percent

B. Report all day-to-day financial and operating decisions to the owner on a regular basis

C. Realize the highest return possible consistent with the owner's instructions

D. Ensure that the rental rates are below market average

91. If an apartment rents for $750 per month and the manager receives a 12 percent commission on all new tenants, how much will the manager receive when renting an apartment, assuming this commission is calculated in the usual way?

A. $90
B. $750
C. $1,080
D. $1,800

92. What is the annual rent per square foot for a 30-foot by 40-foot property that rents for $2,950 per month?

A. $1.20
B. $2.46
C. $24.65
D. $29.50

93. All these could be included in a zoning ordinance except:

A. Objectives for future development of the area

B. Permissible height and style of new construction

C. Style and appearance of structures

D. The maximum allowable ratio of land area to structural area

94. A city passed a zoning ordinance that prohibits all commercial structures more than 30 feet high. A man wants to build an office building that will be 45 feet high. To obtain permission for the building, the man may apply for a:

A. Nonconforming use permit

B. Zoning permit

C. Conditional use permit

D. Variance or zoning change

95. When an area was rezoned as residential, a store was grandfathered in and allowed to continue business. This is an example of:

A. A variance

B. Nonconforming use

C. A conditional use permit

D. An amendment

96. A new structure has been completed to the satisfaction of the inspecting city engineer. What documentation must be issued before anyone can move in?

A. Appraisal report

B. Certificate of occupancy

C. Certificate of reasonable value

D. Conditional use permit

97. Any additional capital or personal property included with a real property exchange to even out the value of a property exchange is called:

A. Cost recovery

B. A REIT

C. Boot

D. Equity build-up

98. One objective of investing in income property is to generate spendable income, also called:

A. Appreciation

B. Basis

C. Cash flow

D. Pyramiding

99. Which of these is an advantage of investing in a real estate investment trust (REIT)?

A. Direct ownership of real estate

B. At least 90 percent of the income must come from real estate

C. Access to the same tax benefits as mutual fund investors

D. Income taxed at corporate rates

100. Which of the following describes straight-line depreciation?

A. Depreciation is taken periodically in equal amounts over an asset's useful life.

B. Depreciation is taken periodically in equal amounts over a maximum of 10 years.

C. The amount of depreciation increases each year until the asset is sold or devalued.

D. The amount of depreciation decreases each year until the asset is sold or devalued.

Answers

1. C. No matter how identical they may appear, no two parcels of real estate are ever exactly alike. Each occupies its own unique geographic location.

2. B. When consumers continue to demand a product for which there is limited supply, the price generally increases.

3. B. Subsurface rights and improvements are included in the definition of real estate. Real property also includes rights and privileges.

4. A. Owners of littoral rights enjoy unrestricted use of available waters but own the land adjacent to the water only up to the average high-water mark.

5. D. The definition of real estate includes fences, buildings, and growing trees. Chattels are personal property. The definition of land would not include fences and buildings.

6. C. An appurtenance is a right or privilege associated with the property, although not necessarily a part of it. Typical appurtenances include parking spaces in multiunit buildings, easements, water rights, and other improvements.

7. B. Whether an item is a fixture or personal property may be determined by method of annexation, adaptation to real estate, or agreement of the parties.

8. B. Personal property is all the property that can be owned and does not fit the definition of real property. The most important distinction between real and personal property is that personal property is movable.

9. D. Because the rose bush is a perennial shrub, it is considered real estate.

10. C. If the owner of the dominant tenement also becomes owner of the servient tenement, or vice versa, the easement terminates. Because the same person owns both properties, there's no need for the easement to exist.

11. B. When two or more people buy property together, it's called co-ownership. A joint venture is a form of partnership in which two or more people carry out a single business project with no intention of establishing an ongoing relationship.

12. C. The brothers are presumed to be tenants in common because they did not indicate themselves as joint tenants with right of survivorship. Joint tenancy requires extra wording. Severalty ownership indicates one owner.

13. C. A trust is a device by which one person transfers ownership of property to someone else to hold or manage for the benefit of a third party. Severalty indicates one owner. Joint tenancy is a form of ownership whereby, as joint owners die, the surviving owners acquire the deceased tenant's interest.

14. C. It appears that the man has condominium ownership because he owns the cottage as well as the interest in the common elements. Cooperative ownership is ruled out because he does not have a proprietary lease. It is not a timeshare because he clearly owns more than the right to use at specific times.

15. B. To create joint tenancy ownership, four unities are required—possession, interest, time, and title—not ownership.

16. D. Under tenancy by the entirety, title may be conveyed only by a deed signed by both parties. Each spouse owns an equal, undivided interest in the property, and the surviving spouse automatically becomes the owner upon the death of the other.

17. D. A benchmark is a permanent reference point used as a reference for marking data, not for expressing a legal description.

18. B. The woman paid $592,416:

$43,560$ square feet $\times 4 = 174,240$ square feet

$174,240$ square feet $\times \$3.40 = \$592,416$

19. B. The man paid $15,000:

$\frac{1}{4} \times 640 = 160$

$160 \times \frac{1}{4} = 40$

$40 \times \frac{1}{4} = 10$ acres

10 acres $\times \$1,500 = \$15,000$

20. B. The buyer's real estate tax proration is $1,600: $\$2,400 \div 12$ months $\times 8$ months $= \$1,600$.

21. D. Documentation for the new loan—preparation of note and mortgage—is the responsibility of the buyer. The seller is responsible for documents necessary to clear any clouds on the title, affidavits of title, and the deed.

22. C. The seller must pay the security deposit to the buyer who will, as the new owner, be responsible for returning the money to the tenant at the end of the lease.

23. D. The transaction would not have been subject to RESPA if the assumption fee had been $50 or less.

24. C. Appraisal fees and credit report fees are paid outside of closing (POC) by the buyer; they are not prorated.

25. C. The earnest money is brought to closing and credited to the buyer.

26. B. The one-lump sum every month to the landlord is a gross lease. In a net lease, the tenant is responsible for paying all or most of the property charges. Percentage leases are generally used by retail establishments and are based on gross sales.

27. A. The tenant typically pays a higher rent with a portion being applied to the subsequent purchase of the property. It differs from a sale leaseback, whereby the owner of the property wants to obtain equity from the building. The owner sells the building and agrees to rent it back.

28. D. Constructive eviction is a result of the landlord not providing essential services—such as the place is unsafe or uninhabitable—conditions that are not met in this situation.

29. B. A form of variable lease is the graduated lease that provides for specified rent increases at set future dates.

30. B. There are two parcels in this description denoted by the word and. The first: $\frac{1}{4} \times 640 = 160$; $\frac{1}{4} \times 160 = 40$. The second: $\frac{1}{4} \times 640 = 160$; $160 \times \frac{1}{4} = 40$; $40 \times \frac{1}{2} = 20$.

$$40 + 20 = 60 \text{ acres}$$

31. D. Township squares are the basic units of the rectangular survey system. Principal meridians and baselines are the two sets of intersecting lines in the system. Ranges are the 6-mile strips of land on either side of a principal meridian.

32. C. A metes-and-bounds description must always begin and end at the point of beginning, encircling the described property.

33. C. The habendum clause is the "to have and to hold" clause that defines the extent of ownership being conveyed.

34. B. A deed is the written document that transfers a real estate interest. Evidence of ownership (title) is written in the deed. An attachment is the process of taking a person's property into legal custody by a court order. A mortgage provides the security for a loan.

35. C. The grantee does not need to sign the deed because the grantee receives the property.

36. C. A quitclaim deed carries no covenants or warranties and generally only conveys whatever interest the grantor has when the deed is delivered.

37. B. The most complete answer is delivered to and accepted by the grantee during the grantor's lifetime.

38. A. A recorded deed is nothing more than that. Other verifications of thorough examinations of recorded documents can affect the title.

39. B. Because land is immobile, it makes sense to record all information about title to the property in the county where it's located. Some owners frequently relocate, and they would be hard to find.

40. B. The Fair Housing Amendments Act of 1988 added disability and familial status. The Housing and Community Development Act of 1974 added sex to the list of protected classes, which is found in Title VIII of the Civil Rights Act of 1968. The Civil Rights Act of 1866 prohibits discrimination based on race.

41. B. The Department of Housing and Urban Development (HUD) handles fair housing complaints on the national level. Most states have enacted substantially similar laws, so the state agency often is involved.

42. C. The Fair Housing Amendments Act of 1988 expanded federal civil rights protections to familial status and disability. The act also changed the penalties by making them more severe and by including additional damages.

43. B. Persons convicted of manufacturing or distributing illegal drugs do not enjoy any protections under the fair housing laws, although disability is a protected class. Individuals who are participating in addiction recovery programs are in a protected class of disability.

44. B. An instruction to not show the home to someone who was not born in the United States violates the Fair Housing Act. The real estate professional should not take the listing with this requirement. He cannot simply ignore the instructions or pretend they do not exist.

45. D. Channeling home seekers toward or away from particular neighborhoods based on national origin, or any of the other protected classifications, is called steering.

46. A. The second wife owns a life estate, and she has the entire bundle of rights except the right to will the property.

47. C. A license is a personal right to enter the property for a specific purpose. There is no buildup of rights.

48. B. The man has granted a fee simple subject to a condition subsequent. If at some point in the future the land is not used as a school, the man or his heirs may exercise the right of reentry by retaking physical possession of the land.

49. D. A lis pendens is a notice filed in the public record affecting the title to property or a claimed ownership interest in it.

50. B. Reporting the status of funds is an accounting responsibility. Obeying the principal's instructions relates to obedience. Revealing relevant information relates to the responsibility of disclosure.

51. C. Both commingling the funds and the practice of conversion are illegal.

52. A. In a buyer representation agreement, the broker acts as the agent of the buyer and must protect the buyer's interests at all points in the transaction.

53. D. Under the exclusive-agency listing, the seller is permitted to sell the house and is not obligated to pay a commission.

54. C. When obtaining the listing, the agent should gather as much information as possible, including the lot size and property conditions. The listing also should include a termination clause. However, when taking the listing from the seller, the agent is not concerned about the seller's future housing needs.

55. C. A broker's agreement to represent a property buyer may be terminated for various reasons, one of which is mutual agreement between the broker and buyer.

56. D. Although the broker can subcontract the work to sales associates, the listing agreement is an employment contract between the seller and the broker.

57. D. The buyer may revoke her offer any time until she is notified that the seller has accepted the offer.

58. B. The offer of a bonus to the top-selling sales-person each quarter is an express contract because the broker clearly stated her intentions in words to the salespeople. It is a unilateral contract because she is obligated to keep her promise, but the salespeople are not obligated to perform.

59. C. Because the seller has promised to sell and the buyer has promised to buy, it is a bilateral contract. It is express because they announced their intentions in writing. The contract is executory because the sale has not yet closed.

60. C. Even changing the smallest of terms, for whatever reason, constitutes a rejection and counter-offer that the other party is not under obligation to accept.

61. C. Earnest money is an optional term in a contract, not a requirement. The essential elements of a contract are offer and acceptance, consideration, legally competent parties, consent, and legal capacity.

62. B. The tax bill is $1,402.50: 0.5 + 1 + 0.5 + 1 + 0.5 + 5 = 8.5 mills or $0.0085 per dollar of valuation: $165,000 × 0.0085 = $1,402.50.

63. A. A real estate tax is levied on an individual property. Few would argue that individuals choose to have the tax levied, hence, an involuntary lien.

64. B. The tax owned on the property is $960: $40,000 × 40% × 3.0 ÷ 100 × 2 = $960.

65. A. A lis pendens is a notice of a possible future lien. If it becomes an actual lien, the effective date of the lien is the date and time the lis pendens was filed.

66. C. A reverse mortgage allows a homeowner aged 62 or older to borrow money against the equity built up in his home. The money may be used for any purpose.

67. A. The evidence that a loan has been made is found in the promissory note. A mortgage or deed of trust provides security for the loan. A satisfaction or release indicates that the loan has been repaid in full.

68. D. The man needs $53,360 at closing: $7,360 (points) + $46,000 (down payment).

69. D. A mortgagor is the borrower in a mortgage. In a deed of trust, the borrower is the trustor, and the trustee holds naked title in trust for the beneficiary (lender).

70. D. The promissory note shows that a loan was made. The satisfaction indicates that the loan was fully repaid. Satisfaction of mortgage is also some-times called a release but not a release deed.

71. D. The Federal Reserve helps counteract inflationary trends, creates a favorable economic climate, maintains sound credit conditions, but does not make direct loans to consumers.

72. A. Credit unions were known for short-term consumer loans but have more recently branched out into originating mortgage loans.

73. C. Private mortgage insurance provides the lender with funds in the event that the borrower defaults on the loan. This allows the lender to assume more risk so the LTV can be higher than for other conventional loans.

74. A. Package loans usually include items such as drapes, refrigerator, dishwasher, and other appliances as part of the sales price of the home. A blanket loan covers more than one parcel or lot. A construction loan finances the construction of improvements on real estate.

75. B. To be considered a conforming loan that can be sold in the secondary market, the borrower's monthly housing expenses and total other monthly obligations must not exceed 36 percent of total monthly gross income.

76. B. The property's market price is $210,000, while its appraised value (and most probable market value) is $215,000. The seller accepted the lower price because of the pressure to close on the new house.

77. C. A newly constructed house may be appraised using the cost approach and omitting depreciation.

78. D. The buyer's house benefits from being a smaller one alongside larger, more prestigious ones (i.e., progression). Buyer B's house is appropriately valued for its neighborhood.

79. C. The value of the land is not relevant to this problem. The cost of the building is divided by the number of years of its useful life and multiplied to determine the depreciation after 24 years:

$$\$265,000 \div 50 = \$5,300$$
$$\$5,300 \times 24 = \$127,200$$

80. D. The title insurance policy lists coverage and exceptions to the policy. Unrecorded documents have not been examined. The chain of title traces ownership. The abstract is the most complete documentation of recorded liens and encumbrances.

81. C. Title insurance does not protect against claims of parties in possession because the grantee should have visited the property; nor does it cover unrecorded liens. Easements and restrictive covenants are found in the deed and should be known to the grantee.

82. C. The sales associate might be treated as an independent contractor for income tax purposes, but the salesperson must still work directly under the broker's name.

83. D. Because the broker introduced a ready, willing, and able buyer to the seller prior to the seller's cancellation of the listing agreement, the broker is entitled to the commission.

84. D. What the brokers agree to regarding splitting the commission is not relevant to the total cost to the seller. The seller paid $19,500 in commission fees: $325,000 × 6% = $19,500.

85. C. The seller's total cost is $18,500: $400,000 × 4% + $2,500 = $18,500.

86. C. The agent is hired by the principal. The customer or facilitator is a third party.

87. A. An agency agreement may be terminated by either destruction of the property or death of either party. In this case, destruction of the property occurred first.

88. B. A special agent is one who is hired for a limited time and given limited authority. A broker taking a listing is generally a special agent.

89. C. An offer on the property does not terminate the agency relationship; however, the death of either party, destruction of the property, or expiration of the term does terminate the relationship.

90. C. The role of the property manager is to achieve the objectives of the property owners, generate income for the owners, and preserve and/or increase the value of the investment property.

91. C. The manager will receive $1,080: $750 per month × 12 months × 12% = $1,080.

92. D. The annual rent is $29.50 per square foot:

$$30 \times 40 = 1,200 \text{ square feet}$$
$$\$2,950 \times 12 = \$35,400$$
$$\$35,400 \div 1,200 = \$29.50$$

93. A. A zoning ordinance might include restrictions for permissible height and style of new construction, style and appearance of structures, and the maximum allowable ratio of land area to structural area. Objectives for future development of the area might be found in a comprehensive plan.

94. D. Because the man's building does not yet exist, it does not qualify for nonconforming use. A conditional use permit is issued for a special use that meets certain standards. A variance, if granted, permits the landowner to use the property in a manner that's otherwise prohibited by the existing zoning.

95. B. Because the store had been there legally before the zoning ordinance, it's permitted to continue operating, usually until its use changes or the building is destroyed.

96. B. Once the completed building has been inspected and found to comply with the building codes, the municipal inspector issues a certificate of occupancy or occupancy permit.

97. C. Boot is any additional capital or personal property included with the exchange transaction to balance the value of the exchange. The IRS requires that tax on the boot be paid at the time of the exchange by the party who receives it.

98. C. Cash flow is the total amount of money remaining after all expenditures have been paid.

99. C. Investors in REITs do not have a direct investment in real estate. Generally, shareholders, not the REIT, pay the tax on profits distributed.

100. A. Different depreciation rules apply for property purchased before 1987—the accelerated cost recovery system (ACRS).

Sample Real Estate Documents

These are sample forms for you to look at to gain a general knowledge of the content needed for each form. Each state agency will provide you with a catalog of specific forms required for the state in which you practice. Remember, unless you are a practicing attorney you cannot write contracts and should always use the forms provided to you by your state agency or managing broker.

Listing Broker (Co.) _____ (_____) By _____ (_____)
                                                          office code   *individual code*
Selling Broker (Co.) _____ (_____) By _____ (_____)
                                                          office code   *individual code*

Provided as a member service by the
INDIANA
ASSOCIATION OF
REALTORS®, INC.

PURCHASE AGREEMENT
(IMPROVED PROPERTY)

1 Date: _____
2
3 A. **BUYER:**_____ ("Buyer")
4   agrees to buy the following property from the owner ("Seller") for the consideration and subject to the following
5   terms, provisions, and conditions:
6
7 B. **PROPERTY:** The property ("Property") is known as _____
8   in _____ Township, _____ County, _____,
9   Indiana, _____ (zip code) legally described as: _____
10   _____
11   together with any existing permanent improvements and fixtures attached **(unless leased or excluded)**, including,
12   but not limited to, electrical and/or gas fixtures, home heating fuel, heating and central air-conditioning equipment
13   and all attachments thereto, built-in kitchen equipment, sump pumps, water softener, water purifier, gas grills,
14   fireplace inserts, gas logs and grates, central vacuum equipment, window shades/blinds, curtain rods, drapery poles
15   and fixtures, ceiling fans and light fixtures, towel racks and bars, storm doors, windows, awnings, TV antennas,
16   wall mounts, satellite dishes, storage barns, all landscaping, mailbox, garage door opener with controls AND THE
17   FOLLOWING: _____
18   _____
19   _____
20   _____
21   _____
22   EXCLUDES THE FOLLOWING: _____
23   _____
24   **The terms of this Agreement will determine what items are included/excluded, not the Seller's Disclosure**
25   **Form, multiple listing service or other promotional materials. All items sold shall be fully paid for by Seller**
26   **at time of closing the transaction. Buyer should verify total square footage, land, room dimensions or**
27   **community amenities if material.**
28
29 C. **PRICE:** Buyer will pay the total purchase price of ($ _____) _____
30   _____ Dollars for the Property. If Buyer obtains an
31   appraisal of the Property, this Agreement is contingent upon the Property appraising at no less than the agreed
32   upon purchase price. If appraised value is less than the agreed upon purchase price, either party may terminate this
33   Agreement or parties may mutually agree to amend the price.
34
35 D. **EARNEST MONEY:**
36   1. **Submission:** Buyer submits $ _____ as earnest money which shall be applied to the
37   purchase price at closing. Unless indicated otherwise in this Agreement, the listing broker shall act as Escrow
38   Agent and shall deposit Earnest Money received into its escrow account within two (2) banking days of
39   acceptance of this Agreement and hold it until time of closing the transaction or termination of this Agreement.
40   Earnest money shall be returned promptly to Buyer in the event this offer is not accepted. If Buyer fails for any
41   reason to timely submit Earnest Money in the contracted amount, Seller may terminate this Agreement upon
42   notice to Buyer prior to Escrow Agent's receipt of the Earnest Money.
43   2. **Disbursement:** Upon notification that Buyer or Seller intends not to perform, and if Escrow Agent is the
44   Broker, then Broker holding the Earnest Money may release the Earnest Money as provided in this Agreement.
45   If no provision is made in this Agreement, Broker may send to Buyer and Seller notice of the disbursement by
46   certified mail of the intended payee of the Earnest Money as permitted in 876 IAC 8-2-2. If neither Buyer nor
47   Seller enters into a mutual release or initiates litigation within sixty (60) days of the mailing date of the certified
48   letter, Broker may release the Earnest Money to the party identified in the certified letter. If the Escrow Agent is
49   the Broker, Broker shall be absolved from any responsibility to make payment to Seller or Buyer unless the
50   parties enter into a Mutual Release or a Court issues an Order for payment, except as permitted in 876 IAC 8-2-2
51   (release of earnest money). Buyer and Seller agree to hold the Broker harmless from any liability, including
52   attorney's fees and costs, for good faith disbursement of Earnest Money in accordance with this Agreement and
53   licensing regulations
54   3. **Legal Remedies/Default:** If this offer is accepted and Buyer fails or refuses to close the transaction, without
55   legal cause, the earnest money shall be retained by Seller for damages Seller has or will incur. Seller retains all
56   rights to seek other legal and equitable remedies, which may include specific performance and additional
57   monetary damages. All parties have the legal duty to use good faith and due diligence in completing the terms
58   and conditions of this Agreement. A material failure to perform any obligation under this Agreement is a default
59   which may subject the defaulting party to liability for damages and/or other legal remedies, which, as stated
60   above, may include specific performance and monetary damages in addition to loss of Earnest Money.

61 E. **METHOD OF PAYMENT: (Check appropriate paragraph number)**
62   1. ☐ **CASH:** The entire purchase price shall be paid in cash and no financing is required. Buyer to provide proof of
63   funds within _____ days of acceptance.
64   2. ☐ **NEW MORTGAGE:** Completion of this transaction shall be contingent upon the Buyer's ability to obtain a
65
66   ☐ **Conventional** ☐ **Insured Conventional** ☐ **FHA** ☐ **VA** ☐ **Other:** _____ first
67   mortgage loan for _____ % of purchase price, payable in not less than _____ years, with an
68   original rate of interest not to exceed _____ % per annum and not to exceed _____ points. Buyer
69   shall pay all costs of obtaining financing, except _____
70   _____
71   _____ .
72   Any inspections and charges which are required to be made and charged to Buyer or Seller by the lender,
73   FHA, VA, or mortgage insurer, shall be made and charged in accordance with their prevailing rules or
74   regulations and shall supersede any provisions of this Agreement.
75
76   3. ☐ **ASSUMPTION: (Attach Financing Addendum)**
77   4. ☐ **CONDITIONAL SALES CONTRACT: (Attach Financing Addendum)**
78   5. ☐ **OTHER METHOD OF PAYMENT: (Attach Financing Addendum)**
79
80 F.   **TIME FOR OBTAINING FINANCING: Buyer agrees to make written application for any financing necessary**
81   **to complete this transaction** or for approval to assume the unpaid balance of the existing mortgage within _____
82   days after the acceptance of this Agreement and to make a diligent effort to meet the lender's requirements and to
83   obtain financing in cooperation with the Broker and Seller. No more than _____ days after acceptance of the
84   Agreement shall be allowed for obtaining loan approval or mortgage assumption approval. If an approval is not
85   obtained within the time specified above, this Agreement may terminate unless an extension of time for this
86   purpose is mutually agreed to in writing.
87
88 G. **CLOSING:**
89   1. **DATE:** The closing of the sale (the "Closing Date") shall be on or before _____ , or
90   within _____ days after _____ , whichever is later or this Agreement
91   shall terminate unless an extension of time is mutually agreed to in writing. Any closing date earlier than the
92   latest date above must be by mutual written agreement of the parties.
93   **If closing cannot occur by "Closing Date" due to any government regulation or lender requirement, the**
94   **date of closing shall be extended for the period necessary to satisfy these requirements, not to exceed 7**
95   **business days.**
96   2. **FEE:** The settlement or closing fee incurred in conducting the settlement charged by the closing agent or
97   company shall be paid by ☐ **Buyer (included in allowance, if provided)** ☐ **Seller** ☐ **Shared equally.**
98   3. **CONTINGENCY:** This Agreement: ☐ **is not** contingent upon the closing of another transaction;
99   ☐ **is** contingent upon the closing of the pending transaction on the property located at _____
100   _____ scheduled to close by _____ .
101   4. **GOOD FUNDS:** Notwithstanding terms to the contrary, the Parties agree that as a condition to Closing, all funds
102   delivered to the closing agent's escrow account be in such form that the closing agent shall be able to disburse
103   in compliance with I.C. 27-07-3.7 et. seq. Therefore, all funds from a single source of $10,000 or more shall be
104   wired unconditionally to the closing agent's escrow account and all funds under $10,000 from a single source
105   shall be good funds as so defined by statute. Buyer is advised that the cost incurred to wire funds on behalf of
106   the buyer to the closing agent's escrow account for the closing of this transaction shall become an expense to
107   the buyer and the actual cost incurred shall appear on the closing statement.
108
109
110 H. **POSSESSION:**
111   1. The possession of the Property shall be delivered to Buyer ☐ **at closing** ☐ **within** _____ **days beginning**
112   **the day after closing by** _____ ☐ **a.m.** ☐ **p.m.** ☐ **noon or** ☐ **on or before** _____
113   **if closed.** For each day Seller is entitled to possession after closing, Seller shall pay to Buyer at closing
114        $_____ per day. If Seller does not deliver possession by the date and time required in the first
115   sentence of this paragraph, Seller shall pay Buyer $_____ per day as **liquidated damages**
116   until possession is delivered to Buyer; and Buyer shall have all other legal and equitable remedies available
117   against the Seller.
118   2. **Maintenance of Property:** Seller shall maintain the Property in its present condition until its possession is
119   delivered to Buyer, subject to repairs in response to any inspection. Buyer may inspect the Property prior to
120   closing to determine whether Seller has complied with this paragraph. Seller shall remove all debris and
121   personal property not included in the sale.
122   3. **Casualty Loss:** Risk of loss by damage or destruction to the Property prior to the closing shall be borne by
123   Seller, including any deductible(s). In the event any damage or destruction is not fully repaired prior to closing,
124   Buyer, at Buyer's option, may either **(a) terminate this Agreement with prompt return of earnest money to**
125   **buyer or (b) elect to close the transaction,** in which event Seller's right to all real property insurance
126   proceeds resulting from such damage or destruction shall be assigned in writing by Seller to Buyer.

127 4. **Utilities/Municipal Services:** Seller shall pay for all municipal services and public utility charges through the
128   day of possession.
129

130 I. **SURVEY:** Buyer shall receive a **(Check one)** ☐ **SURVEYOR LOCATION REPORT**, which is a survey where
131   corner markers are not set; ☐ **BOUNDARY SURVEY**, which is a survey where corner markers of the Property are
132   set prior to closing; ☐ **WAIVED**, no survey unless required by lender; at **(Check one)** ☐ **Buyer's expense**
133   **(included in allowance, if provided)** ☐ **Seller's expense** ☐ **Shared equally.** The survey shall (1) be received
134   prior to closing and certified as of a current date, (2) be reasonably satisfactory to Buyer, (3) show the location of all
135   improvements and easements, and (4) show the flood zone designation of the Property. If Buyer waives the right to
136   conduct a survey, the Seller, the Listing and Selling Brokers, and all licensees associated with Brokers are released
137   from any and all liability relating to any issues that could have been discovered by a survey. This release shall
138   survive the closing.
139

140 J. **FLOOD AREA/OTHER:** If the property is located in a flood plain, Buyer may be required to carry flood insurance at
141   Buyer's expense. Revised flood maps and changes to Federal law may substantially increase future flood
142   insurance premiums or require insurance for formerly exempt properties. Buyer should consult with one or more
143   flood insurance agents regarding the need for flood insurance and possible premium increases. Buyer ☐ **may**
144   ☐ **may not** terminate this Agreement if the Property requires flood insurance. Buyer ☐ **may** ☐ **may not** terminate
145   this Agreement if the Property is subject to building or use limitations by reason of the location, which materially
146   interfere with Buyer's intended use of the Property.
147

148 K. **HOMEOWNER'S INSURANCE:** Completion of this transaction shall be contingent upon the Buyer's ability to obtain
149   a favorable written commitment for homeowner's insurance within _____ days after acceptance of this Agreement.
150

151 L. **ENVIRONMENTAL CONTAMINANTS ADVISORY/RELEASE:** Buyer and Seller acknowledge that Listing Broker,
152   Selling Broker and all licensees associated with Brokers are NOT experts and have NO special training,
153   knowledge or experience with regard to the evaluation or existence of possible lead-based paint, radon, mold and
154   other biological contaminants ("Environmental Contaminants") which might exist and affect the Property.
155   Environmental Contaminants at harmful levels may cause property damage and serious illness, including but not
156   limited to, allergic and/or respiratory problems, particularly in persons with immune system problems, young
157   children and/or the elderly.
158

159   Buyer is STRONGLY ADVISED to obtain inspections (see below) to fully determine the condition of the Property
160   and its environmental status. The ONLY way to determine if Environmental Contaminants are present at the
161   Property at harmful levels is through inspections.
162

163   **Buyer and Seller agree to consult with appropriate experts and accept all risks for Environmental**
164   **Contaminants and release and hold harmless all Brokers, their companies and licensees from any**
165   **and all liability, including attorney's fees and costs, arising out of or related to any inspection, inspection**
166   **result, repair, disclosed defect or deficiency affecting the Property, including Environmental Contaminants.**
167   **This release shall survive the closing.**
168

169 M. **INSPECTIONS: (Check appropriate paragraph number)**
170

171   Buyer has been made aware that independent inspections disclosing the condition of the property are available
172   and has been afforded the opportunity to require such inspections as a condition of this Agreement.
173

174   1. ☐ **BUYER WAIVES THE RIGHT TO HAVE INDEPENDENT INSPECTIONS**
175   Buyer **WAIVES** inspections and relies upon the condition of the Property based upon Buyer's own
176   examination and releases the Seller, the Listing and Selling Brokers and all licensees associated with
177   Brokers from any and all liability relating to any defect or deficiency affecting the Property, which release
178   shall survive the closing. Required FHA/VA or lender inspections are not included in this waiver.
179

180   2. ☐ **BUYER RESERVES THE RIGHT TO HAVE INDEPENDENT INSPECTIONS (including Lead-Based Paint)**
181   Buyer reserves the right to have independent inspections in addition to any inspection required by FHA, VA,
182   or Buyer's lender(s). All inspections are at Buyer's expense (unless noted otherwise or required by lender) by
183   licensed independent inspectors or qualified independent contractors selected by Buyer within the following
184   time periods. **Seller shall have water, gas, electricity and all operable pilot lights on for Buyer's**
185   **inspections. Seller must make all areas of the Property available and accessible for Buyer's**
186   **inspection.**
187

188   **INSPECTION/RESPONSE PERIOD:** Buyer shall order all independent inspections after acceptance
189   of the Purchase Agreement. Buyer shall have _____ days beginning the day following the date of
190   acceptance of the Purchase Agreement to respond to the inspection report(s) in writing to Seller (see
191   "Buyer's Inspection Response").
192

193   Inspections may include but are not limited to the condition of the following systems and components:
194   heating, cooling, electrical, plumbing, roof, walls, ceilings, floors, foundation, basement, crawl space,

195 well/septic, water, wood destroying insects and organisms, lead-based paint (note: intact lead-based paint
196 that is in good condition is not necessarily a hazard), radon, mold and other biological contaminants and/or
197 the following: _____
198 If the **INITIAL** inspection report reveals the presence of lead-based paint, radon, mold and other biological
199 contaminants, or any other condition that requires further examination or testing, then Buyer shall have
200 _____ additional days to order, receive and respond in writing to any additional reports.
201
202 **If the Buyer does not comply with any Inspection/Response Period or make a written objection to any**
203 **problem revealed in a report within the applicable Inspection/Response Period, the Property shall be**
204 **deemed to be acceptable. If one party fails to respond or request in writing an extension of time to**
205 **respond to the other party's Independent Inspection Response, then that inspection response is**
206 **accepted.** A timely request for extension is not an acceptance of the inspection response, whether or not
207 granted. A REASONABLE TIME PERIOD TO RESPOND IS REQUIRED TO PREVENT MISUSE OF THIS
208 ACCEPTANCE PROVISION. Factors considered in determining reasonable time periods include, but are
209 not limited to, availability of responding party to respond, type and expense of repairs requested and need of
210 responding party to obtain additional opinions to formulate a response.
211
212 If Buyer reasonably believes that the Inspection Report reveals a **DEFECT** with the Property (under Indiana
213 law, **"Defect" means a condition that would have a significant adverse effect on the value of the**
214 **Property, that would significantly impair the health or safety of future occupants of the Property, or**
215 **that if not repaired, removed, or replaced would significantly shorten or adversely affect the expected**
216 **normal life of the premises**), and after having given Seller the opportunity to remedy the defect Seller is
217 unable or unwilling to remedy the defect to Buyer's reasonable satisfaction before closing (or at a time
218 otherwise agreed to by the parties), then Buyer may terminate this Agreement or waive such defect and the
219 transaction shall proceed toward closing. BUYER AGREES THAT ANY PROPERTY DEFECT
220 PREVIOUSLY DISCLOSED BY SELLER, OR ROUTINE MAINTENANCE AND MINOR REPAIR ITEMS
221 MENTIONED IN ANY REPORT, SHALL NOT BE A BASIS FOR TERMINATION OF THIS AGREEMENT.
222
223 N. **LIMITED HOME WARRANTY PROGRAM:**
224 Buyer acknowledges the availability of a LIMITED HOME WARRANTY PROGRAM with a deductible paid by Buyer
225 which ☐ **will** ☐ **will not** be provided at a cost not to exceed $ _____ charged to ☐ **Buyer** ☐ **Seller**
226 **and ordered by** ☐ **Buyer** ☐ **Seller.** Buyer and Seller acknowledge this LIMITED HOME WARRANTY PROGRAM
227 may not cover any pre-existing defects in the Property nor replace the need for an independent home inspection.
228 Broker may receive a fee from the home warranty provider and/or a member benefit. The Limited Home Warranty
229 Program is a contract between Buyer/Seller and the Home Warranty Provider. The Parties agree that Brokers and
230 their companies shall be released and held harmless in the event of claims disputes with the Home Warranty
231 Provider.
232
233 O. **DISCLOSURES: (Check one)**
234 1.   Buyer ☐ **has** ☐ **has not** ☐ **not applicable** received and executed SELLER'S RESIDENTIAL REAL ESTATE
235 SALES DISCLOSURE.
236 2.   Buyer ☐ **has** ☐ **has not** ☐ **not applicable** received and executed a LEAD-BASED PAINT CERTIFICATION
237 AND ACKNOWLEDGMENT.
238
239 P. **TITLE APPROVAL:** Prior to closing, Buyer shall be furnished with ☐ **a title insurance commitment for the most**
240 **current and comprehensive ALTA Owner's Title Insurance Policy available** in the amount of the purchase
241 price or ☐ **an abstract of title continued to date**, showing marketable title to Property in Seller's name. Seller
242 must convey title free and clear of any encumbrances and title defects, with the exception of any mortgage
243 assumed by Buyer and any restrictions or easements of record not materially interfering with Buyer's intended use
244 of the Property. A title company, at Buyer's request, can provide information about availability of various additional
245 title insurance coverages and endorsements and the associated costs.
246
247 **Owner's Title Insurance Premium** and that portion of Title Service Fees incurred to prepare the Owner's Policy
248 (including title search and examination and commitment preparation), to be paid by ☐ **Buyer (included in**
249 **allowance, if provided)** ☐ **Seller** ☐ **Shared equally.**
250
251 **Lender's Title Insurance Premium** and that portion of Title Service Fees incurred to prepare the Lender's Policy
252 (including title search and examination and commitment preparation), if applicable, to be paid by ☐ **Buyer (included**
253 **in allowance, if provided)** ☐ **Seller** ☐ **Shared equally** ☐ **Other** _____
254 .
255 The parties agree that ☐ **Seller** ☐ **Buyer** will select a title insurance company to issue a title insurance policy and
256 will order the commitment ☐ **immediately** or ☐ **other:** _____
257 .
258 Pursuant to Federal and State law, Seller cannot make Seller's selection of a title insurance provider a condition of
259 this Agreement.
260
261 Seller agrees to pay the cost of obtaining all other documents necessary to perfect title (including the cost of the
262 deed and vendor's affidavit), so that marketable title can be conveyed.

263 Q. **TAXES: (Check appropriate paragraph number)**
264   ☐ **1.** Buyer will assume and pay all taxes on the Property beginning with the taxes due and payable on
265   _____ , _____ , and all taxes due thereafter. At or before closing, Seller shall pay all
266   taxes for the Property payable before that date.
267   ☐ **2.** All taxes that have accrued for any **prior calendar year** that remain unpaid shall be paid by Seller either to
268   the County Treasurer and/or the Buyer in the form of a credit at closing. All taxes that have accrued for the
269   **current calendar year** shall be prorated on a calendar-year basis as of the day immediately prior to the
270   Closing Date.
271
272   **For purposes of paragraph 1 and 2:** For the purpose of determining the credit amount for accrued but unpaid
273   taxes, taxes shall be assumed to be the same as the most recent year when taxes were billed based upon *certified*
274   tax rates. This shall be a final settlement.
275
276   ☐ **3. FOR RECENT CONSTRUCTION OR OTHER TAX SITUATIONS.** Seller will give a tax credit of
277      $ _____ to Buyer at closing. This shall be a final settlement.
278
279 **WARNING:** THE SUCCEEDING YEAR TAX BILL FOR RECENTLY CONSTRUCTED HOMES OR FOLLOWING
280 **REASSESSMENT PERIODS MAY GREATLY EXCEED THE LAST TAX BILL AVAILABLE TO THE CLOSING AGENT.**
281
282 **Buyer acknowledges Seller's tax exemptions and/or credits may not be reflected on future tax bills.**
283
284 **Buyer may apply for current-year exemptions/credits at or after closing.**
285
286 R. **PRORATIONS AND SPECIAL ASSESSMENTS:** Insurance, if assigned to Buyer, interest on any debt assumed or
287   taken subject to, any rents, all other income and ordinary operating expenses of the Property, including but not
288   limited to, public utility charges, shall be prorated as of the day immediately prior to the Closing Date. Seller shall
289   pay any special assessments applicable to the Property for municipal improvements previously made to benefit the
290   Property. Seller warrants that Seller has no knowledge of any planned improvements which may result in
291   assessments and that no governmental or private agency has served notice requiring repairs, alterations or
292   corrections of any existing conditions. Public or municipal improvements which are not completed as of the date
293   above but which will result in a lien or charge shall be paid by Buyer. Buyer will assume and pay all special
294   assessments for municipal improvements completed after the date of this Agreement.
295
296 S. **TIME:** Time is of the essence. Time periods specified in this Agreement and any subsequent Addenda to the
297   Purchase Agreement are calendar days and shall expire at 11:59 PM of the date stated unless the parties agree in
298   writing to a different date and/or time.
299
300   **Note: Seller and Buyer have the right to withdraw any offer/counter offer prior to written acceptance and**
301   **delivery of such offer/counter offer.**
302
303 T. **HOMEOWNERS ASSOCIATION/CONDOMINIUM ASSOCIATION ("Association"):** Documents for a **mandatory**
304   membership association shall be delivered by the Seller to Buyer within _____ days after acceptance of this
305   Agreement, but not later than 10 days prior to closing pursuant to I.C. 32-21-5-8.5. Brokers are not responsible for
306   obtaining or verifying this information. If the Buyer does not make a written response to the documents within _____
307   days after receipt, the documents shall be deemed acceptable. In the event the Buyer does not accept the
308   provisions in the documents and such provisions cannot be waived, this Agreement may be terminated by the
309   Buyer and the earnest money deposit shall be refunded to Buyer promptly. Any approval of sale required by the
310   Association shall be obtained by the Seller, in writing, within _____ days after Buyer's approval of the documents.
311   Fees charged by the "Association", or its management company, for purposes of verification of good standing
312   and/or transfer of ownership shall be shared equally by Buyer and Seller. Start-up or one time reserve fees, if any,
313   shall be paid by Buyer.
314
315   **Buyer acknowledges that in every neighborhood there are conditions which others may find objectionable.**
316   **Buyer shall therefore be responsible to become fully acquainted with neighborhood and other off-site**
317   **conditions that could affect the Property.**
318
319 U. **ATTORNEY'S FEES:** Any party to this Agreement who is the prevailing party in any legal or equitable proceeding
320   against any other party brought under or with relation to the Agreement or transaction shall be additionally entitled
321   to recover court costs and reasonable attorney's fees from the non-prevailing party.
322
323 V. **ADDITIONAL PROVISIONS:**
324
325   1. Unless otherwise provided, any prorations for rent, taxes, insurance, damage deposits, association dues/
326   assessments, or any other items shall be computed as of the day immediately prior to the Closing Date.
327
328   2. Underground mining has occurred in Indiana, and Buyers are advised of the availability of subsidence
329   insurance.

3. The Indiana State Police has created a registry of known meth contaminated properties which can be found at www.in.gov/meth. Click on "Clan Lab Addresses." Broker is not responsible for providing or verifying this information.

4. The Indiana Sheriff's Sex Offender Registry (www.indianasheriffs.org) exists to inform the public about the identity, location and appearance of sex offenders residing within Indiana. Broker is not responsible for providing or verifying this information.

5. Conveyance of this Property shall be by general Warranty Deed, or by _____ , subject to taxes, easements, restrictive covenants and encumbrances of record, unless otherwise agreed.

6. If it is determined Seller is a "foreign person" subject to the Foreign Investment in Real Property Tax Act, Seller will pay applicable tax obligation.

7. Any notice required or permitted to be delivered shall be deemed received when personally delivered, transmitted electronically or digitally or sent by express courier or United States mail, postage prepaid, certified and return receipt requested, addressed to Seller or Buyer or the designated agent of either party.

8. This Agreement shall be construed under and in accordance with the laws of the State of Indiana and is binding upon the parties' respective heirs, executors, administrators, legal representatives, successors, and assigns.

9. In case any provision contained in this Agreement is held invalid, illegal, or unenforceable in any respect, the invalidity, illegality, or unenforceability shall not affect any other provision of this Agreement.

10. This Agreement constitutes the sole and only agreement of the parties and supersedes any prior understandings or written or oral agreements between the parties' respecting the transaction and cannot be changed except by their written consent.

11. All rights, duties and obligations of the parties shall survive the passing of title to, or an interest in, the Property.

12. Broker(s) may refer Buyer or Seller to other professionals, service providers or product vendors, including lenders, loan brokers, title insurers, escrow companies, inspectors, pest control companies, contractors and home warranty companies. Broker(s) does not guarantee the performance of any service provider. Buyer and Seller are free to select providers other than those referred or recommended to them by Broker(s). The Parties agree that Brokers and their companies shall be released and held harmless in the event of claims disputes with any service provider.

13. By signing below, the parties to this transaction acknowledge: 1) receipt of a copy of this Agreement; and 2) information regarding this transaction may be published in a multiple listing service, Internet or other advertising media.

14. Any amounts payable by one party to the other, or by one party on behalf of the other party, shall not be owed until this transaction is closed.

15. Buyer and Seller consent to receive communications from Broker(s) via telephone, U.S. mail, email and facsimile at the numbers/addresses provided to Broker(s) unless Buyer and Seller notify Broker(s) in writing to the contrary.

16. Buyer discloses to Seller that Buyer holds Indiana Real Estate License # _____ .

17. Where the word "Broker" appears, it shall mean "Licensee" as provided in I.C.25-34.1-10-6.8.

W. **FURTHER CONDITIONS (List and attach any addenda):** _____
_____
_____
_____
_____
_____
_____
_____
_____
_____
_____
_____
_____
_____
_____

398 X. **CONSULT YOUR ADVISORS:** Buyer and Seller acknowledge they have been advised that, prior to signing this
399   document, they may seek the advice of an attorney for the legal or tax consequences of this document and the
400   transaction to which it relates. In any real estate transaction, it is recommended that you consult with a
401   professional, such as a civil engineer, environmental engineer, or other person, with experience in evaluating the
402   condition of the Property.
403
404 Y. **ACKNOWLEDGEMENTS:** This ☐ **is** ☐ **is not** a limited agency transaction. Buyer and Seller acknowledge that
405   each has received agency office policy disclosures, has had agency explained, and now confirms all agency
406   relationships. Buyer and Seller further acknowledge that they understand and accept agency relationships involved
407   in this transaction. By signature below, the parties verify that they understand and approve this Purchase Agreement
408   and acknowledge receipt of a signed copy.
409
410 Z. **EXPIRATION OF OFFER:** Unless accepted by Seller and delivered to Buyer **by** _____ ☐ **A.M.** ☐ **P.M.**
411   ☐ **Noon,** the _____ day of _____ , this Purchase Agreement shall be null and void and all
412   parties shall be relieved of any and all liability or obligations.
413
414   This Agreement may be executed simultaneously or in two or more counterparts, each of which shall be deemed
415   an original but all of which together shall constitute one and the same instrument. The parties agree that this
416   Agreement may be transmitted between them electronically or digitally. The parties intend that electronically or
417   digitally transmitted signatures constitute original signatures and are binding on the parties. The original document
418   shall be promptly delivered, if requested.
419
420
421
422
423 BUYER'S SIGNATURE _____ DATE _____ BUYER'S SIGNATURE _____ DATE _____
424
425
426 PRINTED _____ PRINTED _____
427
428 AA. **SELLER'S RESPONSE: (Check appropriate paragraph number):**
429
430 **This _____ day of _____ , at _____ ☐ A.M. ☐ P.M. ☐ Noon**
431
432 ☐ **1. The above offer is Accepted.**
433
434 ☐ **2. The above offer is Rejected.**
435
436 ☐ **3. The above offer is Countered. See Counter Offer. Seller should sign both the Purchase Agreement and**
437   **the Counter Offer.**
438
439
440
441
442 SELLER'S SIGNATURE _____ DATE _____ SELLER'S SIGNATURE _____ DATE _____
443
444
445 PRINTED _____ PRINTED _____

Provided as a member service by the
INDIANA
ASSOCIATION OF
REALTORS®, INC.

BUYER'S EXCLUSIVE AGENCY CONTRACT

1 This Contract is entered into and shall commence on _____ ,
2 by _____ (Broker) and
3 _____ (Buyer),
4 Buyer employs Broker for the purpose of exclusively assisting Buyer to locate property described below or other
5 property acceptable to Buyer, and to negotiate terms and conditions acceptable to Buyer for purchase of property. This
6 Contract shall terminate at midnight on _____ .

7 A. **BROKER AGREES** to diligently attempt to locate property acceptable to Buyer; to negotiate price, terms and
8 conditions acceptable to Buyer, for the purchase of property; and shall act in the Buyer's best interest during the
9 term of this Contract.

10 B. **DESCRIPTION (INCLUDING, BUT NOT LIMITED TO, LOCATION, PRICE RANGE AND OTHER TERMS):**
11 _____
12 _____
13 _____

14 C. **BROKER'S COMPENSATION:**

15   1 .   **Retainer Fee:** Buyer has paid Broker a non-refundable retainer fee of $ _____ .
16 This amount shall be credited to the total amount due at time of closing any transaction accomplished
17 under this agreement including, but not limited to, a lease with option to purchase.

18   2.   **Commission:** In consideration for the services to be performed by Broker, Buyer also agrees to pay
19 Broker a commission of $ _____ or _____ % of the total purchase price; however,
20 the total commission paid to Broker shall not be less than $ _____ . In the event seller pays
21 a commission under a listing agreement and Broker, with the consent of Buyer, is to receive any portion
22 thereof, that portion shall be credited against Buyer's financial obligations to Broker. Broker shall use
23 Broker's best effort to cause the seller or seller's agent to satisfy the Buyer's obligation to Broker.

24 The commission shall be due, earned and promptly paid if:

25   a.   Buyer or any other person acting for Buyer or on Buyer's behalf, acquires any real property or
26 interest as described herein during the term of this Contract through the services of Broker or
27 otherwise.

28   b.   Buyer or any other person acting for Buyer or on Buyer's behalf, acquires any real property or
29 interest described herein, which was disclosed to Buyer by Broker during the term of this Contract
30 or within _____
31 _____ after termination of this Contract.

32   3.   Other: _____
33 _____

34 **Broker's commission for services rendered, in respect to any broker, is solely a matter of negotiation**
35 **between the Broker and the Buyer and is not fixed, controlled, suggested, recommended or maintained by**
36 **the Indiana Association of REALTORS®, Inc., the local Board/Association of REALTORS®, the MLS (if**
37 **applicable) or any person not a party to the contract.**

38 D. **AGENCY DISCLOSURES:**

39   1.   **Office Policy.** Buyer acknowledges receipt of a copy of the written office policy relating to agency.

_____
(Property Address)

40   2.   **Agency Relationships.** I.C. 25-34.1-10-9.5 provides that a Licensee has an agency relationship with, and
41   is representing, the individual with whom the Licensee is working unless (1) there is a written agreement to
42   the contrary; or (2) the Licensee is merely assisting the individual as a customer. Licensee (Broker)
43   represents the interests of the Buyer as Buyer's agent to buy the Property. Licensee owns duties of trust,
44   loyalty, confidentiality, accounting and disclosure to the Buyer. However, Licensee must deal honestly
45   with a seller. All representations made by Licensee are made as the agent of the Buyer.

46   3.   **Limited Agency Authorization.** Licensee or the managing broker may represent Seller as a
47   seller agent. If Buyer wishes to see the Property listed by Licensee or the managing broker,
48   then Licensee has agency duties to both Buyer and Seller, and those duties may be different or even
49   adverse. Buyer knowingly consents to Licensee acting as a limited agent for such showings.

50   If limited agency arises, Licensee **shall not disclose** the following without the informed consent in writing,
51   of both Buyer and Seller.

52   (a)   Any material or confidential information, except adverse material facts or risks actually known by
53   Licensee concerning the physical condition of the Property and facts required by statute, rule, or
54   regulation to be disclosed and that could not be discovered by a reasonable and timely inspection
55   of the Property by the parties.

56   (b)   That a Buyer will pay more than the offered purchase price for the Property.

57   (c)   That a Seller will accept less than the listed price for the Property.

58   (d)   Other terms that would create a contractual advantage for one party over another party.

59   (e)   What motivates a party to buy or sell the Property.

60   In a limited agency situation, the parties agree that there will be no imputation of knowledge or information
61   between any party and the limited agent or among Licensees.

62   Buyer acknowledges that Limited Agency Authorization has been read and understood. Buyer understands
63   that Buyer does not have to consent to Licensee(s) acting as limited agent(s), but gives informed consent
64   voluntarily to limited agency and waives any claims, damages, losses, expenses, including attorneys' fees
65   and costs, against Licensee(s) arising from Licensee's(s') role of limited agent(s).

66 E. **CONSENT TO REPRESENT OTHER BUYERS:**

67   Buyer understands and agrees that Broker may from time to time represent other buyers who may be interested in
68   acquiring the same property as Buyer may wish to acquire. Buyer expressly waives any claim, including, but not
69   limited to, breach of fiduciary duty or breach of contract based solely upon Broker's representation of other buyers
70   who may be seeking to acquire the same property as Buyer, even if the other buyer represented by Broker does
71   acquire that property.

72 F . **FURTHER CONDITIONS:**

73   _____
74   _____
75   _____
76   _____
77   _____

78 G. **ACKNOWLEDGEMENTS:**

79   1.   Buyer has read and understands this Contract.

80   2.   This Contract contains the entire agreement of the parties and can only be changed in writing and signed
81   by all parties.

82   3.   This Contract is binding upon all the parties, their heirs, administrators, executors, successors and assigns.

83   4.   Buyer has been advised to seek professional advice on legal, financing, property inspections and/or tax
84   matters.

_____
(Property Address)

Page 2 of 3   (Buyer Exclusive Agency Contract)
Copyright IAR 2016

85 5.   Buyer has received an executed copy of this Contract.

86 6.   Broker holds a valid Indiana Real Estate License.

87 7.   Buyer acknowledges that if Broker's commission will be paid by a third party (seller or cooperating broker),
88   that such a relationship may impose limitations on the range of properties that Broker may show to Buyer.

89 8.   Buyer consents to receive communications from Broker via telephone, U.S. mail, email and facsimile at the
90   numbers/addresses provided to Broker unless Buyer notifies Broker in writing to the contrary.

91 9.   Buyer acknowledges that Broker has no duty to disclose the racial, ethnic or religious composition of any
92   neighborhood, community or building, nor whether persons with disabilities are housed in any home or
93   facility, except that the Broker may identify housing facilities meeting the needs of a disabled buyer.

94 10.   Where the word "Broker" appears, it shall mean "Licensee" as provided in I.C. 25-34.1-10-6.8.

95 This Agreement may be executed simultaneously or in two or more counterparts, each of which shall be deemed an
96 original, but all of which together shall constitute one and the same instrument. The parties agree that this Agreement
97 may be transmitted between them electronically or digitally. The parties intend that electronically or digitally transmitted
98 signatures constitute original signatures and are binding on the parties. The original document shall be promptly
99 delivered, if requested.

100 _____   _____
101 AGENT   IN LICENSE #   BUYER'S SIGNATURE   DATE

102 _____   _____
103 BROKER OR COMPANY NAME IN LICENSE #   PRINTED

104 _____   _____
105 ACCEPTED BY: MANAGING BROKER   BUYER'S SIGNATURE   DATE

106   _____
107   PRINTED

_____
(Property Address)

Page 3 of 3   (Buyer Exclusive Agency Contract)

LIMITED AGENCY AGREEMENT

(Licensee represents both Seller and Buyer or both Landlord and Tenant)
(Managing Broker personally represents a client and affiliated Licensee represents other client)

1
2 This Limited Agency Agreement ("Agreement") is dated _____ , _____ .

3 **A. BUYER/TENANT** ("Buyer"): _____
4
5 _____ .
6
7 **B. SELLER/LANDLORD** ("Seller"): _____
8
9
10 _____ .
11 **C. SUBJECT PROPERTY** ("Property"): _____
12
13
14 _____ .
15 **D. NAME OF LIMITED AGENTS(S)** ("Licensee"): _____
16
17
18 _____ .
19 ("Purchase price/listed price" shall also mean "lease rate," if applicable. "Licensee" shall refer to any broker
20 acting as agent for a party. "Limited agent" means a licensee who, with the written and
21 informed consent of all parties to a real estate transaction, represents both the Seller and Buyer.)
22
23 **E. LIMITED AGENCY AUTHORIZATION:** The Licensee is authorized by Seller and Buyer to represent
24 both of them in this transaction. Seller and Buyer understand that this limited agency relationship may create
25 certain conflicts of interest, and that Licensee is representing two parties whose interests are different or
26 even adverse.
27
28 **F. ADDITIONAL DISCLOSURES:** Seller and Buyer acknowledge that Licensee **shall not disclose** the
29 following without the informed consent, in writing, of both Seller and Buyer:
30
31   (1) Any material or confidential information, except adverse material facts or risks actually known
32   by the Licensee concerning the physical condition of the Property and facts required by
33   statute, rule, or regulation to be disclosed and that could not be discovered by a reasonable
34   and timely inspection of the Property by the parties.
35
36   (2) That a buyer will pay more than the offered purchase price for the Property.
37
38   (3) That a Seller will accept less than the listed price for the Property.
39
40   (4) What motivates a party to buy, sell or lease the Property.
41
42   (5) Other terms that would create a contractual advantage for one (1) party over another party.
43
44 Seller and Buyer acknowledge that there will be no imputation of knowledge or information between any
45 party and the limited agent or among Licensees.
46
47 Seller and Buyer acknowledge that they do not have to consent to the limited agency in this transaction.
48
49 Seller and Buyer consent voluntarily to Licensee's limited agency capacity and waive any claims, damages,
50 losses, expenses, including attorneys' fees and costs, against Licensee arising from Licensee's role of
51 limited agent.
52
53 **G. PRIOR AGREEMENTS:** Seller and Buyer understand this Agreement does not replace prior agreements
54 with Licensee to represent Seller or Buyer. However, where this Limited Agency Agreement contradicts or
55 conflicts with prior agreements, this Limited Agency Agreement shall supersede.
56

(Property Address)
Page 1 of 2 (Limited Agency Agreement)
Copyright IAR 2016

57 **H. CANCELLATION:** If the Seller and Buyer do not enter into an agreement relating to the Property or if the
58 transaction fails to close, Seller and Buyer agree that this Agreement is automatically cancelled and the
59 Licensee's role of limited agent is terminated.
60
61 **By signature below, the parties verify that they understand and approve this Limited Agency**
62 **Agreement and acknowledge receipt of a signed copy. This Agreement may be executed**
63 **simultaneously or in two or more counterparts, each of which shall be deemed an original, but all of**
64 **which together shall constitute one and the same instrument. The parties agree that this Agreement**
65 **may be transmitted between them electronically or digitally. The parties intend that electronically or digitally**
66 **transmitted signatures constitute original signatures and are binding on the parties. The original document**
67 **shall be promptly delivered, if requested.**

_____ _____   _____ _____
BUYER'S SIGNATURE   DATE   BUYER'S SIGNATURE   DATE

_____   _____
PRINTED   PRINTED

_____ _____   _____ _____
SELLER'S SIGNATURE   DATE   SELLER'S SIGNATURE   DATE

_____   _____
PRINTED   PRINTED

Prepared and provided as a member service by the Indiana Association of REALTORS®, Inc. (IAR). This form
is restricted to use by members of IAR. This is a legally binding contract, if not understood seek legal advice.
Form #40. Copyright IAR 2016

_____
(Property Address)

Page 2 of 2   (Limited Agency Agreement)

MUTUAL RELEASE FROM LISTING CONTRACT

1   Date _____

2   _____ as Seller
3   and _____ as Broker/Company
4   entered into an Exclusive Right to Sell Listing Contract ("Listing Contract") on _____
5   regarding the property known as _____ ,
6   _____ (city), _____ (county), Indiana _____
7   (zip code) and legally described as _____
8   _____ (the "Property").

9   The parties to the Listing Contract agree as follows: (**check appropriate paragraph letter**)

10 ☐ **A.**   Seller and Broker and its agents release each other from all rights, duties and liabilities in respect to the Listing Contract
11   and agree that the Listing Contract shall be rescinded and of no further force or effect whatsoever. However, it is
12   agreed that if the Property is sold, optioned, leased, or exchanged by Seller or any other person within _____ days
13   after termination of the Listing Contract to any person procured in whole or in part by the efforts of the Listing Broker,
14   cooperating broker, or Seller, Broker shall be entitled to the commission established in the Listing Contract. However, this
15   provision shall not apply if the Listing Contract is released and the Property is listed exclusively with another licensed broker.

16   **OR**

17 ☐ **B.**   Seller and Broker agree to withdraw the Property from the market, but understand that this does not terminate the Listing
18   Contract. Broker will cease to advertise and/or market the Property. If Seller decides to sell at any time before expiration
19   of the Listing Contract or under conditions as outlined in the extension clause of the Listing Contract, the Listing Contract
20   is still in effect and a full commission shall be due and payable in accordance with the Listing Contract. Seller shall not
21   list the Property with another Broker during the remainder of the term of the Listing Contract.

22 Seller agrees to pay Broker $ _____ as compensation for services rendered to date, whether A or B is checked above.

23 Further conditions: _____
24 _____
25 _____
26 _____

27 This Release may be executed simultaneously, or in two or more counterparts, each of which shall be deemed an original, but all of
28 which together shall constitute one and the same instrument. The parties agree that the Release may be transmitted between them
29 electronically or digitally. The parties intend that electronically or digitally transmitted signatures constitute original signatures and are binding on
30 the parties. The original document shall be promptly delivered, if requested.

31 By signature below, the parties acknowledge receipt of a signed copy of this Release.

32 _____   _____
33 AGENT   IN LICENSE #   SELLER'S SIGNATURE   DATE

34 _____   _____
35 BROKER OR COMPANY NAME   IN LICENSE #   PRINTED

36 _____   _____
37 ACCEPTED BY MANAGING BROKER   SELLER'S SIGNATURE   DATE

38   _____
39   PRINTED

_____
(Property Address)
(Mutual Release From Listing Contract)

MUTUAL RELEASE FROM PURCHASE AGREEMENT

1 Date: _____

2 Buyer(s) _____ ;
3 Seller(s) _____ ;
4 Listing Broker _____
5 By _____ Agent; and
6 Selling Broker _____
7 By _____ Agent
8 release each other from all rights, duties, and liabilities in respect to the purchase and sale of property known as
9 _____
10 _____ , Indiana, Zip _____ (the "Property")
11 and agree the Purchase Agreement dated _____ , and accepted
12 _____ shall be rescinded and of no further force or effect whatsoever.
13 It Is further agreed by all parties that the earnest money deposit of _____
14 _____ Dollars
15 ($ _____) shall be: **(check one)**

16 _____ **returned to Buyers;**

17 _____ **paid to Seller;**

18 _____ **other** _____
19 _____
20 _____
21 _____
22 _____
23 _____

24 This Release may be executed simultaneously or in two or more counterparts, each of which shall be deemed an
25 original, but all of which together shall constitute one and the same instrument. The parties agree that this Release
26 may be transmitted between them electronically or digitally. The parties intend that electronically or digitally
27 transmitted signatures constitute original signatures and are binding on the parties. The original document shall be
28 promptly delivered, if requested.

29
30 BUYER'S SIGNATURE   DATE   SELLER'S SIGNATURE   DATE

31
32 PRINTED   PRINTED

33
34 BUYER'S SIGNATURE   DATE   SELLER'S SIGNATURE   DATE

35
36 PRINTED   PRINTED

37
38 SELLING BROKER OR COMPANY NAME   LISTING BROKER OR COMPANY NAME
39 (Indiana License #)   (Indiana License #)
40
41 AGENT   AGENT

42
43 MANAGING BROKER   MANAGING BROKER

Prepared and provided as a member service by the Indiana Association of REALTORS®, Inc. (IAR). This form is
restricted to use by members of IAR. This is a legally binding contract, if not understood seek legal advice.
Form #26. Copyright IAR 2016

OPTION TO PURCHASE PROPERTY

1 Date: _____

2 This Option to Purchase Property is entered into between _____

3 _____ ("Seller"), located at _____

4 _____ and

5 _____ ("Buyer"),

6 located at _____

7 _____ in consideration of and subject to the following terms and conditions:

8 **1.   GRANT OF OPTION**

9   Seller grants and conveys to Buyer the exclusive and irrevocable option to purchase (the "Option") the following described real

10   estate and other property (the "Property") located in _____ City, _____

11   County, Indiana, which is commonly known as _____

12   _____ , and is legally described as: _____

13   _____ .

14 **2.   OPTION MONEY**

15   Buyer pays Seller the sum of _____

16   dollars ($ _____) (the "Option Money"), the receipt of which Seller acknowledges as consideration

17   for the Option.

18 **3.   TERM, EXERCISE/NOTICE**

19   A.   **TERM.** Buyer's right to exercise this Option shall commence on the above date and shall continue until and including the

20   _____ day of _____

21   (the "Option Period").

22   B.   **EXERCISE/NOTICE.** This Option shall be exercised by Buyer's written notice to Seller of Buyer's election to purchase. The

23   notice shall be deemed received when personally delivered, transmitted by facsimile, sent by express courier or sent by

24   United States mail, postage prepaid, certified and return receipt requested, addressed to Seller or the designated agent

25   of Seller prior to the expiration of the Option Period.

26 **4.   CLOSING AND DISPOSITION OF OPTION MONEY**

27   If Buyer exercises this Option as described above, the transaction shall be closed in accordance with the terms and conditions of

28   the **attached Purchase Agreement.**

29   A.   The Option Money ☐ **shall** ☐ **shall not** be credited to the purchase price.

30   B.   If the Option is not exercised, then Seller shall retain the Option Money as consideration for the granting of this Option.

_____

(Property Address)

31 **5. EXPIRATION AND APPROVAL**
32   This Option is void if not accepted in writing on or before _____ ☐ **A.M.** ☐ **P.M.** ☐ **Noon**
33   _____ , _____ .

34 **6. TERMS BINDING**
35   All terms and conditions are included and no verbal agreements shall be binding.

36 **7. ACKNOWLEDGEMENTS**
37   Buyer and Seller acknowledge that each has received agency office policy disclosures, has had agency explained, and now
38   confirms all agency relationships. Buyer and Seller further acknowledge that they understand and accept agency
39   relationships involved in this transaction. By signature below, the parties verify that they understand and approve this
40   Option to Purchase Property and acknowledge receipt of a signed copy.
41   This Option may be executed simultaneously or in two or more counterparts, each of which shall be deemed an original, but all
42   of which together shall constitute one and the same instrument. The parties agree that this document may be transmitted between
43   them electronically or digitally. The parties intend that electronically or digitally transmitted signatures constitute original signatures and are
44   binding on the parties. The original document shall be promptly delivered, if requested.

45 _____
46 BUYER'S SIGNATURE   DATE   BUYER'S SIGNATURE   DATE

47 _____
48 PRINTED   PRINTED

49 **(Check appropriate paragraph letter)**
50 ☐ **A.**   As the Seller(s) of the Property described herein, the above terms and conditions are accepted this _____ day
51   of _____ , _____ at _____ ☐ **A.M.** ☐ **P.M.**
52   ☐ **Noon.**

53 ☐ **B.**   **The above Option is** ☐ **rejected OR** ☐ **countered this** _____ **day of** _____ , _____ .

54 _____
55 SELLER'S SIGNATURE   SELLER'S SIGNATURE

56 _____
57 PRINTED   PRINTED

_____
(Property Address)

58   **ACKNOWLEDGEMENT**

59 STATE OF INDIANA   )
60   ) SS:
61 COUNTY OF   )

62 Before me, a Notary Public, within and for said County and State, personally appeared _____
63 _____ , who acknowledged the execution of the foregoing Option To Purchase
64 Property. Witness my hand and Notarial Seal this _____ day of _____ .

65   _____
66   Notary Public

67   _____
68   Printed

69 My Commission Expires: My County of Residence:

70 _____   _____

71 STATE OF INDIANA   )
72   ) SS:
73 COUNTY OF   )

74 Before me, a Notary Public, within and for said County and State, personally appeared _____
75 _____ , who acknowledged the execution of the foregoing Option To Purchase
76 Property. Witness my hand and Notarial Seal this _____ day of _____ .

77   _____
78   Notary Public

79   _____
80   Printed

81 My Commission Expires: My County of Residence:

82 _____   _____

Prepared and provided as a member service by the Indiana Association of REALTORS®, Inc. (IAR). This form is restricted to use by members of IAR. This is a legally binding contract, if not understood seek legal advice. **Form #27.** Copyright IAR 2016

_____
(Property Address)

Page 3 of 3   (Option To Purchase Property)

Index